THE GODDESS EXPERIENCE

What makes you happy?

gisèle
xx

Gisèle Scanlon

THE GODDESS
EXPERIENCE

What makes you happy?

*experiences are what matter
to me the most...*

*Come with me on my Goddess
adventure and feel the sunshine.*

HarperCollins*Publishers*

HarperCollins Publishers
77–85 Fulham Palace Road,
Hammersmith, London W6 8JB

www.harpercollins.co.uk
Visit www.AuthorTracker.co.uk
for exclusive updates on Gisèle Scanlon

Published by HarperCollins Publishers 2008
1

Copyright © Gisèle Scanlon 2008

Gisèle Scanlon asserts the moral right to
be identified as the author of this work

A catalogue record for this book
is available from the British Library

ISBN-13: 978-0007274710

Artwork by Gisèle Scanlon
Cover, text layout Peter O'Dwyer
Photography by Peter O'Dwyer & Thomas Ball

Printed and bound in Italy

Mixed Sources
Product group from well-managed
forests and other controlled sources
www.fsc.org Cert no. SW-COC-1806
© 1996 Forest Stewardship Council

FSC is a non-profit international organisation established to promote the
responsible management of the world's forests. Products carrying the FSC
label are independently certified to assure consumers that they come
from forests that are managed to meet the social, economic and
ecological needs of present and future generations.

Find out more about HarperCollins and the environment at
www.harpercollins.co.uk/green

THE GODDESS EXPERIENCE

Who makes me happy?

Peter for his daily inspiration, Mum & Dad just for being brilliant!, Babs, Mike, SeànÒg and Granny for keeping it real. Marianne Gunn O'Connor for her guidance and friendship, Pat Lynch, Thomas Ball for all their help, Charlie and Alex, Matt and Helena for the ice-cream, Anne and Philip, Maggie and Gerry. Claire Bord my editor without whom this book would not have been possible, Amanda Ridout, Lynne Drew, Nicole Abel, Laurie Chiltern, Moira Reilly, Tony Purdue and all the team at HarperCollins.

Freddie and Chris, Pat and Margo, Jon Lewis, Conor & Chloe, Mjar, BrenB and Lisa, Richard and Lucy, Billy, Valerie and Robyn. Zoe at Paul Smith and the wonderfully kind Brigitte Stepputtis at Westwood, Pádraig, Eoin and Elaine and Amanda Fatherazi and her embroidered blue tit on the cover, to each and everyone of you this book would not have been possible without your generous time and help. Next time we catch up, the milky tea is on me, yay!

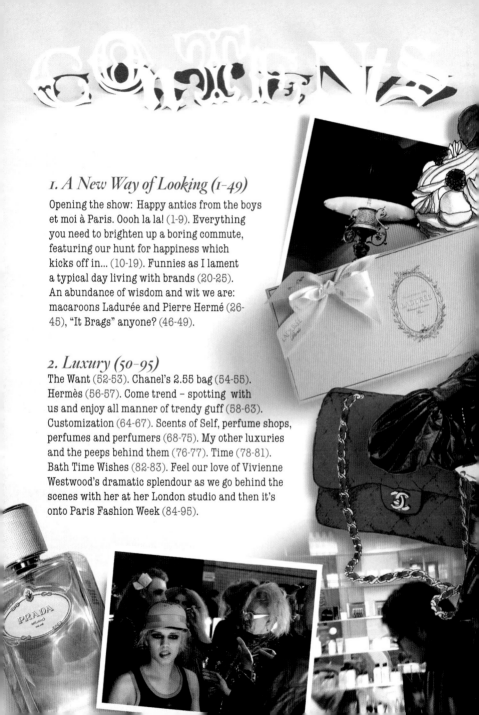

1. *A New Way of Looking (1-49)*

Opening the show: Happy antics from the boys
et moi à Paris. Oooh la la! (1-9). Everything
you need to brighten up a boring commute,
featuring our hunt for happiness which
kicks off in... (10-19). Funnies as I lament
a typical day living with brands (20-25).
An abundance of wisdom and wit we are:
macaroons Ladurée and Pierre Hermé (26-
45), "It Brags" anyone? (46-49).

2. *Luxury (50-95)*

The Want (52-53). Chanel's 2.55 bag (54-55).
Hermès (56-57). Come trend – spotting with
us and enjoy all manner of trendy guff (58-63).
Customization (64-67). Scents of Self, perfume shops,
perfumes and perfumers (68-75). My other luxuries
and the peeps behind them (76-77). Time (78-81).
Bath Time Wishes (82-83). Feel our love of Vivienne
Westwood's dramatic splendour as we go behind the
scenes with her at her London studio and then it's
onto Paris Fashion Week (84-95).

3. Fashion (96–143)

Bags – where else could you see so many designers' obsessions with python, eel and crocodile skins? Here is where (98-103). Bag addresses, care tips (103). The Hook Report... Yes, there's only one book that digs clutch bags, investigating toilets and door hooks in equal measure, and you're holding it in your mitts. (104-105). Building the basics (106-107). Inside Secrets (108-109). Inside Care Secrets (110-111). What's Her Secret – why the perfect look is not just for fashion shoots (112-113).

Petite (116-117), Curvy (118-119), Pear-shaped 120-121), Busty (122-123) or Skinny and tall (124-125); whatever your shape you lot can deck yourselves out like Christmas trees with these splendid shape enhacing fashion tips. Denim – my favourite denim finds for your delectation (126-127). Flat Hunting – oodles of splendid shoes (128-129). Flat Mates – enough high shoe suggestions to make your toes bleed and eyes water (130-131). Trainers (132-133). British design hero Paul Smith does a show and tell of stripes, chairs and opens his secret basement vault to us (134-143).

4. Shopping (144–161)

The Luxurious Goddess (146-147).
The Urban Goddess (148-149).
The Home Goddess (150-151).
The Sex Goddess (152-153).
The Earth Goddess (154-155).
The Office Goddess (156-157).
Secret Shops (158-159).
Secret Value (160-161).

...and I like Boudica

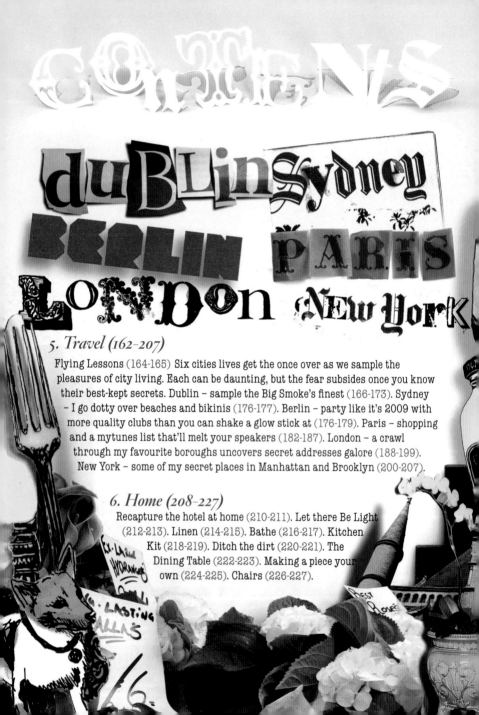

CONTENTS

dUBLIN Sydney BERLIN PARIS LONDON New York

7. Food (228-263)

8. Beauty (264-295)

9. Happy? (296-323)

Lauren Laverne (306-307) - that's right, our favourite Northern lass joins us to strike music warrior poses, talk culture and give us a bevy of juicy bits. A bit of reading (304) and Pat McCabe lets us inside his imagination (305). A bit of art with Chloe Early (310-311), music with Scroobius Pip (302), art with Damien Hirst (303) and fashion with Anna Piaggi (308). Oh and I've got secret finds (301). But don't tell anyone... Shhhhh! The hunt for the perfect cuppa (312-319)... go buck-wild in a bakery as we take you on a teatime tour of the very best tea and gateaux hang-outs. Happy is...taking the time to enjoy the pleasures of a sticky-fingered tea-time trawl. Eat more cake, drink more tea, that's my motto. Jeez, it's all too much. Happy days, folks, happy days.

Milky tea

My ickle broken hare

love him because he's not perfect

frosty brrrr!

new

I bring this everywhere

A NEW WAY OF LOOKING

After much deliberation on a clear frosty morning, I **gathered my bits and bobs** around me (camera, paint, brushes, pens), opened the first page of a fresh new notebook (the book you're holding now) and wrote the word new in black pen.

Waiting for the kettle to boil and distractedly thinking about how **much I** loved tea, making it, milking it and sipping it slowly, I stared at **this little** word in front of me. Hovering there, all tiny and bare on a huge iceberg of white paper, it gave me 'the fear'. I made a cuppa, made some doodles of the cup and turned the word new over and over in my noodle for ages, racking my brain. I set my pen down, cupped my face in my hands and time stopped. What was I doing? What did the future hold? What was **I** going to write?

I should have been scribbling plans for the future, but something was nagging and dragging me backwards, something was standing between me and the writing of this first chapter. What was it? I wasn't sure. After a fair bit of head scratching – will I, won't I, what if it's awful, etc. – I gave in. Damn it. Three, four, five more strokes of the pen around the fingers of this drawing and I could feel myself shutting down gradually, like the light dying on the inside of a fridge. It wasn't sadness that I was feeling but frustration. I closed my notebook and packed it away in my handbag; I'd give it another go the next day.

Peter

Gisèle x

Charlie

The following day I boarded a 7.30 flight to Paris for work with Peter the boyfriend and Charlie our British soul mate. Peter spells quick humour, adventure, that distinctive laugh and then calm (cool as a cucumber in a crisis). Charlie spells good stories, good booze, lots more laughing and wicked fun. Arriving in Charles de Gaulle, we were in particularly high spirits, the guys looking forward to having each other's camaraderie while I poked my head into shops, cafés and markets to look for the 'new'.

The most beautiful bedroom, the secret find, the most sensational yet underpriced dinner in a 'local' jammy bistro, the secret back door into the Louvre and, shhhhhh, don't tell anyone, the banjaxed vending machine spitting out Double Deckers for free, next to that newsstand opposite Zara, just up the rue from the Champs-Elysées. 'Photograph it, or better still, bring me back one with French writing on it, as proof that you did find it, Gisèle.' It's always the way – before you leave, kind friends offer their five sizzling hot travel tips, don't they? Hurried, half-scribbled, half-explained nuggets/new hot places for you to find. The words banjaxed and jammy thrown in for my benefit, because they know even these words alone get me excited. This time though I didn't tell anyone I was travelling, just Peter and Charlie, because they were coming with me. This time I would truffle-hunt inside each nook and cranny on my hands and knees, get down and dirty with the locals (not so much the celebrities). What had I planned? Ah yes, here it is, looking back to the first page of my notebook, one tiny sketch of a little goddess and one little word 'new'.

Over a low-key lunch in a small café the next day Peter, Charlie and I chewed this over. I asked, 'What am I here for? What really matters? Why do I feel this time that my hunt is well... different?' They said, in unison, 'because *you're* different... because *you're* a girl.' I hate to generalize, but in my experience, it's men who are the impatient ones, with these sorts of questions. They mark a dividing line between the genders, like fashion and football, chicken and beef, cocktails and beer.

Frustration like this always makes me turn to the teapot, and one raspberry tart and three cups of warm, milky tea later and Charlie inquired why my tea was this colour, Peter smiled knowingly. An uncomfortable silence crept around our chairs. I had nothing to say for myself, except, 'I like lots of milk, because I think it makes me happy.' Like warm milk at bedtime, I get the same effect. Three cups of tea, two jugs of milk and a slice of cake, thank you very much, *garçon*, and *merci*. Cheerful, we stepped out, into sun showers and puddles, full of raspberry cake and tea. With Peter on stills, Charlie on film and me scribbling away beside them, we set off across the city in search of the 'new'.

I'd earmarked a visit to the Colette store on the Rue St Honoré. It houses all of the newest music, books, beauty and fashion from all over Europe and is one of my favourite browsing spots. Maybe I'd find a few little new things there to get me started. We spent most of the journey on foot talking about Parisians, and our waiter at the tea and cake place. He had been a bit, well, how can I put this? Rude! We agreed finally that Parisians are not rude, not really, only standoffish. If the British and Irish are like peaches (warm, fuzzy exterior but bruise us badly and you'll glimpse a strong little core), the Parisians are like pineapples, spiky and prickly on the outside but sweet (sometimes a bit tough) once you break through. I'd gone off pineapples a few weeks previously and we all agreed that we'd gone off the Little Palace Hotel which we had booked into the first night. The place was nothing remotely like a palace and had a Grand Canyon-like split between beds for two. We cheered up at the thought of moving to the Hôtel Bourg Tibourg later that evening; their double beds had no splits, far from it, but the Little Palace we'd definitely gone off.

3

And all three of us had also gone off worrying about tempting foodie smells coming from business class on airplanes as we flew economy (leaves us more money in our pockets to get out and about and walk the world). And we'd gone off, as if we'd ever really been on, schlebrity, Jim Davidson, George Bush and *Big Brother* all in one breath. What must that house smell of? Ambition? Socks? (*Big Brother*? The White House? Both?) I wouldn't do *Big Brother* for millions if you asked me: eight weeks, no pens, count me out, guys. And I thought of something even more disastrous … jiffy bags. Got one from a PR once with four bottles of suncream, stuffed it in my luggage quickly, it burst, and grey flecky, furry stuff got everywhere. Creams came out unscathed though. I could have ranted happily all the way to Colette, or Cool It as I like to call it, about my little 'passions' but instead, turning a sunny corner, I decided to put the negative brakes on. I made a pact with myself to start concentrating on a Happy List to be, you know, be grateful, well, no, not grateful, what's the word, to be more … more happy. That's it! To concentrate on happy stuff and see where it would take me, from this moment on.

I realized instantly how lucky I was to have the opportunity to go on this adventure with two very happy people; Peter and Charlie. I'd never really questioned happiness before. So what was it? And where could it be found? Was Paris a good starting place? Something I'd read somewhere previously sprung to mind that 50% of happiness is within our own control. David Lykken (I think that's what the chap's name was) of the University of Minnesota found out that 50% of our happiness is genetic. The other half, he found, is subject to our thoughts and decisions. So whether you were born genetically happy or sad 50% of your happiness is completely within your own control. At least I'd 50% to play with…

happy list

On we went, keen as mustard, bouncing along towards Colette, finding out what made the three of us happy. We all liked The Boosh and their crimping, (Julian Barratt and Noel Fielding are wicked) and we all liked Stephen Fry, actor, writer and BBC2's *QI* programme linchpin. Sticking with BBC2, we also liked *The Culture Show's* Lauren Laverne. I said I liked Jon Snow, the anchor of *Channel 4 News*; Peter is more of a Jeremy Paxman man (calls him PaxTHEman, by the way). We all loved Jon Stewart and *The Daily Show* on Comedy Central and I liked parsnips, reindeers and rabbits, but Charlie and Peter wrinkled their noses up at these, preferring to get all excited about YouTube instead.

We all agreed though that we loved David Attenborough and Vivienne Westwood simply because they were themselves and were very, very individual and inspiring. And I liked hyacinths, snail-mail and bicycles. We had another think and decided that we all loved chocolate, good burgers, our mobiles and our families. And then Peter said he loved Polaroid cameras, trainers and road works because of the acrid smell of fresh tar on old gravel. And I liked the word gravel because it sounded sharp like gravel itself. After then Charlie came in with street art, hip-hop, Christmas and Michel Gondry. We turned another corner and all smiled at each other the moment we saw these …

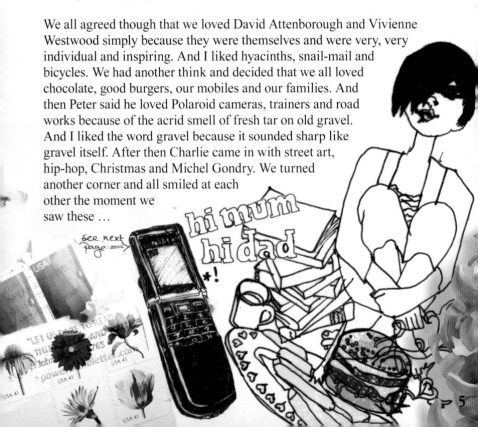

see next page ⇒

hi mum
hi dad

Ta-dah! Feast your eyes on these … teensy, tiny pens measuring just under two centimetres. Must be some of the tiniest pens in the world. Thank you, ladies and gentlemen, for your attention, safe home and good night. Giggling excitedly, we piled into the tiny pen shop, Styl' Honoré at 1 Rue du Marché St Honoré. My happy list continued in my head as I perused the jars stuffed with graphite pencils and coloured pens. Inks, nibs and inkwells lined the shelves along the specialist pen store. Wonderful. It was by some distance one of the coolest shops I'd ever been in. My mum would love this place; she loves coloured pens and pencils (especially highlighters). My Happy List continued because the owners wished us a cheery good evening. I like that, I like that millions and I love the smell of new pen shops, all booky and leathery, and I love the French word for pen: '*stylo*'.

The best thing about this shop (apart from the erasers that looked like real peanuts) was that we hit it off with the couple who owned it (Catherine and Patrick Arabian) immediately. Turns out Patrick is a French pen specialist and customizes nibs for fountain pens from all over the world; naturally the conversation focused on pencils and pen trivia (let me just say at this point that it's always others who call it trivia, I like to look at it more as, ummmmm, knowledge) and then Catherine produced a second eraser shaped like a mini bar of chocolate and pots of thick black ink, ink which she and her husband have been hand-making for eighteen years.

Fishing my notebook from my handbag, I laid it open on the counter and Catherine gently applied some black ink onto the pages. She used a tiny cream bone-handled dip pen which she then customized for my hand (extra la-di-da). She removed bits of black rubber, that had passed at one time or another through the store, from her husband's pen and added them carefully to my dip pen to make it more comfortable for me to handle. It was thrilling and special end to end. I liked these people and I liked Catherine's phrase, 'I'm giving your pen little black rubber hats,' when in reality they looked quite salacious (like little black condoms). I liked Catherine a lot, she had really cool hair.

Styl' Honoré, 1 Rue du Marché St Honoré, 75004 Paris (tel: +33 1 42 60 43 39)

Sketchy Time

Blue tit

Their syrupy thick black ink dripped off the dip pen and onto my open notebook on the counter. Now on the first page was my one drawing, their drippy black ink above it and the word 'new' to its right. (Look back to page 0.) The ink dribbled down the page and gave a sort of drippy black inky hair look to the little goddess sketch. Lovely! I'd found a new pen and new black inky hair for my sketches. 'Blackest ink in the world,' they told me. I thought to myself, 'It's all happening now.' Had to wait for the ink to dry though, to appreciate how black it really was. Ever waited for ink to dry? Takes ages. To pass the time I had to Hammer hum 'naaa na na na na na na na … Can't touch it!' (three times) and then 'Stop! Sketchy time!'

'We have other colours too,' explained Catherine. 'Be careful of your fingers, the ink is drippy.' I loaded the pen up with ink and moved it across to the page carefully, tongue stuck out in concentration. 'Why is it,' I said, thinking I was speaking softly but it came out all shouty, 'why is it that I always …' Splash! The coloured ink ran into where the pages met and off the page and down onto the counter. Catherine came to the rescue quickly with a very big piece of kitchen roll, already full of ink stains. I folded my notebook page in half to blot up the excess ink and popped in my handbag. I bought the pen, fifteen of their coloured inks, some pencils, the two rubbers (lovin' them) and of course three teensy weensy pens from the window, one for each of us. When I reopened my notebook an hour later in a taxi, I was left with this …

see next page ⇒

I see a silhouette
of a little man.

I know this as the ink thingy that psychiatrists hold up in movies to see if you're a deranged psycho killer or a lunatic. To shrinks it's known as a Rorschach ink blot (pronounced 'roar' as in what a lion does and 'shack' as in a small little beaten-up house).

So what else? According to Wikipedia, 'the test was created by Hermann Rorschach in 1921 and is used by psychologists to reveal deep thoughts and significant information about the taker's personality or innermost secrets.' Whoooa, sexxaay, I'm lovin' this! Even turning it upside down, I saw a guy smiling wearing sunglasses. What do you see?

I could go on, but I won't, except to say ... it's almost a mirror image on each side of the folded page in my notebook, apart from a few tiny spots here and there. When looking at this page you can choose to see something sad or something happy. It's *your* call. It's *your* perception. What you see is unique to *you*. The best thing about this ink accident though is this (shrinks, look away now) ... as I stared at it in the back of a cab whizzing through Place Vendôme, Paris, and we all laughed at the different things it could look like, it really got me thinking and I said to the boys, "What if I filled this notebook with experiences and notes on hunting for happiness? What if I tried to find out what makes us all happy?" Peter and Charlie both warmed up their cameras; the hunt for happiness was on ...

So where to start? Well, what about this then? Me clutching my notebook tightly and its ink stains in the back seat of a Parisian taxi and Charlie leaning his head out of the back window like a Labrador filming the shops as they melted past. Peter riding shotgun next to the driver (and us all lovin' the term 'riding shotgun') as we whizzed through a little chicane and pulled up outside the Ritz …

We waited, and waited, then we waited. Hold, hold, hold.

That *Braveheart* moment was brought to you courtesy of our taxi driver, Victor. *Bonjour* Victor, here is the vote of the Irish and British jury, *douze points*, you're a top bloke, you're *the* top bloke. You're a star. *Merci.*

Victor had pulled his taxi 'in' (instead of 'up', 'around' or 'alongside') the front door of the Ritz to get us 'out of the way of the busy traffic'. (His excuse for us to have a look, you have to love him for it.) Just for a moment we peeped past the doorman; it looked like a Ferrero Rocher ad inside, all goldy and iridescent and sparkly, proper ambassador's reception. Gold leaf everywhere, table lamps bigger than your head, chandeliers that would take out an elephant (*Snap! Crash! Sizzle! Bang!*) and glass cases stuffed with so much shiny stuff my eyes watered with the glare. How could I tell this from one brief peepathon? Did a little birdy tell me? Am I bionic? Don't make me laugh.

I've known the lay of Ritzland for years now, from wandering in out of the cold like Oliver Twist at (excuse the name drop) Paris Fashion Week. It's easy, you just walk in, take a seat and pretend you belong there. Simple, and why not? Have a tea or a coffee or something while you're at it. Breathe in the air, it smells gorgeous and it's free (last time I checked anyway). I booked a massage here once in the spa, it was excellent, even brought the slippers and some writing paper home for a friend who wanted them. Seriously!

15, Place Vendôme   75041 Paris Cedex 01

0 - E-MAIL MANAGEMENT : mgt@ritzparis.com - E-MAIL RÉSERVATION resa@ritzparis.com
3 36 69 - TÉLÉFAX (33) 01 43 16 31 78 / 01 43 16 31 79 - RCS PARIS B 572 219 913 - SIRET 572 219 913 00017

Then another time I had a glass of champagne here and toasted the memory of a few Ritz regulars: Marcel Proust (dined here), Coco Chanel (lived here), F. Scott Fitzgerald (introduced his pal Ernest Hemingway to the place). Back then Hemingway would try to scrape together enough money for one drink a week. Then he became successful and all la-di-da and moved in.

A barman at the Ritz told me once that the Bloody Mary was invented there for Hemingway as the 'odourless' cocktail. Liked his drink, did old Ernest, fooled his fourth wife Mary Welsh for years drinking Bloody Marys; she couldn't smell them on his breath when he got home. I know loads of mad stuff like this about the place and it's free. Go on, take it. But the drink, that's expensive. A glass of champagne in the Hemingway bar costs €20. That's twenty euros and zero pence, for one glass, no gold in it or anything, though if you nurse it long enough, they fill you up with plenty of free nibbles (nuts, Twiglets, that sort of thing). Others call this cheap skating (skatery, skatitis, whatever). I call it service. Did this thing a few times with friends where we had a race to see who could drink the slowest and bag the largest selection of nibbles, but I've never gone the whole hog here. At €730 a night, I've never sprung for a room.

Beep, beep! A problem, a small car problem in the shape of a traffic jam blocking us in; a crowd had gathered, taking photos on the Ritz doorstep. The most likely cause I thought was some schlebrity, some Wag weighed down by an 'It brag', sauntering around the front pouting for the paps. 'Takes all types,' my granny says. Yes, she's right and I was wrong, it wasn't a Wag at all. The object of their affections was a fancy-smancy car parked up on the footpath. Don't ask me the brand name (a Lamborghini, Porsche or something, bright blue that's all I know). This scene was way too spendy for my liking, we were out of there in a flash.

Ritz Paris 15. Place Vendôme 75041 Paris

TÉLÉPHONE (33) 01 43 16 30 30 - E-MAIL MANAGEMENT : mgt@ritzparis.com - E-MAIL RÉS
TÉLÉFAX RÉSERVATION (33) 01 43 16 36 68 / 01 43 16 36 69 - TÉLÉFAX (33) 01 43 16 31 78 / 01 43 16 3

€60 for 3 glasses of champagne.
Ker-razy!

CAR PORN

Sitting back against the seat of the taxi, I thought to myself, car porn that doesn't even make Peter and Charlie happy. Spendy, tacky cars, bit pointless. Hardly going to feature on my Happy List now, is it? And the Ritz? Expensive, smells it, nice for a brief visit, but not going to blag it's way onto my Happy List just because of that. I mean, I could never imagine me or my friends ever paying €730 for a hotel room unless for a honeymoon or anniversary. I shook myself out and reasserted my independence. You'll be OK, Gisèle, expensive hotel suites don't necessarily mean happiness, just live for the moment (or so I told myself, – makes me feel all edgy and exciting and no one can hear me if I say it quietly enough). Just look for happiness by doing your 'micro hunting' thingy (my madey-uppey word, for looking around you for tiny specks of happiness right here and now, sounds plausible enough, doesn't it?). Things like hair not sticking to lip gloss, straight in at number 1 on my Happy List filed under beauty and a quality candle which can make your house smell like a hotel in under an hour (see opposite page). Little things like that.

Then, Charlie swung the camera into the taxi and went all Spike Jones on me. 'So let's try a little piece,' he smiled. 'You're going to tell the camera where you are and where you're going and why it's special, what's good about it.' We were on our way to my favourite hotel, a small place that smells even better than the Ritz and is a fraction of the cost, so I though, yeah, mention that ... 'Ummmm, OK,' I stuttered. 'I'm on my way to Hôtel Bourg Tibourg, Bourg di Tibourgy di Tibourgy, hang on until I check the thingy' (meaning my notebook). Flapping and pausing to find the correct pronunciation, was it warm in the car, or was it just me?

I tried again. 'I'm on my way to Hôtel Bourg Tibourg.' Then I weaved on, 'You know that guy on *Sesame Street*?' (I was a bit shell-shocked and what I actually meant to say was 'the Swedish chef on *The Muppet Show*'.) 'You know how I remember the name of the hotel? He goes, "Hurdy Burdy Hotel di Tibourgy". That's how I remember it, because I'm not good at French.' I squirmed. Charlie helped me out with 'That's it, but you're not talking to me, you're talking to the camera.' 'Why can't I talk to you?' I asked. 'Well, you can talk to me, but you're supposed to be telling the camera where you're going.' 'Oh, ahhh, we're going to, ah, Hôtel Bourg Tibourg and it smells absolutely divine. There, and that's why I stay there every single time.' Phew! Got it!

THE CANDLE

Charlie swung the camera back out the window to film the passing city and I gushed to Peter about the black Bougie candles they burn at Hôtel Bourg Tibourg. I couldn't wait to get my hands on one, they smell really special and they burn them at Hôtel Costes too, (Hôtel Bourg Tibourg's more expensive big sister). You can walk in off the street to either hotel and buy one for €38. Bargain! (ish). Scented with black musk, seeds of coriander, juniper and lavender and a touch of rose it's unforgettable. It makes my house smell like Paris when I burn this candle and helps me bring the Costes experience home, it really does! And the soaps, shower gels and all of that hotel paraphernalia in the bedroom have the same scent as the candle. I just bag them cos they're free, you're supposed to; anyway, I see it as recycling, otherwise they'd just chuck them out. When I run out at home I buy them online.

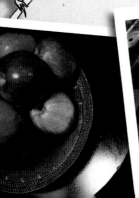

Rose Breasted grosbeak

Costes candles and bath products are available to buy at reception at **Hôtel Bourg Tibourg,** 19 Rue du Bourg-Tibourg 75004, Paris (tel: +33 1 42 78 47 39; www.hotelbourgtibourg.com) and at reception and online at **Hotel Costes,** 239 rue St - Honoré 75004, Paris (tel: +33 1 42 44 50 00; www.hotelcostes.com). Also avaiable from Colette (page 184) and **Neiman Marcus** www.neimanmarcus.com or **Beauty Habits** www.beautyhabit.com in the US.

VICTOR'S HAPPINESS

Victor our taxi driver pootled along at 30, maybe 40mph ... talking about Paris and wait until you hear what he had to tell us ... Charlie flipped the camera back into the car, just in time to hear him deliver this little nugget... quite normally at first Victor said, '[Paris] it's a nice city. Isn't it?' 'It's beautiful,' I replied. Victor went on, 'It is beautiful, like a woman.' We all laughed with him about this. 'What type of woman?' Peter quizzed. 'This is a type of woman that you shall be with her, but not to live with her.' We all laughed even more.

Victor loved Paris, no doubt about that, but he didn't have much faith in very beautiful women, thought they were a bit thick. 'Of course when she's [a woman] too nice, too beautiful, so there is nothing in the head, I mean the beauty attracts the first, it does not permit the brain work.' I mulled this over myself for a moment. Was he talking about all beauties here? Surely not. The funny thing was, Victor would have probably said the same thing to Johnny Depp if he was in his cab with the missus, Vanessa Paradis, beside him and she's beautiful and smart. I know, small talk, you're thinking, nothing special so far, when are we going to get to the good stuff? But wait, there's way more. Patience!

You think I'm joking? Check the film of this cab ride with Victor at www.thegoddessguide.com if you think I've popped the cork too early on this one. Victor is brilliant, dramatic, elusive and in surround sound, with lavish pictures, moving ones of course, so much more eloquent than my own humble scribblings here. But meanwhile, by way of a modest trailer, allow me to pass on a few more of Victor's philosophies. Trust me, he's worth it.

Victor also didn't rate money. He had his own take on life. He was in a different world. Except he wasn't. I was about to learn great things from Victor, about Paris, obviously, but the real lesson came unexpectedly at the beginning of the paragraph after this one and then more, much more in the paragraph after that ... 'You can get great Iranian tea or coffee in the 15th Arrondissement,' he told us in his French Iranian accent. At least that's what I think it was anyway, didn't ask him.

Victor sounded like Ben Kingsley in *House of Sand and Fog* (great 2003 movie, best acting Kingsley's ever done). At that moment a siren whined in the traffic and I, obsessed, got right tingly about it too and scribbled this into my small green Smythson notebook: 'Like the sirens on Parisian emergency vehicles. Love all emergency vehicles. They sound different in every city around the world. Must check this out.' Along with 'Check Iranian tea in the 15th Arrondissement.'

Victor broke me from my thinking. 'I like *after tea*,' he said. And I asked tentatively 'What's after tea? ... Dessert?' This sort of filming/camera caper is all about reading silences. A tricky business when you think for a split second that your taxi driver is looking in the mirror at you and accusing you of thinking about sex. I don't know, to this day. Was he pure as the driven snow? Watch the little movie on www.thegoddessguide.com and make your own call.

'After tea, what is after tea in alphabet?' he teased roguishly, innocently?

After a long pause (I thought 'what's after tea in the alphabet?') 'U,' I replied. 'You like me.' We all laughed. 'I like you too. You're nice,' I said.

'You are nice too,' he joked. It was all very 'Borat'. And then there was this warm silence that sloshed around the car, like my milky tea feeling.

I broke it with 'What makes you happy?'

I like you too
You're nice

'To see the people, they are happy,' Victor answered. 'To see other people happy,' I repeated like a parrot. 'You see right now, have a look.' He waved his arms towards the sunny streets. I went, 'Yeah.'

Tufted Titmouse

'In one week before it wasn't like this, you see all the people around?' And I went 'Yeah' again. 'So when they are happy you get the sense of happiness. What we search? No? This is the only thing. Happy!' My first vital clue. 1. Victor was happy to see other people happy.

'Does more money make you happy?' I asked.

'No, not too much, it depends on my capacity. I
don't want too much money. I want just to lead
a serene life, not to bother anybody, not to get
bothered.' He said that last bit with truckloads of
passion, especially the serene bit, the word serene
he really emphasized. Another vital clue!
2. He was happy to lead a serene life.

I felt the need to reply urgently, 'That's very
good, I wish I could lead a serene life.'

He went on, 'Yes, yes, in saying it is very good, but in acting, no.'
'
And what's your luxury, like everyday living in Paris?' I asked.

'Working!' he answered. Clue number three. Loved his job. Important.
3. Victor's luxury was his work/job.

'Is your luxury? *Luxe*?' I said.

'What is it, luxury?' he said quizzically. Of course thinking he couldn't
understand my Irish accent, I began to translate. 'De luxe?'

'What is it for?' he cut across me.

'Is that a rhetorical question do you think, yeah?' I hinted nervously.

'Yes, what is it? Can we wear it? What is it? What is the use of it?'
'Clothes, food, good food, is that a luxury?' I clarified.

'No, it's comfort,' he explained. Clue number four surely. 4. Clothes and
food are comforts and here's number five. I've been trying to get to it for
ages … Victor said ...

'Luxury is that when you are not satisfied with natural things so you go for it.'

Have a look at that last sentence again for a moment. 'Luxury is when you're not satisfied with natural things.' 5. Luxuries are things that we buy outside our natural needs. Things we need when we're not satisfied. Brilliant! Isn't he? Victor's resolute refusal to be impressed by anything the three of us thought about luxury, luxe, de luxe, whatever you want to call it glued Charlie, Peter and me together silently in that car. Possibly for ever! At that very moment it felt good to be breathing. Victor was a gem. We could all feel it as he turned left and chirped, 'This is Bourg di Tibourg. So I go this far.'

Desperate to know more, I blurted out, 'What's your favourite thing to do in Paris?'

'To take you to your destination' – clue number six, and seven when he added this: 'to be satisfied. It's OK here?' The goodness just kept on coming. 6. Victor expressed happiness and satisfaction with his work life – his job and 7. He was simply satisfied in the moment. There and then. A big new lesson for me!

'Perfect!' we said as he pulled up outside Hôtel Bourg Tibourg. He got out and I paid him. High in the moment, I even went so far as to ask him about his *Teenage Mutant Hero Turtles* pencil case in which he kept his money, just to hear him talk. 'I love your pencil case? Where did you get that?' He smiled as he handed me back some change. 'Thank you,' I smiled back. 'You are welcome.' He waved. 'Have a nice time, eh?'

Hôtel Bourg Tibourg, 19 Rue du Bourg-Tibourg 75004, Paris (tel: +33 1 42 78 47 39; www.hotelbourgtibourg.com)

Sword-billed Hummingbird

So What makes you happy?

Go on, write it down.
Victor made me happy.
His answers played over in my head
on a happy loop for the rest of the day.

1. He was happy to see other people happy
2. He was happy to lead a serene life.
3. Victor's luxury was his work / job
4. Clothes and food are natural comforts
5. The word 'Luxury' stands for things that we buy outside our natural needs when we're not satisfied with ourselves
6. He loved his city and getting people to their destinations
7. He was simply satisfied. Happy there and then!!!

We checked in at the hotel and Charlie and Peter headed out for a bit of a wander. I broke out the new ink and the new bone-handled dip pen in my hotel room and cracked on with a sketch (love cracking on, me, even if it's only for the sound that cracking on makes or the way it looks and smells as I line up my pens, pencils, little paints and ink bottles.) Anyway I cracked on and painted this ...

18

The word
Labradoodle

Then I noticed that I had painted a few logos inadvertently among my happy stuff. Oops, Victor would be disappointed. Chanel (love a dab of No. 5 before bedtime), Vivienne Westwood (clothes, shoes, anything), Paul Smith (his stripy notebooks; in fact anything with his multicoloured stripiness). My hooded leather jacket. My Angelika Paschbeck scarf, Adidas and Nike (sports shoes), my Nokia phone, my Apple iPod, etc. Were these comforts or luxuries? And why these logos? My friends tell me I've been staying in East London way too long. They've noticed my growing fondness for whizzing round in heels on my bike and girly chats in the evening at the Ten Bells, my local (love the walls, love the tile pattern). 'It'll be all beehives, catty eyeliner and tattoos before long,' they warn. And? I say. Geography doesn't matter. I'd be loyal to these brands (my phone, my bike) wherever I lived. Why?

Why does one Stay Brand Loyal?

OK, so I'm cycling into another world here, a world of fancy -smancy lady talk, but it's only for two paragraphs and then it'll be all back to fun and games ... In my heart of hearts I believe that we stay brand loyal because brands function as extensions of our own identities. They're symbols/logos that we exchange with each other to reach a common territory of understanding. Think yummy mummies in 4 x 4 Land-Rovers, B-Boyz wearing A Bathing Ape, Wags and 'It brags', etc., that sort of thing. Different tribes adopt certain brands collectively and stay loyal to them. A brand often offers an individual status and safety because you melt in, fit in, if you emulate a certain tribe. So you're turned on to a brand because a certain tribe has adopted it. What next? Well, I know we're all guilty now and then of blending in with others but wouldn't it be much more authentic and individual to adopt a brand because it means something special to you alone? With me so far? OK!

When I find a brand that really speaks to me I absorb it, buy it, buy into it, I adopt it and wear it like a badge. I want it around because it makes me feel well, happy, gives me that warm fuzzy feeling. If it stops working for me, I walk away. A brand that I stay loyal to is something that I take inside of me and it becomes an expression of my own self and my own identity. That's when a brand becomes a success, when suddenly you or I are happy with it because it delivers consistently. We happily adopt that brand into ourselves and say, 'This is me.'

'Now I feel much better. Thanks for listening,' I said to the lamp. The hotel room had one on each side of the bed, delicately attached to the wall. They're usually great listeners, lamps. 'You got what I was trying to say there in the previous few paragraphs, didn't you? I've had that stuff locked up in my noodle for ages waiting to get out.' Slightly out of breath after all of that, I hopped up onto my hotel bed and wrestled with the remote control to switch on the telly. It was a Bang & Olufsen, not like my telly at home (belongs to Peter's parents and I love it so much because of that and because of the sounds ... it makes a really nice sound when you turn it on, haven't heard it on any other telly on my travels and makes Jon Snow and Jeremy Paxman sound, what's the word? Creamy.). This other telly though, it meant business, very hi-tech. 'I have these at home too, you know,' I said to the lamp, stroking the sheets all white and foldy like cake icing, 'but none of this other stuff.'

Then some French dude started going at it with his co-star on the telly, and I cringed and turned the sound down. What would the neighbours think? Still the pictures were enough to keep me glancing, they kept me company in a funny sort of way. After five minutes the bed was like a bombsite, full of make-up as if my make-up bag and handbag had exploded. There was stuff everywhere. 'Whoa! Wait a minute,' I said out loud. There was a stunned pause from all five light fixtures. 'Don't move a tassel, guys. Everything I've touched in the last five minutes IS A BRAND.'

A room maid knocked on the door to leave some towels in the bathroom. I tidied up fast and hung around her trying to make eye contact, wanting to tell her my news. 'Listen, I was just telling the lamps earlier,' I said. 'Pardon,' she said, eyes darting quickly towards the closed room door between her and safety. She left quickly and I poked around the room for some more furniture to tell. The bath and the toilet seemed quite uninterested so I checked in the closet in case anyone was hiding in there and I'd almost given up when Peter arrived through the door full of smiles. 'What have you been up to?' he said. 'I just passed a staff member running down the hallway.' 'Nothing! But listen to this. Everything you touch – your camera, your jeans, your runners, your notebook – everything is some type of brand or another and you've chosen it. Everything.' 'Right,' he said and flopped down on the bed to check his emails and have a little chirp.

As Peter tapped away at his laptop, I explained. 'Look, there on your screen, Google, that's a brand; MySpace, that's a brand; Bebo, that's a brand; and your computer, that's a brand, and Gmail, that's a brand and the BBC news website, that's a brand, and our bags, everything in our bags are brands; even my toothbrush with soft bristles which my dentist gave me for free is a brand, not a well-known one, but a brand nonetheless.'

'The Arctic Monkeys, that's a band,' Peter chirped. We laughed. 'And a brand,' he added. I went out onto the veranda with my pen and notebook and started to make a mental list of how many brands I'd personally chosen to share my life with on a normal day at home. Why had I chosen them? I've taken the next two pages and just a few lines to share them with you. If you were to do your own Happy List, would everything you share your life with be worthy of a place? Wanna have a snoop at mine. That OK? Right.

With preparations for Oscar night in LA belting out on the telly and Marion Cotillard being interviewed in French, Peter was gripped by an uncontrollable fit of yawning. He asked, 'How's the list going, G?' checking in politely mere moments before he was about to check out. This is what all normal straight guys do in real life (even the nice ones); when they see anything remotely girlie on the box it's code for SNOOZE. But how could any man snooze through Marion Cotillard? She's stunning! Even her name pronounced 'Cut-eee-yay' is soooo, well, French (we were in Paris for God's sake). Although Cotillard got off lightly being snoozed on just the once; some of Hollywood's greatest women have had Peter snooze on them repeatedly, well, not on them exactly, but you know what I mean.

'Peter, before you nod off there,' I said, popping my head through the window from the veranda, 'to answer your question about my list progress, I've realized that waking up in my own bed at home and breathing fresh morning air is tops.' Nothing more inviting than that exact moment when morning air hits your nostrils, except perhaps night air. Very late at night, air does smell sweet. 'Peter isn't moving, guys!' I said to my audience of winking light fixtures. 'Keep an eye on him, will you, and give me a shout when he's back in the land of the living. I'll be outside.' Funny how all light fixtures look on quietly as we slip from sleep into unconsciousness, then deep coma and finally death.

Never mind all that though, because back outside I cast around for things to say about my favourite place. I wrote 'My own bed' in bold and then 'Prioritize the waking-up bit and then list the nice bed bits after that.' I have to do this sort of thing, you see, to be able to include the word prioritize on my Happy List.

'Aaaah!' my own bed, that's the waking-up sound, isn't it? And if I send my big right toe out to scout out cold hidden territory and it finds some lurking at the edges of the duvet the sound turns to 'Ooooh!' When my toe pokes out a cold patch, then all the other littler toes scuttle quickly over to join it. I'll lie there for a full ten (ahem, fifteen) minutes Oooohing and Aaaahing with just my toes stuck wriggling in that cool place. Heaven! Then there's the bed itself.* I like poking around every last corner of it: the memory foam pillow, the pillow case, the sheets, the duvet, the vi-spring mattress and even the base of the bed. And the pyjamas and knickers have to be nice too for maximum sound effects. 'Peter,' I said, 'one thing has struck me about my gift-wrapped sleep experience.' 'What's that?' he asked, jolting himself awake again. 'Just waking up in the morning, just lying still, not even moving a muscle, just like you are now, involves about eight brands.' (I'd given them pink numbers and it made counting them quicker.) 'That's a good start,' he said smiling.

After a quick trip to le toilet I remembered that I like Andrex toilet paper and not because of the puppies, and, looking at my Crest Extra Whitening Clean Mint toothpaste (gets my teeth sparkly clean) and my nondescript toothbrush and Glide dental floss laid out in the hotel bathroom, I counted four more brands. Wow, I'd have to fly through my general-day-at-home list to get it done quickly. So here goes. Deep breath ...

In the morning I like long showers† – shower gel, body scrub, face wash. And shampoo and conditioner every third day, because I prefer my hair a bit 'unwashed' (not dirty). And I like the shower nozzle and putting the shower on ice cold before I get out (makes boobs perkier) and fluffy towels – is there anything nicer? And then I like coating every limb in body oil (Decléor's Aromessence Body Concentrate, it's organic with a nice smell). And I like body cream for my legs, and lotion containing glycolic acid for my upper arms (prevents bumpy bits and bingo wings), and I like cellulite cream, foot cream, hand cream, deodorant and perfume. Twenty-five brands and counting.

And I like a mist of water for my face (that's free and not a brand at all, but I still like it), and moisturizer (with fake tan, if I'm feeling pasty), sun block, eye cream and lip balm, and I like to put something on my neck so I don't end up some day looking like a chicken.

*See page 210 to construct the perfect sleep.
†For the perfect shower experience see page 274.

Thirty brands. Extraordinary! Thirty brands before I even have time to get dressed in the morning. Oops, is that the postman? And I like Calvin Klein bras, Agent Provocateur knickers, but Marks & Spencer ones if I'm on a lazy day at home. And Gandolfi ballet slippers and ballet socks (cheap as chips but extra fine) and my Angelika Paschbeck hooded top and bottoms. We're at thirty-six now.

And for breakfast I like? Barry's tea, always Barry's, the kettle, my vintage cup, milk – four more brands – and the perfect piece of toast involves – count 'em, go on – good bread (one), toaster (two), butter (three) and a knife (four). Four more brands again. Five if you count jam, six if you add a jam spoon and seven if you don't want to get crumbs everywhere and you use a plate. That's eleven brands for tea and toast. Twelve, thirteen, fourteen and counting if you want orange juice and an egg and a piece of cheese. Fifty brands so far! You get my drift.

And then after breakfast there are the brands that aren't obvious at first like when you turn on your computer; checking emails (Gmail is a brand) and watching film (YouTube is another) and the special sound the keys make only on my brand of computer when I type really fast with two fingers. I love that, I love that lots, makes me sound extra professional. And I like acting all important holding big newspapers that are now small newspapers like The Times and the Guardian. And I like words in these papers like 'presumably' and 'allegedly' and all the words that end in 'ly'. And I like kitchen roll for tea spillages when I read headlines like 'Small Fishermen Facing Extinction' in the Guardian dated 25 March 2008. How small?

And I like Marie round the shop who sells me the posh papers. ('How is the book going? Are you going to put us in it, Gisèle?' Yes, I am, guys, there you go and thanks a mill for all the milk and smiles.) See in a way, they're a brand too, yes they're people, peeps that I'm very fond of, but people can be brands and these guys are the best. And I like passing men on the street on their way to work who wear nice suits and shiny shoes and smell gorgeous when – go on, count it – one, two, three seconds later the smell trails behind them. The word for that is sileage, like when a plane in the sky leaves a thin white line (and I love that word sileage and the thin white lines planes leave in the sky). All brands the lot of them: colognes, airplanes and the company-owned men in shiny black shoes.

Back at the desk, I like notebooks and thumb tacks and staplers and pink staples and Blu-Tack and Tippex and Post-its (three world-renowned brands right there that each of us use at least once or twice a week). Brands, brands and more brands, there's no getting away from them, logos everywhere and even the people who make me happy during a tea break like Oprah … sure she's one of the biggest brands in the world.

And what's for dinner? Chicken from Tom, my local butcher, another brand. And who is on the box tonight? Stephen Fry, Jeremy Paxman, etc., the guys that Peter, Charlie and I talked about on our Happy List, all brands, every single one of them. And countries and cities on the news, they're all brands too. Like London and the Olympics (Yay!) and China and the Olympics (Boo!). (The world's largest gathering of people peeing in a cup, with footprint fireworks and a lip-synching little girl. Who'd a thunk it eh? One word …fake!) And then after dinner, stuff on TV makes Peter yawn again. I read in a book called *Blink* by Malcolm Gladwell (he's a brand, by the way) that when you read the word yawn it prompts you to yawn. Well, have you yawned yet? I have.

And I'm a brand at Christmas

Tea Break

So to set the scene, Peter and I are in Paris in a hotel room, and I've finished my four hours of painting and list making and feel that it's just impossible to work past four hours without a tea break, and anyway little drops of rain have started dropping onto my notebook (look Paris rain), that's when I decide it'd be best if Peter the boyfriend doesn't work either. 'Petes,' I say, while cleaning my paint brushes, 'what would happen iffffffffff ... I fainted with the lack of a tea break? What if I died because of tea deprivation? Surely there's a word for that syndrome? Have you any thoughts on this?' 'I don't think that's possible,' he says, grinning at my mischief. God forbid I'd be melodramatic. Mental note to self, this fainty, girly approach is only for whiny gals. In fact, it's total crrrrrrrrrrap.

Three, four, five minutes and he's still engrossed in his computer, hasn't moved a muscle, like when he's watching sport. In the sports world they call a situation like this 'a Big Ask'. Meanwhile, same venue, second act in the saga of the gender divide, that is, why girls and boys are different: 'Petes? What if the rain came in, splashed on your computer, you got electrocuted and I died trying to save you. Do you think the Parisian coroner's office would be able to pinpoint our time of death by our empty stomachs? I saw this thing on CSI where time of death is ascertained (lovely word that) within two hours of your last meal.'

'I think you're goimg mental,' he smiles, I think you need lunch and tea babes. 'Yep, that is a great idea,' I say, halfway backwards out the door. Worth mentioning, I think also, that I gingerly packed Snailey (the squidgy snail) in his little box and popped it in my bag to take with us, as always. (To read about the day Snailey was born see page 228).

I carry Snailey, the plastercine snail, to restaurants because a) he reminds me to take things slowly, to take time out to appreciate new food experiences with friends and b) it's fun to see other people smile at him perched on the table while I eat and have friendly chirps. It's a very good sign of a place, if staff smile back at him, he likes that, he likes that lots.

Yes, Londoners, New Yorkers, Berliners and the French and now Parisians have all come to know and love the seducer that is simply known on the continent as Snailey. You'll see him crop up all over the book when we're eating and gathering recipes. He's a proper A-list shellebrity, gets grovelling service from maître d's in restaurants from Marylebone to Montmartre. 'Mr Snailey, always a pleasure to have you with us, sir, your usual table by the window? We've ordered in the special; salad we know ... no salt.' Etc. Stuff like that.

Today we decide to treat ourselves at Ladurée's flagship tea salon on the Champs Élysées and I scribble the bones of this paragraph down partly on a napkin and then into my notebook after finishing a club sandwich and one cup of tea. If the truth be told, I'm feeling all J.K.ish at this very moment (that's Rowling, not Jamiroquai) and anything is possible. Ooooooh yeah, keep it coming! I start to draw and write this while sipping my tea ...

I like the cups, the saucers, the vast quantities of carbohydrates, the light green menus, the elaborate receipt stubs, the plush red chairs and the whole Ladurée experience. It's very French and elaborate and gold, gilty, glitzy. Like it, like it? Love it, love it lots. It's Saturday, I'm in Paris and I'm happy ... Looking about me, I scribble, cake and tea still popular then? *Délicieux* and most definitely yes!

The Club Ladurée sandwich, at – wait for it – €16, isn't really what I came for, but I'm hungry and it's substantial; more a reconnaissance mission really; research for my perfect club sandwich recipe which I've perfected globally and recreated with my favourite bread on page 298 so that I can make it affordably for a group of friends at home.

The Club Ladurée sandwich in itself is a lovely experience but way too expensive. The menu reads as follows: 'Toast, mayonnaise, salad, chicken, hard-boiled egg, green salad, tomatoes, grilled bacon, green salad, served with Ladurée French fries', each component of the sandwich mentioned as it appears on the delicious, delicate pile. The first thought that strikes me is why does it come in three triangles instead of four as per usual elsewhere? There's no real logic, but it does and it's good.

The French fries? There aren't enough of them (four, I ask you) but they're gorgeous. And the tea (awful) is the complete opposite of George Orwell's essay on how to make the perfect cup. At Ladurée as a dedicated hot-beverage hunter I'm not best pleased with the tea list. I chose a pot of the Darjeeling Namring from the menu thinking that it would be plain and simple. It isn't. The peach flavour isn't me at all. A pot of tea costs €6.80 here. That's six euros and eighty cents for a pot (two cups) of peachy tea. Ridiculous, *non*? (Ridiculous spelled the same in English as in French but pronounced the French way today of course).

'Er, this tea,' I say as casually as I can, 'not got the plain type like breakfast, have you?' 'Nu sooooray,' says the waiter, 'we 'ave only ze tea what's there,' in his best Inspector Clouseau while pointing at the menu of fifteen flavoured teas. No problem, I nod, fine, excellent … and then I retire to the bathroom and, in the cubicle out of sight, chew on my knuckle and concentrate on my new thing, which is counting backwards from ten while thinking of the word 'cheery uppage'. Makes me smile. Calms me down. In a situation like this you need to shake yourself up and look at the positive. Face the world with a smile rather than a scowl.

Returning to the table, I smile at Clouseau as he plonks my treat on the table, a *millefeuille au vieux rhum brun*. '*Caramelized puff pastry, vanilla cream flavoured with old dark rum*', at least that's what it says on the menu. Even to look at it makes me ''appy' as the French would say. Cake always gives me a massive dose of cheery uppage when on tour. With the tea problem now ancient history, I sink my fork into the millefeuille and listen to it break like brittle sticks.

Millefeuille, eh? Fantastically complicated piece of kit, layers and layers of puff pastry with hand-combed icing, no two are the same, bit like the human being. I've made my decision after several trips to Ladurée's – their many branches across Paris, their branch in Harrods and the Burlington Arcade in London – but it's this trip that has sealed it for me, the *millefeuille au vieux rhum brun*, the *religieuse à la rose* and the *Saint Honoré rose-framboise* are their three best cakes.

The *religieuse* is basically two cream puffs of choux pastry, one popped on top of the other and filled with flavoured confectioner's custard. It comes in chocolate, strawberry, rose, blackcurrant and caramel (hyperventilate). Got its name from some cardinal waaaay back (the priesty type, not the bird). Cardinals wear scarlet blood-like red robes symbolizing their willingness to die for their faith. Tough job that.

The *Saint Honoré rose-framboise* has nothing to do with priests, it's flaky pastry, choux pastry, light rose-petal confectioner's custard, raspberry stew, Chantilly cream flavoured with rosewater, rose syrup fondant and fresh raspberries. Yummeeeeeee! So ask yourself this? Are you salivating? Has my cakecentricity made you want to go out and eat something sweet? Is this like Malcolm Gladwell a few pages back with his yawn in his book *Blink* all over again, is it? He says that by reading the word yawn, you'll yawn eventually. So have you? Yawned yet, that is. Or is it me?

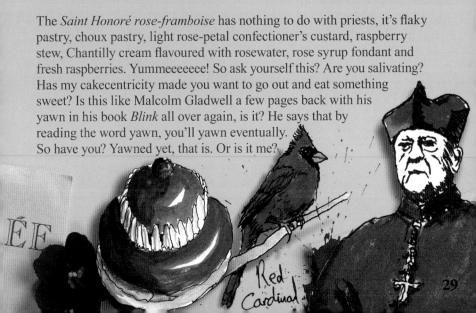

Red Cardinal

So that's that, and what else? I have nothing further to add about Ladurée except to say it was Saturday and as I descended their staircase high on sugar, Peter had to tie me down by anchoring me to his armpit in case I floated. Looking downstairs, I wasn't seeing double, there really was a very long queue that ran all the way out the door for their macaroon counter. So why the queue? Hadn't trends labelled the macaroon passé, like past it, like RIP, like dead?

Obviously these shoppers didn't give a fiddler's about trends or their predictors and what they went on about. So here's my question, who gets to tell the French that their macaroons and tea have kicked the bucket? Who gets to tell us that cupcakes are hot this week and apple pie the next? Apart from eejits like me that is. Full of fake confidence, i.e. cake confidence, i.e. sugar, I decided to ask. I sauntered over to the top of the queue and the tension mounted. The whole of the line watched, upwards of thirty people, Peter, Clouseau, attractive young waiters, dogs, the lot.

Queue La La

'Is everyone here to buy the macaroons?' Yes? No? Maybe? Too tired from queuing to remember? Peter nudged me and whispered, 'Try it in French, otherwise they'll ignore us.' 'Ummm, *bonjour*,' sieving my brain for school French from my orals, '*je m'appelle Gisèle, et je suis irlandaise.*' (Translation: I am Gisèle and I am Irish.) The lady third in the queue smiled at my efforts, face registering part confusion, part boredom, part pity. Mostly pity. I felt as small as a wren (the smallest bird in Ireland), I went on, head down, nonetheless: '*J'adore ma bicyclette comme les Français. J'adore les macarons et this is my boyfriend qui s'appelle Pierre.*' (Translation: I love my bike like the French, I love macaroons and this is my boyfriend Peter.) I think they got the last bit because Pierre's the French for Peter. Everyone knows that.

'This is going well,' I said to myself: the lady fifth in the queue was smiling and showing pity too. Fair enough, no drama yet, but then it got interesting, because I had not one, not two, not three, but four people queuing who looked quite approachable (sugar does this to me) so I nudged a bit closer and repeated, 'Is everyone here to buy the macaroons?' '*Oui*,' said the lady third in line in a twisty scarf and greeny sweater. '*Moi aussi*,' said another with a nice bag. '*Et moi*,' said a youngish woman. But she was only pretending to be Parisian because she flashed a ten-tooth smile, go on, count 'em, ten teeth exposed across the top row just like Julia Roberts – only Americans smile like that.

And there it was, the tiny question that each of us has to ask ourselves in order to find clues that will hopefully bring us that little bit closer to happiness. *Why*? *Why* were these people prepared to queue for close to an hour for a few little macaroons? *Why* didn't they go around the corner to another pastry shop where there was no queue at all? *Why* was the American pretending to be French, Parisian even? *Why* hadn't I worked harder to learn more French words for my orals at school?
'*Why* are you queuing for Ladurée macaroons?' I asked the lady with the twisty scarf first.

'*Ils sont étonnants*,' she said. 'Riiiiiiiiiiiiight!,' I replied. '*Oui, ils méritent d'être remarqué*,' a second lady added. 'Aaaaaahaaaaaa!' I mumbled. Some people cope with social anxiety by talking too fast, too loud or too much; I just clam up. Noticing my struggle, the smiley American lady pushed forward (her name was Jane by the way). '*Ils sont remarquables*,' she explained. Sounded like remarkable, so I nodded. 'In English?' 'The macaroons are outstanding, notable,' she answered.

And then she said, 'They're Pierre Desfontaines's.' 'Who?' 'Pierre Desfontaines, that's why they're special. He was the grandson of Louis Ernest Ladurée, the miller who founded this place, the Ladurée bakery, in 1862.' It seems that this Pierre Desfontaines fellow was the main man. I remember her telling me that and his first name because Pierre means Peter. The second bit I had to write down along with this other stuff: seemingly Pierre stuck two macaroon shells together with buttercream *ganache* in 1930 and Ladurée haven't looked back since. 'Before that, the original French macaroon had no filling and was stuck together warm from the oven and fused as it cooled' – at least that's what Jane said anyway. Who was this woman? She looked normal enough. Was she Professor of Cake and Buns at Yale or Harvard, maybe? My pathetic attempt to wind her down failed miserably so I kept scribbling, afraid if I stopped she'd think I was thick.

MACAROON WAR

So is all of my scribbling a waste of paper? On the contrary, Jane turned
out to be fascinating, and it was only through time spent scribbling that
I worked that out. She told me that 'a macaroon war has broken out in
Paris'. Picture it, bakers in fork-proof vests, French kitchen equipment
and piping bags loaded and ready, peering out from behind a barricade of
macaroons. Ooooooh yeah, I'm on fire now. 'Patisseries wage war on each
other across Paris every day to see who can create the wildest and most
over-the-top flavours,' she went on (she even said OTT for over the top to
explain how hot the war was). 'And the other patisseries – you should see
the packaging and flavours that they come up with,' she laughed. 'Chilli
and olive, balsamic vinegar and tomato.' *'Non, merci,'* I said. 'I don't fancy
the sound of them at all.'

Peeping behind Jane, I could see flashes of colour as the neat rows of sugary macaroons were lined up like big coloured buttons sandwiched together with buttercream *ganache* in their centres. 'Com 'ere Jane, what's the bluey-greeny one?' I asked. ('Com 'ere' is Irish for listen.) 'Herbaceous *anis vert* (aniseed),' she explained. 'Yuck! Aniseed, can't stand it. And the jet-black one with the browny filling?' '*Réglisse* (liquorice).' 'Hate the stuff. Black liquorice, spawn of satan. And the very light-green one, Jane. What's that?' '*Citron vert-basilic* (lime-basil).' 'Diiiiiiiiiiisgusting.' 'It's the au courant flavour in Paris,' she smiled. *Au courant* should mean current, shouldn't it? Oh yes, quite the linguist, me.

'These macaroons were in the movie *Marie Antoinette* directed by Sofia Coppola. Did you see it?' she asked. I had, so I said yes. 'Coppola's people employed Ladurée to make the cakes and macaroons and they were almost as important as the actors,' she giggled. Yes, in 2006 Sofia Coppola gave the Ladurée macaroon maximum exposure in her movie and then American Vogue gave Kirsten Dunst, who played the lead role, their April 2006 cover dressed as Marie Antoinette.

Suddenly Ladurée's macaroons were everywhere and the lines of green bags queuing at the Gare du Nord Eurostar were proof that this was a huge trend. The macaroon tipped and crossed the worlds of fashion, movies, luxury and travel. It even crossed the Channel to London when Ladurée opened its new tea shop in Harrods and a second branch in the Burlington Arcade.

These macaroons, I thought, restless back in my hotel bedroom, there's something about them. I studied my notebook, chewing my finger. Scrawled right next to all the stats on the number of buns scoffed and Snailey's smile mark (6 out of 10) was Jane's explanation. 'She was nice,' I said to the lamp. 'Eh?' said Peter, looking up from his laptop and surveying my notebook. 'Jane, the lady in Ladurée, she was nice.' 'She was, wasn't she?' he reflected. 'Yeah, they deserve the six Snailey smile points you've given them here and she was extra smiley.' So on behalf of Snailey I added one more. Ladurée smiles from Snailey 7/10.

'Ummmm, what do you think that first lady meant about the macaroons with her *étonnant*, Peter?' 'Here, have a look on the laptop yourself,' he

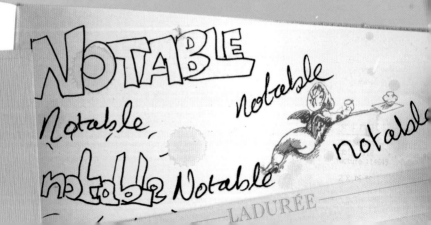

LADURÉE

said as he stood up to unpack a bag. I truffled around t'internet. *'Ils sont étonnants'*… tap, tap, tap, tap … 'Remarkable.' She said, 'They are remarkable.' And the second lady said, *'méritent d'être remarqué'* ... tap, tap, tap … that means 'notable' or 'noteworthy'. And Jane said, *'Ils sont remarquables,'* that's remarkable, outstanding and that word notable again. There's a whole bunch of other stuff here on the computer about *'remarquable'*; it means 'extraordinary, remarkable, exceptional, noteworthy and notable'. Notable – isn't that just such a lovely word?

I wrote notable into my notebook because it sounds like n-o-t-e , which kind of made me want to do it. Then I looked it up because I thought it simply meant to make a note of something, but guess what? It also meant a whole bunch of other cool stuff as well.

I scribbled this alongside 'notable'… Something notable is something worth noticing. Something exceptional. Interesting. Important. Significant. Extraordinary. Uncommon. Outstanding. Something special. Notable means something remarkable and distinguished. (Is this making any sense?)

And I couldn't write this next bit down fast enough, it nearly took the fingers off me … Notable does not mean perfect, ideal, gorgeous, stunning or beautiful.

What else? Oh yeah, notable means that something is worthy of notice, worth talking about, worthy of being noted, remembered and recorded, it's worthy of scribbling down in your Happy List in your notebook in pink, so I did. Ladurée's *millefeuilles* and their macaroons are notable! I wrote.

I was not alone in my praise. The four Ladurée shops in Paris sell over 12,000 buttercream-*ganache*-filled macaroons every single day – that's over four million macaroons a year. Jane wasn't kidding. Yep! Ladurée's sales figures are spectacular. I poked around t'internet again looking for their advertising. Nothing! A nice woman in their head office told me that they run no TV ads, no magazine ads and not one single giant billboard in Paris. So how have they achieved all of this success?

I believe that Ladurée's success came from their storytelling. When Jane buys macaroons at Ladurée she's not buying a sugar treat (she could buy that anywhere), she's buying the Ladurée story wrapped in their green Ladurée box and ribbon. Jane embraced Ladurée's story ... their macaroons were – hold on, what's the word she used – 'outstanding, notable', that's it, and their guy Pierre, sure, wasn't he the first to come up with the creamy bit in the middle idea? 'And isn't the first always the greatest?' she said; she got real excited saying that bit.

Or how about when she told me that she'd been living in Paris for over eight years and that the most exciting thing for her was when Hollywood came to town to feature 'my macaroons'. Her voice gave me that funny shiver you sometimes get up a mountain, or under the spell of a good book, as she carefully arranged Ladurée's story end to end for me. This is the same story she tells herself every time she queues for ages for those macaroons. That's the story that makes her return repeatedly. Ladurée's success was outside any trend forecaster. The macaroon would never be RIP as long as Ladurée had people like Jane.

Jane had convinced me with her story that Ladurée was worthy of my new word 'notable' and worth all of this space in my notebook. And here we are, now you know the story too. I suppose a few more pages showing the many macaroon warriors battling it out and the most beautiful flavous can't hurt, can it? Yes, I have proof of purchase and my own little add-on! There! Where? There! A green cuboid Ladurée box which when empty will be perfect for housing all my scissors. A box with their name on it in goldy writing which will remind me of my Ladurée experience every time I need to fish out a pair of scissors at home to cut a piece of paper, thread or tape. But first I'd have to scoff its contents to find the nicest flavours.

It was eleven thirty – way too late to go on with this now, I thought to myself, I'll tackle this tomorrow. I stuffed my notebook and pen in my bag and left the hotel to find Peter and Charlie. They'd gone to a bar across the road earlier to have a few drinks and, looking through the bar window, I could see them deep in chats. As I pulled up a chair and ordered, I sensed an awkwardness. I suppose they'd been chirping on about the hot barmaid in graphic detail ... is that what they do, do you think, when we're not around? Or do they just talk about sportsy stuff? Because I'm sure I heard Peter clearly use the words exquisite, Marion and Cotillard (and I thought he had snoozed right through her Oscar preparations on the telly, obviously not, becasue he pronounced it 'Cut-eee-yay' and everything).

a LITTLE BIRDY TOLD ME

Jamacian Tody

PARIS – –: **Ladurée Bonaparte**, 21 rue Bonaparte - 75006 Paris (tel: +33 1 44 07 64 87); **Ladurée Royale**, 16 rue Royale - 75008 Paris (tel: +33 1 42 60 21 79). **LONDON – Ladurée at Burlington Arcade**, 71 -72 Burlington Arcade, London W1J 0QX (tel : +44 207 491 9155) **Ladurée at Harrods**, 87/136 Brompton Road (tel: +44 203 155 0111). **BERLIN – Ladurée** Berlin, Espace Gourmet, Galeries Lafayette GmbH, Französische, Strasse 23, 10 117 Berlin (tel: + 49 30 35 12 3897). **See www.laduree.fr**

So, next day, a beautiful morning, up with the sparrows, I planned to spend a happy half-hour chomping back and forth between different Ladurée flavours. (Not ALL on my own.) In the front room of Hôtel Bourg Tibourg, I'd ordered a gallon of tea and Peter and Charlie pitched up to help me. Excellent! This was shaping up to be a great day. I was so freaking excited that the boys decided that there was nothing for it but to turn the tasting into a boy-type competition … with scoring of course and a list of rules and everything.

'The first rule of snack club: do not talk about snack club,' said Peter. 'The second rule of snack club, do not talk about snack club,' added Charlie. Beyond that, there were these … Charlie called them 'mere technicalities', adding, 'Are we all agreed that we take a few bites of a macaroon, make a quick note of the flavour, score it out of ten and then get an average?' I suggested we wash each bite down with a great big slurp of milky tea to … you know, clean the palate. 'It'll make it proper professional,' I explained. The boys stared at me blankly. OK! Clipboards and pens at the ready. Click! Click! Click! Macaroons at the ready. No kicking, no biting, no gouging of eyeballs, no illegal use of elbows and, gentlemen, no below-the-belt punches please, etc.

I dug out Snailey and laid him on the table to keep the competition friendly. 'What are those people doing?' A lady seated at the next table elbowed her husband. He replied, 'What people?' 'Those people there?' 'How should I know?' he snapped. She came by and asked, 'Excuse me, do you mind me asking what this is?' 'Snack club,' I chirped. Peter shot me a *shhhhhhh* glance. Too late. 'What's snack club? Ummmm, we taste things with our friends and give them scores, that's all.' 'Why?' 'Well, I'm trying to make a Happy List and fill my notebook up with little things that make me and my best friends happy. At the moment it's snacks,' I replied. 'And how do you decide who or what gets in?' she pressed.

Lily of the Valley 10/10

'Gut feeling,' I said (tapping just below the ribs where gut feeling lives). Then I took a bite of a greeny macaroon with a whitish filling (lily of the valley) … 'Mmmmmmm, this one's goooooooood! Ten out of ten, would you like one?', I asked the lady. She declined and slipped away. 'Not so good to start so high,' Peter advised. But it was my overall favourite so beginner's luck. Sitting there munching, I played name that feeling. Joy was the first thing that came to mind; yes, I was full of joy, but there was something else … but I couldn't quite place it.

All done. I shook the sticky crumbs from my fingers then I drew a line under my macaroon fetish and wrote case closed for now in my notebook. And for extra safety around the bit that said 'Ladurée is the most "notable" I put a big full stop. A big one like this. I should have left it at that, but I made one last mad dash around the other pastry shops in the city (call it snack club research) – you know, just in case I'd missed something. Messy, crumbly, sticky business, scoffing macaroons, but the G's got to do what the G's got to do. What do you reckon? Do you think that I could find anything better, anything more notable, a more notable story than I found at Ladurée yesterday? I doubted it.

Well, let me tell you, after checking out all of what, ten, twelve or more pastry shops listed one after another in my notebook, Ladureé was still the winner. So save yourself a fortune and the cake face (we don't want one of those now, do we?) and take my word for it; after hours of chewing macaroons the length and breadth of Paree, Ladurée was still the bizz, except for one challenger to the crown and that was Pierre Hermé. Surely you'll be wanting to know a little bit about him, won't you? Here goes, it won't take a tick …

OK. Well, as Peter and I rocked up to the front door there was a long queue down rue Bonaparte and you know how excited queues make me. A queue like this just to get in the door means there's something worth queuing along the street to get in to. Right? So what was it? To cut a long queue short, it's not the biggest patisserie in Paris, it is not even the most famous, so why were people queuing? Wouldn't it have to have a story like Ladurée's to cause all of that interest? I stood in line and geared myself up to ask the girl in front of me what exactly that story was.

For more underground snack club meets check out www.thegoddessguide.com.

39

'So are the croissants really good in this place then?' I asked the girl in front of me and to answer she swung right around and faced me. 'Pierre Hermé is zee couture *pâtissier*,' she answered, 'he does not do *des croissants*.' She fixed me with a Parisian stare when she said the '*des croissants*' bit. She continued, 'Like zee fashion, he does *deux* [two] different collections *par année* [each year].' 'So is this place *très cher* then?' I asked. 'It's €1.50 *pour* a *petit macaron* and €3.60 *pour* the laaaaarge ones,' she explained. Laaaaarge ones? Did she say laaaaarge ones? I looked at Peter. Now you're talking. Laaaaarge ones, I like the sound of that.

'*Oui*, laaaaarge,' she said, in the most beautiful Parisian drawl. She was chic, yes, but seemed kinda regular (like me), so why was she so prickly? As I was just about to ask her a bit more about the laaaaarge macaroons, a guy broke the queue and nearly kilt me in the process. 'Zat's a delivery boy. He has come to pick up *macarons*, small cakes for a *patron* [a regular local], he jumps zee queue because zee order is very laaaaarge,' she explained. How laaaaarge? I asked. Three hundred euros, somesing like zat. 'For cake's sake, that's not laaaaarge,' I explained, 'that's mahussive.' She taught me to say 'laaaaarge' and I taught her to say 'mahussive'; we were quits, what can I say?

So anyway, getting away from nearly getting kilt and back to, er, wotsisname, Pierre Hermé. This Pierre Hermé chap is a living breathing pastry chef then, eh? My French lesson continued: it's Pierre Hermé, py-air air-meh, not peeeee-hair her-mayyyyy, she explained patiently. Apart from that last bit she was great company, (she waaaaas) so I let it slide and put it down to prickly Paris pineapple syndrome (see page 3). So did I ever get to the bottom of py-air air-meh? Did I ever get to the end of the py-air air-meh queue even? The answer, emphatically, is yes. Read on.

On we all went shoving along towards the front door and as we stepped in from Rue Bonaparte, Nathalie told me her name and thawed. She suddenly went all shake-your-shoes-off, let's-have-a-laugh on me. 'Zee *macaron* is zee queen of pastry,' she smiled. 'You see everybodies [loved the way she said that] can make zee *croissant*, but only zee best can make zee *macaron*.' And finally I plucked up the courage to ask, 'What exactly in the name of God are they made of?' 'Egg whites, white almond powder sieved *deux fois* [twice], sugar and lots of *patience* [patience said the French way of course (pah-see-ance)]. And zee filling,' she said, 'zee filling is *très important*.' Just as she said that bit I saw my first Pierre Hermé macaroon glowing in the distance. Nathalie was spot on, these looked 'well nice' (another phrase I taught her, along with 'gutted', 'ker-razy' and 'ching-ching' – my word for her *très cher* (expensive)).

She then in
turn told me that
even though Pierre
Hermé confections were
'ching-ching', he himself was
'well nice' and that if he was better-
looking, less humble and spoke English, he could be a
'mahussive' celebrity. 'It's ker-razy that he isn't,' she
exclaimed, shaking her head. 'I know,' I said, in a
jokey way and added – ho-ho – 'He'll have to start
throwing a few Fs around like Gordon Ramsay.'
There was an icy silence and I watched her reaction
unfold through my fingers. All that plus me going,
'Umm ... errr ... and er ... do you think that would
help?' '*Mais non*,' she gasped. Fun and games
... fun and games, I tell you; don't think the
Frenchies like the F-word at all.

Seriously though, turns out that Pierre Hermé is
a very modest man, a very nice man and hasn't
sought international celebrity anywhere. Apart
from a boutique in Tokyo, he has only three
tiny shops in Paris. 'He is zee artiste,' Nathalie
explained. 'When he dies, there is no other artiste
like him for the magnificent *macaron* flavours. He
invents zee flavours like no other. When he dies
everybodies in Paris gutted.' I must stop now before
I start to believe my words 'ker-razy', 'mahussive',
'well nice', 'ching-ching' and 'gutted' should be in
common use in everyday language in France.
Imagine? One can only dream …

Pierre Hermé, 72 Rue Bonaparte and 185
Rue Vaugirard, Paris, France (tel.: +33 1 43
54 47 77, www.pierreherme.com)

Plonking myself down back at the hotel, it suddenly dawned on me, so suddenly that I had to scribble this down fast before the thought escaped me for ever (has that ever happened to you?). I made little notes along the lines of … lacking Ladurée's famous history, Pierre Hermé has had to trade on something else; he's had to find another way to get people's attention so they'll queue up along the street for his macaroons. He's had to tell an equally good if not better story than Ladurée. Hmmmmm!

As I opened the box, the other two snack club members watched in silence. 'What do you think, guys?' (Will they be better, worse or the same as Ladurée? We took a nibble of each, mouthfuls punctuated with things like 'What do you think of this? What do you think of that? Hold on, what's this one?' Americano Pamplemousse (Campari and Grapefruit), Huile d'Olive and Vanille – I know, some very weird-sounding names but the tastes? The tastes ambushed me like the excitement I felt on my first day on t'internet. I was suddenly overwhelmed and excited all at the same time and (this surprised me) I got all emotional. Nearly spilt my tea with the joy!

As we bonded busily over brews, something inside me shivered (another lovely word that). I thought of all the people involved in the making and marketing of this little tiny box of goodies, people who had to get up extra early that morning (that's ker-razy early in the baking world) to help make these little sugar circles that made us smile brighter smiles. Snailey awarded eight points for that alone. And another point was awarded for the joy of la-di-da-ing it up in Paris, drinking milky tea and chomping posh things as a mini-break (a break from the usual routine), I said, 'Guys, this man has poured his heart and soul into this little bosca [pronounced bus and ca, it's the Irish word for box]. Can't you just taste the truth?'

I drifted off into my own little world imagining the Macaroon War raging in Paris and Pierre in his bunker making little sugar love bombs. I could see it vividly, Pierre sporting his snack club cakey-bakey face, cool, calm and in the zone, whisking, folding, baking, tasting and then voilà! ... flavours. Eureka! Take that! Candied chestnut cream with a layer of matcha tea ganache (yum). And that! White-truffle hazelnut macaroon with lightly toasted Italian hazelnut in a thick white-truffle ganache (double yum). And that! Yellow passion fruit macaroon filled with milk chocolate (triple yum). And here's is zee laaaaarge macaron - a rose Isaphan sandwiched with rose cream, lychee and raspberries. 'Extraordinary,' the G said to herself, surveying the flavours, shaking a bit with excitement. 'This is utter genius. This is instant joy.'

With this in mind, we evaluated both experiences. No one, as the cliché goes, remembers those who finish second. Or fifth, or tenth. Sorry? We did. Ladurée came a good second and loads more followed on after that (see my list of great cakey-bakey macaroons shops on the next page). Say what you like about the Pineapply Parisians though, they've still got the best pastries. There wasn't a lot else to be said after that, we agreed, except that Ladurée's macaroons in second place were a bit crumbly and gritty in comparison to Pierre Hermé who with his unique flavours deserved to be the winner.

And the queues? Pierre Hermé's was more, more … what's the word? Local … that's it, less touristy, more Parisians and more locals collecting laaaaarge orders (always a good sign). We'd slowly unravelled Pierre Hermé's scripted planned market-y/PR-y message in snack club. We'd examined each bite for fakey bakeyness and were genuinely impressed with what we found. Pierre Hermé was authentic. His macaroons were notable because he was so real. So righty ho then! That's the Pierre Hermé story. Is it better than the Ladureé one, do you think? Given the choice, right now, which ones would you buy?

We spent four days and three nights in Paris and did loads of other cool stuff besides queuing and holding secret snack club meets in the lobby of Hôtel Bourg Tibourg. Each day the locals (the Pineapply Parisians) shared more and more notable titbits with us (said like that, titbits sounds like little tiny birds delivered the messages. Doesn't it, though?). Were we happy? Were we what … Ecstatic, more like: I was so lucky to have found tons of authentic fashion, food and secret places with the help of the locals (see pages 180-187).

Meanwhile, I got thinking about all the notable things we'd experienced, little morsels of happiness that were now but tiny memories. "Just three mouthfuls in one macaroon, did you know that? That's not bliss, it's only fleeting happiness," who said that? Yeah, I needed something with a bit more shelf life, something a bit more robust, something a tad laaaaarger to give me longer happy time. Something from the fashion world puuuuuurhaps? What do you think? I decided to poke around there next. Gulp! It was Paris Fashion Week, something was bound to kick off.

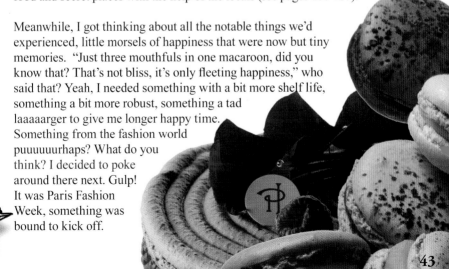

43

Best macaroon cakey bakey shops (worldwide)

Aren't macaroons a teensy, tiny bit of affordable luxury? While queuing in Paris the locals explained, 'We don't get to dine out in Paris's haute restaurants, but macaroons are a tiny treat at €1.50 each.' Yet another reason to love them then, eh? Everyone has a favourite address. Here are mine ...

Paris

Pierre Hermé, 72, rue Bonaparte, 75006 (tel: +33 1 43 54 47 77, www.pierreherme.com) means you can have your own tasting - snack club style. Ooooo yeah! Keep and eye out forPierre Hermé's exquisite flavours which change with the seasons. His most famous creation is a rose-flavored macaroon with rose cream, lychees, and fresh raspberries. Yummers!

Ladurée, Champs-Elysée, 75, avenue des Champs Elysées - 75008 (tel : +33 1 40 75 08 75, www.laduree.fr) is the hugest of tea salons, however it's usually overrun with tourists so the locals prefer the older and first ever Ladurée shop, **Ladurée**, 16, Rue Royale 75008 (Tél : +33 1 42 60 21 79).

Ladurée, 21 rue Bonaparte, 75006 (tel:+33 1 44 07 64 87; www.laduree.fr) just down the street from...

L'Artisan de Saveurs, 72 rue du Cherche-Midi, 75006 (tel: +33 1 42 22 46 64, www.lartisandesaveurs.com). A tea salon and take-out, love the grilled tea-flavoured macaroon filled with chocolate ganache.

Dalloyau, place Edmond Rostand, 75006 (tel: + 33 1 43 29 31 10, www.dalloyau.fr). Delicate macaroons (champagne flavour anybody?) make this a fave with the locals. There are six branches in Paris.

Fauchon, 24–26 place de la Madeleine, 70008 (tel: +33 1 70 39 38 00, www.fauchon.com). Everything is va va voom here, gold leaf on the bread, feminine boxes of chocolates and sophisticated macaroons.

Gérard Mulot, Magasin Saint Germain, 76 rue de Seine, 75006 (tel: +33 1 43 26 85 77, www.gerard-mulot.com). A comprehensive boulangerie-pâtisserie and gourmet take-out with two locations in Paris. The classic chocolate and more exotic coconut or passion fruit are well nice.

Jean-Paul Hévin, 231 rue Saint-Honoré, 75001 (tel: +33 1 55 35 35 96, www.jphevin.com). Beautiful chocolate macaroons in this tearoom and shop.

Hévin2, 16 avenue de la Motte-Picquet, 75007 (tel: +33 1 45 51 99 49, www.jphevin.com). Lush!

Lenôtre, 36 avenue de la Motte-Picquet, 75007 (tel: +33 1 45 55 71 25). Difficult to do this justice. In a city that prides itself on the quality of its patisseries, Lenôtre is regarded as one of the very best. Founded by Gaston Lenôtre, the man who wrote the definitive book on pastry, it now has seven branches in Paris and even gives classes on how to make them.

Titbit

Want to learn how to make the perfect macaroon yourself? Ecole Lenôtre, Pavillon des Champs-Elysées, 10 avenue des Champs-Elysées, 75008 (tel: +33 1 42 65 97 60, www.lenotre.fr), runs classes in its cookery school on the Champs-Elysées three times a week. At €115 a lesson, for three and a half hours, they're expensive.

New York

Bouchon Bakery and Café, Time Warner Center, 10 Columbus Circle, Third Floor, New York, NY 10019 (tel: +1 212 823 9366, www.bouchonbakery.com). Good classic macaroons.

Fauchon, 442 Park Avenue, New York, NY 10022-2604 (tel: +1 212 308 5919, www.fauchon.fr). Best in NYC. Fauchon also does a mean gold leafed bread and really high quality hand-crafted chocolates.

Payard Patisserie & Bistro, 1032 Lexington Avenue between 73rd and 74th Streets (tel: +1 212 717 5252, www.payard.com). The best macaroons in New York – after Fauchon that is.

London

Hard as I try, I can never make London be Paris.
Do you think that paying in sterling affects the
taste of the macaroon? Regardless, here is where to
get a macaroon fix worthy of Marie Antoinette.

London

Ladurée, Harrods, 87/135 Brompton Road, Knightsbridge, London SW1X 7XL (tel: +44 203 155 0111).
This British outpost offers everything available in Paris (macaroons, millefeuilles, madeleines, tea) but
it costs a bomb and lacks atmosphere. If you're around that area it's good for macaroon take-outs.
Otherwise go to Ladurée, 71–72 Burlington Arcade, London W1J OQX (tel: +44 207 491 9155), a much
more authentic experience.
Maison Blanc, 7 Old Church Street, Kensington, London SW3 5UK (tel: +44 207 795 2663, www.
maisonblanc.co.uk). This is a cute salon de thé with good classic macaroons. Offers loads of other French
stuff too, like viennoiseries and other pastries. There are tons of locations around London; see the website.
Paul Boulangerie, 122 Brompton Road, Knightsbridge, London SW3 1JB (tel: +44 207 584 6117, www.
paul.fr). At £7.10 for twelve good macaroons or £2.50 each for the large ones, better value than most
places and also a decent selection of tarts and viennoiseries, as well as good sambos. Catching a train? Try
Paul Boulangerie, Unit 33, The Lawn, Paddington Station, London W2 1HB (tel: +44 207 402 8866), to
get your fix or take some home.
Sketch, 9 Conduit Street, London W1S 2XG (tel: +44 207 659 4500, www.sketch.uk.com). This is one
of Snailey's favourite places to have macaroons and a cuppa. The macaroons are good here, the china
gorgeous and the staff are the friendliest in London. Sketch also has a pastry counter in Fortnum & Mason.
Yauatcha, 15–17 Broadwick Street, Soho, London W1F 0DL (tel: +44 207 494 8888). Serves tea and
cake like no other place in London. Phenomenal cake, amazing macaroons and beautiful packaging,
what's not to like? Snailey isn't a fan for a start, thinks the staff don't know what a smile is.

Tokyo

Jean-Paul Hévin shop, Omotesando Hills, 1F 4-12-10 Jingu-Mae Shibuya-Ku (tel: 03 5410 2255).
Pierre Hermé, Hotel New Otani, 4-I kioi-cho, Chiyoda-Ku, Tokyo 102-8578 (tel: +81 (0)3 3221 7252,
www.pierreherme.com). Only heard recently, Pierre Hermé is a superstar in Tokyo.

Sydney

Lindt Concept Store and Café, 53 Martin Place (tel: +61 2 8257 1600,
www.lindt.com.au). Flavours are superb (from passion fruit and, of course, all
things Lindt-chocolatey.) There are two other branches in Sydney.

Berlin

Ladurée, Espace Gourmet, Galeries Lafayette GmbH, Französische Strasse 23, 10 117
(tel: +49 30 3512 3897). One more good reason why Berlin is rockin'!

Titbit

Parisian macaroons are nothing like the coconut paper-light macaroons popular
in the US, and while the Europeans call them 'macaroons' and the French call
them 'macarons', at the Lindt place in Australia they call them 'delice'. Ker-razy!

Battle of the

What next? Oh yeah, time surely, before heading back stage to look for happiness in the world of fashion, to squeeze in one more observation. My most treasured memory of the whole Paris trip was when I was casually queuing in a shop to test more stuff for snack club. Picture the scene: for two days I'd queued with ten dozen or so ladies doing bun battle. But there was another war being fought in Paris along the queuing trenches and it involved neither cake nor chocolate; it centred around this... the season's 'It Brags'. Lined up like soldiers going to war they were; heads down these ladies, thrusting their leather armour studded with logoed hardware like shields against the world (et moi, 'stand back I say, stand back').

Funny business, handbags. The French and I: same taste, different competitive streak though. I wonder if I am entirely alone in harboring a sneaking admiration for their cheeky chicness? Am I? I probably am. Fashion, eh? Fickle world... Shall I? Shan't I? Will I just give my 'It Brag' a tiny shove forward, just an inch or so, nothing much, just a nudge to show that, you know... I'm still in the game, and you know what? For the first time in my life I didn't engage in that inch by inch, bitter hand-to-hand combat. I froze.

It wasn't that I was a scaredy cat or anything, no, I just hid there in that cake queue, clutching my new belief tight to my chest for fear of damage. I held it close, held it back, behind the cheeky French, safe in the knowledge that I'd go unnoticed. So there I was clutching to my "It Brag" and this new idea of myself, looking for meaning in widening circles. I dunno, do you think I was stupid? I stood there quietly and made this observation...to thrust my "It Brag" forward even an inch at that moment in time, to go all fashion showey offey would have let the side down. What do you think?

To tell you the truth, I had never thought a lot about what motivated me to buy an 'It Brag'. All this analysis over a bag might seem barking, but it's not, not entirely anyway. You've got to accumulate the facts, and then stare these facts straight in the face, and then you can start doing something to change yourself. Right? All I knew was that every season there was an 'It Brag' name checked in the fashion industry and I did as I was told like everyone else and bought it. One costs around eight hundred quid usually; why, my friends, why?

'It Brags'

Friends? Yeah that's it, my friend made me do it. Even though there were two of us shopping, one of us touted a picture and many sketches of a particular 'It Brag' around the shops. There they all were, stuck into her notebook, pictures of 'It Brags' with the words MUST BUY written in pink ink above them, stats and notes on everything, especially the hardware. You'd never guess who that was?

Back to Paris. Standing in that queue I was melting and managing quite successfully to pass blame on again, this time to the French, a group of whom (and I speak as I find) had arrived during Paris Fashion Week, touting 'It Brags' and were refusing to budge up. No different then, than the front row battle at the catwalk shows. And then it struck me… to avoid the 'It Brag' battle, I had spent the length of the queue looking for someone else to blame. So far I'd blamed a) the fashion magazines for being too numerous and containing sixty per cent advertising of which most is the season's 'It Brags' b) the fashion magazines again who are too keen to include said same 'It Brags' in loooovly editorials, c) my friends and d) the French. Yeah, the French, they made me do it.

Bullshit the lot of it. Here's the truth, I have a history with Desire; we go way back. He eyeballs other people's nice new shiny stuff, winks and elbows me, and then I want in, plain and simple. Posh writers call it status anxiety, 'Desire' and his pal 'Inadequacy' are the ones who make me buy. Recently, however, I've been questioning their motives.

Back on page 1, the very first page of this journey, while alone in my kitchen I first questioned it… after making and milking my tea and poking around in my ageing 'It Brag' for my pencil case. I asked myself… Isn't the 'It Brag' like a carton of milk? Shouldn't there be a bar code printed on the side with a best before date? Shouldn't there? Sensational admission! Can't believe I just wrote all that down. But I have, so there.

But my clarity was short lived. For that whole day in Paris, I felt Desire and Inadequacy slip along the Parisian streets looking to seduce me.

47

When by myself, window shopping, I'd catch glimpses of them, but then they'd duck into doorways or slip around corners at the sound of Peter's and Charlie's laughs. Desire finally caught me and nuzzled up against me. I recoiled against the counter at Sadaharu Aoki, a Japanese patisserie. With only him for company, we glanced at the French/Japanese pastries... macha eclairs, black sesame macaroons and yuzu tartlets. He waited like he does at home, when he wants me to hit the shops on quiet Sundays, (calm but uneasy), he was waiting for an opportunity to strike.

I could feel him all over me and then he whispered; his voice dark and husky he slowly filled me to my fingertips. 'If only you had a spare quarter of a million pounds, Gisèle, everything would be better wouldn't it?' (I melted and shopped from the ladies who queued), 'Yeah,' I said, 'you're right, I'd get that, and that bag, and one of them, and I'd like one of them, and two of those (one shoe is no good on its own right?), and one of them to match those,'... fairytale stuff that; made me wish I owned America. Desire encouraged, 'Yesssss, that's my girl.'

I brooded. Around this point Inadequacy stepped in, carefully carving his way through the cake shop, immaculate, shirt collar open, hair greased back... He turned his attention in my direction. 'How did you find me?' I asked. Like the mercury in a barometer plummeting, my confidence fell when he spoke. 'A quarter of a million wouldn't be nearly enough, Gisèle, for everything you're longing for, better make it a round 500 grand, what do you think?' But the money is irrelevant really because it was the shiny stuff that I was really after. If I owned more shiny stuff, people would be more interested in me. Face it, without shiny stuff, I was bland.

'Spivvy impostors,' I snapped. Inadequacy guessed he'd crossed the line and apologized. 'Oooo, I'm so sorry, honey, did I upset you? There, there... tell you what, why don't you just ignore the two of us and all this silly "It Brag" business?' 'Yes, I have a much better idea, darling,' rasped Desire ... (here it comes, no surprises) '...instead of worrying about a new "It Brag" why don't you buy loads of cake instead?' The air froze, the jig was up, and I was banjaxed; the boys had raised a full-blown, category-six insecurity and it blew around my head. But this time, I welcomed it, took a deep breath and relaxed. Because that's what you have to do isn't it? So G, would it be bag or cake, shoes or tea, sink or swim?

I had drowned at this point so many times in the past. I didn't mean to do it, I just jumped in without thinking and bought loads of stuff. I'd love to be able to go back to all the places I've spent that type of money in and have them greet me with a smile and a refund. Maybe if I explained properly... 'Listen, I bought this "It Brag" four months ago because I wanted other people to look at it and think that I was special. It was simple fear, fear of rejection; could I have my money back please?'

This fear also creeps into my writing. You'd think it was pathetic, really, if you could see me: sitting at home, staring at a few misspelled scrawls in my notebook, desperately trying to be honest about a subject but also wanting to convey the experience and the fun I'd had. At one time I used to be one of those proper writers who just wrote facts about this and that. Straight, old-school writing, but I can't do that anymore. Thing is, you can come straight from a funeral and write straight stuff like that. No, to push on with life and my hunt for happiness I'd started to write more fun in, it helps me to stand my ground with 'Desire' and 'Inadequecy'. 'Listen, lads, if you don't mind... I'm a bit busy, it's my turn to order anyway.'

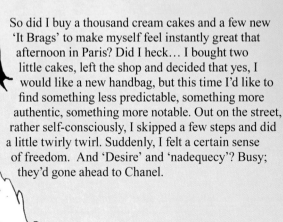

So did I buy a thousand cream cakes and a few new 'It Brags' to make myself feel instantly great that afternoon in Paris? Did I heck... I bought two little cakes, left the shop and decided that yes, I would like a new handbag, but this time I'd like to find something less predictable, something more authentic, something more notable. Out on the street, rather self-consciously, I skipped a few steps and did a little twirly twirl. Suddenly, I felt a certain sense of freedom. And 'Desire' and 'nadequecy'? Busy; they'd gone ahead to Chanel.

Waiting for a taxi on my own in Paris, it began to rain and I did a few more twirly twirls like a ballerina, at the taxi rank. Twirly twirls make me feel loose, free and happy. Do you know what I mean when I say 'loose'? OK let me rephrase that. Do you know what I mean when I say 'free'? You're in a really good mood and you feel free of bother, light as a feather. You go all running-in-the-rain-in-your-bare-feet-without-a-care-in-the-world on yourself. You're happy! It's simple. Having shaken off Desire and Inadequacy and leaving the Japanese Parisian patisserie with two small buns, I believe I had just experienced how that feels.

So my hope was to hold onto that feeling as I cast around for transport. Why? Dunno. I just know that that milky tea happiness feeling was really nice and it made me feel brave. See, it's at times like this that I get the courage to glimpse inside myself just for a split second, and I asked: Gisèle do you have a wish? (Apart from finding a taxi, before you get soaked that is). Would you like to be able to make that wish come true? What would you need to make it happen? Well? Money? Time? I felt at that very moment that anything was possible. I really felt that. Was this luxury? Freedom to live life, my way? A taxi splash broke my thought.

Pootling along towards Colette to meet Peter and Charlie, I heard a screech as a 4x4 clipped a bike beside my taxi on the slippery tarmac. I could see a cyclist on the ground and the 4x4 driver who hit him shrugging her shoulders apologetically in that 'I'm not getting out. Yesss I need my 4x4 in zee citeeee for zeee children's bikes,' kinda way. He came away unharmed, thankfully, peeling his handlebars from the grill of her mahussive vehicle (his bike was a write-off. Pity, nice model). All this made me question that lady's choice of ride. I mean, who needs to be driving a tank about town anyway? But that was one of her luxuries; too spendy for me though. I knew my luxury had more to do with freedom.

Outside of lovely things, I do like having the time to spend with lovely people. Travelling alone in the past, I would not have much to write about if I hadn't talked to drivers and folks along the way. Ho ho ho. Already you're laughing at my Gi Gi country mouse naivety. If it's at a steering wheel and it looks anyway human, you'll engage with it. Well, yes, I will, because drivers are in fact the eyes and ears of a city. Snailey loves them. To be honest, now that I think of it, it's a great luxury for me to be driven about by a local who is really in tune with the streets. Remember Victor? This driver looked nice enough so I opened with, '*ummm, bonjour, je m'appelle Gisèle.*' Oooooops! He was a scowly young man who hadn't yet got to "hello" in the English language. Yes, he lightened up a tad when I said the *bonjour* bit, just enough for me to be sure that I wasn't being driven across Paris by an extra from the cast of Shaun of the Dead.

As we slipped along the wet streets and waited at different corners, I could feel the tension mounting, my eye caught an iron kiosk selling newspapers, maps and porn mags. Going round it a revolving advert caught my eye. Perfume, now there's a luxury that I'm just ker-razy about. As we drove along I started to see them everywhere, and I was mesmerized by their rotations. I thought: it's a good job this Goddess is in a fast moving car and has somewhere to get to… stop too long in front of one of these and you'd go ker-razy with lust. There were a ton of these ads; they were everywhere. Each one gave me a little nudge, towards 'the want'. Each one that is except the one for 'a Royale with Cheese'.

And, because I didn't have anything else to do except soak up the scenery, I started to covet all of the other luxury things besides perfume that were rotating on those newspaper kiosk ads. There was tons of stuff, like stuff to make me smell nice, look nice, feel nice and stuff to zapp my cellulite in six *semains*, (isn't that six weeks?). All the things I'd like to own but really didn't need were lining themselves up on a wish list in my brain, unbeknownst to me. A list built purely on lust. I had a quick fantasy about living in a white house, with white carpets, white flowers, white birds and thin thighs smooth as silk – that's the way I would like my life to actually be and fantasies being so fragile I thought I'd better crack on before I get to the realization bit and then the disappointment will set in – that bit's soul destroying isn't it? We passed four luxury-brand stores in a row, swish, swish, swish, swish and I kept my cool and kept my head down (pat on the back G). Didn't want a bag, didn't want a wallet, didn't even want a key-ring. At that point, there and then, I wanted nuffink. Then we stalled outside Chanel behind a Renault; I peeped sideways out the car window and damn it if I didn't start to drool…

THE WANT

It's fair to say that if Gabrielle "Coco" Chanel hadn't existed I would have had to invent her. Seriously! I am fascinated by her. She created a whole load of stuff, the soft jacket, costume jewellery and even the suntan (she went off on holidays, collaborated with the sun, got a tan and made it into an instant fashion trend). She was a courtesan before rising to become a fashion designer, would you have guessed that? And today, apparently, there are over 20 Coco Chanel film projects in the pipeline so she's still hot. But enough of my guff about all of this stuff because she had invented (drum roll please) a bag to better the 'It Brag' and it was staring back at me from a Chanel window in Paris so let's blame her for my continuing bag lusting. With me?

Yes, let's blame Coco. The Chanel 2.55 (reissued in 2005 by Karl Lagerfeld) was giving me 'the want' big time. See, it wasn't 'It Braggy' at all. The design had only been adjusted slightly by Lagerfeld for the reissue and this 2.55 was so utterly Chanel it wasn't an 'It Brag' it was outside all of that. How? you ask. Well, it's an icon, a classic, it's too cool, been around too long to be an 'It Brag'. While other brands were giving their 'It Brags' the hard sell by pushing them onto the catwalk all fashion week, Chanel had chosen to only show two bags in its autumn 2008 show. Knowing all of this was only making my decision harder. Maybe if I convinced you first, It'd be ok for me to buy?

It was the Fendi baguette in the autumn of 1997 and the *Sex and the City* crew that got the whole 'It Brag' thing rolling in the first place... then Gucci, Balenciaga, etc. they all followed suit and a mahussive luxury goods industry was born. So how does it come about, this 'It Brag' status thing? How does a luxury brand market luxury leather goods? From where I've been sitting, the 'It Brag' becomes 'It' on the catwalk, before a model has even removed her after-show lipstick, because it's carefully planned. It has to be because perfume, bags and shoes offer us a tiny slice of that brand so we buy in (millions of us) and that's what brings the brands in the big moolah. After a show, a luxury brand limits supply of a bag, publicizes the fact that there's a mahussive waiting list and Bob's your aunty (fashion, remember?) – it becomes (they hope) an instant 'It Brag'. Hey, Desire, what you doin' here?

So why was Chanel any different? One word. Authenticity, or my new word 'notable', seeing as that was my word du jour for all thing coolio in my notebook. This bag had been around for ages. Way back in 1929 Coco Chanel created this style in both black and navy jersey and added a chain strap to it, because of her irritation at constantly losing her strapless purses. The strap idea was inspired by soldiers' satchels and Chanel simply stated that she wanted to free up women's hands; so a bag to swing on the shoulder was born. No big deal so far. You're right!

But in February 1955, Chanel returned to Paris and her beloved rue Cambon and relaunched her career (she was 71 by the way, so there's hope for the rest of us). She developed the bag into the iconic 2.55 quilted Classic (the name 2.55 refers to the bag's birthday, February 1955). But this is no ordinary luxury item, ladies and gentlemen, because it's still considered a highly sought after classic within the industry, even today. So much so that various designers 'borrow' and take inspiration from the diamond leather idea and the chain strap from season to season. But Chanel wouldn't have minded, cos she once said this, 'Come to my place and steal all the ideas you can.' I would have loved to have met her, she sounds cool.

CHANEL 2·55

Okey dokey, so here we are, with me actually trying to get my mits on a Chanel 2.55 quilted classic. Staring at it in the window I ticked down my list of well-known fashion titbits about it… It takes six people 10 hours to complete the 180 separate processes to create it and this swish little formula hasn't changed since 1955. Chanel still uses the diamond pattern similar to jockeys' tops, which Chanel herself had seen at the racecourse and requested. She also asked that the shoulder straps be heavy gilded chains (same as the ones she secretly slipped into the linings of her jersey jackets to ensure they hung perfectly from her narrow little shoulders, (good tip that).

Over fifty years on and it is still instantly recognizable anywhere in the world as a symbol of French quality and a classic. See how it's waaay cooler than the one season best before date I'd imagined printed on the side of my 'It Brag'? Those double Cs spell luxury, no doubt about it. Chanel's luxury goods (handbags, shoes and fragrances like Chanel No 5) are all of the highest quality and have pure luxury staying power. Karl Lagerfeld, the creative director, has done a very good job of making sure of that.

But new me, new beginning, and all of that. So? Yes, I could have found the finance. And the time? We were stuck in a traffic jam so I could have hopped out, easy-peasy style. Alternatively I could have asked the taxi driver to go to Gabrielle Geppert, 31 Rue de Montpensier, Galerie de Montpensier, Jardin Palais Royal 75001 France (tel: +33 1 42 61 53 52). She sells perfect vintage bags including a whole space dedicated to Chanel (loads of nice 2.55s there). Buying second-hand is a good investment, you see (vintage 2.55s don't lose their value). Or back in London, French Touch, 11 Shelton Street, London WC2 (tel: +44 207 240 2680) sells a range of new and vintage accessories including quilted Chanel handbags, Louis Vuitton luggage and Hermès silk scarves. Luxury goods aplenty. And of course there's ebay. So did I? Jet off to Gabrielle's for a vintage 2.55 classic while in the neighbourhood? Oh 'the want' was terrible, but I did not. I thought, I need a bag for my notebook and my pens and the vast amount of junk that I cart around with me daily, so I'll leave the adopting of this beautiful little baby to someone else I think.

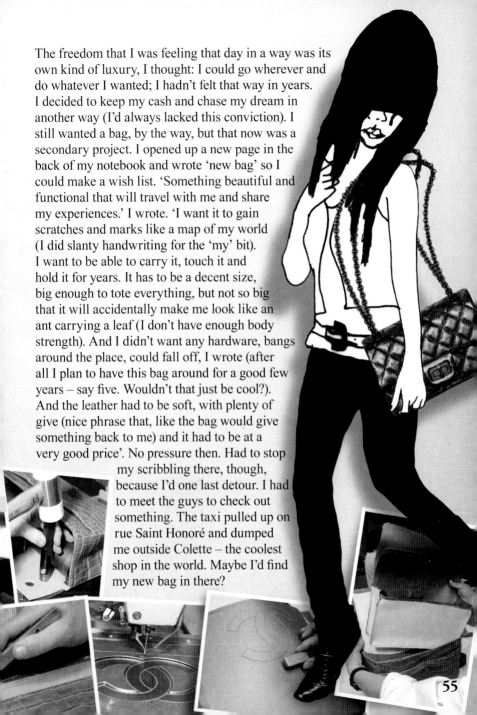

The freedom that I was feeling that day in a way was its own kind of luxury, I thought: I could go wherever and do whatever I wanted; I hadn't felt that way in years. I decided to keep my cash and chase my dream in another way (I'd always lacked this conviction). I still wanted a bag, by the way, but that now was a secondary project. I opened up a new page in the back of my notebook and wrote 'new bag' so I could make a wish list. 'Something beautiful and functional that will travel with me and share my experiences.' I wrote. 'I want it to gain scratches and marks like a map of my world (I did slanty handwriting for the 'my' bit). I want to be able to carry it, touch it and hold it for years. It has to be a decent size, big enough to tote everything, but not so big that it will accidentally make me look like an ant carrying a leaf (I don't have enough body strength). And I didn't want any hardware, bangs around the place, could fall off, I wrote (after all I plan to have this bag around for a good few years – say five. Wouldn't that just be cool?). And the leather had to be soft, with plenty of give (nice phrase that, like the bag would give something back to me) and it had to be at a very good price'. No pressure then. Had to stop my scribbling there, though, because I'd one last detour. I had to meet the guys to check out something. The taxi pulled up on rue Saint Honoré and dumped me outside Colette – the coolest shop in the world. Maybe I'd find my new bag in there?

55

Bags again. Indulge me. It had taken me twenty minutes to get to Colette with the heavy rain and traffic. Twenty! The guys were running late so I sheltered under Colette's canopy. What is it about rain? The sense that you're always about to drop something vital in it: gloves, scarf, umbrella, phone, bag… Splash! A girl standing beside me dropped her 'It Brag' under the watchful eye of Colette's doorman. Sopping wet it was, as she fished it from the pavement, a great big whopper it was too. I can't say I much liked her attitude, she gave me 'the daggers' – the oddest look – when I tried to help her. Did I have cream all over my face from the buns or something? Ink on my face from my pen? Was my hair like a bird's nest? I had a look in Colette's window to check. Seemed normal. I stood there smarting after I'd pulled a muscle trying to help her lift the bag from the water. Left shoulder, as it happens. It hurt.

My phone rang. 'I'll see you at the Colette entrance in ten minutes.' 'That's fine, but could you make it five, Peter please?' Relationships eh? It's all in the timing. I noticed her giving me the 'What bag are you carrying and how much did it cost?'' stare. Jaysus BeJaysus, thanks be to God I'd gotten over that 'It Brag' bullshit completely because I was hatching a… murder fantasy? Very seductive. I don't usually think like this. And then… 'Hey what are you doing here all on your own ?' Desire had caught up with me. He slipped his arm round my right elbow and whispered, 'Look, she's got a black crocodile Hermès Birkin bag.' 'Niiiiiiiiice,' I said. Isn't that one degree away from the definition of slippery sadness? Standing there receiving the 'I've got a better bag than you' stare from my left and your man on my right bending my ear. Between them they were melting my resolve (and my brain cells).

Desire asked why I couldn't get my act together and treat myself to one of those big bags immediately. 'Look, it's roomy and you'll fit all your notebooks and pens in there and it's handmade at Hermès by one person, pure luxury.' The girl carrying it shoved its lux-ness towards me and I looked longingly. 'Erm, there's the small matter of £10,000, and a waiting list.

And I don't think I'll be scrounging that up from under the sofa cushions any time soon do you?' 'What about ebay?' Desire questioned. 'A dodgy plasticky one would set me back £300.' 'And if money were no object?' 'There's a black crocodile one for £44,000' (only bidders with at least 10 feedbacks, please). Forty-four thousand pounds, I thought. Shock and befuddlement. What a waste of moolah, how many red velvet cupcakes would that buy?* 'You've checked it out then?' he teased. 'I check a lot on things on ebay, Mister. I just happened to see the bag by accident, is all. Anyway, I don't want one.' I turned my back to try and shake him. 'It's cold out here,' he said, eyeing the twinkling shop interior. 'Follow me in, I'll be inside.' So did I? Follow him inside that is… of course I did. Who wants to be a Hermès-lusting lamb left out in the rain?

*23,783 red velvet cupcakes from The Hummingbird Bakery (see page 318)

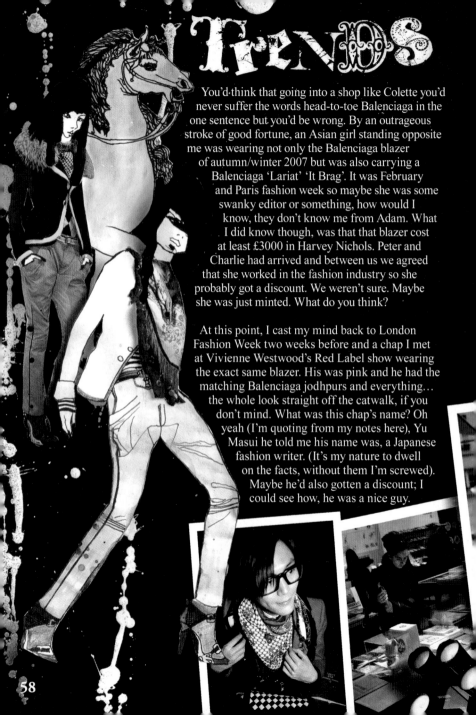

TRENDS

You'd think that going into a shop like Colette you'd never suffer the words head-to-toe Balenciaga in the one sentence but you'd be wrong. By an outrageous stroke of good fortune, an Asian girl standing opposite me was wearing not only the Balenciaga blazer of autumn/winter 2007 but was also carrying a Balenciaga 'Lariat' 'It Brag'. It was February and Paris fashion week so maybe she was some swanky editor or something, how would I know, they don't know me from Adam. What I did know though, was that that blazer cost at least £3000 in Harvey Nichols. Peter and Charlie had arrived and between us we agreed that she worked in the fashion industry so she probably got a discount. We weren't sure. Maybe she was just minted. What do you think?

At this point, I cast my mind back to London Fashion Week two weeks before and a chap I met at Vivienne Westwood's Red Label show wearing the exact same blazer. His was pink and he had the matching Balenciaga jodhpurs and everything… the whole look straight off the catwalk, if you don't mind. What was this chap's name? Oh yeah (I'm quoting from my notes here), Yu Masui he told me his name was, a Japanese fashion writer. (It's my nature to dwell on the facts, without them I'm screwed). Maybe he'd also gotten a discount; I could see how, he was a nice guy.

Good taste both of them… because the fit on these blazers was nothing short of genius, with shoulders tailored so sharply thay'd take your eye out if I'm to be honest. Can't argue with a nicely cut shoulder and for a split second I experienced 'the want'. But the episode left me with a profound question. Ready? It being the fashion world and Paris fashion-week, were they not shittin' themselves that they'd run into each other wearing the same look at some point? Imagine the shock, horror; like turning up to a wedding and everyone wearing the same Coast dress but in different colours. £3000 for the likelihood of bumping into someone else in the same jacket. No thanks. Or worse still, someone looking swisher in the high street version. Wouldn't you kick yourself? Wouldn't you die though?

Peter and Charlie got back to browsing and rolled their eyes wide over a glass case full of shiny gadgets. 'Take your pick,' Charlie said, 'but choose only one thing. What'll it be?' 'Dunno! Don't do gadgets much.' I said. 'They're soooooooooooooooo boysey.' Harsh I know, but an opinion widely shared among my female friends. Besides there were candles and beauty products and fragrance and trinkets propped up in every nook and cranny. I skipped around stroking them and cooing. And books, beautiful, beautiful books. How was it that one girl, standing beside a copy of Banksy's book *Home Sweet Home* put it? Ah yes (I'm quoting from my notes again here): 'If I had loads of money,' she said, 'I'd buy everything in here.' I secretly agreed. 'Hey would you really?' I asked. 'Yeah,' she replied. 'Do you want to come outside and have a chat about that?' She nodded, 'Yeah, sure.' Sometimes it's tough to say 'no' to 'the want'.

Her name was Magda and she was wearing a chequered black-and-white Arafat keffiyeh, pronounced caff-eye-yeah (not seen in fashion in 20-odd years, since CND marches, Gisèle! I hear you say). Be that as it may, I still asked her about it. 'Where'd you get your scarf?' 'I got it in a shop in Paris called Noir Kennedy in the fourth.' she admitted. 'Was it expensive?' I added. 'Not really, 20 Euros or so.' See, this is how I roll; normal folk, the peeps who live in a place, they always give the best shopping tips. Always. (I checked the shop out later and it's definitely not one to pass up if you love skinny jeans and punk rock stuff. Here's the address: Noir Kennedy, 22 rue du Roi de Sicile , Paris 75004 (tel: +33 1 4274 5558).

Back to the scarf, 'Why did you buy it?' I continued. 'I thought it was cool, everybody was wearing it, so I just thought, this is the cool thing to have.' I was curious about its symbolism so I asked, 'Do you know of any political things attached to it?' 'It's ahhh, for the freedom of Palestine right? And aaaam, yeah, I don't really know about it. But I still wear it,' she smiled. Looking down I saw Victor the taxi driver's tea tip in my notebook from waaaaay back and I found myself wanting to ask her Victor's questions too, so I did. 'What makes you happy?' I asked. 'Oh, to party.' 'And if you had loads of money what would you buy?' 'The entire shop,' she laughed. Charlie filmed the whole lot; you can see hers and a whole host of other keffiyeh stories on www.thegoddessguide.com.

Ten minutes later, same place, different keffiyeh, (this time a blue one, it was lovely) and belonged to Alex (Alexandre). 'Where did you get your scarf?' 'Actually this one comes from Berlin.' You're familiar with 'the want' that I experienced for the Chanel 2.55 quilted bag earlier? I judged it too small at the time but 'the want' returned when I saw a lady whip out of Colette's door behind Alex with a laaaaaaarge Chanel quilted bag swinging from her shoulder (it's all in my little keffiyeh movie if you want to watch it) and what with Alex's lovely blue keffiyeh being extra lovely and everything happening in the blink of an eye I lost my cool. Steady on, G, steady on.

Alex continued, 'the thing is, there's a lot of people ask me where I get this one [the scarf] and it was in a very cheap tourist place. But I got it blue.' 'Why?' 'Maybe because of Colette; I work in the store, it's the colour of the store. I don't know, I think it was more ahhhh original, I don't know.' 'Do you put any

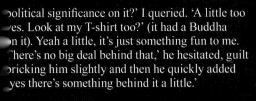

political significance on it?' I queried. 'A little too
~es. Look at my T-shirt too?' (it had a Buddha
~n it). Yeah a little, it's just something fun to me.
~here's no big deal behind that,' he hesitated, guilt
~ricking him slightly and then he quickly added
~yes there's something behind it a little.'

A few minutes later a chap named Murat Turkil
~olled by and around his neck? An intricately
~mbroidered keffiyeh. 'Where did you get your
~beautiful, beautiful scarf?' I quizzed. 'I made it
~n my own,' he beamed. It was gorge so I asked
~or a few more details. 'It's all about flowers and
 had those colours and I liked them very, very,
~nuch and I thought that maybe it can be a nice
~dea to put embroideries on and I made it. It's
~handmade of course.'. 'Where had he bought the
~riginal keffiyeh before embroidering it?' 'The
~riginal came from the East part of Turkey, which
~s really very, very famous with their keffiyeh. I
~ust talked to one of my friends, he was visiting,
~ind he just brought lots of them to me and I just
~nade it. We call it 'purhiu'; in Turkey; different
~kinds of colours like red, black and white and blue
~symbolizes different kinds of status. Black means
~something different, if you put red it's something
~different and it is something which is Arabic of
~course, the origin.' 'Do you know the difference in
~he colours then?' I asked. 'I have no idea about it,'
~he laughed loudly. 'It's all about fashion. I have no
~dea what it is.'

And G of Arabia took the opportunity at this point to wrap her own keffiyeh round her neck against the damp chilly Parisian weather. Which sand-duned Oasis had I bought mine in? Berlin six months previously, it was by a German fashion designer by the name of Angelika Paschbeck www.paschbeck.de, she's a secret fashion genius (shhhhh!). OK, I'll admit it. I'm Angelika Paschbeck ker-razy right now, she's a designer to be reckoned with; she's 'notable', her clothes are timeless investment pieces, and seeing as scarves have always been my thaaang, I see her Fummel & Kram www.fummelundkram.com embroidered scarves lasting me a good 10-20 years. Anyway I'd never met anyone with anything similar and that felt kinda special, straight onto my Happy List. Angelika Paschbeck's embroidery, I wrote in my notebook, helps set my little scarf apart.

At this point a very snazzy French man sided up beside us. His name was Geoffroy de la Bourdonnaye. I said to myself, 'If I had the chance to get the name Geoffroy de la Bourdonnaye into the notebook and blew it, I'd never forgive myself.' So off we went. Turns out Geoffroy was the CEO of Liberty of London (a great, great shop). What was he doing talking to me? He'd been eyeing up Murat's embroidered keffiyeh and was looking into researching it for the store for autumn/winter. See, that's how trends roll; peeps with a good eye spot something special. People like Geoffroy. He was slick (James Bond style) and he ran Liberty of London, God damn it, so I decided to ask him a few questions about luxury. He looked very luxurious himself.

You'll recall the astoundingly profound saga of Victor the taxi driver way back at the beginning of my journey? He thought 'luxury is that when you are not satisfied with natural things so you go for it'? Well, I was itching to know what Geoffroy thought, 'What makes you happy, Geoffroy?' 'What makes me happy in general? People smiling. I think it's contagious. And I think when people feel good, they usually dress good and look good and it's contagious and I think it makes me happy for sure.' 'What's your luxury?' 'My relationships with my

family and my friends, all the things that you're given and you don't really value until you miss them.' 'What would you buy if you were given loads of money?' 'Time.' Did you see that one coming, reader? Cos I didn't. You can see all of this on www.thegoddessguide.com.

Now, if I worked for a big fancy-smancey cool-hunting business, they'd make me charge you many millions of dollars for this next bit of privileged information. As a Goddess Experience reader, however, you are très important – so here it is for free. Come a little bit closer, I have to whisper.… trendspotters, cool-hunters and CEO'S of big stores, (people like Geoffroy) identify hot new ideas and products daily from the fringes of society and over time, they share them with the rest of us. What else? Well, I wanted to know how it all worked, so I asked…

'What impressed you about the scarf Geoffroy?' 'Craftmanship, the quality of the detail, the florals. You could see that it was done in a country which cares for detail and quality of detail.' 'So the scarf could crop up in Liberty of London next season?' 'We're always looking for brands which are not easily found in Western Europe.' But guess what? The fashionistas wearing the Balenciaga look (remember the blazer and jodhpur peeps earlier?), well, they were also wearing a Balenciaga keffiyeh. Balenciaga had several keffiyeh type scarves embellished with coins and tassles in their collection that season and there was even a waiting-list. And? The keffiyeh had suddenly become fashionable. The only difference being that Alex's blue scarf and Murat's embroidered scarf were giving me more of 'the want' Why? Because they were 'personal' more unique and more 'notable' than something off the catwalk, that anyone could buy. I liked Murat's best, because it was a one-off and was hand customized.

CUSTOMiZZatiON

Customization and personalization, go way back (I'm talking waaaaaaay). In the past you'd go to the cobbler and he'd make your shoes for you and the shirt maker would make your shirts (oh the bliss) and then we entered an era of industrialization where the shirt made on the production line became the 'it' thing because peeps thought that it was cooler to wear something more, what's the word? Modern, that's it, and now drum roll please... customization is making a comeback. Fed up with mass-produced stuff, peeps are hand embroidering and personalizing stuff. I spent a fair bit of time thinking about that and the more I thought, the happier it made me. Customization puts us back in the driving seat. In a ubiquitous world, customisation is the new luxury. For the first time in a very long time, we now get to choose.

Converse

Take Converse (www.converse.com), you can order a gazillion colours of canvas, it seems, for the outside of your Converse and a different kind of rubber band across the toe, and so the probability that someone else is going to order the same shoes as you is highly unlikely. Makes me faint with 'the want', this.

Nike

You can customize a Nike shoe twenty-eight ways now (www.nike.com), and it'll be the only one with that colour combo in the world, Happy List anyone? See runners page 134. Same with Adidas (www.adidas.com).

Etsy

Etsy www.etsy.com is a sort of ebay, where really creative people put one-off handmade customized items up for sale. It's a vast marketplace with everything from a hand-embroidered t-shirt, £110, to a vest for your dog, £10. The trawl is worth it and if you fancy having something bespoke (say a skirt or something), you post a design request and peeps will battle it out to hand make your item for the best price. Lovin' it!

Take this red little vintage kimono clutch bag that I found on Etsy, by Who's the Fairest (www.whosthefairest.etsy.com). Get this, the designer is based in Australia, I like her stuff, within a week I can have it tucked under my arm going to a party, and as she says herself 'I guess thats the best thing about online shopping!'

Tees

At Bountee (www.bountee.com) anyone can submit a t-shirts design; the most popular are voted on to the home page and cost £15 to £20 to order. Spreadshirt (www.spreadshirt.com) allows a bit more creativity for non designers. There's a library of little logos and colours to choose from. Simple.

From tees to teas – create a tea for a friend

Blends For Friends (www.blendsforfriends.com) is a UK based company that creates custom-blended tea. £27 plus postage for 100 grams of loose-leaf tea, created by master blender Alex Probyn especially for you or a loved one. The tea arrives packaged in a gift-wrapped tin caddy with a bespoke label with your friend's name on it. There's a similar site in Australia, World Par-Tea (www.worldpartea.com) and The Shaded Leaf (www.theshadedleaf.com) custom blends teas in the US.

Extra nice tees

Design your own t-shirt on this genius website. Choose one, add your own words and then it comes in a beautiful patisserie box complete with cute ribbons and a sweet little treat... (cupcake, biscuit? It's a surprise, I'm not telling.) Head to Luna & Curious, 198 Brick Lane, London E1 (tel: +44 207 033 4411) or order online at www.tshirtpatisserie.co.uk.

The Promise

Shopping on Etsy and buying handmade customized things allows me to reconnect with the world... to go back to a time when we bought our bread from the baker and shoes from the cobbler, for me it's a wonderful experience. The opposite to buying a top in Primark and throwing it away a few weeks later; where's the emotional attachment in that? I like buying things that I can grow with.

Life is so disposable these days, it makes me think of all those disposable landfill plastic coffee cups and twizzle sticks. Peeps in the UK alone, drink 70 million cups of coffee a day. A large proportion of these are consumed from ceramic mugs at home but when we're out and craving a fix? It's always a paper cup isn't it? Here's a thought, bring your own cup, these ceramic coffee cups by Rob Brandt are £5.95 at wwwthorstenvanelten.com and are highly ironic.

Aaaaaanyway! Coffee. The reason I'm droning on about it is that a cup of coffee was my very first customization and personalization experience. 'I'll have a double shot skinny mega soy latte, purleeeese.' Lovely feeling that, when you get to choose. That's customization at its most basic; Starbucks started that, but I'd had my fill of Starbucks in Beverly Hills, Los Angeles, about five years ago. Their coffee doesn't interest me in the slightest and the experience doesn't excite me anymore. Small little coffee shops, they're what rock my world now, with smiling owners. Snailey loves them too. Coffee places like Monmouth Coffee Company, 2 Park Street (tel: +44 207 645 3585, www.monmouthcoffee.co.uk) across from Borough Market its cappuccino's are legendary and it has a great communal table. And then there's Amoul, 14 Formosa Street, Maida Vale (tel: +44 207 286 6386, www.amoul.com), a family run deli with a couple of tables and excellent coffee and teas.

Back in Paris, leaving Colette, I
snapped this Coke can squashed in the gutter
and it sent me into chirpy overdrive. We buy a Coke and
cart it around as we wander, a nomadic wander across the world
– the pop safe inside the can – and then after consumption we
chuck it like a paper coffee cup. Squashed and fading in
the sun, was the can now worthless? Full, it created 'the
promise' that creates 'the want' in me. I realized that
sometimes my happiness is just based on 'the promise'
alone. Packaging can promise so much can't it?
Take these…

I went into ker-razy overdive at the meer sight of this
pink KitKat packaging. I found it on www.jlist.com,
a website, that pedals all things japanese. I love the
fact that KitKat means 'good luck' in japanese and
sales of these unusual flavours go mental at exam
time. You can also get green tea, red apple flavours
etc and there's another website,
www.cybercandy.co.uk where
I have been spending far to
much time typing **in the words**
KitKat Wa Guri **(a chestnut**
KitKat). Leaving the soft
stuff behind, it was time
to move onto **the hard**
stuff...

Nestle®
Kit Kat®

春はきっとやってくる。
満開のさくらを願って。　〈桜葉1.5%使用〉〈サクラン系香料使用〉

うつく

SCENTS OF SELF

I'm a real sucker for perfume. My knowledge started with my mother; her Chanel No. 5, Guerlain Vetiver and Guerlain Mitsouka raining down on me as a five year old; the Guerlain scents, fresh, simple, a little spicy and earthy, both full of oak moss. The Mitsouka; bergamot, jasmine, may rose, oak moss and vetiver, quite feminine. The Guerlain Vetiver; orange, bergamot and lemon on a base of oak-moss, tobacco and vetiver; masculine - which my mother thinks smells classy (it does). I heard somewhere recently that Elle McPherson has worn Guerlain Vetiver for the past 25 years. Elle is in good company then.

The Chanel No. 5? Well most peeps know what that's all about; jasmine, which leaves the skin smelling warm and powdery (happy list word that if ever there was one), it's a clean smell, well befitting a girl who was raised in the country, which is who I am. Or, which is who I was. Because those country girls, we grow up, move to Dublin, travel around the world, go to Paris and all that stuff changes you. Especially the Paris bit. There were kissy, wissy couples everywhere, smouchy, wouchy kids clamped to each other on benches, a blurr as our cab whizzed by. The whole thing got to me reader. Suddenly, I wanted to be irresistible like in Scent of a Woman when Al Pacino's character recalls a woman he met briefly by declaring, "Ooh, but I still smell her." I wanted a fragrance that could do that.

Grassroots

I headed straight to Guerlain's flagship store in Paris to track down both of Mum's fragrances (Vetiver and Mitsouko). They're classified as chypres (sheep-ras) in the perfume world - (moss, grass, heather, earth, vetiver). Vetiver is in fact a weed with a huge root system which in the past was put in linen drawers. A perfumer has to work very hard to extract scent from this root as fanatics desire purity. Guerlain's Vetiver is it, currently at its best.

At La Maison de Guerlain perfumery on the Champs-Elysées my eyes watered at the sight of the glass perfume bottles sharing a wall with tall translucent tubes of amber fragrance. I went into luxury over load when I was told that I could design the bottle by adding a monogram and choose a ribbon colour. "You can even bring in a favourite old perfume bottle and have it filled," they explained to me. Wow! Mitsouko produced by Jacques Guerlain in 1919 is legendary, so I took three Guerlain samples; one Mitsouko, one Vetivert and a Shalimar too, because "dabbed on the breast bone and spritzed lightly in hair it's seductive", they said.

Then, I found my way to Chanel's flagship store on rue Cambon, Paris. Man, but at times like this, I'm thrilled I'm a girl. Shutting my eyes to the handbags inside I eyed a little bottle and walked straight to it "Extrait Chanel No. 5" the shop assistant said. "Do you hear that Snaily? She said "Extrait" "it's made from the world's most expensive jasmine" she continued. I already knew that, because Joy, a perfume launched in 1930, (available at Fortnum and Mason in the UK) is laced with natural jasmine and natural Bulgarian rose and has long been known as one of the costliest perfumes around. I also knew that both Joy's and Chanel's jasmine come from fields in Grasse in France. See told you, I'm a perfumaniac, a geek.

"It's, £250 for 30ml." Ouch! A mahussive splurge on one bottle of scent. "Jaysus hold on, I'm not made of money Mrs." I popped the No. 5 extrait on a tester, weighed up my options and dammit, if I didn't go and buy a bottle of my secret weapon Chanel's Cuir De Russie eau de toilette, from the 'les exclusives' range instead (it's leathery but more about that later).

I swung by Jean Patou's next and popped their Joy extrait (£250 for 30ml) onto a tester and shoved it deep into my hand bag along with all the others. An hour later and the scent of the testers rose deep from within my handbag. What do you think Peter? "Hmmmmmm smells like a little garden in there, grassy and flowery, not really you G.

Righty ho, it was time to box clever, I decided to go on
a bit of a fragrance dabbing hunt with Snailey the next
morning, a dabathon, better still, a dabathon across Paris,
better still a dabathon across Paris where at each stop I'd
also ask, "can I buy this in London too?" And if I did well,
then people from Camden to Croyden would be hopping
up and down and…wait there one minute, sticking with
the maths, I think I have discovered an equation where I
schlep across Paris tracking down bottles and dividing them
by one year's usage and then, at the very last minute naming the
best. Most shops were lovely and helpful but some were prickley
pineapples places, so I'm not even going to include them. Perfume
shops can be frightening places can't they, hushed as funeral parlours
with rude staff circling like vultures, can't be doing with that Snailey can we?

Traveling out with Snailey, the fragrance world before us, we stopped off at
Sephora. A one-stop shop for a whole host of easy to find fragrances across
the world, I wanted to check out a few more chypres and some florals (white
flowers, roses that sort of thing). After a bit I narrowed my hunt down to
the white flowers: Gardenia in the shape of Marc Jacobs Gardenia Essence
(an intoxicating burst of gardenia, jasmine with a hint of Turkish rose petal)
or Tom Ford's Velvet Gardenia Private Blend eau de parfum, £90, by Tom
Ford Beauty (tel: +44 (0)870 034 2566 for UK) both intensely feminine.
Hmmmmmmm! Or how about other whites?

How about lily of the valley for instance …a bottle of Chloé Eau De Parfum
£35, was stuffed with it; a dry sweet white floral note of lily of the
valley and magnolia gradually fading to reveal a combination of
rose and amber. Still in girly territory then. My Chypre habit
slowly creeping back up on me I reached for a bottle of Gucci
by Gucci and it felt better, I ooed and ahhed a bit at it and then
Narciso Rodriquez musk for her - a woody-oriental with tons
of musk sent me into overdrive, then it was back to the florals
with Estée Lauder's, Beyond Paradise, containing hyacinth,
honeysuckle and jasmine, it was breathtaking, like a well
practised orchestra every note sat perfectly (for anyone
interested), it is the perfect floral and it's readily available in
most department stores. Still too girly for me though.
The following morning the most pleasant part of this scent
hunt was what remained on my sleeve, a lingering echo
of Narciso Rodriquez Musk For Her, so I popped back to

Sephora and bought it (lovely bottle too)
and while there gave the highly popular
Prada's Infusion d'Iris eau de parfum
a spritz. What was not to love here?
Instant dressing- table appeal and the
subtle iris note with just a touch of
mandarin, and guess what? The
super-size version came with a
tiny sized decanter bottle which
is a travel bonus, (this little lot
costs £200 but is also available
in 50ml spray for £45, tel:
+44 207 499 4420). At
more than $30,000 a kilo,
absolute of iris is the most
expensive natural material
in perfumery. Not really my
thing though.

And then I hopped across to Editions
de Parfum Frédéric Malle (see page 74).
Frédéric Malle has got the greatest perfumers
falling over each other to compose for him. Why?
He encourages his gallery of noses to use only the
best raw materials. The results are extraordinary a
gallery of the world's finest fragrances and they're
also available in London at Les Senteurs (see page
75) so stick with me on this…the Iris Poudre was
Irisey and powdery. The Lys Méditerranée
fashioned from ginger lilies was created by
one of the most renowned white perfume
noses on earth: Edourd Fléchier. And their
Tuberose fragrance Carnal Flower was
seductive, erotic and borderimg on Al
Pacino Scent of a Woman territory,
again all beautiful, beautiful florals,
feminine and light. The guys love
these by the way, still I craved
something else.

The following day it was back to Sephora to test two popular rose fragrances; Stella McCartney's Stella Eau de Parfum Natural Spray (£26 for 30ml) a clear, pure heart note of rose, smells rich and mysterious, rose and amber like passing a hedge of wild roses on a damp August morning.

Paul Smith's Rose Eau de Parfum (£48 for 100ml) was next; Paul's wife Pauline had the rose cultivated especially for him by the famous English botanist, Peter Beales. No blooms are harvested, crushed or distilled in the perfume process, instead the living flowers are isolated in a glass bell and special equipment 'inhales' the scent molecules and then they're recreated in the lab. It was very fresh, addictive (almost). Later that day at Parfums de Rosine (see page 74) - a parfumerie dedicated to the rose their Twill Rose was a spectacular blend of Turkish rose and ivy. How I yearned to be able to carry off these florals. The harsh truth is that they just don't suit me, too girly.

It was at Serge Luten's shop in the Salons du Palais Royal Shiseido, that things started to look a bit well, more G(ish). It began to look promising with Iris Silver Mist; a burst of Iris that smelt of a cold, damp forest heaped with rusting metal. Beautiful! Luten's Iris Silver Mist is a cold floral, no powder here, just steely earthiness. It came in a clear, bell-shaped flacon – available only in Paris- so could not travel in a suitcase; I thought about bringing it back as hand luggage, I said to Snailey, we're into dressing table territory here.

In fairness, with all of these fragrances I sat down and tested them nice and slowly, wrist to neck, like you're supposed to. Just did three a day because anymore and it becomes a bit of a joke. It made me think of the days when women did this kinda thing daily.

What a luxury, to take the time to get dressed and apply fragrance sitting at a dressing table. And dressing tables need bottles don't they? So it was time to stop testing and time to commit. So while I accept that the chypres and florals are beautiful fresh little things, I will leave their enjoyment to others. As with speed walking (Olympic style), liquorice, mime-artists and moths.

So, did I ever reach my Al Pacino moment? Did I drive the men of Paris wild with my new perfume, well? Kind of… leaving the Iris Silver Mist aside at Serge Lutens I bought a bottle of Shiseido Feminite De Bois Eau de Parfum (also available in Harrods, London). Think cedar boxes, old wood, sweet yet complicated. Extraordinary! This store stocks both Shiseido and Serge Lutens fragrances (the Bois de Violette is very like the aforementioned Féminité du Bois) so I bought a bottle of Serge Lutens Féminité du Bois as well please. And Serge Luten's Ambre Sultan was my kinda thing also (spicy and oriental). I tippy-toed back out onto the street my clothes and skin scented with dark, mysterious orientals; musks and smokey leathers a dressing table must-have, there was just one more more stop, Caron (see page 74).

Caron, has one of the greatest perfume Baccarat crystal fountains to be found anywhere in the world, I can't take that away from them, (if I could I'd put it in my house and bathe in Caron Tabac Blond eau de parfum). Caron Tabac Blond is from the leather-tobacco family. It smells of secret letters, bookcases, open fires, leather chairs and is tobacco heightened with tuberose and vanilla on a long-lasting musk base. So I had them fill a flacon for me (criminal not to). £90 later and I left with the beautiful stoppered bottle in my hand, perfect for my dressing table fantasy. I also bought a pink swansdown powder puff and some of Caron's dusting powder, because they're dressing table must-haves. You can even bring in a flea-market bottle or a family heirloom and they'll fill it for you here. And can I get all this in London? Yes, at Roje Dove, Harrods (see page 74). How much do I love Caron? I want its babies.

Back in a taxi, I justified my purchases with some good old fashioned mathematics. If I dabbed a bit on every day and night, - the boxes tattered round the edges, the bottles a blur of G fingerprints, at this rate of usage, they should last me, let me see here, that divided by 365 days give or take, that's 2.50p a day on scent, yes, 2.50p a day for one year, that's not that much in the broader scheme of things, is it? And then I thought, hang on there G… why are you wasting time on wondering which scent will create an Al Pacino moment? Surely a personal fragrance should dance on tables with you on a Saturday night and read the papers with you on a Sunday morning. A signature scent should age with you and help you sort out the boys from the men. Whoooo haaaa!

My favourite perfume shops and perfumers

Paris

Annick Goutal, 14 rue de Castiglione Paris (tel: +33 1 42 60 52 82, www.annickgoutal.com) Also available in Liberty of London and Les Senteurs (London). Annick Goutal known for Leau d'Hadrien now has Les Nuits d'Hadrian - a sensual musk that lasts all night. The candles are lush too.

Boutique Chanel, 31 rue Cambon, 75001, Paris (tel: +33 1 42 86 26 00) www.chanel.com. The 'les exclusifs' range of which Cuir De Russie (the leather scent I bought) is one is available at Chanel boutiques. Chanel No 5. extrait is available at most Chanel beauty counters.

Caron, 34 Avenue Montaigne, Paris (tel: +33 1 47 23 40 82, www.parfumscaron.com). Fill a gorgeous bottle in Paris or at Roja Dove, in Harrods (see below), or buy bottled Caron from Les Senteur, London (see below). Caron is also available in New York – Caron 675, Madison Avenue (tel: +1 212 319 4888).

Editions de Parfum Frédéric Malle, 37 Rue de Grenelle (tel: +33 1 42 22 77 22, www.editionsdeparfums. com). Extraordinary experience in Paris. Available at Les Senteurs, London and Barneys across the US.

Guerlain, 68 avenue des Champs-Élysées, Paris (tel: +33 1 45 62 52 57, www.guerlain.com) – where I started my journey; remember Mitsouko, Samsara and Vetiver?

L'Artisan Parfumeur, 24 boulevard Raspail, Paris (tel:+33 1 42 22 23 32, www.artisanparfumeur.com). Their Dzongkha Eau de Toilette is the temples of Bhutan in a bottle (also see below).

Parfums de Nicolaï, 80 rue de Grenelle, Paris (tel: +33 1 45 44 59 59, www.pnicolai.com). The granddaughter of famous nose Pierre Guerlain, she's also based in London at 101a Fulham Road, London SW3 (+44 20 7581 0922). Her fragrances are also available from Les Senteurs, her Eau de Iisque – divine.

Parfum de Rosine, 43 Galerie Montpensier, 75001,Paris (tel : +33 1 42 60 47 58, www.les-parfums-de-rosine.com). Also available at Les Senteurs.

Salons du Palais Royal Shiseido (Serge Lutens), 142 Galerie de Valois, Jardins du Palais Royal (tel: +33 1 49 27 09 09, www.salons-shiseido.com). This violet-coloured boutique is enchanting and sells Serge Luten's exclusive perfumes (20 different scents, €95 each). For an extra fee they'll even etch your initials onto the bottle. Serge Lutens scents are also available at Les Senteurs London.

London

Angela Flanders perfumery, 96 Columbia Road, London E2 (+44 20 7739 7555) bespoke scent service.

Guerlain, (tel: +44 20 7563 7563 for store details) there are Guerlain counters at department stores.

Roja Dove Haute Parfumerie, Fifth Floor Urban Retreat, Harrods, London SW1 (tel: +44 20 7893 8333, www.rojadove.com or for mail order tel: +44 20 7893 8797).

Jo Malone, 150 Sloane Street, London (tel: +44 20 7730 2100, www.jomalone.co.uk). Her lime, basil & Mandarin range is universally coveted. Also available online.

L'Artisan Parfumeur, 17 Cale Street, London SW3 (020 7352 4196) sells a great range of fragrances which it creates itself. Buy from the store or online at www.mkn.co.uk/perfume. They offer a scent sample service and also have concessions at Harvey Nichols, Liberty, Fenwick and House of Fraser.

Les Senteurs, 71 Elizabeth Street, SW1 (tel: +44 20 7730 2322, www.lessenteurs.com) an old style perfumery and a gem of a shop, I love this place with a passion. If you're looking for something unique then this is the place to come. My whole Parisian experience Caron, Serge Lutens, Frédéric Malle they stock them all here. And Snailey loves the staff, they're extra smiley and very knowledgeable. Better still, request their mail order catalogue, choose a few fragrances and for £2.50 they'll decant some of your favourites into tiny little scent phial and post them out to try.

Miller Harris, 21 Bruton Street (tel: +44 20 7629 7750, www.millerharris.com). See the scent range here and Lyn Harris also offer a bespoke service. She offers the most beautiful citrus fragrances and candles.

Ormonde Jayne, 12 The Royal Arcade, 28 Old Bond Street, London (tel: +44 20 7499 1100, www.ormondejayne.com. Owner, Linda Pilkington's, signature perfume called Ormonde woman is a luxurious treat containing black hemlock, it'll transport you to another world, stunning! This is a proper Luxurious Goddess perfume and a beautiful store to visit in London. Linda is both talented and friendly!

Penhaligons, 16 Burlington Arcade, W11 (tel:020 7629 1416, www.penhaligons.com). There are a good few branches across London, their bottles are lovely on dressing tables. Bluebell is popular.

Santa Maria Nouvella, 117 Walton St. London (tel: +44 20 7460 6600). Beautiful soaps, the best moisturizing milk on the planet and Nostalgia one of the best leather scents in my opinion on the market. Made by Dominican monks since the sixteenth century, the packaging is ultra vintage.

Scent Systems, 11 Newburgh Street, London W1 (tel: +44 20 7434 1166, www.scent-systems.com) Great choice, exclusive and elusive, modern fragrances.

Vienna
Knize & Co, 1st district Graben 13, Vienna. (tel: +43 1 51 22 11 90) The best leather scent on the market.

New York
Bond No.9, 680 Madison Ave., 61st St. New York (212-838-2780) www.bondno9fragrances.com. Laurice Rahm celebrates different New York post codes with different fragrances. Also at Harvey Nichols.

Slatkin & Co www.slatkin.com available to buy in London from Harrods or online at www.bqhair.com In the US buy online from www.neimanmarcuse.com or visit Neiman-Marcus or the Fred Segal store.

Other Little Luxuries

And here are some more things I consider to be luxuries in my life...

Ali Hewson's Edun

Photograph by Helena Christensen

I like being able to buy a fashion label where the money I spend is helping other people in the developing world, take Ali Hewson's Edun (www.edunonline.com) clothing line (nude backwards) for example. She teamed up with Rogan Gregory a designer whose denim label and cottons are totally organic and with Bono they launched the totally organic clothing line Edun in 2005. A collection of separates including tees, dresses and super skinny jeans, they're produced in factories in three continents, where the pieces are made using existing resources within a community to help the people who live there. I like the sound of this, her cause is very genuine and I'm not alone in my praise, Gwyneth Paltrow and Helena Christensen are just two Goddesses who love Edun. In a way this is the new luxury, where more then big corporations reap the rewards. So what does Edun's founder consider luxurious.

What makes you happy? The perfectly fitted Wellington boot...
What is your luxury? Time to wear them...

Lainey Keogh

Irish knitwear designer Lainey Keogh's cashmere is so fine it feels as fine as fairy spun gossamer. Her talent is to take the finest cashmere and fashion tiny luxurious sweaters, cardigans and scarves and cashmere coats. Hollywood is besotted with her for her originality. Being wrapped in a piece of her cashmere on a chilly day feels like total luxury.

What makes you happy? Knowing we are all tuning in to "planet earth", knitting cashmere "off-grid", making something beautiful here at home in Ireland, witnessing our human family come ever closer each day, knowing some lainey pieces enabled a new treatment center for the"Chernobyl children's project" in Bella Russe, donating "shopping days" to charities who care for children worldwide, vibing our hero's and heroines, loving my loved ones, being able to make the right choices, living dreams, downloading visions and creating and enjoying success together with my fellow passionistas.
What is your luxury? Freedom to choose, having all the time in the world to... Enjoying good health and knowing everything is possible.

Lainey Keogh (tel: +353 1 679 3299, www.laineykeogh.com)

Carolyn Quatermaine

And everything about Carolyn Quartermaine's fabric painting is luxurious, her delicately designed screen-printed chairs are luscious and giant lace silk organza panels intricately painted are the stuff of fairytales. Everything she does is covetable, her work gives me a serious care of 'the want'.

What makes you happy?
Garden wild roses, blowsy and dewy make me happy
What is your luxury? Luxury is walking through rainwater puddles in summer, barefoot, after a storm...

Carolyn Quartermaine works from her studious in London and the South of France (tel: +44 207 373 4492, www. carolynquartermaine.com).

But these were all lovely things and although I like having them share my life, I see the time that is needed to enjoy them as a bigger luxury. That got me thinking about the luxury of..v.

77

Time passes. It's the major flaw in the equation. Air, water, procreation, photosynthetesis, the miracle of non-stick lipgloss; all great, but time cocks-up the lot. In short: to have the time and freedom to lay back and admire the clouds is a luxury. I was just gearing myself up to do that, when I tripped across this...

What big city do you live closest to? Do you walk fast in this city? Faster than anywhere else? Now ask yourself this... Do you think overall that your city has the fastest walkers in the world? Yes? No? Maybe? Too tired from walking fast to slow down and think?

My mother phoned and mentioned casually to me that she'd been shopping in Dublin and that the pace had really heated up there. She was right. Scientists have discovered that it is the fifth fastest city in the world. 'Seriously?' she laughed. 'Yes, Mum. Humans around the world are walking faster now than a decade ago and they're walking fifth fastest in Dublin.' 'How do they know that?' she asked. 'Well there's this guy, Professor Richard Wiseman, he's a psychologist and he headed up an experiment in 2007 with British Council researchers where they secretly timed the speed of thousands of pedestrians walking in 32 city centres across the globe.'

'So what city has the fastest walkers, G?' 'Singapore' 'And Dublin came fifth?' 'Yep, Mum, after Copenhagan (2nd), Madrid (3rd) and Guangzhou (4th).' God I was proud that I could rattle off the facts with www.paceoflife.co.uk open in front of me. Have you ever done that? Examined information with a stare so hard that it would melt a teddy bear's eyes? 'Surely the South Americans came way down the bottom,' she suggested. 'Well not really, Mum, as Brazil's Curitiba came in 6th, just above Berlin (7th) then New York (8th), Utrecht (9th), Vienna (10th) Warsaw (11th) and only then did London figure in 12th . 'And aren't you always telling me that yourself and Peter find London and New York seat of the pants crazy?' 'Yep! I know! I'm as surprised as you, Mum.'

A little later I poured over Richard Wiseman's table of results and was particularly shocked that London came in at the number 12 spot below Dublin. Paris at number 16 was no great surprise, things are pretty laid back there, but Tokyo at number 19 was unbelievable. I've been to many of the cities tested on the list and can say hand on heart that Tokyo definitely seemed faster than let's say... Madrid. Incidentally Blantyre in Malawi (official population of 646,235 people) has the slowest walkers of all. My mother opined that 'it might have something to with them walking slowly due to the heat.'

Anyway science had spoken and I had noticed other little road signs along the way that time and the times were a changin'...

In the US, peeps don't even have the time to take proper holidays anymore. Expedia does an annual Vacation Deprivation Survey there every year and in 2007 the results showed that Americans on average took only 14 days holidays per annum. A fortnight, I tell you, a fortnight! Can't express how queasy that made me feel, 438 million days to their employers free of charge. No bonuses or nuffink. Meanwhile in Tokyo folks don't even have time to spend on a luxuriously long haircut; ten minutes for 1,000 yen (€6) at QB ('Quick Barber') House (www.qbhouse.co.jp) it's all the rage. The fastest haircut in the world, they say. In their 338 stores in 2007 they did 9.5 million of them.

On the other side of the world I did a straw poll of my own friends and asked them what they thought about it. 'Time's my great luxury,' said Tom, a photographer in London, 'Time's my luxury,' chirped Anne, a London based PR. 'Time for me too,' said Philip, her husband... 'there's not enough of it.' You get the gist, reader. And headline after headline in the papers pointed to proof that Time is the new currency, so how can we earn ourselves more of it? I spotted a few little things that might help. First the trivial...

Hasbro Games www.hasbro.com have introduced a sort of Honey I Shrunk the Game! version of the classics. (Deep breath.) They've made an 'express' version of Monopoly. I know, sacrilege. The 'Speed Die Edition' uses speed dice to speed up the action! And their Scrabble accommodates (wait for it) two words at a time. When we were kids, Monolopy went on for ages, for days it sprawled across the kitchen table, 'Don't move the board, eat around it, lads.' That was the best part, the anticipation; this express version isn't in the spirit of things is it? But it saves time.

Pushing the Monolopy aside, I recalled a few occasions in my life (well, three, four at a push), when time lost its pegs and floated away, taking with it my normal human day for me. Like the time I crossed part of the Sahara with Berber guides, hot days, cold nights, they set fires with skinny blue matches. Or more recently a trip I took to Las Vegas – daylight means nothing there, regular meal times, usually a nudge for me to take some nutrition don't exist. Vegas visitors (mainly Americans) walk around the fruit machines and not an apple or a banana between them. I love America but boy, does Las Vegas mess with your time perception. I strolled around happy and free for 48 hours and no bedtime. No clocks anywhere, you forget to sleep.

Leaving the poker and the black jackers to their fun and sleeplessness, I climbed into bed and googled 'Time' on the laptop. My favourite finds were Personal Porter (www.personalporter.com.au/P2), Luggage Forward (www.luggageforward.com) and Virtual Bellhop (www.virtualbellhop.com), door-to-door luggage delivery services that have sprouted up around the world. No more waiting at baggage carousels, searches by security staff and lost luggage.

And how about not having to treck to the shops to stock up on the staples like Blacksocks (www.blacksocks.com), offers a 'sockscription'. You choose a sock type and how many times a year you'd like them delivered, send payment and relax. Now how good a luxury is that? Or when is the last time you remembered to buy a new toothbrush? Recycline (www.recycline.com), offers a toothbrush subscription service (click 'Buy Now' to see the details) where you can choose to have a new brush delivered every two, three, four or five months. Toothbrushes and socks are the very basics, but these are only little time savings; to gain yourself some real time you should check out this…

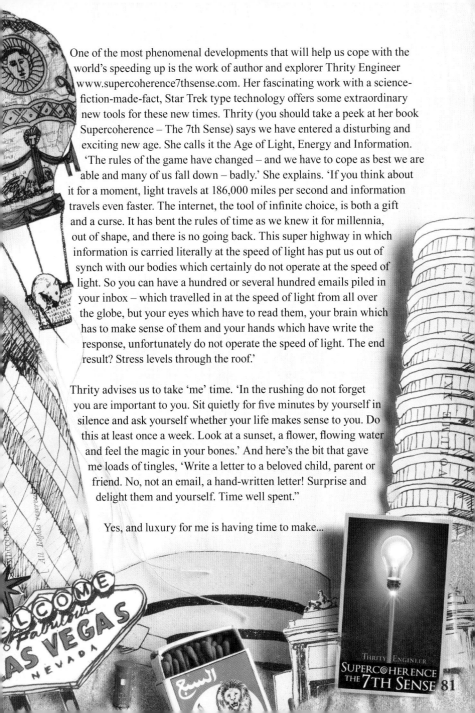

One of the most phenomenal developments that will help us cope with the world's speeding up is the work of author and explorer Thrity Engineer www.supercoherence7thsense.com. Her fascinating work with a science-fiction-made-fact, Star Trek type technology offers some extraordinary new tools for these new times. Thrity (you should take a peek at her book Supercoherence – The 7th Sense) says we have entered a disturbing and exciting new age. She calls it the Age of Light, Energy and Information. 'The rules of the game have changed – and we have to cope as best we are able and many of us fall down – badly.' She explains. 'If you think about it for a moment, light travels at 186,000 miles per second and information travels even faster. The internet, the tool of infinite choice, is both a gift and a curse. It has bent the rules of time as we knew it for millennia, out of shape, and there is no going back. This super highway in which information is carried literally at the speed of light has put us out of synch with our bodies which certainly do not operate at the speed of light. So you can have a hundred or several hundred emails piled in your inbox – which travelled in at the speed of light from all over the globe, but your eyes which have to read them, your brain which has to make sense of them and your hands which have write the response, unfortunately do not operate the speed of light. The end result? Stress levels through the roof.'

Thrity advises us to take 'me' time. 'In the rushing do not forget you are important to you. Sit quietly for five minutes by yourself in silence and ask yourself whether your life makes sense to you. Do this at least once a week. Look at a sunset, a flower, flowing water and feel the magic in your bones.' And here's the bit that gave me loads of tingles, 'Write a letter to a beloved child, parent or friend. No, not an email, a hand-written letter! Surprise and delight them and yourself. Time well spent."

Yes, and luxury for me is having time to make...

THRITY ENGINEER
SUPERCOHERENCE
THE 7TH SENSE 81

BATH-TiME wiSHEs

I know it's only a simple little thing, but finding time to ladle richly scented oil into a bath and then being able to relax in it and dream impossible dreams is a Cleopatra-like luxury. So which bottles deliver the most luxurious soak? This works Deep Relax bath oil by This Works, 18 Cale Street, London SW3; (tel: +44 207 584 1887 mail order +44 8452 300499; www.thisworks.com) or at Harvey Nichols is preservative free and packed full of vetivert, lavender and camomile. Cath Collins Neroli Bath Oil £11 (tel:+ 44 (0) 844 815 7390, www.cathcollins. com) turns the bath water milky and moisturises skin. Ren's Moroccan Rose Otto Bath Oil at Space NK (tel: +44 (0)845 22 55 600, www.renskincare.com) does the same but is steam distilled from Moroccan Rose petals harvested at dawn so makes the bath water smell of pure rose scent. Another rose treat is Claus Porto Rose Soap at Liberty (tel: +44 207 734 1234, www.liberty.co.uk) beautiful packaging and wonderfully scented. Follow this by slathering Renew Nourishing Rose Body Oil, £27, by Aromatherapy Associates (tel:+44 20 8569 7030, www.aromatherapyassociates.com) on after your long bath to make legs feel cashmere-soft. These last two products are delicately scented with roses and I only recently found out that that's stress-relieving too. A spritz of Vivienne Westwood's Boudoir perfume completes the rose experience. She's waaaay up there on my Happy List, I'd love to meet her some day.

82

Jamaican Tody

Scarlet tanager

Rose breasted Grosbeak

Vivienne Westwood
BOUDOIR

AROMATHERAPY
ASSOCIATES

RENEW

ROZA
PARADISE ROSE
Clear Perle

AROMATHERAPY
ASSOCIATES

REVIVE

NOURISHING ROSE
BODY OIL

125MLE   4.18FL OZ

Vivienne Westwood

Eeeek. So. Excited. Can't. Breathe. I'm sitting next to Vivienne Westwood in Paris. But first let me rewind the tape and tell you how this all came about...

I'm sure tons of peeps receive invites from Westwood inviting them to go behind the scenes at the studio, to discover the 'history' before meeting the designer, Vivienne Westwood. I'm also sure that a lot of people write up their piece and have done with it. Well, working in fashion all my life, I know a special thing when I see it and after setting the phone down and jumping up and down on the one spot for ten minutes with excitement I confirmed that yes, I would be thrilled to accept Westwood's invitation (sending a rejection back would be stupid, right?) and could I bring Peter to take photos and Charlie to film everything in the studio in Battersea? 'Yes' was the answer. And could we go backstage at the London Red Label show? 'Yes' again. And could we go backstage in Paris and talk to Vivienne loads and maybe hang out with her for a bit? 'Yes' came the reply. On my Gaaaaaaaaaaaawd! Two words Ec-Static. I spilt my tea with joy.

So, to London and there's a newspaper on Vivienne Westwood's desk with her picture on the cover. Underneath it reads 'She's back on London catwalk after 10 years.' It's the morning after her Red Label show at London Fashion

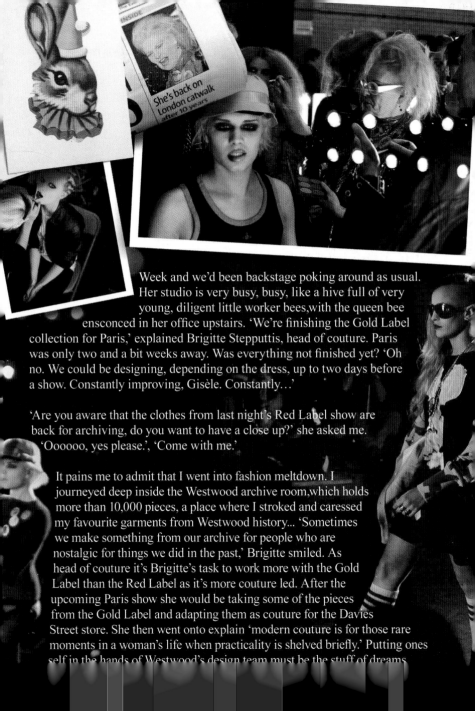

Week and we'd been backstage poking around as usual. Her studio is very busy, busy, like a hive full of very young, diligent little worker bees,with the queen bee ensconced in her office upstairs. 'We're finishing the Gold Label collection for Paris,' explained Brigitte Stepputtis, head of couture. Paris was only two and a bit weeks away. Was everything not finished yet? 'Oh no. We could be designing, depending on the dress, up to two days before a show. Constantly improving, Gisèle. Constantly…'

'Are you aware that the clothes from last night's Red Label show are back for archiving, do you want to have a close up?' she asked me. 'Oooooo, yes please.', 'Come with me.'

It pains me to admit that I went into fashion meltdown. I journeyed deep inside the Westwood archive room,which holds more than 10,000 pieces, a place where I stroked and caressed my favourite garments from Westwood history… 'Sometimes we make something from our archive for people who are nostalgic for things we did in the past,' Brigitte smiled. As head of couture it's Brigitte's task to work more with the Gold Label than the Red Label as it's more couture led. After the upcoming Paris show she would be taking some of the pieces from the Gold Label and adapting them as couture for the Davies Street store. She then went onto explain 'modern couture is for those rare moments in a woman's life when practicality is shelved briefly.' Putting ones self in the hands of Westwood's design team must be the stuff of dreams.

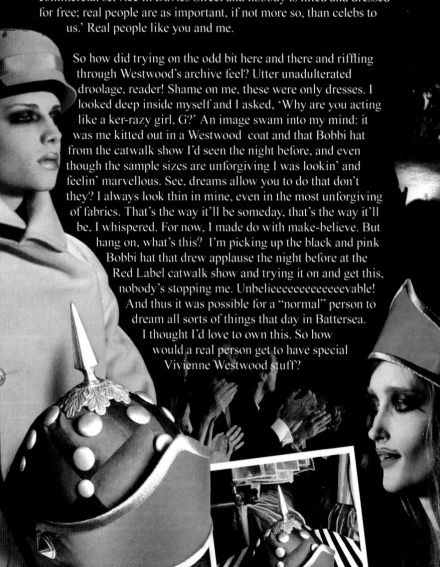

'Paris haute couture business today is all about publicity stunts. Dresses are taken from the runway and sent to the Oscars, for example; in other words the celebs are just walking billboards for the designers, not paying customers. Westwood's Couture Collection is a commercial service in Davies Street and nobody is fitted and dressed for free; real people are as important, if not more so, than celebs to us.' Real people like you and me.

So how did trying on the odd bit here and there and riffling through Westwood's archive feel? Utter unadulterated droolage, reader! Shame on me, these were only dresses. I looked deep inside myself and I asked, 'Why are you acting like a ker-razy girl, G?' An image swam into my mind: it was me kitted out in a Westwood coat and that Bobbi hat from the catwalk show I'd seen the night before, and even though the sample sizes are unforgiving I was lookin' and feelin' marvellous. See, dreams allow you to do that don't they? I always look thin in mine, even in the most unforgiving of fabrics. That's the way it'll be someday, that's the way it'll be, I whispered. For now, I made do with make-believe. But hang on, what's this? I'm picking up the black and pink Bobbi hat that drew applause the night before at the Red Label catwalk show and trying it on and get this, nobody's stopping me. Unbelieeeeeeeeeeeeevable! And thus it was possible for a "normal" person to dream all sorts of things that day in Battersea. I thought I'd love to own this. So how would a real person get to have special Vivienne Westwood stuff?

The prêt-a-porter Red Collection is the affordable collection, and prices range from £120 at her stores and in department stores. The prêt-a-porter Gold Collection is more expensive and prices start at £500. For made-to-measure in Davies Street the dresses start at £1,500, for a couture-type service. This is less than half the price charged by traditional couture houses. Jean-Paul Gaultier's haute couture was said to start at £5,000 when it launched in 1997, and Ungaro quotes £7,000. And Chanel haute couture? £15,000 for a suit, no less. Westwood, I learned, is unique because she follows every line of a piece personally, right through until completion. She does the sketches with Andreas, her husband, in her office and like Madame Vionnet, who invented the bias cut and the ingenious Grecian drape column dress, Westwood drapes miniature toiles on tiny puppet-sized tailor's dummies for every single dress.

'She works on cutting principles with little mannequins,' Brigitte explains. 'Every design is made up of 100 small decisions. What she's built up over all of these years is a studio in London where she makes all of the prototypes for the Gold Label, which I can then offer to my customers in Davies Street with personal fittings and a made from scratch service as couture. It's made especially for you; the whole team here at Westwood would be working on a dress.'

I began to wonder if I'd ever get to meet Vivienne. 'Where is she?' I asked. 'She's upstairs with Andreas and they're deep in a dress design. It's taken them four days. Four days! They've rejected many, many toiles of this one style so until they've got that sorted…' she lapsed into silence. 'Are there any dresses ready for Paris then?' 'Yes, yes of course, come, come let me show you how we make a dress before you meet Vivienne.'

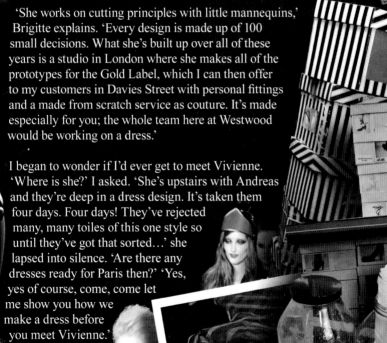

The story of a Vivienne Westwood dress

1. The basic drawings/concept story is devised by Vivienne and Andreas.
2. They decide which material will best tell the story they wish to tell. This season was about the jungle and soldiers and Vivienne had enlisted the help of children from Miss Bell's class in Nottingham to paint on the fabric for the clothes.
3. The drawings and materials matched, they're put on a board and the baby dummies start to arrive from Vivienne's office a few metres away from Stephan.
4. Stephan makes the little dummies into big dummies and the pattern makers draw up their patterns.
5. They cut the patterns in a specific Westwood style; one straight rectangular piece is cut and draped and moulded to create shape. This is a very unique pattern, very difficult to master and sets Westwood's clothes apart because of the specific drape.
6. They make a toile from calico (a cheap cotton material) on a dummy because using an expensive material at this stage is just a waste of fabric if there are changes to be made (there always are).
7. The toile is then fitted on a real model.
8. If it looks good at the fitting then Westwood goes ahead and has her team make the garment (say a dress) up in the expensive fabric.
9. It's fitted again on a real model and then if everything looks good, seams are finished and it's 'cleaned' (trimmed of hanging threads, buttons holes are finished off by hand and buttons and hand stitched details are added – the garment is made perfect and steamed and put on a hanger and covered in plastic.)
10. The dress is taken with the rest of the collection to the catwalk show.
11. At a model fitting, adjustments are made to the dress before the show so that the garment suits the model.
12. The music, stage set, make-up and hair and styling are all created and discussed to enhance the garment's story.
13. The dress is shown on the catwalk where buyers and the press see it for the first time.
14. Buyers arrive at the atelier or showroom the following day to see the garment up close and place an order for their shop. It's at these meetings that buyers sometimes request that the dress might be changed slightly from the original to suit their customer base.
15. Members of the press (stylists, editors), having seen the show, make appointments to see the collection and garments to consider it for a fashion shoot.
16. The dress is shot in a fashion shoot or appears in a newspaper (short lead) or a magazine (long lead) and a reader instantly wants it.
17. The reader goes into a store and buys the dress, then the Westwood story continues with the new owner.

The service at Davies Street takes the experience one step further, you can have any of Westwood's designs created by the Westwood team from scratch for you. In my humble opinion this is where every bride should go for her wedding dress.

Vivienne Westwood, 6 Davies Street, Westminster, W1K (tel: +44 207 629 3757, www.viviennewestwood.co.uk).

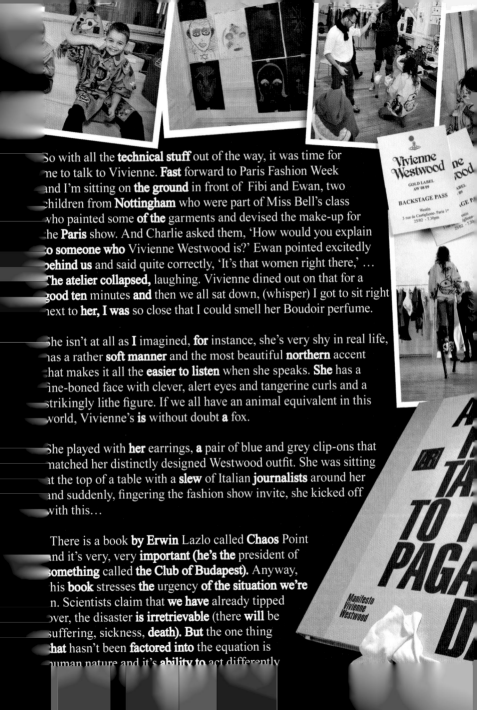

So with all the **technical stuff** out of the way, it was time for me to talk to Vivienne. **Fast** forward to Paris Fashion Week and I'm sitting on **the ground** in front of Fibi and Ewan, two children from **Nottingham** who were part of Miss Bell's class who painted some **of the** garments and devised the make-up for the **Paris** show. And Charlie asked them, 'How would you explain **to someone who** Vivienne Westwood is?' Ewan pointed excitedly **behind us** and said quite correctly, 'It's that women right there,' … **The atelier collapsed,** laughing. Vivienne dined out on that for a **good ten** minutes **and** then we all sat down, (whisper) I got to sit right next to **her, I was** so close that I could smell her Boudoir perfume.

She isn't at all as **I** imagined, **for** instance, she's very shy in real life, has a rather **soft manner** and the most beautiful **northern** accent that makes it all the **easier to listen** when she speaks. **She** has a fine-boned face with clever, alert eyes and tangerine curls and a strikingly lithe figure. If we all have an animal equivalent in this world, Vivienne's **is** without doubt **a** fox.

She played with **her** earrings, **a** pair of blue and grey clip-ons that matched her distinctly designed Westwood outfit. She was sitting at the top of a table with a **slew** of Italian **journalists** around her and suddenly, fingering the fashion show invite, she kicked off with this…

There is a book **by Erwin** Lazlo called **Chaos** Point and it's very, very **important (he's the** president of **something** called **the Club of Budapest).** Anyway, his **book** stresses **the** urgency **of the situation we're** in. Scientists claim that **we have** already tipped over, the disaster **is irretrievable** (there **will** be suffering, sickness, **death). But** the one thing that hasn't been **factored into** the equation is human nature and it's **ability to** act differently

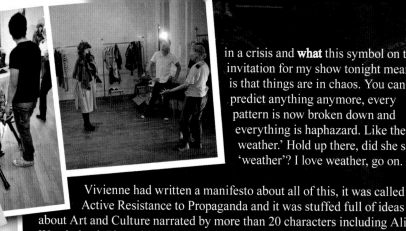

in a crisis and **what** this symbol on the invitation for my show tonight means is that things are in chaos. You can't predict anything anymore, every pattern is now broken down and everything is haphazard. Like the weather.' Hold up there, did she say 'weather'? I love weather, go on.

Vivienne had written a manifesto about all of this, it was called Active Resistance to Propaganda and it was stuffed full of ideas about Art and Culture narrated by more than 20 characters including Alice in Wonderland, Pinocchio and (my favourite) the pirates. She was paraphrasing for the Italians 'It's not just enough to say we need cleaner air and leave it to the scientists to develop these things, it's ordinary people that will ensure a change and I believe in public opinion and this is why I'm telling all of you this today.' There was a stunned silence from the table, mainly because the Italians hadn't understood one word she'd just uttered. The translators got going on explaining it. To soak up the whole behind-the-scenes atmosphere check out the little movie of all of this at www.thegoddessguide.com.

So what about fashion?
'The fortunes of "made in Italy" is changing,' she explained. 'People in Italy are finding that the things that used to be made in Italy are now being made in China. As a result people are starting to wear less fashion and are investing instead in well-made European, sustainable things. Like if you buy something really good and it costs a lot you have to question whether it's genuine, authentic. Did a lot of skill go into making it? I am against people being conned into paying big money for stamped out clothing which is rubbish.' Good point. Eyeing one of her male employees wearing a very unusual jacket she exclaimed, 'I think a certain amount of status can be earned these days from wearing a piece of clothing over and over again.'

At this point she bit her index finger
nervously, before continuing 'You don't have
to buy my clothes; get your kid to paint it for
you. Put a flower in your hair, whatever, do
something different to demonstrate your individuality!'

I plucked up the courage and asked Vivienne, 'A lot of my friends
would buy and wear your clothes, maybe not the Gold Label
but the Red Label. They find that your clothes give them that
individuality but how can they further that themselves?'
She explained that her shop at 430 The Kings Road offered
really good bargains, and if you just bought a piece, wear it
over and over again and individualize it.' 'Like a uniform of
individuality?' I added. 'Yes, add badges, pins, customize.'
Whoa, whoa, whoa, sweet child of mine, did she just say
'customize'? "It's the easiest way to celebrate authenticity."

Anyway, later I got her on her own to talk about more
personal things.

I'd had a quick gab with Andreas her husband before
speaking to her and he's a real doll; there's a bit of the pirate
about him. He loves the Irish (good start) and introduced me to
Pep Gay, the lead make-up artist who had flown in from New
York to do the make-up. Seriously, if you ever want to know
how to do perfect, natural looking eyeliner, check out the
movie of Pep backstage at www.thegoddessguide.com.

Anyway, we asked Vivienne if Andreas had changed the way
she looked at things and the way she worked now.

'Definitely, I would say so, yeah. For the better! He's just really
different – he's a visual person and I'm a literary person, I see things
from a story point of view and he doesn't care, he just sees things from

CHAOS POINT

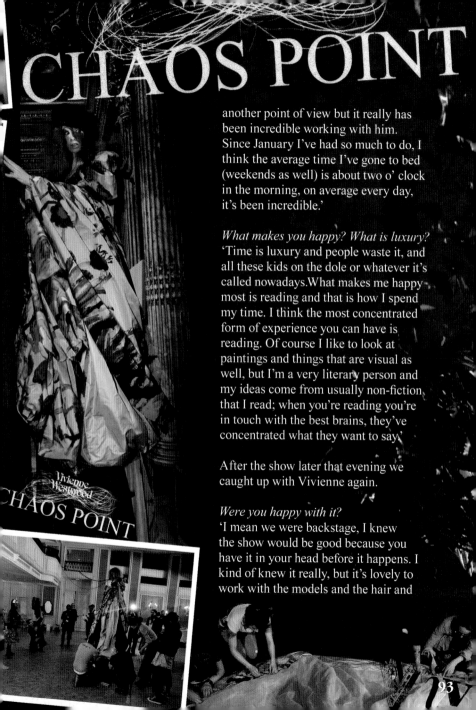

another point of view but it really has been incredible working with him. Since January I've had so much to do, I think the average time I've gone to bed (weekends as well) is about two o' clock in the morning, on average every day, it's been incredible.'

What makes you happy? What is luxury?
'Time is luxury and people waste it, and all these kids on the dole or whatever it's called nowadays.What makes me happy most is reading and that is how I spend my time. I think the most concentrated form of experience you can have is reading. Of course I like to look at paintings and things that are visual as well, but I'm a very literary person and my ideas come from usually non-fiction that I read; when you're reading you're in touch with the best brains, they've concentrated what they want to say.'

After the show later that evening we caught up with Vivienne again.

Were you happy with it?
'I mean we were backstage, I knew the show would be good because you have it in your head before it happens. I kind of knew it really, but it's lovely to work with the models and the hair and

Vivienne Westwood

make-up people and everything like the flowers in the décor and the room. **Everything is** very, very important. The clothes – that's my responsibility, **but** then the problem **is** to get all the other things right and I think I knew it would be good because we had **got** them right.'

*The response was phenomenal; the press **side** were standing up **and clapping.***

'Were they? **I'm** not **quite** sure what they were doing because I was quite serious at **the** end of it all for some reason. I knew that **it** was a very powerful thing. Yeah it was a whole concept **and the** idea that human beings are more wise than they know **they are, I** don't know, and that why **we** had all these different heights and **the** stilt walkers and everything. When people **talked** to me **about** the stilts I **said** maybe they weren't **on** stilts maybe **it was just** magic, you know **that** the **impression I** wanted **to** create. Yeah.'

*Tomorrow the buyers come in, are **you apprehensive** about that?*
'No, it's **not my** responsibility. I'll take a few days off but soon **as** I **go** back **to** work I'm having to work **on** the next collection. That's **the** way it is. **You** know?'

So **we await** the press over the next couple of days… I'm **sure it'll be** great. I'll be too busy doing the next thing.'

And taking time off.
'I've got two things in **my** life: fashion, which I really enjoy. For years I didn't want **to** do **it,** I just did it out of duty because if I didn't **do it, it** wouldn't exist. The story of my life is that when I finish this pair of trousers, the minute it's over for the designer it's old. I can read my book. I've got a category called "all these other things", which I hardly ever get time to do but I do make time whenever I can to read. I don't go on holiday, I don't do things, **I** just read and I go to museums and I think and that's what all these other things are about. My manifesto is about me having to try and communicate these things because after all that investment in trying to understand how the world could be better I think it's sane and not arrogant in any way, I think it's wonderful to try and tell people what I think is important and that's what my manifesto is about, how people can change the world."

Vivienne Westwood, **44** Conduit Street, W1 (tel: +44 207 439 1109, www.viviennewestwood.co.uk).

You probably feel a bit funny about me now, sharing as we just have the closeness of the last 95 or so pages. The macaroons, the perfume, Victor, Vivienne… so far this experience has been one heck of a journey of discovery for me and up until now that's the way the dice has rolled. See, I don't pretend to understand life completely so I have to do a lot of poking about in it. If you feel like I invited you around for dinner and served you cake and tea instead, while twirly twirling about in the kitchen rabbiting on about all kinds of stuff, well then I'm truly sorry. Or maybe you're a cake and tea kinda person, in which case you're going to want to stick around to meet Paul Smith. He loves tea, serves it in stripey little cups.

Aaaaaanyway, here are some crackin' fashion pages and not a speck of twirly twirl guff among them. See, I set aside a different notebook altogether for my fashion stuff and it's stuffed full of answers to questions that many of my friends have asked me since my last book; practical stuff like where to get a pair of Christian Louboutins resoled in 'that' exact same red colour. Or is there any place that does a good white shirt or gives good advice about jeans? One friend even asked where she could find boots for chubby Irish calves. See, I'm even choosing to ignore making an obvious farm joke here because of the seriousness of the subject. So, where to start? Well I'm off upstairs first to doll myself up a bit seeing as it's fashion speak. You can come with me if you like.

Shut the door, sit down there on the bed and be honest with me. Does my ass look big in these trousers? Have you ever noticed how your bedroom reeks of expectation, it's the planning room, the centre of activity when choosing your sartorial identity each day. "Yeah, you're right. Trousers too daytime, I'll try this dress instead then.' Anyway, as I was saying, the bedroom, or more to the point the bedroom mirror, where you take one last look and give yourself the seal of approval before facing the world; the shoes (good), the dress (nice), the make-up (subtle), the hair (shiny), and the accessories? Hello Inadequacy. 'Sorry I'm late, G,' Inadequacy said, 'Saturday evenings are tragic. They're my busiest night each week. So what do we have here then? Which of your closest friends led you to the tills at

Topshop holding this little number?' 'Yeah, yeah whatever!' 'Will you go all wobbly tonight ten minutes before you take on that crowded room, G?'

'Could you close the door on your way out, please, I'm with very important people.' Yes, easy peasy this time to shake Inadequacy, but he had a point about the crowd thing. 'They' stare, 'they' raise eyebrows, 'Who is she?', 'Is that paint on her fingers?' 'They' seem to think that 'they' are fab! Under normal circs, I'd let this slide but feeling, as ever, the pressure to provide answers I exclaimed, '"They" – little fashioney clones who've ripped their new look straight off the back of some WAG in a WAG mag – "they" wouldn't know fashion if it jumped up and bit them on the keesters.' See I just can't be doing with people who decide that we should all look identical. Do you agree with me? If there's one thing I've lived and learned in the last one hundred pages or so it's that authenticity is unique and is the opposite of sameness. Against a bland background it shines. Authenticity is honesty... 'I am what I am' so I'll step outside the crowd and stand on my own, alone if I have to. Your clothes should reflect this.

'So does this dress look OK then? Do you think I'll need a jacket if I'm left in the corner near the door on my own?' Inadequacy mused, 'Do you think that look is going to impress the whisperers, G?' 'Listen, mate, where were you when I met some of the fashion world's greatest mavericks? Nowhere. So see ya.' Take Vivienne Westwood for example, her style has nothing to do with perfection, it's an attitude; you find what suits you and let those shapes magnify your strengths repeatedly. Style should be all about you and you expressing your individuality, and with that in mind, my friends, 'they' can kiss my Westwood-clad ass.

Righty ho G, calm down there before you give yourself a coronary and open up your notebook, I tell myself. I'm lucky enough to get to see the catwalk shows and sketch and note down what I feel is unique. In the weeks after the shows I gradually add bits and pieces that I find until I've filled my notebook with my trend list for the season. It's a drool list, a dream list. I'm not a slave though, it's not a shopping list, just something for me to glance at once in a while and prod myself with notes like 'Oooh yes, new shooooooos and a coat are much needed. Now let me just open up my little notebook and see what shapes are in here?' Plus it just looks so nice, all my little fashioney ideas in the one place. So what's the first thing that I want to add to my wardrobe? Hmmm, let me see...

BAGS

I need a new bag me thinks. So where to start looking; it has to be unique, one that isn't a WAG bag, something deserving of my new word 'notable'. Eyeing my notebook I quite fancied Pauric Sweeney's bags, (very, very luxurious). When it comes to expertise he's as accomplished as Bottega Veneta, Chloé and all the other big brand names, but there's a difference, he doesn't do "It Brags" he's too cool. I've know Pauric for many years (he's Irish) and he's always been ahead of the "it" curve. As well as his own collection he's even taken on a job to revamp the über –luxury brand Tod's (his collection for them hits the shops next season).

So what makes a Pauric Sweeney bag so good then? His leathers come from very advanced tanneries; sting ray, lizard, python and crocodile all sourced and used in accordance with the Washington Convention and the attention to detail is phenomenal – it's the direction in which the luxury world is moving; independently owned companies offering a finish and a guarantee that their items are of the highest of quality. I stroked a Pauric Sweeney patent bag at Harvey Nichols (also available in 180 other worldwide locations and The Design Centre, Powerscourt Townhouse Centre, Dublin) and then I called him, who better to ask about luxury.

'Hey Pauric, what is luxury do you reckon? 'The realisation that we live, in the best of all possible worlds.' 'What's your luxury?' Freedom. Time. Love and humility.' See what did I tell you, a real laid back coolio. I went on... 'if you had a million quid what would you do or buy?' 'I'd get advice from the KLF Foundation.' 'And why do your freind's love you Pauric?' 'I try my best.' Nice to see the nice guys in fashion isn't it reader? Seeing as Pauric is the hot bag guy at the mo, I decided to ask his honest opinion on the whole "It Brag" thing. 'What's the deal with the demise of the "It Brag" Pauric?'

'It's a paradox as niche bags become elevated due to their niche values and 'under-the- radar' status and inevitably become "it bags" due to increased popularity and extensive media coverage, therefore the term "it bag" namesake becomes redundant. Perhaps a new name should be used to describe the hot niche bag of the season. The 'YOU' bag or 'ME' or 'NO' bag may be more appropriate.' Hmmmmm! I like the sound of the 'ME' bag, especially if it's one of his. You should take a look at this collection in Harvey Nichols, they're magnificent. His silver python bag is the stuff of dreams. Drooool!

Pauric Sweeney, Tel: +39 055 263 8259, www. pauricsweeneybags.com) and see Harvey Nichols, Browns, Dover Street Market, Galerie Lafayette, Luisa Via Roma and Net-a-porter.

Photograph by Takashi

99

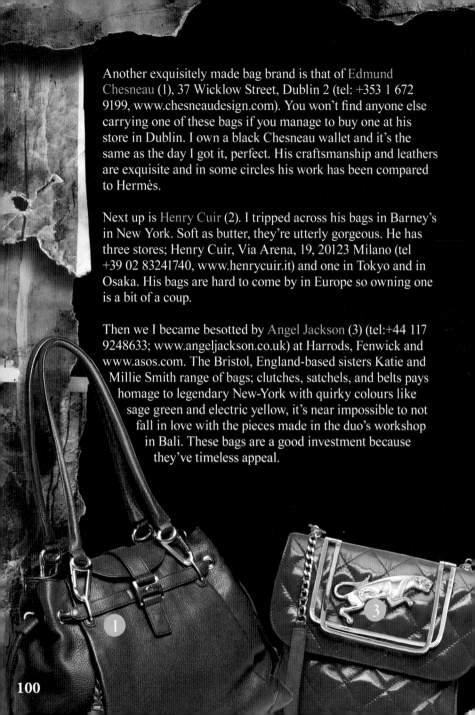

Another exquisitely made bag brand is that of Edmund Chesneau (1), 37 Wicklow Street, Dublin 2 (tel: +353 1 672 9199, www.chesneaudesign.com). You won't find anyone else carrying one of these bags if you manage to buy one at his store in Dublin. I own a black Chesneau wallet and it's the same as the day I got it, perfect. His craftsmanship and leathers are exquisite and in some circles his work has been compared to Hermès.

Next up is Henry Cuir (2). I tripped across his bags in Barney's in New York. Soft as butter, they're utterly gorgeous. He has three stores; Henry Cuir, Via Arena, 19, 20123 Milano (tel +39 02 83241740, www.henrycuir.it) and one in Tokyo and in Osaka. His bags are hard to come by in Europe so owning one is a bit of a coup.

Then we I became besotted by Angel Jackson (3) (tel:+44 117 9248633; www.angeljackson.co.uk) at Harrods, Fenwick and www.asos.com. The Bristol, England-based sisters Katie and Millie Smith range of bags; clutches, satchels, and belts pays homage to legendary New-York with quirky colours like sage green and electric yellow, it's near impossible to not fall in love with the pieces made in the duo's workshop in Bali. These bags are a good investment because they've timeless appeal.

also love Mimi Maka (4), across town in Shoreditch, I ... urred against her Jack Shopper silver leather tote £90 at ... her shop Mimi leather bags, 40 Cheshire Street, London E2 ... tel: + 44 207 729 6699, www.mimimika.com). Her Mimi ... Grace coin purse £40 in gold with a little zip running along the ... bottom was also very cute to go inside it. Berry crafts samples ... of her handbags (£90- £100), purses (from £25), belts (from ... £25.00) and laptop bags (from £155) on the premises and they can ... be customised. Her bags are gorgeous and she's even stocked in ... Bergdorf Goodman and Takashimaya in New York. I liked the ... silver tote for practicality and it was a good price at £90.

Finally I happened upon the Jenna style Beirn (5) (pronounced 'burn') bag in New York (see www.beirnbag.com for stockists). They're available also online at www.vivre.com - a great little website this with tons of bag choices and www.plazatoo.com another crackin online bag shopping site. I love this bag for many reasons, firstly the Jenna style is a hobo shape so it fits my lifestyle perfectly, it comes in tons of glorious colors and there's loads of room for my stuff. Yay! The bags are made from water snake and glossed with something called Mowilex, this makes them both shiny and waterproof (they're immune to liquids). Thinking back to my rainy bag experience outside Colette on page 56 I though you could drop this in a huge puddle (my favourite new word that) and it'd survive, I tell ya, it's genius. Decision, decisions, log onto www. thegoddessguide.com and find out which bag I bought in the end.

'Addresses of bag peeps I love for you...

Angel Jackson, (tel: +44 117 924 8633; www.angeljackson.co.uk) and at Harrods, Fenwick and www. asos.com. Anya Hindmarch, 15-17 Pont St, London SW1 (tel: +44 207 838 9177, www.anyahindmarch. com). Ballantyne, 153a New Bond St, London W1 (tel: +44 207 495 6184). Be&D, (www.beandd.com and see Harvey Nichols and www.net-a-porter,com). Bracher Emden (tel: +44 207 235 2745, www. bracheremden.com) and Harrods and Selfridges. Browns, 24-27 South Molton St, London W1 (Tel: +44 207 514 0016, www.brownsfashion.com) gives really good advice when bag shopping. Cartier, 175-175 New Bond St, London W1 (tel: +44 208 080 0330, www.cartier.com) Connoly Luxury Goods, Washington House, 40-41 Conduit Street, London W1S (tel: +44 207 439 2510) . Corto Moltedo, (www.corto.com) see Luisa Via Roma, Net-a-porter and Selfridges. Gérard Darel, 78 St John's Wood High St, London NW8 (tel: +44 207 586 9027, www.gerarddarel.com) and stockists. Devi Kroell, (tel: +1212 228 3201, www. devikroell.com) and see Browns, London and 10 Corso Como in Milan. Lanvin bags are stocked at Dover Street Market, 17-18 Dover Street, London W1 (tel: +44 207 518 0680, www.doverstreetmarket.com). Edmund Chesneau, 37 Wicklow Street, Dublin 2 (tel: +313 1 6729199, www.chesneaudesign.com). Marc Jacob's former head accessories designer Joy Gryson now creates her own range Gryson (www.gryson. com) which is really slick. Henry Cuir (www.henrycuir.jp) available in Barney's, New York. Jamin Puech, 54 Ledbury Road, London W1 (tel: +44 207 221 3059, www.jamin-puech.com) and see Fenwick, Harvey Nichols and Liberty. Janet Collin, (www.janetcollin.com) at Joseph, 77 Fulham Road, London, SW3 (tel: +44 207 823 9500,) and branches. Liberty, Great Marlborough St, London W1 (Tel: +44 207 734 1234, www.liberty.co.uk) have their own range of bags and matching diaries etc. Longchamp, 28 New Bond Street, W1S (tel: +44 207 493 5515, www.longchamp.com) Martine Sitbon's MS, (www.ruedumail.com). Melí Meló, (tel: +44 207 835 1363, www.melimelo.it) and Harrods. Michael Teperson, (tel: +39 055 210 524, www.michael-teperson.com) and Harrods, Fortnum & Mason and Joseph. Mulberry, (tel: +44 207 229 1635, www.mulberry.com) Nook & Willow, (tel: +4 4 (0)151 548 0432, www.nookandwillow. com) and see www.asos.com. Pierre Hardy, Jardins du Palais Royal, 156 Galerie de Valois, Paris (tel: +331 4260 5975, www.pierrehardy.com) and see Dover Street Market. Smythson, 40 New Bond St, London W1 (tel: +44 870 521 1311, www.smythson.com) and branches/stockists. Steven Harkin, (tel: +44 162 177 4703, www.stevenharkin.com). Susannah Hunter, 7 Rugby St, London WC1 (tel: +44 207 692 3798, www.sussanahhunter.com) and stockists. Tanner Krolle, 5 Sloane Street, Knightsbridge, London SW1 (tel:+44 207 823 1688, www.tannerkrolle.com.ru). Wilbur & Gussie, (tel: +44 207 589 1624, www. wilburandgussie.com). Zagliani, see Browns, Harvey Nichols and Matches boutique.

And if you'd only like to dip your toe in the luxury pool why not rent a bag instead?

At Be a fashionista (www.be-a-fashionista.com) there's an endless supply of bags. A new bag will be sent to you every 30 days which you can carry around for a whole month from £29.95 (per month). Similarly www.bagaddiction.c.uk offers exclusive styles and when you get bored, just change from £44.95 per month. Find a gorgeous Hermès Birkin at www.ukbeafashionista.com plus many other fab things, from £29.95 per month and www.fashionhire.co.uk holds iconic styles from labels such as Chloé, Gucci and Fendi, from £9.95 a month for its "Pay as you Go" package with additional hire fees. And www.bagstealorborrow.com starts at $9.95 a month. Rental fees depend on the bag, some of which cost up to $2,500 retail.

CARE TIPS

Interior

More often than not your bag will be lined with canvas, nylon or pig suede. To clean gently tease the interior out and use a standard lint roller, to pick up debris. Or try the fabric-brush attachment on your valuum (without turning it on I might add).

Exterior

Leather is a skin, fact, so treat it like you would your own. Keep it happy with a leather conditioning cream. There's no reason to treat it with a protectant or a silicone spray. Caught in the rain? Run for cover, then dab – don't wipe – moisture away. I know of one gal who moisturises her bags with her face moisturiser, if you're tempted try a hidden patch first.

Bottoms

Structured bags with stiff bottoms often have "feet" (metal rivets incorporated into the base) to protect the leather against sctratches and stains. An idea might be to ask a professional shoe mender to see if they'll add feet for you.

Storage

Store your bag away when not in use by stuffing it with acid free paper and placing it in a beautiful 100% pure cotton embroidered "shoes" storing bag £9 available online at Nina Campbell, 9 Walton Street, London SW3 2JD (tel: +44 207 225 1011, www.ninacampbell.com).

Handles and straps

Residue from lotions can discolour and age material –another good reason to keep handles clean. Also don't overstuff your bag; too much weight can weaken stitching or damage straps.

Hardware

Deep scratches or cracks on metal are virtually impossible to repair. But bag and shoe repair shops can replate hardware to hide finer flaws.

Zippers

Keep these working smoothly by running a pencil or a piece of natural beeswax (found in hardware stores), over a zipper's open teeth.

Wanna clean old leather without damaging it?

Use a warm damp (not wet) cloth lathered up with a gentle soap, such as Dove or Imperial Leather. Rub the leather well, wringing the cloth out and working in the soap until all the dirt has gone. Buff it up with a soft cloth before polishing with leather cream or polish. Test a hidden patch first as some leathers might not react well to water.

Clean you bag

Use an Ecloth available at John Lewis or at www.e-cloth.com to give the your bag a good clean at least once a week. Clean the underside especially.

THE HOOK
REPORT

Don't be fooled by the jaunty tone of this next little rantarooney; it's a serious piece of business. My current obsession is door hooks in public toilets and the lack of them. I've been hitting the world's toilets pretty hard lately, nailing the culprits. Anyone catch the tip about wiping your bag with an Ecloth in among all that guff about caring for your handbag on the last page? Yeah, well you gotta keep one step ahead, keep your bag clean.

Outside toilet doors everywhere people eat, drink, dance and discuss holidays, love, sex and telly, (always telly) and then it's "sorry, where's….(lets call her Sharon shall we?). Yeah where's Sharon? She's been ages! There must be a queue for the loo!" Next thing, Sharon appears trekking her germ-ridden tote from the bog and swinging it gaily off her arm launching it onto the dinner table, along with a grand old dose of whatever the toilet floor had. Think I'm over dramatising this? Read on.

I had notions about doing a mahussive scientific experiment about this one but a lad by the name of Chuck Gerba, (a la-di-da microbiologist with the University of Arizona), beat me to it. Using a hand-held germ meter, he tested the bottom of ten womens bags for ABC News and found that out of ten bags, every one had bacteria. Righty ho, big deal G, a few germs, never harmed anyone. What then? Well, some of the bags (wait for it) contained millions of bacteria. And wouldn't you know it? There's always one! One bag was covered with 6.7 million bacteria. Diiiiiiiiisgusting? And Gerba's findings were made extra sexy with this…five of the bags tested positive for coliform bacteria, (that's human waste to civilians like you and me). No shit G! Yes, shit G and plenty of it! And straight onto the kitchen table with it the moment we come through our own front doors.

Yes, I've said it before and I'll say it again, all public loos need door hooks. So back in the bog I'm planning a revolution, like when Jamie Oliver got the kiddies to bin the chicken nuggets, or when Hugh Fearnley-Whittingstall tried to wean us off battery reared hens. Either way, both spent days filming the stuff and all that palava. I'm talking about a simple project, I'll take a quick snap of every toilet door I encounter, get all excited about those that have hooks and maybe lash a hook or two up in pubs, clubs, shops and restaurants that have forgot to do it themselves, guerrilla style. What do you think? Steady on there G, you're not a revolutionary, and (girly voice) you'll get done for it. Be that as it may, something's got to change.

And don't get me started on clutch carrying…(that's bags not Jamie or Hugh Fearnley-Whittingstall chickens). How do you get a clutch onto a hook on a toilet door? You don't, I've tried and it's impossible, you need a ledge, simple as. But there lies another problem… they're extinct (too many guys and gals using them to powder their noses.) Hence, (lovely word that) I can't see the ledge appeal gaining as much sympathy as the hook thing? And anyway hooks cost buttons and don't encourage coke taking – unless you fancy skewering your nose to a door. I pondered all of this, waaaaay back on page 28 while traumatised by the state of the tea and chewing my knuckles and counting to ten backwards in a loo in Ladurèe, Paris. I experienced my first ever case of hook envy there. There was a fine big hook there for me to sling my bag onto. By heck there was and it set the standard. This was the hook to beat all hooks, I left that loo, every pore, every molecule satisfied. Imagine every loo door in the world with a proper hook? And a ledge too for clutch bags. Maybe I'll sort it in say about 20 years or so. You know me and a challenge. Watch this space!

My embossed, wrapped dress by Proenza Schouler (www.proenzaschouler.com) makes me happy.

BUILDING
the BASICS

Insider Secrets

I'd love to think that Karl Lagerfeld will be designing for Chanel when I'm 99 but, barring a miracle, it just ain't gonna happen. Sigh! Buying a brand at the top of its game is a smart investment – any Chanel quilted bag toting gal will tell you that. But buying good basics is the first step to creating a solid wardrobe, let's start with the classics.

A classic white shirt

Try Maxmara at Harvey Nichols (tel:+44 (0)20 7235 5000, www.harveynichols.com) and Brown Thomas (tel: +33 1 6056666, www.brownthomas.com); Thomas Pink (tel: +44 207 498 3882, www.thomaspink. com), Massimo Dutti (tel: +44 207 851 1280, www. massimodutti.com), Paul Smith (tel: +44 207 235 5000, www.paulsmith.co.uk), Agnès B (tel: +44 207 520 6914, www.agnesb.com)and COS tel:+44 207 478 0400, www. cosstores.com) for ice-white shirts. A blue or greyish tone to a white shirt will make your skin look dull, so white, white, white is key. Check that shoulder, cuffs and around the button holes are well stitched and finished and if you like your shirt fitted, look for cotton with a little bit of stretch (a little elastine) it'll keep its shape better over time.

Best time to buy designer coat

The best time to buy a designer winter coat is early August – the weather is warm (ahem, supposed to be, but stores turn up their air con to try and get their winter stock moving). Here's a fact for you: most department stores, say Harvey Nichols for example, take delivery of their first set of winter coats the last week of July. The early bird will get the most choice.

A cardi

A great way to keep your layering light is to wear a camisole under a cardi. Queene and Belle has a good selection of cardigans with slightly nipped in waists but there are a bit spendy at £379 (tel: +44 01750 23419, www.queeneandbelle.com). For a long cardi in their signature print try Missoni (tel: +44 207 221 0255, www.matchesfashion.com) to buy or for inspiration-they're as good as a coat.

Best time to buy high street coat

In comparison to designer coats, the high street stores (including Topshop) usually receive their coats the first week in September. Topshop and Jigsaw receive deliveries right through the season even into December.

Coat basics at a glance

Petite – Pick a coat to cover your favourite dress, which being petite, should be on or just below your knee. A dress hanging below your coat will shorten you. Stay away from big voluminous styles; translate the trend by choosing a fitted coat with a bell sleeve. The Princess shape suits you. Busty – Avoid heavy boucles and tweeds. The military style can be worn open and will give structure to your shoulders, which will balance big breasts. Tall/skinny – You can wear coats with lots of volume, even the dreaded padded coat. Pear shaped – Choose a belted coat but run from padding. Curvy – Avoid volume, big furs, sheepskin and big front pockets. Opt for a tailored Princess style or military style instead.

Casual with a coat

Team a coat, like a 3.1 Philip Lim coat (www.net-a-porter.com) with a top and leggings and leather boots, to create the perfect casual look.

Titbit

Most of us will buy a coat in black, beige, navy or grey. Lighten a sombre coat with a flash of colour - a huge necklace or scarf.

A polo neck

Put a polo neck over a pair of trousers and it's plain and simple. Put a huge necklace over it and it's, hot.

Bespoke bikini

If you have trouble finding a bikini that fits perfectly, then Biondi, 55B Old Church Street, Chelsea, London SW3 (tel: +44 207 349 1111, www.biondicouture.com) offers a made-to-measure bikini service. They can even add beautiful leather straps and trims.

Time saving tips

Keep a notebook of bits that you covet from magazines and use it for inspiration when shopping. Keep an eye on celebs with your body proportions. Check out Vogue (www.vogue.co.uk) to see catwalk shows and get an idea of what will filter down to the high street. Net a porter (www.net-a-porter.com) do a neat thing where they match and display their garments so you'll get a good idea of what goes with what for most of the key shapes for the season ahead. And ASOS (www.asos.com) shows looks on real models. All will help you create different looks.

INSIDER SECRETS

Little tweaks to a garment can make a huge impact; taking trousers up, or – if there's sufficient hem – down, tightening or loosening waistbands, shortening sleeves. Here are some industry secrets.

The perfect shirt

Is the perfect shirt proving to be elusive? Here's a simple solution: buy a shirt one size too large for you and have it altered to fit you perfectly. If you have a larger bust, have bust darts put in. Ask to have secret hook and "eyes" or snap fasteners put in secretly around the buttons in the chest area. This will help the shirt lie flat across your chest . Many couture designers use hidden hooks to help garments lie smoothly, so try it.

The perfect jacket

Think shoulder, shoulder, shoulder. Everything else is easy (and more affordable) to adjust. When buying a jacket (or coat), make sure the shoulder fits. Sleeve length is simple to change. A tip from fashion shoots that I've been on… bulldog clips are often used in the industry to clip a jacket at either side of the back seam to make it appear figure hugging around the waist and bust line. You can achieve the same effect (minus the clips of course) by having a jacket decreased around the back seam. It's really inexpensive and makes a huge difference.

The perfect skirt

No figure benefits from a large, shapeless sack of a skirt. Have it suit your body shape better by taking it in along the sides or at the back for a more flattering fit around the thighs and bottom. If you have a flat bottom, have your skirt adjusted along the back seam to give the illusion of shape. There are tons of tricks to change a skirt.

The perfect suit skirt

Only buy a skirt cut on the bias if the fit is perfect. Trust me; this style is a nightmare to alter. It's originally cut so that the fabric will fall fluidly and stretch. Any alteration to a bias cut style can create unsightly ripples, which make it look as if the garment is too tight for you and that's counter productive. Tulip skirts are hard to alter also. Opt for a pencil or straight cut if you intend on altering it to suit your figure perfectly. Ask shop assistants to explain shapes.

The perfect jeans

Too long? No probs. A seamstress can work with you to keep as much of the original shape as possible in the leg while making the hem shorter. Take jeans to a tailor who will be able to match the thread used in an alteration to the rest of the jeans (yellow-gold or white usually).

The perfect trousers

You've tried on a pair of trousers and the waist is too big but the hips are perfect. What are your options? Always think hips first, waist later. A seamstress can easily take in a trouser waist at the back vertical seam or at the sides.

Titbit

When you take trousers to be shortened, bring the shoes you intend wearing with them too, to get the length perfect.

The perfect armhole

In plus-size garments, armholes are cut low to allow ample room around the armhole for arm movement and comfort. Sometimes, however, you won't need all that room or bagginess, which can make a jacket or coat look bulky. Have a good seamstress or a tailor see if he/she can reduce the volume of the sleeve and raise the armhole a little.

Titbit

Ask; some retailers will hem and alter your purchase for free.

The experts

Designer Alterations, 220a Queenstown Road, Battersea, London, SW8 (tel: +44 207 498 4360, www.designeralterations.com) is a super, super alteration service. They do fittings at their studio in Battersea and (wait for it) they will even come to your place of work or home. How cool is that?

The perfect poloneck

If you're unhappy with the neck of a poloneck because it appears slack then have it taken in to give you a snugger fit. This one change alone makes an instant impact.

Titbit

There doesn't seem to be an umbrella organisation for dressmakers, but you can get a list from Sew Direct (tel: +44 870 777 9966, www.sewdirect.com) for £1.

Titbit

Had your jeans altered and the hem looks too crisp or new? Run an emery board or a piece of sandpaper along the bottom to distress it and make it look less fresh.

INSIDER CARE SECRETS

Shirt care

Stained collar? Place the stain facing downwards on a piece of white tissue paper. Rub the reverse side of the stain with a circular motion working from the outside of the stain inwards using dry-cleaning solvent, which you can buy at most department stores. Keep changing the tissue to absorb more and more of the solvent and stain. Leave the fabric to dry, and then using a toothbrush and white soap, gently wash the area of the stain. Then wash your shirt as normal.

Coat care

To keep your coat looking as good as new, empty the pockets after each wear. Never hang it on a hook – instead use a thick, padded hanger where the edges of the hanger are nice and wide for the shoulders.

Heavy deodorant stains on t-shirts

However good your anti-perspirant, underarm staining can still be a problem; pre-treat with a liquid laundry detergent. For heavy stains, pre-treat with a pre-wash stain remover. Allow to stand for between five and ten minutes, then wash using a laundry detergent and oxygen (all-fabric) bleach in the hottest water that it is safe to use for the fabric.

Titbit

When blood comes into contact with fabric, act immediately. Treat it with cold water and lift the stain gently with a clean cloth. Don't ever use hot water as it'll set the stain. Don't rub the fabric really hard, as this will cause bobbling.

Blood on wool

The iron and protein content in blood can cause an indelible stain on wool. However, I would suggest, at your own risk, trying water with a hand-wash liquid from the royal launderer and dry cleaner, Blossom and Browne's Sycamore (tel:+44 208 586 7715, www.blossomandbrowne. com). Alternatively take it to a specialist cleaner.

White light deodorant marks

Gently rub a Deo Blitz sponge (£2.99 at Boots, www. boots.com) onto the annoying white marks and stains caused by deodorant on your t-shirt and they'll disappear.

Hats

All hats need to be cared for. Stuff your hat with acid free paper after a big occasion and pack it away carefully in a hat box. If you use it as an ornament in your bedroom felt, feathers and straw will collect dust over time, which is very difficult to shift.

Lipstick on linen shirt collar

Remove lipstick from linen by applying Vaseline petroleum jelly before washing.

Cleaning leather gloves

Pop your gloves on and then with lukewarm water and a mild soap solution, gently rub your hands together as if you're washing them. Then remove the gloves and pat dry with tissue paper. Dry flat, away from heat.

WHAT'S HER SECRET?

Huge boobs but sick of bulky boulder-holder bras?

Bravissimo, 28 Margaret Street, Oxford Circus, London W1W (tel: +44 207 62 5620) have branches nationwide and do a great catalogue service (tel: +44 (0)1926 459859, www.bravissimo.com.). Their bras go up to a size JJ cup. Rigby & Peller, 22A Conduit Street, Mayfair, London, W1S (tel:+44 (0)845 076 5545, www.rigbyandpeller.com) do a wonderful fitting service as well as made-to-measure, with bras off the peg bras running from sizes A-J. Marks & Spencer offer lovely Truly You Underwired Padded Plunge lace bras from £20 (tel: +44 (0)845 302 1234, www.marksandspencer.co.uk) and many other styles, which go from DD-G. Fantasie (tel: +44 (0)15 3676 4334, www.fantasie.co.uk) makes a range of larger sizes and Goddess (www.figleaves.com) has a selection of styles going up to 56FF.

Halterneck top or dress?

An underwear-drawer multitasker is a super investment. The Hawaiian Twist convertible halterneck by Wonderbra is lightly padded for extra uplift. It costs £20 and comes in pink, black and white (tel: +44 (0)1475 504175, www.wonderbra.co.uk). If your dress is see-through, try Marks & Spencer's five way nude padded convertible bra for £16 (tel: +44 (0)845 302 1234,www.marksandspencer.co.uk). For a splash of colour, try the Love Kylie Microfibre seamless bra in aqua for £30 (tel: +44 (0)1925 212212, love-kylie.com).

Wearing a deep v-neck dress to an event?

If you feel you need support and can't go braless (seriously, who among us can?), make a feature of your front with a diamante detail bra, £27 from Splendour (tel: +44 208 964 7820, www.splendour.com) and leave the diamante on show; it looks like a part of the outfit. You could also support the girls with a stick-on bra by Marks & Spencer (tel: +44 (0)845 302 1234). Also effective is the frontless Body, £45 from Ultimo (tel: +44 (0)845 130 3232, www.ultimodirect.com), which has a low, plunging front with diamante or clear plastic between the cups and comes in nude and black.

Titbit

Black lace is a huge trend this autumn/winter. From Givenchy's sheer lace blouses to Stella McCartney's light as gossamer tunics. Choose a nude bra.

cetti's warbler

Strapless dress but don't want droopy girls?

The 'sticky' seams of the Halo Lace Convertible Strapless bra, £36 from Wacoal at Fenwick (tel: +44 207 629 9161, www.fenwick.co.uk), keep it in place all night. Also, the Hide & Sleek strapless cami, £28 by Spanx (tel: +44 (0)845 004 8400, www.mytights.com), will hold in your bust and smooth tummy bulges. Calvin Klein's Perfectly Fit range offers a strapless bra for £26 at Selfridges (tel UK: 0800 123 400; outside UK tel: +44 (0)113 369 8040, www.selfridges.com) and Calvin Klein stores (tel: +44 207 290 5900, www.calvinklein. com). If ample boobs means you need straps, try this: go onto www.figleaves.com, type 'clear straps' into the search box (top right of the web page) and it'll spit back pages of strapless bras in all sizes with clear straps as an option. Buy there and then from Figleaves or track down a brand suggested at your local department store. Tons of choice here and not that expensive either.

Sweater dress or clingy wool skirts

The Secrets Beauty Enhancers Bottom Shaper, £6.99 from Playtex (tel: +44 (0)500 3624 30, www. playtex.co.uk), has a higher waistline and strong fibres to ensure your tummy stays in place. The scary sounding High Waist Girdle, £18 from Marks & Spencer (tel: +44 (0)845 302 1234), is a tummy terminator – high waisted and scalloped to avoid bulge. If you want something less rigid, the Revo-light, £15.50 from Cette (tel: +44 (0)1297 625888, www.cette.com), could be your answer.

WHAT'S HER SECRET?

Lace dress or Victorian blouse, but it's slightly sheer?

For white lace, pick a vest with built in integral support, £14 from Bhs (tel: +44 (0)845 196 0000, www.bhs.co.uk), to avoid the double bra-and vest-straps look. If you're wearing pale colours, then stick to whites and nudes – and look for a secret support vest if you have ample girlies. Black looks best under dark colours, but Prada have added extra interest to this area by placing nude collars, which slip inside a lace dress.

Going braless inside a backless dress?

OK, harsh reality. Unless you're small and pert this can be disastrous. There are always Concealits, £5.95 by Useful Chick Stuff at Harvey Nichols, Topshop and www.asos. com (tel: +44 207 349 7572, www.usefulchickstuff.co.uk). Concealits will hide any nipple action while sagging girlies can be lifted using Liftits, also from Useful Chick Stuff. This super adhesive tape is attached just above the nipple and then you lift up your boob and stick it in place to give a more pert position. These are only suitable for a C cup or smaller and give real shape to boobs. Useful Chick Stiff also has their new DD+ Breast Cups which will give backless, strapless, breast support to women with breasts bigger than a DD cup. Alternatively you could try www.figleaves.com where Natural stick on cups £13 go up to a 38D.

Backless dress

The Arinna nude satin body, £59 from Valisere (tel: +44 (0)1793 720232, www.valisere.com), has convertible straps that can be used as a halterneck, a crossback or a clear-strap option for a deep 'bare-back' look. The Impromptu Stretch Knit Bandeau bra, £14 from La Redoute (www.laredoute.co.uk), has clear straps around the back and between the cups.

Want a smaller bum in trousers?

No need to resort to lipo – instead, buy yourself a pair of Shape Up briefs, £6.99 from Levante (tel: +44 (0)1277 232301, also available at www.tightsplease.co.uk). They'll lift south-spreading buttocks with their strategic support panels. Alternatively, the contour panty, £29 from Flake (tel: +44 20 7493 8442) is practically a bottom in a box. And finally, Magic Knickers has the Magic Slimshort for £25 (www.figleaves.com) which performs posterior miracles by giving you rear a lift while flattering your stomach.

Office Goddess pencil skirt perfection

Try the seam-free Ceriso Brazilian invisible-line knickers, £5 from Marks & Spencer (0845 302 1234) – they won't show through even the slinkiest of skirts. Hot Hips boy-cut briefs, £7 from Sloggi (tel: +44 (0)1793 720232), are a great solution for low-cut skirts. And the seam-free sides and pretty satin detailing of the Toujours French knickers, £22 from Elle Macpherson Intimates (tel: +44 207 478 0280, www.ellemacpher-sonintimates.com), will look just as sexy when you're changing in the evening. at the gym.

Cellulite under a silk gown

So you've tried the gym and gallons of water. Try a pair of Original Footless Tights £13.99 from Spanx (www.tightsplease.co.uk), they're all you'll need for a bump-free bum. Playtex's Secret Beauty Enhancers range includes a thigh and tummy slimmer in black, white and nude for £7.99 (tel: +44 (0)500 362430, www.playtex.co.uk). The Relax support panty, £17 by Cette (tel: +44 (0)1297 625 388, www.cette.com), pulls in from the waist to the knees, giving an overall slimming effect. Great little secrets, this lot. Shhhhhhhhhh!

115

People assume that if you are small, everything looks good, but that's not always the case is it? Although Kylie is the best representation of a pixie petite, without her proportions, finding the perfect pair of trousers is not always a breeze (usually too wide at the waist aren't they?). If you spot something that you feel you really must have, then see page 00 on how to have it altered for your proportions. The following tips should help you look (and feel) lean and tall.

The first thing to remember as a petite is that the perfect fit is imperative. Of all the different body types, you will suffer the most if your clothes are baggy because you'll just look swamped. Invest in basics like little fitted shirts, tees, skinny jeans and a shrunken little leather jacket. Let tee sleeves graze your knuckles under leather jacket sleeves, it creates the illusion of long arms.

Being petite… it's all about elongating your lower half. That means matching your trousers colour to your jacket colour - the same colour top to toe will lenghten your frame. A killer pair of platform heels where the platform seems hidden is your secret weapon, worn under trousers and jeans.

This empire line dress from Burberry Prorsum is the perfect petite solution.

Dresses

An empire line under the bust is great for petites. For dresses/skirts, the ideal length is a couple of inches above the knee or higher if you've got the legs for it.

Bin huge necklaces

Keep your neck area free of huge, clanking heavy jewellery and big dangly earrings. Avoid huge scarves, your neck should be bare to add height.

When shopping

Chose styles that are neat and don't ever hide your bust/waist/hips under yards of material, you need to nip in all of these places to give your tiny frame slight feminine curves and a sense of proportion. A well-cut fitted trench coat is always a great buy.

Elongate your torso

Invest in a good bra to lift your bust and give as much of a gap as possible between your waist and bust line, this creates a taller and leaner silhouette (like a dancer).

Elongate legs

Skirts should be knee length or slightly below for the office. High black shoes and matching black tights add length

Avoid

Long jackets, floor length skirts; high waisted trousers or ultra-low-rise ones. Trouser turn ups or a deep waistband also have a shortening effect. Heavy fabric like Boucle and tweed will bulk your small frame up so is best avoided. Avoid hugely contrasting colours top and bottom as they'll chop your body in half (disaster!).

Suit jackets and coat sleeves need to be kept short

However, suit jackets for work and heavy coats with wide sleeves have to be altered to sit on your wrist bone (wide sleeves that are too long can make it look as if you've borrowed a tall person's coat or jacket.)

Titbit

Low-cut bikini waists elongate the torso and cut-away swimsuits add height.

Addresses for you

ASOS (www.asos.com) for tunics. Ann Taylor (www.anntaylor.com) from size 4; Bershka (tel: +44 207 025 6160; www.bershka.com) from size small; Dolce & Gabbana (tel: +44 (0)870 700 0988, www.dolcegabbana.com) from size 6; Gap (tel: +44 (0)800 427 7895; www.gap.com) from size 8; Harrods (tel:+44 207 730 1234, www.harrods.com) their teenage department goes up to size 18 and is VAT free. H&M (tel: +44 207 323 2211, www.hm.com) from size 8; Jimmy Choo (tel: +44 207 823 1051, www.jimmychoo.com); John Lewis childrenswear (tel: +44 (0)845 604 9049, www.johnlewis.com) – brilliant for t-shirts, sportswear and black trousers and it's cheaper because you don't pay any VAT. Manolo Blahnik (tel: +44 207 352 8622, www.manoloblahnik. com); Marc Jacobs (tel: +44 207 235 5000, www.marcjacobs.com) from size 6; Marks and Spencer Petite Collection (tel: +44 (0)845 302 1234, www. marksandspencer.co.uk) from size 6; Miu Miu (tel: +44 207 235 5000, www.miumiu.com) from size 6; Morgan (tel: +44 (0)800 731 4942) from size 6; Moschino (tel: +44 207 318 0555, www.moschino.it) from size 6; Muji (tel: +44 207 323 2208, www.muji.co.uk) from size 8; New Look 915 teenwear (tel: +44 (0) 50045 4094, www. newlook.co.uk); Next Petites (tel: +44 (0)870 243 5435, www.next. co.uk) from size 6; Prada (tel: +44 207 647 5000, www.prada.com) from size 6; River Island (tel: +44 208 991 4759, www.riverisland. com) from size 8; Sara Berman (tel: +44 207 025 6160, www. saraberman.com) from size XS; Topshop Petite (tel: +44 (0)845 121 4519, www.topshop.co.uk) from size 6; Velvet (tel: +44 207 580 8644; www.velvet-tees.com) for t-shirts with a feminine fit from XS; Zara (tel: +44 207 534 9500; www.zara.com) from size 4. Second-hand designer boutiques and vintage stores are a great source of small sizes; the Victorians were tiny. Marni, DKNY, Ralph Lauren, Paul Smith, Maharishi, Diesel and Tommy Hilfiger all do kid's collections. Many go up to age 18 and because kid's clothes are minus VAT they're cheaper than adult ranges. A good tip if you're in London is to head straight to the Harrods teen department, the variety is mind-boggling.

CURVY

I wish women would love their curves and not treat them as a problem. To all who fall into this category, I say size should simply not be an issue. Buy yourself a few key pieces to put structure to your wardrobe and celebrate those gorgeous curves.

The Basics

A good starting place is to invest in a dress. Anyone over a size 12 should start by checking out Anna Scholtz. The brand also offers jeans (bootcut are the most slimming) and great trousers.

Lingerie

A good bra will lift your bust, give you a waist and lengthen your torso see p 112.

A bit of a tummy

Choose clothes that skim rather than cling – tunic tops over dark, wide legged trousers are a blessing for big hipped girls with a protruding tummy. Slim your bottom half with a darker colour than the top and for best results match top and bottom colour; an unbroken line will appear more streamlined and stop eyes resting on your problem area.

Secret to perfect curve control

Designer Allison Rodger, who dresses Nigella Lawson among others, offers a signature look to her dresses, which have all of the perfect dress secrets to get the most from curves: a low neckline, nipped-in waist and a skirt, which glides over the hips and flares out below the bottom. Look her up, she's brill!

Proportions

If you are carrying extra pounds, a poufy, exaggerated skirt will only add volume and pounds to the waist and thighs, so avoid.

Upper arm dilemma

Look for a bell shaped sleeve in tops and dresses as it camouflages fleshy upper arms. An interesting v-neck or low-cut neckline, cinched in waist and loose skirt, will also help draw attention way from upper arms.

A big bottom

My take on this is that you can show it off in a pencil skirt or disguise it in a drop waisted one. With trousers, give high waisted a wide berth. Shop around from the addresses on the next page for a good pair of leg elongating classic trousers.

Boots

If boots are a problem for curvy legs, try footwear specialist Duo, which has 20 calf widths, ranging from slim to extra wide (see below).

Avoid

High or fussy necklines, bold graphic prints; garish colours; stiff or chunky fabrics (velvet springs to mind); boxy or square jackets; clumpy shoes and boots; padded gilets or anoraks; anything overtly masculine like oversized polo shirts or men's sweaters (even if they are on the catwalk).

Invest in...

tummy control knickers (see p113); a support bra; a ruched one-piece swimsuit; small prints; jersey; crossover or v-neck tops to break up a large bust line; bias-cut or A-line skirts; high heel and boots with a slim heel; statement jewellery; belts; sunglasses.

Titbit

Invest in some fabulous jewellery to draw the eye towards your face neck or wrists.

Addresses for you

Allison Rodger (tel: +44 207 821 7000, www.allisonrodger.co.uk) made to order; Anna Scholz (tel: +44 208 964 3040, www.annascholtz.com) from 8-26; Anne Harvey (tel: +44 (0)1582 399877, www.anneharvey.co.uk) for sizes 16-28; BiB Big Is Beautiful, at H&M (tel: +44 207 323 2211) for sizes 16-30; Boden catalogue (tel: +44 (0)845 677 5000, www.boden.co.uk) go up to a 20; Bravissimo (tel: +44 (0)1926 459859, www.bravissimo.com) for cup sizes up to JJ; Debenhams (tel: +44 (0)8445 61 61 61, www.debenhams.co.uk) for cup sizes up to 20; Dorothy Perkins (tel:+44 (0)870 122 8801, www.dorothyperkins.com) for sizes up to 20; Duo (tel: +44 (0)845 070 5588, www.duoboots.com); Elena Miro (tel: +44 207 734 1333, elenamiro.com) offers an Italian line in plums, olives, lots of sequins and suede, which goes up to 28, and **is** stocked by Harrods, Dickins & Jones, DH Evans and its own store (all London, plus Rackhams in Birmingham). Eskandar (tel: +44 207 351 7333, www.eskandar.com) **is** the Nicole Farhi of the plus-size world: very expensive and stylish. Elvi (tel: +44 (0)1527 400489, www.elvi.co.uk) for 16-plus sizes; Evans (tel: +44 (0)845 121 4516) for sizes 16-32; George at Asda (tel: +44(0)500 1000 55, www.asda.co.uk) for sizes up to 24; Inspire at New Look (tel: +44 (0)0500 454094, www.newlook.co.uk) for sizes 16-24; JD Williams (www.jdwilliams.co.uk) for sizes 12-34; Marina Rinaldi (tel:+44 207 629 4454) for sizes up to 28; Marks & Spencer Plus Collection (tel: +44 (0)845 302 1234, www.marksandspencer.co.uk) for sizes 20-28; MySize (www.mysize.com) for sizes up to 38; Next (tel: +44 (0)870 243 5435, www.next.co.uk) for sizes up to 22; Nitya (tel: +44 207 495 6837, www.nitya-paris.com) from sizes up to 20; Persona (tel: +44 207 580 5075) for sizes 12-28; Rigby & Peller (tel:+44 (0)845 076 5545, www.rigbyandpeller.com) for cup sizes A-J; Simply Be (www.simplybe.co.uk) for sizes 16-47; Sixteen 47 (www.sixteen47.com) at French and Teague for sizes 16-47; 1626 by Florence & Fred at Tesco (tel: +44 (0)800 505555, www.clothingattesco.com) up to size 26.

PEAR SHAPED

Good news, a pear shape is far easier to balance than other problem areas such as bust, wide masculine shoulders or a pregnancy bump. For this body shape, tailoring is your friend. Ultimately, the hourglass is the silhouette that everyone should be trying to achieve and you've got it.

Balance

Make sure your top half balances your bottom half; if you don't have a large bust, buy a padded bra to gain that balance.

Elongate

Elongate from waist to ankle and wear heels where possible.

Shoulders

Wear a slight shoulder pad, I know, the word shoulder pad (Grrrroan!), tucked into an Edwardian-style puff or a tailored, military-style coat won't even be noticed by others. But it functions to trick the eye into seeing a more slender silhouette.

Silhouette

Break up your silhouette lengthwise as well as widthways by choosing bracelet sleeves and wearing lots of bangles. Make sure all the action is taking place on top. And keep it plain from the waist down.

Avoid

Pencil skirts; prints or horizontal stripes on your bottom half; skinny top halves like a poloneck or shrunken jacket, boxy trousers, knickerbockers, short skirts, high waists, light colours on your bottom half; see anything velvet or tiered, run a mile; that goes for skinny stiletto heels, too.

Legs

Choose fishtail skirts, pointy-shoulder jackets, Edwardian blouses, fussy collars, caped jackets, three quarter length Princess line coats that just cut you at the knee or a little below it – you want to show off your legs from the knee down. Wear fake-fur collars, boot-cut hipsters; ethnic or tribal necklaces – Diva at Miss Selfridge do a nice selection; scarves and pashminas, high-heel, stretch suede or moleskin boots.

Westwood

I've always felt that Vivienne Westwood's designs make the most of this body shape. Edwardian style coats and corsets with little puffed and padded shoulders worn over high neck, frilly blouses and a lot going on around the neckline draw instant attention away from a pear shaped bottom. If you fall into this category you should have by now invested in a few things that are empire line; either a smock for the summer months or a dress for the winter.

No Uggs

First things first. No Ugg boots. Most say they've gone waaay out of fashion but there are some who still cling to the comfort.

1930's Style

Pear shapes look good in longer jackets. Styles like 1930s tea dresses really fsuit as well. Don't be afraid of colour.

Travel outfit

An empire line dress which falls just from under the breast area with plenty of room in the skirt is the best combination for your summer dress shape. Smocks are brill too.

It will end in tiers

Avoid tiered skirts
Choose jeans and a kaftan for festival or summer lounging instead of a flouncy, peasant-style skirt, which flares out from the widest part of the hips. I know the peasant skirt is dead but just in case.

Swimwear

Bikini bottoms with wider sides flatter hips, while triangular cups enhance a bust. a high-cut one-piece slims thighs, while plunge-necks create spectacular cleavage and this in turn will help balance wide hips.

Addresses for you

Accessorize (tel: +44 (0)870 412 9000, www.monsoon. co.uk); Anna Scholz (tel: +44 208 964 3040, www. annascholtz.com) for sizes 8-26; Anne Harvey (tel: +44 (0)15 82 399877, www.anneharvey.co.uk) for sizes 16-28; Avoca Anthology (www.avoca.ie); BiB Big Is Beautiful, at H&M (tel: +44 207 323 2211, www.hm.com) for sizes 16-30; Diane Von Furstenberg (tel: +44 207 221 1120, www.dvf.com) for wrap dresses; Diva at Miss Selfridge (tel: +44 (0)1227 784 4157, www. missselfridge.com); Dorothy Perkins (tel: +44 (0)870 122 8801, www. dorothyperkins.com); Ghost (tel: +44 208 960 3121, www.ghost. co.uk); Juliet Dunn (tel: +44 207 584 1059, www.julietdunn.com); Karl Donoghue scarves (tel: +44 207 729 0114, www.karldonoghue. com); Mark Jacobs (tel: +44 207 235 5000, www.marcjacobs.com); Marks & Spencer (tel: +44 (0)845 302 1234, www.marksandspencer. co.uk) for sizes up to 22; Miss Selfridge (as before); Next (tel: +44 (0)870 243 5435, www.next.co.uk); Office (tel: +44 (0)845 058 0777, www.office.co.uk) for two-tone high heels; Per Una at Marks & Spencer (as before); Vivienne Westwood (tel: +44 207 924 4747, www. viviennewestwood.com), and Wallis (tel: +44 (0)845 121 4520, www.

BUSTY

Right, reality check. Some women have paid out pots of cash to have what you've got. So what if you don't get to wear tiny little lacy blouses or coats buttoned up to the neck? Most trends are still yours for the taking – what about v-neck knits? Or sexy wrap dresses? This, baby, is where you come into your own.

Large busts demand attention, which is why few designers – aside from Vivienne Westwood – allow them to dominate a fashion show, choosing instead models with bee stings where boobs should be. It's not in any way strange, it's just that anything larger than a 30AA messes with the line of a tailored garment in a show. Now back in the real world where boobs are allowed, If you've been blessed with biggies then balance and proportion is required.

Invest

A good investment is a three-way support bra (with different strap options), which allow you to wear a variety of tops (see p114).

Balance

Work with a large bust, not against it. Don't wear loose tops, wear a low-cut top, preferably a v-neck, and the secret is to show a little flesh from neck to cleavage. Then wear something slimming (boot cut trousers) on your bottom half to counterbalance your boobs.

Avoid

Scarves, thin spaghetti straps on dresses or tops (which will automatically make the bust look heavier), anything high cut or fussy around the neck; spindly heels that can make you look like Jessica Rabbit (not entirely a bad thing but a bit cartoonish at the end of the day); chokers are out as is heavily beaded ethnic jewellery unless it rests on your cleavage.

Beauty

Make sure the skin on your neck and cleavage is moisturized and glowing, helped along by fake tan or a contouring powder (see p282). Long hair and red lips add extra va-va voom to busty figures but avoid very strong make-up as this can look a bit OTT.

Boom or bust

Wearing floral? Printed or highly patterned frocks can be tricky if you are top-heavy. Solution: make sure the pattern at the top is smaller and less dramatic than the one on the bottom. Reverse the idea if you're small on top.

Basics

Go for hats with height, which draw attention away from your bust. Wrap dresses; v-ballerina or scoop necks; pencil or fishtail skirts,; well-cut trousers, belts low on the hips or hipsters, loose swing jackets and high, high stacked heels.

Wrapping

Wrap tops, wrap dresses and ruching are your friends. Issa, Velvet, Sass & Bide and Diane von Furstenberg excel at these shapes

Too Tight

Never be tempted to wear a bra that's too small in an attempt to minimize your cup size as it will squash you in all the wrong places.

Never cover completely

If you're a top-heavy girl, you should never cover up completely, it'll just add bulk to your bust.

Addresses for you

Alexander McQueen (tel: +44 207 355 0088, www.alexandermcqueen.com); Anna Scholz (tel: +44 208 964 3040, www.annascholtz.com) from 8-26; Anne Harvey (tel: +44 (0)1582 39 9877, www.anneharvey.co.uk) for sizes 16-28; Anonymous (tel: +44 207 727 2348, www.anonymousclothing.com), Bravissimo (tel: +44 (0)1926 459859, www.bravissimo. om) for cup sizes up to JJ; Celine (tel: +44 207 2974999, www.celine.com); Chloé (tel: +44 207 823 5348, www.chloe.com); Diane Von Furstenberg (tel: +44 207 221 1120, www. dvf.com); Dolce & Gabbana (tel: +44 (0)870 700 0988, www.dolcegabbana.com); Dorothy Perkins (tel: +44 (0)870 122 8801, www.dorothyperkins.com); Emma Cook (tel: +44 207 730 1234, www.emmacook.co.uk); French Connection (tel: +44 207 399 7200, www. frenchconnection.co.uk; Frost French (tel: +44 207 267 9991); George at Asda (tel: +44 (0)500 1000 55, www.asda.co.uk); Gharani Strok (tel: +44 (0)870 837 7377, www. gharanistrok.co.uk) Inspire at New Look (tel: +44 (0)500 454094, www.newlook.co.uk); ssa (tel: +44 207 514 0000, www.issalondon.com); JD Williams (www.jdwilliams. o.uk); Karen Millen (tel: +44 (0)870 160 1830, www.karenmillen.co.uk); La Petite alope (tel: +44 (0)870 837 7377, www.lapetitesalope.com); Marks & Spencer tel: +44 (0)845 302 1234, www.marksandspencer.co.uk); Marni (tel: +44 207 730 1234, www.marni-international.com); Patrizia Pepe (tel: +44 207 531 3399, www.patriziapepe.com) Rigby & Peller (tel: +44 (0)845 076 5545, www.rigbyandpeller.com) for cup sizes up to J cup; Sass & Bide (tel: +44 207 235 5000, www.sassandbide.com); Simply Be (www.simplybe.co.uk) Stella McCartney (tel: +44 207 841 5999); Swim Hut (tel: +44 (0)1444 819219, www.swimhut.com) for bikinis up to cup-size DD-plus; Temperley (tel: +44 07 229 7957, www.temperleylondon.com); Vanessa Bruno (tel: +44 (0)870 837 7377, www.net-a-porter.com/Vanessa_Bruno); Velvet (tel: +44 207 580 7377, www.velvetboutique.co.uk).

Skinny & Tall

Everyone assumes that fashion is easier for tall women, but not every tall gal is blessed with Elle MacPherson proportions. Women 5ft 8in and over are catered for by a number of high-street shops. Dorothy Perkins, Topshop, New Look, Evans and Next have followed the lead of pioneer Long Tall Sally. Even Next directory now offers a longer sleeve length, three centimetres longer than standard.

Skinny

If you'd like to create the illusion of curves, then ruffles and puffballs will help. Though the bottom is puffed out, bare arms and a long neck will balance the ruffled skirt. Patterns on your top will create bulk and a military-style cropped jacket will broaden your upper body. If your legs are skinny then you can enjoy all shoe heights from the highest wedges and platforms to the flattest gladiator sandals. Wearing something structured up top, like a shirtdress with wide waist-cincher, will emphasize the waistline and distract from your legs if too skinny.

Sleeves

Be careful with sleeves; shop around until you find a brand that works for you. C&C California offer the most exquisite t-shirts. Team with trousers from Joseph and Jane Norman for jackets. They have long sleeves and are always a bit different to anything else on the high street.

Online

The internet is another great option, MySize, which specializes in taller and larger sizes,allows you to see the clothes on a model your size. Also worth a look is Dizzy Heights, a Kent-based site with fashionable shoes up to size 11.

Large & tall

If you're large and tall stick to one colour but break up your line with different textures and fabrics.

Avoid

Oversized bulky, boxy jackets, they can look too masculine; cropped jackets or all over bold prints.

Buy

Fluid, long and lean Missoni-style cardigans over tube or bell shaped skirts; cropped, fitted trousers.

Shirts

Skirts with pleats, a gentle A-line or ruffles will create instant curves below the hemline and make skinny legs look shapelier.

Layer

You can layer without worrying about looking frumpy.

Addresses for you

Ann-Louise Roswald (tel: +44 207 250 1583, www.annlouiseroswald.com); Day Birger et Mikkelsen (tel: +44 207 267 8822, www.day.dk); Dizzy Heights (www.dizzyheights.org); East (tel:+44 208 877 5900, www.east.co.uk); Evans (tel: +44 (0)845 121 4516, www.evans.co.uk); Inspire at New Look (tel: +44 (0)500 45 4094, www.newlook.co.uk); Jane Norman (tel: +44 207 659 1234, www.janenorman.co.uk); Joseph (tel: +44 207 736 2522, www.joseph.co.uk); Kazoo (www.tall-people.co.uk); Land's End (tel: +44 (0)800 617 161, www.landsend.co.uk); Long Tall Sally (tel: +44 (0)870 990 6885, www.longtallsally.com); Margaret Howell (tel: +44 207 009 9006, www.margarethowell.co.uk); Miory (tel: +44 (0)845 056 3545, miory.co.uk) makes really sharp trouser suits at very good prices for tall women, Marks & Spencer (tel: +44 (0)845 302 1234, www.marksandspencer.co.uk), which has long legs lengths; Mint (tel: +44 208 870 2219); Monsoon (tel: + 44 (0)870 412 9000, www.monsoon.co.uk) MySize (www.mysize.co.uk); New Look (tel: +44 (0)500 454094, www.newlook.co.uk); Next (tel: +44 (0)870 243 5435, www.next.co.uk); Nitya (tel: +44 207 495 6837, www.nitya-paris.com); 1626 by Florence & Fred at Tesco (tel: +44 (0)800 50 5555, www.clothingattesco.com); Tall at Dorothy Perkins (tel: +44 (0)870 122 8801, www.dorothyperkins.com); Tall at Topshop (tel: +44 (0)845 121 4519, www.topshop.co.uk); Tall Women (www.tallwomen.org).

DENIM

Skinny jeans

There's no sign of this trend winding down, at least among the peeps that I hang out with anyway. Keep in mind that unless you have legs like a giraffe you'll have to team these with height-giving heels.

Titbit

For help in finding the perfect fit, Browns Focus (tel: +44 207 514 0000, www.brownsfashion. com does the best denim service in London.

Treat your dark denims like cashmere

If you've spent over £100 on a pair of jeans then let's be real. You'll want the colour to last on them. I know it's a bit of a pain, but dry cleaning them is the best way to preserve colour. Also, wash them as seldom as possible, and when you do, turn them inside out and use a cold, gentley cycle with a small amount of detergent.

Inseam

The inside length of your jeans affects the entire outfit, so the inseam is crucial. The average inseam is 34 inches, but petites should opt for styles with a 32-inch inseam, and leggy ladies (those 5 foot 10 and taller) should look for jeans with a 36-inch inseam.

Titbit

When buying flared jeans, take the shoes you intend to wear with them with you to see if the jeans length will need altering. A flare should cut across the foot.

Titbit

Cream plimsolls by Converse (tel: +44 207 255 9004, www. justconverse.co.uk) look really good with skinnies.

Big bottom

In the denim world, you can buy your jeans based on 'sculpt' (in English that means the size of your butt). The brand Notify offers sculpt sizing: size A for flatter bums, B for a moderate curve; and C for fuller bottoms.

Titbit

Keep your top half slim with a fine C&C t-shirt (Selfridges) underneath **your little** jacket.

Earth Goddess jeans

Mavi do organic denim as do Edun and Rag & Bone. Habitual Organic denim is made from bamboo, and now even Levi's are making jeans from organic denim and recycled buttons.

Day to night jeans

Switch things up a notch by swapping your flats for heels. This outfit might look like it's effortless, but it's really working incredibly hard to dress up a pair of jeans for evening time. Add neat tailoring makes jeans look smart. I know the word waistcoat (groan) is now a dirty word in the fashion industry, but you can't argue that a fitted waistcoat or little jacket gives a flattering top half. The texture of the t-shirt is also important – make sure it's extra luxurious like .

1 questions

Check out www.zafu. com and go through the 11 point questionnaire to uncover jeans suitable for your body type.

Titbit

Sperling's vests and tees look and feel as if they've been washed thousands of times, making them feather light.

8th Amendment

New from this super-cool Aussie denim brand is, Harlow jeans £170, which hug the hips and thigh then flare out beneath the knee. Very 70s and very sexy – I love 'em. From Browns Focus, 38-39 South Molton Street, London. W1K (tel: +44 207 514 0063, www.brownsfashion.com)

Denim address book

Best Skinnies **J Brand** Low Rise 910 Skinny at Browns Focus (as before); **Superfine Black Liberty** skinny leg jeans £135, also at Brown Focus; **True Religion** dark skinny jeans £163 from Selfridges tel: +44 (0)870 837 7377, www.truereligionbrandjeans.com); **Tsubi** Ksubi skinny dry raw (dark) denim, £121 (tel: +44 207 251 9003, www.ksubi.com). Best Flared **J Brand** Love Story Low Rise Jeans £170 at Browns Focus (as before). This brand's denim is so thin **that** jeans have a great fit like trousers. Best Highwaisted Jeans **£120 by Paper Denim & Cloth**, from Questionnaire, (tel: +44 207 **385 7300**)

Denim shops

Trilogy, 33 Duke of York Square, Chelsea, London SW3 (tel: **020 7730 5515**) is by far the best denim shop in London with a huge **range. Gap** is good value with prices starting at £50 (tel: +44 (0)800 427 **789,** www.gap.com). Choose from dark indigo one year old denim **through to** 0-year-old denim in skinny, slouchy and boot-cut fits.

127

FLAT HUNTING

Ballet flats

Wearing my ballet flats makes me smile because they make me feel all girlish. I want to skip along the capital's stairways and do twirly twirls on the spot like a ballerina in a jewellry box. The most coveted flats ever are these Alexander McQueen bejewelled pointed pumps. Ohhhhh how beautiful would they make you feel, twinkling from place to place like a Princess?

Flat flattery

Ballerina pumps have become a wardrobe staple and here's how to make them flatter you... choose a pointed toe if you're lacking in height, it's more leg-elongating. A style cut low over the toes is the most flattering option when worn on bare legs. Wearing flats everyday can shorten calf muscles so alternate them with heels.

Titbit

Avoid pencil skirts or minis, as both styles benefit from leg-lengthening heels. Flats look best with voluminous, loosely pleated skirts that are hemmed just below the knee.

marsh
tit

Titbit

Cute flats are perfect with narrow cropped pants from Joseph (tel: +44 207 590 6200, www.joseph.co.uk), or slim-cut jeans from Superfine at Browns Focus 38-39 South Molton Street, London. W1K (tel: +44 207 514 0063, www.brownsfashion.com).

Slim Cut

Your cute flats will also set off narrow cropped pants from Joseph (as above), or slim-cut jeans turned up above the ankle, such as Miss Sixty tel: +44 (0)870 751 6040, www. misssixty.com).

Titbit

Punctuate a block colour outfit with a flash of vivid leather or a bright bejeweled, silk or satin flat.

Flat hunting addresses

Azzedine Alaïa at Browns, 24-27 South Molton Street, London. W1K (tel: +44 207 514 0016, www.brownsfashion.com); he's made timeless ones for years. Carmen Ho's flats at Joseph (tel: +44 207 610 8441, www.carmenho.com); have exquisite detail. Chanel, 20 Old Bond Street, Mayfair W1S (tel: +44 207 493 5040, www. chanel.com); Chanel invented the pump for daywear – this classic was the first, and is still coveted today. Gandolphi, Gandolfi Dance Shop, 150 Marylebone Road, London, NW1 (tel: +44 207 935 6049, www.gandolfi. co.uk); this is where I buy leather-soled flats for indoors. Repetto, 22 rue Paix ,75002, Paris (tel:+33 1 4471 8312, www.repetto.com); find Parisian Repetto pumps also online at La Redoute Creation (tel: + 44 (0)844 842 2222, www.laredoute.co.uk); order their catalogue – it's gorge. LK Bennett, 31 Brook Street, London W1K (tel: +44 207 629 3923, www.lkbennett.com or +44 (0)844 581 5881 for your nearest stockists.) (Pink pumps right). French Sole (www.frenchsole.com) available from most department stores, (leopard pumps top right). Pretty Ballerina, 4 Brook Street W1K(tel:+44 207 493 3957 www.prettyballerinas.com); (leopard pumps bottom). Sam Edelman, 1370 6th Avenue (at 56th Street), Eighth Floor, New York, New York 10019 (tel: +1 877 932 7726, www.samedelmanshoe.com) – round toe flats with brooch around $99. Scorah Pattullo's suede pumps at www. scorahpattullo-online.com are gorge. Also, seasonal flats by Pedro García, Olivia Morris and Christian Louboutin from www. netaporter.com are good buys.

FLat MATES

Just when I thought I couldn't find space for any more shoes, I found these new fabulous designers. How about that then? Can we say 'gagging for it'? All together now...

Fashion secret

Sexy, sexy, sexy! They're not subtle but they are fabulous. Nicole Brundage, a Texan based in Milan, is a fashion industry secret. Her £214 tan leather shoes at www.nicolebrundage. com, made from the most luscious leather, are just for starters. Salivate!

Titbit

To remove grease stains from leather, rub in washing-up liquid, leave to dry and then polish off.

Titbit

Mix a tiny drop of linseed oil with a tiny drop of vinegar and put on a chamois cloth to buff tan leather. Test a hidden patch first in case the leather is colour treated.

Titbit

Clean wooden heels with furniture polish. This also makes patent leather sparkle as well.

Buy online

Check out these shops and websites for great footwear: www.minnetonka.co.uk or Wilde One's, 283 Kings Road, Chelsea, London. SW3 (tel: +44 20 7352 9531 www.wildeones.com) for fringed moccasins; www. espadrillesetc.com for coloured espadrilles; and www.funkyflipflops.com for flip flops; www.easyspirit. com for gladiator sandals and www.shoestudio.com for, among others, Pied a Terre.

Names to love

I bought booties two years ago from Scorah Pattullo (tel: 44 (0) 207 036 7366, www. scorahpattullo.com) and they served me well. Their shoes are great too. Another great brand is Carvela (tel: +44 20 7546 1888, www.kurtgeiger. com) at Kurt Geiger. The Kurt Geiger shop is located at 198, Regent Street .London W1B (tel: +44 20 3238 0044). Kate Kuba, 26 Brooke Street, London W1K (tel: +44 20 7499 2626, www.katekuba. co.uk) is also great.

Thick ankles

Shop around for a pair of slimming extreme heels. Wedge and platform heels are very good at giving the illusion of a slimmer ankle.

Lengthen your legs

A hidden platform is not only a stable shoe to walk on but it's a super way of adding extra inches to a petite frame. Wear a shoe that's the colour of your trousers or stockings to create the illusion of longer pins if your desire is to look taller. Prefer going bare legged? Try a stiletto or a platform in a colour close to your skin tone.

Christian Louboutin red soles made good as new

Classic Shoes, 23-25 Brecknock Road, London, N7 (tel: +44 20 7485 5275). These guys are brilliant (friendly too). Not only can they restore your Louboutin heels to their former red perfect glory but they can make leather boots more comfy by adding a panel. They'll also stretch shoes for you, and best of all they can even match a replacement heel if one has completely snapped off. How amazing is that?

Create your own

Selve in Mayfair (located above Paxton & Whitfield Cheesemongers) 93, Jermyn Street, London SW1 (tel: +44 20 7321 0200, www. selve.co.uk) offers a made-to-measure service called 'The Shoe Individualizer'. Choose from loads of styles, heel heights and materials (including snakeskin) to create your perfect boot or shoes. To order, you need to book an appointment to visit the Salon for a personal fitting and then it takes about five weeks for the shoes to be hand made. Prices start off at £250.

Break in new heels

Break in a new pair of heels by wearing them around the house for a few days with a thick pair of socks before you intend wearing them out.

Cleaning Leather

To make leather shoes last longer, try cleaning with saddle soap (Grison £4.95) in place of ordinary cleaning products. Then polish using a neutral shoe polish.

Coloured shoes

If you've invested in a pair of shoes made from coloured leather then clean and condition them using Woly Shoe cream £2.80 from www. shoestring.uk.com. It comes in 68 colours including hot pink and dark green.

Flatter your calves

Don't stress yourself about boots that won't zip up. Pied a Terre, 19 South Molton Street, London W1T (tel:+44 20 7629 1362, or www.shoestudio.com) do a wonderful stretchy style in black moleskin every season with a heel which looks great with skirts. It's their best-seller. LK Bennett, 31 Brook Street, London W1K (tel: +44 20 7629 3923, www.lkbennett.com or call +44 844 581 5881) also do really good boots.

Goddess shoes

Treat yourself to Georgina Goodman, 44 Old Bond Street, London, W1S (tel: +44 20 7493 7673, www.georginagoodman.com) unique handcrafted boots and shoes.

Rotate your shoes

Try not to wear the same shoes day after day. They'll last longer and it's healthier for your feet to let the shoes rest and completely dry out.

TRAINERS

How many models of sneakers can you name? Not brand names, but the individual model itself. All right, you've read past the first line on this trainers page so the chances are you can list a few, but for the average punter on the street, the number is waaaaay low. Considering this alone, the Adidas Superstar (shell-toe to you and me) is the king among sneakers for its iconic value. In the 35 years since its original release, the Superstar has undergone technical and cosmetic changes, countless reissues and celebrity endorsements. The cultural impact of the humble basketball shoe has spanned generations and cultures to become one of the most famous shoe silhouettes in the world.

By the mid 80s, the Adidas Superstar crossed over to the street and was adopted by the Run DMC old-school rap artists, but did you know that metal heads like Anthrax were wearing them with their regulation leather strides too?

Years ago you'd have been laughed out of school for wearing Gola, or Patrick, or Mitre for that matter. But nostalgia softens the memory (and taste), and in some quarters, it's now deemed acceptable to wear trainers until recently only sold in Woolworths. So it's party time for the unpopular kids at school; now we can wear our high-tops without a bother.

I'm in a street artist sandwich queuing outside Gloria's, king of the London street art scene, D*face swishes by on his way to **Stolen Space** his gallery on Dray Walk, The Old Truman Brewery 91 Brick Lane, London E1 6QL (tel: +44 207 247 2684 www. stolenspace.com). Two things worth queuing for on Dray walk then, a limited edition runner and a D*Face limited edition print. I luuuurve both to the point of obsession.

VELVET KICKS & BAG

Emma Hope's velvet sneaker bag, £399 at **Emma Hope**, 53 Sloane Square, London SW1X (tel: +44 207 259 9566, www.emmahope.co.uk) comes in antique rose, fuchsia, inky blue and gold. Hope also even offers matching 'Magic Basket' sneakers, which are swathed in the same unlikely shades of luscious velvet.

BEST CLEANER

Principally targeted at sneaker-heads, **Jason Markk P.S.S.** (Premium Sneaker Solution) www.jasonmarkk.com is the best cleaner I've ever used. It's 98% natural, completely biodegradable, and the wave of a hog-hair bristle brush coated in their specially formulated magic potion, get sneakers extra clean. So why is it so good? (Jason Markk, the creator, has a devoted following and wide online acclaim at sneaker-fanatic blogs worldwide). It rids your kicks not only of grass stains but stubborn stains even your mum couldn't move. As well as being on sale at Jason Markk's online store, it's also available through most good sneaker stores: **Ubiq** (www.ubiqlife.com), **Kendo** (www.kendo-la.com) and **Colette** (www.colette.fr) in Paris, among others.

TITBIT

To stop sneaker laces from ripping, wet them before you tie them. The knot dries and remains in place.

TITBIT

Fill a sock with cat litter, tie the end and pop it into a shoe overnight. A sheet of fabric softener left in a trainer overnight also leaves it fresher by the morning.

SUPER SNEAKER WEBSITES

www.sneakerfreaker.com: everything that you would ever need to know about sneakers, and their magazine is the last word on kicks. www.hypebeast.com: a super website with a great forum and a great store.

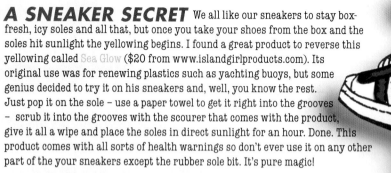

A SNEAKER SECRET

We all like our sneakers to stay box-fresh, icy soles and all that, but once you take your shoes from the box and the soles hit sunlight the yellowing begins. I found a great product to reverse this yellowing called Sea Glow ($20 from www.islandgirlproducts.com). Its original use was for renewing plastics such as yachting buoys, but some genius decided to try it on his sneakers and, well, you know the rest. Just pop it on the sole – use a paper towel to get it right into the grooves – scrub it into the grooves with the scourer that comes with the product, give it all a wipe and place the soles in direct sunlight for an hour. Done. This product comes with all sorts of health warnings so don't ever use it on any other part of the your sneakers except the rubber sole bit. It's pure magic!

CUSTOMIZE ADIDAS

Using a scanning device to measure the exact width, length, and pressure distribution of your feet, the Mi-Adidas counter at Harrods, 87-135 Brompton Road, Knightsbridge, London SW1 (tel: +44 207 730 1234, www.harrods.com) offers customized trainers for a variety of sports from £90. Choose from 147 colour combinations and personalized embroidery options.

CUSTOMIZE NIKE

Are you familiar with the NikeiD concept? Launched in 2000 the service offers you the opportunity to create custom-made shoes from a selection of styles, colour ways and materials, with the chance to further personalize your design with a unique alphanumerical ID of your choosing, stitched onto the shoes. There's a studio in New York and one in London's Nike Town, 236 Oxford Street, London W1C (tel: +44 207 612 0800, www.nike.com). On the ground floor there's the Id bar with 54 styles all of which offer thousands of changes for you. Upstairs Nike has transcended customization, allowing you access to archive shapes, a bespoke service, which allows you to create a runner from scratch. Staff are really amazing here (Snailey loves them) and helped me create what is, in my humble opinion, the freshest pair of Max 90s ever made,

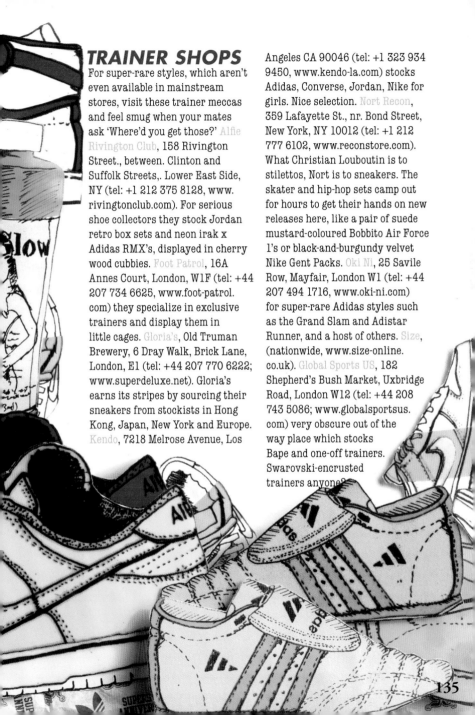

TRAINER SHOPS

For super-rare styles, which aren't even available in mainstream stores, visit these trainer meccas and feel smug when your mates ask 'Where'd you get those?' Alfie Rivington Club, 158 Rivington Street., between. Clinton and Suffolk Streets,. Lower East Side, NY (tel: +1 212 375 8128, www.rivingtonclub.com). For serious shoe collectors they stock Jordan retro box sets and neon irak x Adidas RMX's, displayed in cherry wood cubbies. Foot Patrol, 16A Annes Court, London, W1F (tel: +44 207 734 6625, www.foot-patrol.com) they specialize in exclusive trainers and display them in little cages. Gloria's, Old Truman Brewery, 6 Dray Walk, Brick Lane, London, E1 (tel: +44 207 770 6222; www.superdeluxe.net). Gloria's earns its stripes by sourcing their sneakers from stockists in Hong Kong, Japan, New York and Europe. Kendo, 7218 Melrose Avenue, Los Angeles CA 90046 (tel: +1 323 934 9450, www.kendo-la.com) stocks Adidas, Converse, Jordan, Nike for girls. Nice selection. Nort Recon, 359 Lafayette St., nr. Bond Street, New York, NY 10012 (tel: +1 212 777 6102, www.reconstore.com). What Christian Louboutin is to stilettos, Nort is to sneakers. The skater and hip-hop sets camp out for hours to get their hands on new releases here, like a pair of suede mustard-coloured Bobbito Air Force 1's or black-and-burgundy velvet Nike Gent Packs. Oki Ni, 25 Savile Row, Mayfair, London W1 (tel: +44 207 494 1716, www.oki-ni.com) for super-rare Adidas styles such as the Grand Slam and Adistar Runner, and a host of others. Size, (nationwide, www.size-online.co.uk). Global Sports US, 182 Shepherd's Bush Market, Uxbridge Road, London W12 (tel: +44 208 743 5086; www.globalsportsus.com) very obscure out of the way place which stocks Bape and one-off trainers. Swarovski-encrusted trainers anyone?

PAUL SMITH

'Do you think we could go interview Paul Smith for the book?' asked Peter. Not the easiest question to answer on a Monday morning. 'Aaaaaaaaaam? Don't know.' I replied. 'I'd love to; do you think he'd be up for it?' And off I went to make the call. I can't pretend I wasn't nervous. The first bit of good luck was speaking to Zoe, his PR lady. She wasn't all pushy and unctuous like some PR peeps; she was cool, and she also had a lovely laugh. It was thanks to Zoe that I got a meeting with Paul Smith.

So there we were a month later standing in front of Paul Smith. He is a big smile of a fellow. Within two minutes of meeting him, we're talking bikes. 'Yeah me boiks nice iddinit? Beautiful. You know we did a project with Mercier (www.cyclesmercier.com), they're based in Derby. Sixty years old and there's only nine of them working there and we did this lovely project together and they… you know, measured me for it and it was a really nice experience. I aspired to be a professional racing cyclist as a teenager but then I crashed and ended up doing this thing called fashion. But last year they just rang me up and said, "You know it's our 60th anniversary? Is there any chance we could do something together?" So I said, "Yeah I'd love to".' Two minutes later and he'd hopped up on his boik and was cycling around the office. 'Bikes rule my world,' he beamed. 'Yes they're the hot, hot thing right now.' He was bang on; we'd been all over Europe and even in America bikes are big, big news. But Paul Smith had been into them for ages, this was not the only emerging zeitgeist in which he was ahead of the curve.

One of the most engaging things about
Paul Smith, something that makes him
a popular figure in his office and (by
fashion standards) in the whole industry,
is that he seems genuinely interested in
other people. You might balk reading
that last sentence if you live in the normal world, but
in fashion, niceness can be scarce and even scarcer in a
designer who's very high up in the pecking order.

He's a restless host, constantly scanning around for fun
and mischief. For the next hour, we talk about all sorts;
from Nottingham to his first 12ft square shop, where his
artist wife and business partner Pauline designed their
pieces in the Seventies.

Since then, hunting and sourcing the most eclectic of finds has become
his trademark and a lucrative business. Japan is his biggest market now,
where he has 200 shops, accounting for more than 80 per cent
of the profit. He is by nature easy-going, 'The days of class
distinction are gone forever,' he says.

What makes you happy?
'Just being fit and healthy and alive, that's it.'

What's your luxury?

'Time. Silence. Time. Wild flowers. Fields.'

What is luxury, then?

'Well the preconceived idea of luxury is something that costs money. But for me the privilege of freedom is luxury for me, the privilege of silence, the privilege of being able to make your own decisions, it's very different to a lot of people's luxury.'

And why do your friends like you?

'Probably because I'm not full of shit.' (Yes he said shit, reader, and I love him for it). 'You know I tell it, say it, as it is, I'm a very normal bloke, down to earth, very loyal, very well mannered and I'm happy! I tend to make people laugh. My wife said she fell in love with me not because I was good looking, but because I made her laugh'

I dunno, I beg to differ with you there Paul, but anyway.

'Because I made her laugh, that's what she said! She fell in love with me because I made her laugh.'

I love that you said you're not full of shit, Paul. There's a real lack of genuine people in the fashion industry isn't there?

'Not just in the fashion industry. There's so much false celebrity in the world today. I mean, if you look at a lot of the people who started their careers, say, on television because they were interested in cooking, or architecture or books or something and then suddenly the programme is not about that anymore, it's about them.'

'Yeah,' I said, 'like so and so's cooking a bun, but the bun could be shite.'

'Nowadays there's so much interest in self-promotion, and falseness, and the whole thing about celebrity. And of course with digital cameras as well, even everyday people immediately want to look at the picture you've just taken of them to see how they look.'

We've been to Paris for all of the shows, we're not really interested in that blingy, blingy stuff and all of that palaver.

'I'm so lucky because I've been with the same lady since I was 21 and we're just very, very happy with each other; we're happy with our lot, we've never been motivated by money, we've just been motivated by the joy of life. The joy of touch, the joy of conversation, the joy of emotion. Obviously it's very nice to be successful as well, 'cos that's also a joy, but I think that because we've got a lot of stability at home it means that I'm not sort of searching for anything, I don't feel the need to go to all the private views and the kissy, kissy parties. It doesn't appeal to me.'

When you started out, you were with the Missus then were you?

'She was the one that really gave me the encouragement to open my own little business. Basically, from the age of eleven to eighteen the only thing I lived for was cycling and I aspired to be a professional racing cyclist, which I never would have achieved because I wasn't brave enough and I wasn't strong enough. But anyway, that's what I thought in my head and then I had a bad crash, ended up in hospital for three months. When I came out I arranged to meet a few guys that I'd met in hospital, one of them said why don't we go to the Bell Inn, which is a pub in Nottingham, where I come from, and by chance it was

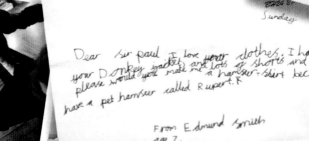

Sunday

Dear Sir Paul I love your clothes. I have got your Donkey jacket and lots of shorts and T shirts please would you make me a hamster shirt because I have a pet hamster called Rupert.

From Edmund Smith age 7.

14

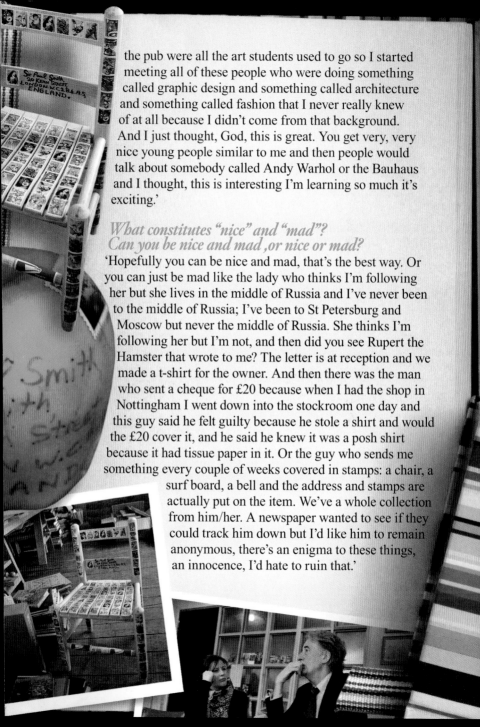

the pub were all the art students used to go so I started meeting all of these people who were doing something called graphic design and something called architecture and something called fashion that I never really knew of at all because I didn't come from that background. And I just thought, God, this is great. You get very, very nice young people similar to me and then people would talk about somebody called Andy Warhol or the Bauhaus and I thought, this is interesting I'm learning so much it's exciting.'

What constitutes "nice" and "mad"?
Can you be nice and mad, or nice or mad?

'Hopefully you can be nice and mad, that's the best way. Or you can just be mad like the lady who thinks I'm following her but she lives in the middle of Russia and I've never been to the middle of Russia; I've been to St Petersburg and Moscow but never the middle of Russia. She thinks I'm following her but I'm not, and then did you see Rupert the Hamster that wrote to me? The letter is at reception and we made a t-shirt for the owner. And then there was the man who sent a cheque for £20 because when I had the shop in Nottingham I went down into the stockroom one day and this guy said he felt guilty because he stole a shirt and would the £20 cover it, and he said he knew it was a posh shirt because it had tissue paper in it. Or the guy who sends me something every couple of weeks covered in stamps: a chair, a surf board, a bell and the address and stamps are actually put on the item. We've a whole collection from him/her. A newspaper wanted to see if they could track him down but I'd like him to remain anonymous, there's an enigma to these things, an innocence, I'd hate to ruin that.'

So the thing I wanted to ask you about was the experience of going into a shop and buying something on the internet. What's the difference?

'Well the difference is huge. The first thing about buying on the internet is that it's massively convenient and massively impersonal. One of the things that I work really hard on is my shop, particularly the one in Covent Garden. It came with old mahogany fittings. You can smell the beeswax polish that we clean the shop with every morning; it's the first thing that greets you when you walk through the door. The second thing you'll be greeted with is a smile. It's so important to make people feel welcome. If a lady comes in with a man and a baby, just don't be nice to the one that's shopping, treat them all equally. Just think about things.'

Do you think email is going to change the way we interact?

'Email is a big problem because the British Library are very concerned as to how they are going to be able to record people like they used to do. Previously with old letters, there would be a box of letters and they'd be able to say that was the box from this famous writer or this famous poet, but now so much disappears all the time.

The interesting thing about Pauline, my wife, and I is that we don't use email at all and we don't have a mobile phone. We don't have an answer machine. We don't have a computer at home. Pauline only ever writes letters, ever. And we've got "nice" and "mad" letter boxes here 'cos we get lots.'

You remind me of my neighbours at home in Ireland. Good stories, fun.
'People forget that's what life's about, it's not about greed and wealth, it's about conversation and we're on the earth for such a very short time and it's absolutely not about that. It's about touch, it's about meeting new people and sharing.'

Speaking of which… This had been so great, surely I couldn't cope with anymore excitement. 'Would you get the key for the magic room, Zoe?'

Did he say magic room?

I felt I'd just about got the hang of him by the time we had to leave. Well, I'd gotten the hang of his niceness; the hang of hanging on his every word. Now he was treating us to the magic room and my head was about to explode with happiness. He whipped out of the office, with us all in quick pursuit, his energies directed towards getting us to the magic room and showing us his stash of goodies. His collection lay inside a warren of doorways and passages in the basement, tucked deep within the building. He left us there to rifle through it before he moved onto the next thing, the next chair, the next book, the next market, leaving me little time to ask him any more. He told all four of us that his time with us had been, how'd he put it? 'Smashing'. I really ought to go back and meet him again, maybe even go outdoors with him. What do you think? This time we could take our bikes.

Paul Smith, Westbourne House, 122 Kensington Park Road, W11 (tel: +44 207 727 3553, www.paulsmith.co.uk).

SHOPPING

Can a girl be any happier than when she's shopping? I think not. Six weeks ago, I twisted my ankle shopping but I carried on (oh the courage), even after it was killing me with pain. OK, it wasn't as dramatic as a mahussive head wound spilling with blood, (yeah blood and a big white bandage like in the movies when they've got toothache, that sort of thing). Still, to shop? To buy? To twist your ankle and still keep going? What pushed me through the pain? The 'want' that's what. The 'want' and history repeating itself. On my very first shopping trip to Dublin I tumbled down the entire length of an escalator in Roches Stores. I quickly forgot about the bloody palms and knees, though, as I was enthralled by the smells, bright lights and the promise of new shooooooooos.

Understanding 'the want' or shopping, means understanding human beings (or human beans) as my godson calls them, which I suppose isn't far from what I'm talking about, because looking for value when shopping can be equated to shopping for a can of beans, can't it? That being the case, I shop for beans A LOT! I've always nursed a curiosity about what makes us buy stuff; do I like retro sweets because my Granny had a shop that sold loads of them when I was little? And fashion. My training started early for shoes and bags... Mum loves those.

Lying awake one morning and wondering, I started to tick off in my head all the things I'd bought that lay silently in the room around me. Then 'the want' crept in and I did a mental check of the things that got away: the perfect black eyeshadow, the perfumes that said different things to me, L'artisan Parfumeur Dzonka (I'm sultry), Tiare de Chantecaille eau de parfum (I'll make you feel light as air). Lying there, all these wished-for items seemed to say 'Well you could have had me but you chose not to'. Since meeting Vivienne Westwood, and more recently Paul Smith, I had become more of a hunter than a gatherer. And the shopping trip where I twisted my ankle? Well I sat down that evening and had a good long chat with myself. It went along the lines of...

Most of the time, you don't want to buy anything, it's the experience you're after. Right? The browsing, the spotting, the picking up, the touching, the smelling, the feeling of leather fragrance, fabric... just stuff. London, Dublin, Berlin, New York, I poke around always looking for the most interesting little places that offer the best experience. There is only one problem with this..., although finding good shops means the experiences are magnificent, they also give me a mahussive case of 'the want'. Oh, 'the want', I tried to pin down when this want first started, recently holding a pair of shoes in London I was whisked up into the air like Dorothy in the *Wizard of Oz* and transported back to my very first 'big shopping day'. I still get that little frisson of excitement thinking about it.

Growing up (though not as far as I would have liked to) my parents took us shopping, and made it into a sort of pilgrimage. But anyway, back in the day, to use an urbanism I'm currently fond of, we'd sit in the car in silence, engine ticking over, looking out at a statue of the Virgin Mary in the spotlight, like the bat light in the sky in Batman, Mary in the beam of the car's headlight, our breath steaming up the windows waiting for Mum and Dad to finish their quiet little travel prayer. Bring us safely there and back was the gist of it and... we waited. And waited. And then a quick U-turn and Dad would swing the car around and we'd head North East for the 8th of December, Ireland's big Christmas shopping day. Like country mice visiting town mice my younger brother, sister and I, in our pyjamas, would stuff pillows and blankets around us in the back of the car and snuggle down at 4am for the four hour driveathon. The planning was always flawless. I'm sure this is what has led me to need my comfy blanket and my special pillow on any long trips today.

So you can understand, surrounded by this type of planning and glamour as a child, I was always going to adore shopping experiences. I find a sort of freedom in being able to enjoy all things killer: killer 10 pound vintage handbags, killer stationery, killer Italian Vogue, killer books, books and more books, and killer flats (of course) nothing else for a sprained ankle like a new pair of flats (any excuse eh?). See, I like killer stuff and if it's a particularly good killer then I always say to myself, 'Go on G, treat yourself,' in a tough old world we need little treats, don't we? Here are the Goddesses and the things that they find killer, which one are you?

145

LUXURIOUS GODDESS

She's immaculate, even when working that just-fell-out-of-rock-star boyfriend's-bed look. The Luxurious Goddess (LG) is never seen without the latest 'It' accessory. She ticks all the fashion boxes and sets trends that the high street set their watches to (she did soft goth, like, three years ago), she likes to be first with everything before it goes mainstream and loves limited editions.

Heroines: Coco Chanel, Audrey Hepburn, Sofia Coppola, Kate Moss

One off pieces

Made from vintage silk-brocade Japanese obi belts and rare kimonos, each piece from Sai So (www.sai-so.com) is a one-off. From throws to a make-up bag £180, that is so gorgeous it could be easily used as a clutch bag.

Throw

The cotton wool throw by Duth designers Scholten & Baijings, Sandvikweg 2b, 1013 BA Amsterdam (tel: +3120 420 8940, www.scholtenbaijings.com) and also available at Vitra, 30 Clerkenwell Road, London EC1M (tel: +44 207 608 6200, www.vitra.com) from £220 to drape over your sofa or chair. Oh "the want".

The candle

Le Labo Santal 26 candle at Liberty of London, (tel: +44 207 573 9469, www.liberty.co.uk) or see www.lelabofragrances.com

Shoes

From Dries Van Noten to Christian Louboutin the Luxurious Goddess fills her room with the lot of them.

Limited edition scent

As cute as a Christmas bauble, L'Artisan Parfumeur's limited edition Mure et Musc perfume, £165, comes in a delicious blackberry bottle at L'Artisan Parfumeur, 17 Cale Street, London SW3 (020 7352 4196).

A limited edition find

Online retailer 20ltd (www.20ltd.com) sells no more than 20 items at a time, each of which are highly exclusive and only available in small numbers. Goods currently on offer range from GBP 2,900 white buffalo horn sunglasses (edition of 10), to a £9,000 hammock covered in cashmere and black fox fur. All items are exclusive to 20ltd, and not sold anywhere else.

Decanted scent

An antique French glass perfume bottle from the Jasmine di Milo Boutique at Harrods, £89.99 filled by Roja Dove Haute Parfumerie, Fifth Floor Urban Retreat, Harrods, London SW1 (tel: +44 207 893 8333, www.rojadove.com or for mail order tel: +44 207 893 8797) with Caron Tabac Blonde perfume £120.

Bobbi Brown

It's a great gift and even a good one to buy for yourself, a luxurious collection of Bobbi's most essential, Professional Brushes, £180 (www.bobbibrown.co.uk).

The gal who has everything

Crabtree & Evelyn's metal toothpaste tube rolling key (tel: +44 (0) 20 7361 0499; www.crabtree-evelyn.co.uk) might only cost £1.50 but pop it on the end of any tube and roll it down until the tube runs out. Brilliant!

URBAN
GODDESS

Creative, clever and very opinionated, she is
a blend of cultural sponge and streetwise gal.
Literature, art, schlebs – she has something
to say about all of them. Her style is
unconventional and earns her respect because
of her originality and authenticity. She ain't
afraid to be honest. Fashion-wise she dresses
unapologetically, flouts rules and snubs the big
designer names except for up and comers and
of course, Vivienne Westwood.

Heroines: Vivienne Westwood, Gwen Stefani,
Bat For Lashes, Lauren Laverne

The Drawers

There's no queue for these beautifully sculptural
chest of drawers from Established & Sons (tel:+44
207 608 0990, www.establishedandsons.com) there's
a waiting list (same thing really isn't it?). At £1,763
they certainly are a hot little item to own. They
slide both ways can stand anywhere in the
house. They're a real Urban Goddess item. Did
I mention she loves her furniture?

Proust

French writer Marcel Proust's
questionnaire has been used for years by
Vanity Fair to help showcase interviewees
personalities. Now his questions have been
published in this large leather -bound book
£152 by Assouline (www.assouline.com).

Book Wallpaper

The Urban Goddess loves books even on
her wallpaper by Tracey Kendall
(www.traceykendall.com).

Parteeeeee shoes

Georgina Goodman, 44 Old Bond Street, London, W1S (tel: +44 20 7493 7673, www. georginagoodman.com) sexy but in a very urban way.

After Parteeeeeee toes

A pair of foldable flats £25 by Viva La Diva (tel: +44 (0)870 601 0870, www.vivaladiva.com). They fold over and come in a little pouch so you can throw them in your bag and pop them on when your toes are all danced out.

Committee

And how about the hot British design duo Committee, Gallop Workshop, 198 Deptford High Street, London SE8 (tel:+44 20 8694 8601, www.gallop.co.uk). Their Turquoise Monkey Curiosity for Lladro's Recyclos collection (www. lladro.com) is new but was inspired by an old curiosity they found. It's just one example of stuff they find in curiosity shops and make into one-off pieces. Urban Goddesses love Committee.

Hella Jongeruis

This handmade ceramic piece by Hella Jongerius's is divine. Vessel, 114 Kensington Park Road, London W1 (tel: +44 207 727 8001, www. vesselgallery.com)

Titbit

Wrap her gifts in Emily Burningham wrapping paper £1.50 per sheet (www. emilyburningham.com).

Mind the Gap

The Patrick gold leather Oyster card holder £20 by Mimi, 40 Cheshire Street, London E2 (tel: +44 207 729 6699, www.mimimika.com).

Every book in the world (almost)

Two words, Abe Books (www.abebooks.com), a website which brings together over 15,000 specialist book sellers. I've found some of my fave books here and I use it all the time to find bookey pressies.

Under the radar labels

Brittique (www.brittique.com) is a good place to shop online if you're an Urban Goddess. You'll find dresses by San Francisco designer Kirribilla here (tel: +44 777 1 981 672, www.kirribilla.com) or exquisitely tailored pieces from Louise Amstrup (www.louise-amstrup.com). She trained under Alexander McQueen, Jonathan Saunders and Sofia Kokosalaki and her pieces are exquisite.

A ring

As it has one of the best selections of contemporary jewelry online, you can go wrong with a ring from www.kabiri.co.uk.

HOME GODDESS

She's a home bird, who prides herself on a beautifully kept nest box. She'll churn out scones in the morning and cupcakes for tea, even when there are a million other things to do. The Home Goddess is always on the lookout for little things to make her nest more special, is never seen without a little notebook to keep notes on different food she's found and she just adores little teacups and flowers. Her treat is beautiful baths, beautiful flowers and beautiful candles. Her nest is all fresh linen, sparkling surfaces and hotel deluxe.

Heroines: Nigella Lawson, the Number One Home Goddess of them all.

An Aiveen Daly chair

Aiveen Daly, 2 Letchford Gardens, Kensal Green, London NW10 (tel: +44 208 962 0044, www.aiveendaly.com) fashions vintage upholstered silk chair that are the ultimate indulgence. She hand-works silk into pleats, ruches, corsetry & frills and each chair takes 6-8 weeks to create. This yellow silk love knot chair is £715 plus fabric.

Flowers

Plant a victorian baby bath, (£140 at Portobello) with Hyacinths, £30 at Jo Boggon, 106 Askew Rd, London W12 9BL (tel +44 207 493399,www.joboggon.co.uk) or Marks & Spencer around November as a gift for her.

Titbit

Tie her gifts up with pretty ribbon £10.50 from VV Rouleaux, 102 Marylebone Lane, London W1U (tel: +44 207 224 5179, www.vvrouleaux. com). She even knows the word to describe it – passementerie (the art of elaborate trimmings). Wooooooo!

Kitchen goodies

Pink and cream milk pot, £15.00 (also comes in black) from Labour And Wait, 18 Cheshire Street, EC2 6EH (tel: +44 20 7729 6253, www. labourandwait.co.uk) and see www.dotcomgiftshop.com for teapots, cups, cake plates, cake stands.

Monogrammed linen

Volga Linen, 17 Langton Street, Chelsea, London SW10 (tel:+44 207 352 5616, www. volgalinen.co.uk) a great wedding list idea too.

ROSE

FILIPPO BERIO OLIVE OIL

Titbit

Pop the rind of a piece of Parmesan cheese into a bottle of Olive Oil to add Umami to it. Gift it to someone with a voucher for a cookery course.

151

SEX GODDESS

A dirty, pretty little thing, she's faultless from her hair to her toenails.
Even when casual she looks groomed. Secretly she's an expert with beauty
products and lingerie. She'll often show a little quirky detail (a low cut t-shirt
or a bra strap poking from beneath her dress). She adores her stilettos and has
a wardrobe full of Choos, Louboutins and Manolos. She favours subtle allure
over overt sexuality and she's an expert at layering sensual scent.

Heroines: Dita von Teese, Jennifer Lopez, Jessica Alba.

Bath Oil

Dark Amber & Ginger Lily
Bath Oil, £52 by Jo Malone
(tel: +44 207 720 0202,
www.jomalone.co.uk) with
notes of cardamom, orchid
and kyara wood.

Body Cream

No Louboutin loving Sex Goddess would dare to
neglect her pins, a gorgeous jar of Maitresse Silk
Stockings, £38, by Agent Provocateur (tel: +44 845
688 3343, www.agentprovocateur.com) is an ideal
gift. After exfoliating it's applied and gives legs a
tinted silky sexy finish – no tights required.

Lingerie

www.figleaves.com think of a name and they'll have it, even little labels like Princess
Tam Tam. At www.sexypantiesandnaughtyknickers.com there's an array of flirty
underwear with feminine ruffles, chiffon nighties come in the most divine packaging
(silver mirrored boxes and tissue paper sexy enough for you?). A pink baby-doll
nightie by Myla (tel: +44 (0)870 7455 003, www.myla.com) is a lovely treat. And
then there's Essenziale, 13 Grafton Street, London W1S (tel: +44 207 629 6454,
www.essenziale.uk.com) which carries La Perla black label, and a small elite range
from others including pieces from Guia la Bruna lingerie range. Breathtaking! Dolce
v (www.dolcev.com) a superb lingerie website stocks really great labels and Tocca
Laundry Wash £12 for you to hand wash them.

Bespoke Lingerie

A Lee Klabin bespoke hand-stitched corset at Blue Poppy Couture, 171 Westbourne
Grove, London, W11 (tel: +44 207 792 9667, www.bluepoppycouture.com) is the
ultimate luxury gift. Think dark smooth feathers, boned torsos and hand-stitched
velvets and silks. They cost from £500 to £3,000-plus and take three weeks to
make with fittings. Rigby & Peller, 22a Conduit Street, London W1 (tel:+44 207
491 2200, www.rigbyandpeller.com); for made-to-measure enquiries contact
Rigby & Peller, 2 Hans Road, London SW3 (tel:+44 207 589 9293). Madame V
(tel: +44 (0)870 740 5333www.madamev.co.uk) offers seductive lingerie with
private customer fittings and evenings in their studio. Harrods also stocks
the Madame V collection in limited editions (kimonos can be monogrammed).

Bespoke Bikini

Bespoke swimsuits/bikinis at Biondi, 55b, Old Church St, London SW3 (tel: +44 207 349 1111, www.biondicouture.com)

Shoooooos

Iris, 124 Draycott Avenue, London (tel. +44 20 75 84 12 52) and 61 Ledbury Road – London (tel: +44 207 229 1870, www.iris-shoes.it) Owned by the Joseph fashion group they sell Marc Jacobs, Chloé, Viktor & Rolf, Gaultier and Paul Smith.

The Candle

John Galliano for Diptyque candle £38 at Dyptique, www. diptyqueparis.com and in most department stores.

Vintage gifts

A vintage mirror and brush sets or a brooch, all from Linda Bee (tel: +44 207 629, 5921) at Gray's Antique Market, 58 Davies Street, London W1.

Mirror Mirror

Huw Griffith's bespoke mirrors are customized reclaimed antiques that he finds in France. Each mirror is unique, they range in price from £1000 to £2500 at www. designersguild.com or www.huwgriffith.com

EARTH GODDESS

Well travelled, well educated eco chick. Fiercely against animal testing, even if it means sacrificing her favourite face cream. She loves her bike but wears Stella McCartney heels to ride it. Being an Earth Goddess doesn't mean a drop in style, quite the opposite, her jeans label is now the hottest name in fashion because eco is now huge news. Style wise she loves Katherine Hamnett, Ciel and Edun for single-handedly inventing stylish eco-fashion. She loves Fresh and Wild shopping for food.

Heroines: Ali Hewson, Stella McCartney, Helena Christensen

It's in the bag

The Jackson sisters work with the Masai in Kenya and various other groups to bring beautifully-made products to Britain. This woven bag is from Vietnam £89 at The Jacksons, 5 All Saint's Road, London W11 (tel:+44 207 792 8336, www.thejacksons.co.uk).

Divine

Shepherd England's handmade lamb's-wool scarf in geometric prints by Gemma Shepherd can be worn as a pussy bow or coiled, £120 at Shepherd England (tel:+44 (0)1233 733 096, www.shepherdengland.com).

I take it all back

Care by Stella McCartney and Kiehl's will recycle your empties. M.A.C. gives a free lipstick for every six returned.

Pure luxury

Jatamansi Organic Body Care range by L'Artisan Parfumeur, L'Artisan Parfumeur, 17 Cale Street, London SW3 (tel: +44 207 352 4196, www.artisanparfumeur.com) contains Himalayan plant extracts and pink grapefruit, this Jatamansi Bath Lotion £45 is totally free of chemicals as is the non-toxic Jatamansi Scented Candle, £34.

Green skincare ranges

Aromatherapy Associates (mail order tel: +44 20 8569 7030, www.aromatherapyassociates.com) – Aromatherapy Associates Deep Relax Oil, £30. Bamford, 169 Draycott Avenue, London sw3 (tel:+44 207 589 8729, www.bamford.co.uk) - Bamford Botanic Geranium Bath Oil, £16. Burt's Bees, (www.myburtsbees.co.uk)-Burt Bees Lip Balm £3.49. DHC (www.dhccare.com DHC Deep Cleansing Oil £16 removes make-up naturally. Dr Hauschka (www.drhauschka.co.uk) - Dr Hauschka, Rose Day Cream £12. Erbaviva (www.erbaviva.com) – Erbaviva Body Lotion. Jo Wood Organic (www.jowoodorganics.com and at Harvey Nichols) - Jo Wood Usiku Organic Body Dew, £45. ID BareMinerals (www.bareminerals.com also at www.hqhair.com) - Bare Minerals Bare Essentuals Mineral Veil £21. Brilliant powder make-up. Jane Iredale (www.janeiredale.com) Longest Lash Mascara in Jet Black £26. Jurlique (www.jurlique.com) at Fenwick, 68 Bond St, London, London W1A (tel: +44 207 629 9161) and Fresh and Wild stores - Chamomile Hydrating Essence, £26 and Jurlique Citrus Silk Finishing Powder £24. Kiehl's, 29 Monmouth Street, WC2 (tel: +44 207 240 2411, www.kiehls.com) - Kiehls Crème de Corps Nurturing Body Washing Cream, £16.50. Korres (www.korres.com) - Korres Lightweight Tinted Moisturiser SPF 30, £18. Lavera (www.lavera.com) Lavera Basis Sensitiv Protection Body Lotion, £7.50 and their lip-glosses are chemical free. Liz Earle (mail order tel: +44 1983 813 913,www.lizearle.com) - Liz Earle Naturally Active Skincare Daily Eye Repair, £12.25. Louise Galvin at Daniel Galvin hair salon, 58-60 George Street, w1 (tel: +44 207 486 9661, www.danielgalvin.co.uk) - Louise Galvin shampoo and conditioner Sacred Locks haircare collection starts at £22. Neom (www.neomorganics.com) at Selfridges and Brown Thomas, Dublin. Neom Luxury Unwind Skin Treatment Organic Bath and Body Oil, £32. Dr Andrew Weil for Origins (www.origins.co.uk) - The Way of the Bath Matcha Tea Body Scrub, £35. Ren (www.renskincare.com or at Space NK) - Ren Otto Bath Oil, £26. Spiezia (tel: +44 (0)870 850 8851, www.spieziaorganics.com) – Organic Body Oil £12. The Organic Pharmacy, 36 Neal Street, London, WC1 (tel: +44 207 836 3923 mail order tel: +44 207 228 2852) as well as skincare Organic Glam is their range of mineral make-up (lipsticks, eye shadows, blushes foundations that are 100% natural) - The Organic Glam Lipstick £16.95 is very good as is the Sheer Tint in Bronze Glow £29.95. The 100% natural Self Tan £29.95 is fantastic. This Works, 18 Cale Street, London SW3 (tel: +44 207 584 1887, www.thisworks,com mail order +44 (0)845 230 0499). In the Zone Bath and Shower Oil, £30. Stella McCartney Care (www.stellamccartneycare.com) - Stella McCartney Care 5 Benefits Moisturising Cream, £46.

Laptop case

This Laptop case £59.99 (they also do iPod cases) is made from re-energised Columbian lorry tyres from Tread (tel: +44 207 471 1706)

OFFICE GODDESS

She runs ten laps around Hyde Park, has an express facial at Jo Malone and finds time to pick up an Annick Goutal candle and a new white shirt from MaxMara. Sound like your boss? If you aspire to get everything done and you're highly organized then there the touch of the Office Goddess about you. She loves, loves, loves her work and everything to do with it. She's smart, clever and a snappy dresser. Her blackberry is her best friend.

Heroines: Madonna and Oprah

Office Security

All Day All Year by Sisley, (tel: +44 207 491 2722, www.sisleya.com) creates a genuine protective UV shield around the skin and protects it for up to eight hours while sitting inside a window at an office desk. It's an Office Goddess must-have.

For her car

A Welsh travel blanket £65 from Labour and Wait 18 Cheshire Street, London EC2 6EH (tel: +44 207 729 6253, www.labourandwait.co.uk)

Soap Stars

Claus Porto Fantasia Soaps £60 at Liberty (tel: +44 207 734 1234, www.liberty.co.uk) A beautiful, beautiful gift for a friend at the office, the packaging is gorgeous and each soap has a wonderfully different scent.

Kiss and make-up

Why not treat two of your Goddess best friends from your office to their make-up before a night out together? At Becca, 91a Pelham Street, London SW7 (tel: +44 207 225 2501, www.beccacosmetics.com) you can book the store after hours for yourself (plus a minimum of two people, from £60 per person) for private party preparation.

Chocolate

Office Goddesses-even dieting ones – love chocolate as a present, but don't give anything but the best like these exotic chocs from www.artisanduchocolat.com whose couture range includes flavours like tobacco, cardamom and rose, all intricately decorated and beautifully wrapped in the most luxurious box. Or chocolate champagne truffles from Charbonnel et Walker, One The Royal Arcade, 28 Old Bond Street, London, W1S 4BT (tel:+44 20 7491 0939, www.charbonnel.co.uk) (lovely packaging too).

Case Closed

The perfect something for the Office Goddess who has everything...a Kydd snakeskin embossed leather white laptop case, £485 or a Blackberry purses (they start at £165.00) from Victoria May London (tel: +44 207 253 2048, www.violetmaylondon.com). These leather cases are very luxurious and there's a bespoke design service which allows you the opportunity to have a case beautifully crafted and individually styled to suit your boss, a client or better still, you. The current range includes laptop cases & bags, laptop sleeves, document wallets, business card holders and Blackberry wallets. One of these is an excellent, excellent gift idea.

Staple buy it

Sterling Silver Crocodile stapler by Richard Jarvis, £475, Quebeck House, 60 Pall Mall, London SW1 (tel: +44 207 925 2211, www. richardjarvisofpallmall.com) also comes as a Hippo and a Lion is a cute little gift to brighten up your deck.

SECRET SHOPS

The cat's whiskers

Lik Neon, 106 Sclater Street, E1 (tel: +44 (0)7876 323 265, www.likneon.com).
Owner Janice Taylor is a true maverick and always greets me with a huge smile. Her
collection of jewellery and labels from new designers is fresh, original and inspiring.
Everything has a handwritten price sticker and there's a real sense of fun about the
place. Her cats lie in the window and in baskets dotted around the store. This shop
makes me extra happy and only Beyond The Valley in Soho beats it as my favourite
shopping experience.

A good start

Start, 59 Rivington Street (Menswear),
(Womenswear and Accessories), 42-44
Rivington Street London EC2A (tel: +44
207 729 3334, www.start-london.com). Yes,
this is a very good place to start – like a
mini Browns it does great denim
labels (Tsubi, Nudie, J Brand, Cheap
Monday, Acne) and they stock
Laura Bohnic and Karen Walks.
Smiles all round too
from the peeps behind
the tills, so Snailey
simply adores it!

Art books

Galignani, 224 rue de Rivoli,
+44 33 1 42 60 76 07, because
you can find loads of art books
there.

Now this is lovely

Dover Street Market, 17-18 Dover
Street, W1S (tel: +44 207 518
0680 www.doverstreetmarket.
com) Comme des Garcons,
Junya Watanabe, Alber Elbaz
for Lanvin, John Galliano,
Givenchy, Judy Blame,
Veronique Branquinho,
Undercover, Arts and
Science, Universal Utility,
and Raf Simons…what a
line up. I get lost in this
Emporium for hours.

The greatest little shop in the Universe (official)

Beyond The Valley, 2 Newburgh Street, London SE1 (tel: +44 207 437 7338, www.beyondthevalley.com) a hip, hip store (correction the hippest in London) run by the most extraordinary bunch of friendly people on the planet. Snailey loves, loves, loves this shop. It is a pandora's box of up and coming designers. Oh and before I faint with the excitement let me tell you that the things you find in here are one-off and very special. They were my favourite store in my last book and they're still going strong.

Spread the love

Labour of Love, 193 Upper Street, N1 (tel: +44 207 354 9333, www.labour-of-love.co.uk). Worth visiting Islington for this one. Staff are sweet (wait up it's Snaily time) and the stock is brilliant. Vintage is sourced by the owner Francesca and (deep breath) they stock Beatrice Ong shoooooooooooes, Louise Amstrup draped dresses and Baum and Pferdgarten here (amazing dresses).

Authentic vintage

The Girl Can't Help It, G100 G90, G80, at Alfies Antique Market, 13-25 Church Street, NW8 (tel: +44 207 724 8984). Lovin Alfies antique market and the oldiness of it all and its quality. All the garments are well sourced and they're dripping with authenticity. Think pin curls and 40s and 50s cocktail dresses to die for and you're in the right ballpark.

Florentine dream

Santa Maria Novella, 117 Walton Street, SW3 (tel: +44 207 460 6600 www.smnovella.it) A Florentine perfumerie that stocks the most beautiful soap and beauty products.

Buy and sell

Bang, Bang, 21 Goodge Street WT (tel: +44 (0) 207 631 4191). A dress agency, designer consignment store and vintage shop all together. You can sell off old designer gear here for a nice bit of cash. There's tons of vintage, (two seasons old) Marc Jacobs, Prada, and some smaller labels. Have a poke about in the basement which is stuffed full of incredibly cheap finds.

Faux sure

Black Out 11 London, 51 Endell Street, London WC2 (tel: +44 207 240 5006) This little shop in Endell Street, has the best faux fur coats and Fifties party dresses. It's a treasure chest.

SECRET VALUE

A cashmere sweater

Burberry Factory Shop, 29-53 Chatham Place, London E9 (tel +44 208 328 4287). Right, you either love Burberry or you hate it. Personally, I love it. Have you seen how cool the Burberry Prorsum catwalk shows are? Check out www.style.com. There ain't nothing wrong with 50% off a flawless high quality British classic cashmere jumper, I can tell you, logo smogo, the clothes are quality. (Opening times: Monday-Saturday 10am-6pm; Sunday 11am-5pm).

Jean/streetwear

Carhartt Warehouse Outlet, 18 Ellingfort Road, London E8 (tel: +44 208 986 8875). One of my best friends, Charlie told me about this one. Half price street wear and jeans (sometimes they're discounted more). Nothing wrong with that right? A few trips here and your casual wardrobe is sorted. (Take the Hackney Central rail or Bethnal Green tube. Opening times: Monday-Saturday 11am-6pm; Sunday 12pm-5pm).

Vintage wallpaper

EW Moore and Sons, 39-43, Plashnet Grove, Upton Park, London E6 (tel: + 44 208 471 9392, www.ewmoore.com). Used a lot by industry insides this place carries small one-off runs of vintage wallpapers. Small run means limited availability so it's unlikely that anyone else will have the same. Visit in person or they deliver. (Upton Park tube. Opening times: Monday-Saturday 9am-5pm).

A £10 tea dress

The East End Thrift Store, Unit 1a, Waterman's Building, Assembly Passage, London E1 (off Mile End Rd), (tel: +44 207 423 9700, www.theeastendthriftstore.co.uk). For years you've bemoaned the fact that you can't find a bargain in London, well hang up your moaney shoes, because this place is cheap (will less than a tenner do you?). Students get 10 per cent discount, look out for their fun parteeeeeeeeees. (Whitechapel tube. Opening times: Monday-Sunday 11am-6pm).

Discontinued Perfume

East End Cosmetics 131 Middlesex Street,London E1 (tel: +44 20 7626 4015, www.eastendcosmetics.com). I really loved Yves Saint Laurent's Nu Eau de Parfum, which was created by the nose, Jacques Cavallier, for Tom Ford when he was still at Yves Saint Laurent in 2001. Yves Saint Laurent no longer makes Nu, but guess what? I found an intact bottle, stashed away safely here. They have tons of discontinued products like this and loads of beauty bargains. (Liverpool Street tube/rail. Opening times: Monday-Friday 10am-5.30pm; Sunday 9.30am-4pm).

Paints and brushes

Atlantis, 7-9 Plumbers Row, London E1 (tel: +44 207 377 8855, www.atlantisart.co.uk). Hard to find, but worth poking around for. Sells paints, cans, stretched canvases – a must visit if you're a graffiti artist, illustrator or fashion student (Aldgate East tube. Opening times: Monday-Saturday 9am-6pm, Sunday 10am-5pm).

Mani and pedi tools

USA Nails & Beauty Supply, 235 Mare Street, London E8 (tel: +44 208 985 6888) A gazillion varnishes and pedicure tools including electric heel buffers can be bought directly from this wholesale. (Take the Hackney Central rail. Open Monday-Sunday 11am-9pm).

161

Why should I go anywhere? I can get tea and sympathy at home. Sand and salt water is so overrated anyway. You can't bring a laptop to the beach – did you know that? Sand gets in the keys. At first they start to make a sort of crunching noise and after a bit they just cease up. A friend told me that. Honestly? I do beaches only if I'm banjaxed and need to flake out somewhere and anyway the beauty routine is a big ask when you're talking about exposing that much skin. I prefer more action, a bit more variety and anyway, I can roam the planet from my living room, so why go anywhere at all?

Just now I got interested in street view in Google Maps and spent ten minutes whizzing up and down rue du Mont Thabor in Paris. You move your mouse along and you can see every single shop front along that street in a 360 degree angle. I swung the camera around a bit outside the door of Editions de Parfumes, Frédéric Malle's shop on rue du Mont Thabor (you know, just to let them know I was passing). Not in any shape, form or description is this the same as being there though; there were no noises and there was no smells.

I closed my eyes and called on my memory. Carnal Flower, a heady tuberose, is what I caught as I whipped past Frédéric Malle's shop door three years ago and then the petrol of a Citroen as it flew past and nearly kilt me. Yeah, travel is a noisy business; a noisy, smelly business. I do a lot of it these days, and it's not all simple. Shuffling through airport scanners can get a bit tedious, browsing the duty free for a squirt of something and then, Jaysus, an eyeful of Tom Ford juice and a tearful departure. The wet goodbye they call that, mine fuelled by eyefuls of Estée Lauder schlebrity perfume. The routine is always the same in the leaving, setting out into the big bad world, international woman of mystery with Snaily playing sidekick. It's rarely smooth.

These are short trips, mostly a week here, a week there, four days in Berlin – just the right amount of time to get a feel for a place, to ask the people on the streets where's good for food and fashion and then to go and browse, queue a little, eat a bit and then browse some more. The weeks travelling for these pages were so spontaneous that I skipped around a lot and did at least six little twirly twirls in each city; yes it was one big twirl of time, like throwing a pebble in water, one good piece of luck kept rippling farther and farther. I got a good run at it this time and tracked down some crackin' secrets. What a great adventure I had. We all want to be able to use that word, don't we, when we talk about travel, yeah adventure and authenticity – they're nice travel words.

And the coming home bit, the bit where you relive the experience while your pals listen patiently to you recall it, that's all part of the travel experience too isn't it? The I-saw-King-Kong-on-top-of-the-Empire-State-building and I'm absolutely sure he was in disguise, cos he was wearing a wig and a moustache and everything. Can anyone else ever really appreciate fully the experience that you've just travelled through? Excellent question reader and one I intend to ponder here for one brief second. Stay with me. So I'm back from wherever and I'm telling you that the air was actually sweeter there. Do you believe that the air was actually sweeter? I swear I tasted it and it was. And the grass, you wouldn't believe how much greener the grass was. Waaaaaay greener on the other side? And the sky? Name a blue, go on, the sky was bluer. And the beach? Sand you say? Well, where we were was a bit more er, stoney.

Incidentally (this might be useful), the quality control manager of stones and gravel at a Dubrovnik seaside resort told me that sandy beaches are bad for laptops. Yeah, haven't you heard? Stoney beaches are the new black. Good tip that. You get my drift don't you? No mention of the grey skies, the torrential downpour, the humiliating water-skiing accident and the near-death food poisoning. One by one, we take the crunchy with the smooth on holiday. But the good times are great when they're great aren't they? And don't you just love the way that on holidays sometimes you…

Walk down a small street and peep though a window where fairy lights illuminate a table and a handwritten menu. You stop. Is there any better feeling? My heart takes a picture at times like this. So here are the people, places and things that it has captured so far (see if you can spot King Kong).

FLYING LESSONS

How does a plane fly? Heck if I know, I didn't talk to the pilots for this page, just loads of cabin crew and Sir Paul Smith – the most frequent flyer of them all. So buckle up ladies and gentlefolk, it's gonna be a smooth ride.

The perfect in-flight kit

Pack your own in-flight kit before embarking on a flight. It should contain wipes (steer clear of wipes they give away on aircraft – the lanolin in those can be an irritant.) Go for ones such as Dermalogica's skin purifying wipes or Take It Away Towelettes, £16, by Estée Lauder (tel: +44 87 0034 2566, www.esteelauder.com) are also good. A face mask like Aromatherapy Associates rose hydrating mask available mail order (tel:+44 20 8569 7030, www.aromatherapyas-sociates.com) or an eye mask like Guinot's eye mask (tel:+44 13 4487 3123, www.guinotuk.com) then a serum (see page 272) and Elizabeth Arden's eight-hour cream for lips, knees and elbows.

Or pop an Alpure Altisource Extreme Intensive Hydration ReSourcing Mask, £30 for 12 (tel: +44 80 0123 4000, www.alpure.ch or from Selfridges) into your kit too. Applied mid-flight its moisture-boosting formula leaves skin dewy and hydrated. Pack a few more in your luggage for sun-baked skin, chapped hands and ski burn..

Paul Smith's top three travel tips (boys will love these too)

'I take a little bottle of Aromatherapy Associates Support Breathe Essence (tel: +44 20 8569 7030, www.aromatherapyassociates.com) as an essential piece of kit. A few drops on a handkerchief inhaled deeply during a flight prevents me from picking up other people's colds and flus. Otrivin Decongestant Nasal Spray applied 30 minutes before take-off and landing helps if you suffer from blocked sinuses, painful ears or pressure headaches.

Flying always dehydrates me; I pack Aesop Rind Aromatique Body Balm, in the 50ml size. These three travel products are all small bottles ehich you can easily take on a flight. They're great because they make the flying bit a more enjoyable experience.'

JUNE 7/JUNE 8 2008

City Travel

Upon arrival in a hotel, I pop a tube of Origins No Puffery Eye Mask, £16.50 (tel: +44 87 0034 2888, www.origins.co.uk) in the freezer of the mini bar to chill. Yes! Sometimes hotels I stay in have no mini bar so I ask for a huge bucket of ice instead. Just before heading to bed I bury my No Puffery to chill for the morning; applied before breakfast, it instantly erases morning-after eyes and cools and tightens eye skin. It's jet-lagged supermodule's (supermodel's) dirty little secret (among other things of course).

Hydrate

Apply a super-hydrator like Dermalogica's skin hydrating booster and then a moisturizer such as Dermalogica's anhydrous barrier repair when flying. Any skin that's exposed to the air should get a shot of body lotion. Continue this routine for a day or so after landing. Drink buckets of water – prior to flying, during and for a day after your flight if schlepping around a city. .

Tanning Tips

Don't exfoliate for two weeks before going on your holidays. If you let your skin thicken it'll have a greater natural protection against UVA and UVB and you'll get a better tan. Clarins Sun Wrinkle Control Cream SPF15, £15.50 (tel: +44 80 0036 3558, uk.clarins.com). Sunscreen with high SPF is crucial; put it on in your hotel room each morning before you head to the beach and add Clarins Sun Wrinkle Control Eye Contour Care SPF30, £15.50, around the eyes, as normal sunscreens can often make your eyes run. The Lancaster Precious Sun range is also a good option, £55 (tel: +44 80 0376 0688, www.lancaster-beauty.com). In the evening cool your skin with Lancôme's excellent After Sun Cooling Hydrating Gel, £20.50, followed by Lancôme Soleil Reconfort After Sun Milk Tan Extender, £20.50. To boost your tan use Lancaster's fabulous Tan Maximizer, £21, apres sun.

Make-up

If you must wear make-up choose mineral-based make-up for flying. ID Bare Minerals (www.bareminerals.com) or Jane Iredale (www.janeiredale.com) are 100 per cent preservative free and are made using crushed minerals, which aren't absorbed into pores like other make-up.

Make-up Bag

Only one bag will do. The clear plastic travel bag from Joni Galvin, My Make-up (www.mymakeupdirect.com) is one of the most useful things I own for travelling, the perfect size for airport security checks.

165

duBLin

Usually when something unlikely such as a building, or a monument, or a bridge is said to "whisper" or "shimmer", or pirouette or whatever across Europe, China, whatever... it's a mahussive knees-up for the city that it's built in. Not so with the 'Dubs', hang around with them and after a few pints it's clear that the city isn't built on monuments but on 'the craic' – they're still laughing at the new spire on O' Connell Street. You don't have to strain or pretend to be having fun in Dublin, it's proper loud, booming, laughter and it's what makes the Irish tick (loudly). I have gradually come to believe that Dublin is built on the people's laughter, here's how you can join in the fun.

Introduce a few Dublin terms into your vocabulary

Even if you've landed from Mars, after two days in Dublin, howyaaaaaa (hi) and Jaysus (Jesus) will pour off your tongue as easily as Guinness and rashers will pour on to it. Bull, you say. I guarantee, you won't even notice it's happening until it's too late my friend. Dublin slang has some of the best words: like the drink link you had to visit to get cash to pay for a few scoops (drinks); the dickey work the lady made of your hang sangwich (ham sandwich); or the smirting (smoking and flirting) everywhere now outside pub doors. To really consider yourself a local though, you have to order your hungover lips around a Spar Sunday special– a breakfast roll with sausage, egg and rasher finished off with lashings of red sauce (there you go again...that's our special word for tomato ketchup). Oh yes, quite the linguists the Irish, Joyce would be soooo proud.

A true Dub knows...

• that Dublin inhabitants are known locally as Dubs or 'The Dubs'.
• that Dublin is Dubh Linn in Irish (Gaelic), which means Black Pool.
• that the spire in O' Connell Street is known locally as the stiletto in the ghetto.
• that the silent 'L' is always pronounced loudly in the word 'film'. Repeat, 'fi-lum'

Sleep Luxury

The Merrion Hotel, Upper Merrion Street, Dublin 2, (tel: 353 1 603 0600, www.merrionhotel.com). The deep plush couches, relaxed afternoon tea, beautiful art work and crisp white linen mark this place out as the business. Slap bang in the centre of the city, it also offers two really great restaurants; The Cellar Restaurant (very affordable and very good food) and Restaurant Patrick Guilbaud (expensive but divine). A room costs €250 per night for a Queen double.

Sleep Mid Range

The Dylan Hotel, Eastmoreland Place, Dublin 4 (tel: +353 1 660 3000, www.dylan.ie). This is the new kid on the block and has been getting great reviews from friends of mine who've visited. Hip, young and typically boutique, a room costs €199 per night here, for a luxury double.

Sleep Mid Range

Number 31, 31 Leeson Close, Dublin 2 (tel: +353 1 676 5011, www.number31.ie) is known for it's unique décor; a mix of modernism and Georgian splendour. Famous for its sunken lounge, its secret garden and its crackin breakfast, rooms start at €150 for a double.

Breakfast

Know that breakfast and brunch is better across the road from the Dylan hotel; once you're over the hype of eating breakfast in bed at the Dylan (lush): you'll come to appreciate The Espresso Bar Cafe, 1 St Mary's Road Ballsbridge, Dublin 4 (tel:+353 1 6600585). Brekkie ranges from poached egg on toast with crispy bacon and relish to porridge with toasted almonds and honey or French toast with bacon, winter berries and syrup. Weekend brunch is a must here. Open Sat 9am-9.15pm, Sun brunch 10am-5pm.

Best seafood

Cavistons, 58-59 Glasthule Rd, Sandycove, Co. Dublin (tel: +353 1 2809120, www.cavistons.com) tale the DART to Sandycover for an afternoon of fresh fish.

Best Burger

Jo'Burger, 137 Rathmines Road, Dublin 6 (tel: +353 1 4913731, www.joburger.ie). Jo Burger's organic burger as a main with the best coloured coleslaw I've ever had - no joshin, it was pink I tell ya! Pink!

Best lunchtime treat

Fallon & Byrne, 11-17 Exchequer St, Dublin 2 (tel: +353 1 4721010; www.fallonandbyrne.com). The best lunchtime soup and a sandwich. Check out the one euro corkage fee from the wine store on Monday nights, known as Happy Mondays and often sore headed Tuesdays for Peter.

Butlers Chocolate Cafe

24 Wicklow Street, Dublin 2 (tel: +353 1 6710591, www.butlerschocolates.com). The best hot chocolate and chai lattes.

Cake and a cuppa

The Cake Café, 62 Pleasants Place, Dublin 8 (tel: +353 1 4789394, www.thecakecafe.ie). The chocolate cake is really good here as is the tea. This place is cute with a capital C, the toilets even flush with rainwater.

That's not my name

L'Gueuleton, 1 Fade Street, Dublin 2 (tel: +353 1 6753708, www.lgueuleton.com) has no name over the door, and even if it had, I couldn't pronounce it. There's a queue here for dinner most nights and you know me and queues don't you? The French Onion Soup with Gruyere Croute to start is scrummilicious!

Have a slice of real Italian pizza

Run by Italians, The Steps of Rome, 1 Chatham Court, Dublin 2 (tel: +353 1 670 5630) offers authentic slices (rosemary and potato is the yummiest).

Dinner – Italian

If it's a special someone you're taking to dinner then go all out and treat yourselves at Town Bar and Grill, 21 Kildare Street, (tel: +353 1 6624724, www.townbarandgrill.com) a modern Italian which has become the city's hottest place. I love the potato rosti here and the monk fish. Dinner comes in at around €60 a head.

Dinner – French

Alternatively L'Ecrivain, 109a Lower Baggot Street, (tel: +353 1 661 1919, www.lecrivain.com) is French and totally exquisite and the wine list is absolutely divine. I can't rave enough about their Degustation (ten-course taster menu), at €120 per person – this doesn't include drink but you get to taste the best of what Dublin has to offer, food-wise. L'Ecrivain recently received a five-star review in The New York Times.

Secondhand books and food

Visit The Winding Stair, 40 Ormond Quay, Dublin 1 (tel: +353 1 8727320, www.winding-stair.com) To browse second-hand books and book a table at the upstairs restaurant, overlooking the Ha'penny Bridge. Food is good here and is included in the 2008 edition of the Michelin Guide for Ireland.

A beautiful mess

Grogans, 15 South William Street, Dublin 2, (tel: +353 1 6779320). Great for a pint and a chat. The place is a lovely mess of wonderful paintings and people.

Squeeeeeeze!

The Dawson Lounge, 25 Dawson Street, Dublin 2, (tel: +353 1 6710311; www.dawsonlounge.ie) is Dublin's smallest pub. Your challenge, should you choose to accept it is to see how many of your mates can squeeze in here.

Escape

The Long Hall, 51 South Great Georges Street, Dublin 2, (tel: +353 1 475 1590) isn't that long and isn't really a hall either. It's a cute little hideaway from the hassle of the crowds.

Oasis of chaos

The Bernard Shaw, 11-12 South Richmond St, Dublin 2 (tel: +353 85 7128342; www.bodytonicmusic.com). The Bernard Shaw is run by club promoters Bodytonic who set up shop in this 113-year-old boozer and have bands and DJs playing 6 days a week.

BEAUTY

Hair

Dylan Bradshaw, 5 Johnson's Place, Dublin 2 (tel: +353 1 671 9353, www. dylanbradshaw.com) Don't let the slick look of Dylan's salon fool you for a second, inside the people couldn't be friendlier. Dylan has tended to the heads of Bono, The Corrs, as well as a ton of international schlebs, but it's his team's understanding of everyday hair problems that make this salon the best by miles.

Laser hair removal

Bodyclinic, 24a Wicklow Street, Dublin 2. (tel: +353 1 633 9900, www.thebodyclinic.ie) has the latest technology for hair removal in the form of the class 4 laser 'Candela'. Treatment areas include bikini (brilliant for holidays), under arms, back, upper lip, chin, chest and legs. Open 7 days a week Mon-Fri 8am-8pm, Sat 9am-6pm, Sun 10am-6pm

Label heaven

5 Scarlet Row, 5 Scarlet Row, Essex Street West, Temple Bar, Dublin 8 (tel: +353 1 6729534) for Eileen Shields shoes and Irish labels Sharon Wauchob and Helen James, as well as international Eley Kishimoto and Bali Barrett.

BUY

Sexy smalls

Beneath, 1 Cows Lane, Temple Bar, Dublin 8 (tel: +353 1 6745983, www. beneath.ie). An excellent lingerie fitting service stocking cups measuring from A to F. Brands there include Lejaby, Freya, Pureda, Fantasie, Maidenform, DKNY, Calvin Klein, Honeydew and Sally Jones.

Beautiful boutique

Cherche Midi, 23 Drury Street, Dublin 2 (tel: +353 1 6753974). Named after owner Frances O'Gorman's favourite shoe-shopping street in Paris, Cherche Midi stocks designers Emma Hope and Jane Brown, as well as Kate Spade, Sonia Rykiel, Givenchy and Christian Lacroix.

The Design Centre

Powerscourt Townhouse, 59 South William Street, Dublin 2 (tel: +353 1 6795718, ww.designcentre.ie). Some fantastic Irish lines available include Linda Farrow vintage sunglasses and stunning Julien Macdonald gowns. There are also several Irish and international labels here as well as Pauric Sweeney bags. Lush!

Hot labels

Smock, 31 Drury Street, Dublin 2 (www.smock.ie). Karen Crawford and Susuan O Connell have the most wonderful buying skills. Labels here include Mayle, Masion Martin Margiela, A.P.C and Vivienne Westwood. One of my favourite shops in the city and the staff are always full of smiles.

Goodie Bag

Chesneau, 37 Wicklow Street, Dublin (tel: +353 1 6729199, www.chesneaudesign.com). Edmund Chesneau is a design genius; his bags are so carefully crafted that's they're practically Hermés (but at a fraction of the price).

Antique jewellery

Rhinestones, 18 St. Andrews Street, Dublin 2 (tel: +353 1 6790759, www. rhinestones.ie). Specialising in antique jewellery, it's a super shop for gifts.

Jewellery

Vivien Walsh, 24 Lower Stephens Green, Dublin 2 (tel: +353 1 4755031, www.vivienwalsh.com). A very talented jeweller who really knows her craft.

Twirly Dresses

Rococo, 1 Westbury Mall, Dublin 2 (tel: +353 1 6704007). Brilliant selection of dresses to do twirly twirls at parties.

Fairytale dresses

Chica, 25 Westbury Mall, Clarendon Street, Dublin2 (tel: +353 1 6719836, www. chicaboutiqueonline.com). Wonderful fairytale dresses and sparkly pumps and tons more Goddess stuff.

Rock it!

Lara Boutique, 1 Dame Lane, Dublin 2 (tel: +353 1 01 6707951, www. laras.ie). A wide range of labels including Rock & Republic jeans, Replay jeans, Pinko, and Terry de Havilland famous wedge shoes.

BUY

Lingerie

La Petite Coquette, 22 South William Street, Dublin2 (tel: +353 1 7079973, www.lapetitecoquette.ie). Beautiful, beautiful lingerie.

Party dresses

Tulle, 28 Market Arcade, South Great George's Street, Dublin 2 (tel: +353 1 6799115). A hidden treasure-trove of exclusive labels including Malene Birger, Sass and Bide, Betsey Johnson, Sanimi, and Leona Edmiston. Check out Leona Ebelsten, an Australian designer they stock (www.leonaedmiston.com) whose dresses are to die for; and staying down under, Rachel Gilbert's dresses – also sold here too – they're birthday and wedding must-haves.

Urban oasis

Circus, Powerscourt Townhouse, First Floor, South William Street, Dublin 2 (tel: +353 1 672 4736, www.circusstoreandgallery.com) sells unique labels and spots the hot new think even before it's hot. The space converts into a gallery in the evening time, to showcase art as well as fashion.

Hip labels

Indigo and Cloth, 27 South William Street, Dublin 2 (tel: +353 1 670 6403, www.indigoandcloth.com) In a basement under the ribbons and bows shop, this store sells labels for guys and gals that are the definition of the word 'hip'.

A one-off find

A Store is Born, 34 Clarendon Street, Dublin 2 (tel: +353 1 2857627). Only open Saturday, this is a collection of internationally sourced vintage items – good for cashmere cardigans and coats. Everything is in very good condition.

Sales bargains

Browse and jostle at Brown Thomas, Grafton Street (locally known as BT's) during sale time. It's our Selfridges and the designer handbag section (ground floor) and shoes (first floor) offers excellent value in the sales!

Bits and bobs

Toejam Carboot Sale, The Bernard Shaw, 11-12 South Richmond Street, Dublin 2 (tel: +353 85 712 8342) is a carboot sale in the car park of the Bernard Show pub the first Saturday of every month. It's mighty 'craic' full of all sorts of characters.

The perfect lace dress

Jenny Vander, 50 Drury Street, Dublin 2 (tel: +353 1 6770406). Bags, shoes, clothes, jewellery, the best vintage in the city and helpful and friendly staff.

Book shops

Dubray Books, 36 Grafton Street, Dublin 2 (tel: +353 1 6775568). Chapters Bookstore, Ivy Exchange, Parnell Street, Dublin 1 (tel: +353 1 8723297, www.chapters.ie). Cathach Books, 10 Duke Street, Dublin 1 (tel: +353 1 6718676, www.rarebooks.ie). The Secret Book and Record Store, 15A Wicklow Street, 2 Dublin (tel: +353 1 6797272).

Tee time

Versus, 1/2 Smock Alley, Temple Bar Dublin 2 (www.turtlehead.ie). The best t-shirts in the city. Tom Waits bought some t-shirts here recently.

Blanket Statement

Avoca, 11-13 Suffolk Street, Dublin 2 (tel: +353 1 6774215, www.avoca.ie). Large scones, blankets, books, everything and anything a Goddess could need.

So are you having a good time then? Have you… Ridden the hour long Dart train to Sandycove to have seafood at Cavistons. Visited Johnny Fox's Pub in the Wicklow Mountains for food and serious Irish dancing. Settled in for overpriced drinks at the Horseshoe bar in the refurbished Shelbourne Hotel. Gone for a spin on the 'Funderland' Ferris wheel (Big Wheel) at the RDS (Christmas). Had the best beef burrito and juice at Nude, Suffolk Street (owned by Norman Hewson, Bono's bro). Felt that your Irish host has watched all this through gritted teeth as you got stocious while he/she chauffeured you around the place. 'No fair' I say, 'no fair!'

Make sure that you at least bring home one of these little treats to remember Dublin by:
A wool blanket from Avoca Handweavers, 11-13 Suffolk Street, Dublin 2 (tel: +353 1 677 4215, www.avoca.ie) Second hand books form The Winding Stair café/ bookshop to browse secondhand books overlooking the Ha'penny Bridge. A wallet or bag from Chesneau, 37 Wicklow Street, Dublin 2, (tel: +353 1 672 9199, www.chesneaudesign.com)

Ice cream and gelato

Pompei's, 126 Roscoe St, Bondi, (tel: +612 9365 1233). No visit to the beach is complete without an ice-cream! The range of sorbet and gelato is hand-made daily by George Pompei and includes flavours such as white nectarine, blood orange and a special take on old favourite mango. Divine!

Bespoke shoes

At the Andrew McDonald Store and Workshop, 58 William St Paddington, (tel: +612 9358 6793, www.andrewmcdonald. com.au) one can sketch up a shoe and then learn in just ten days on their Intensive Shoemaking Course how to make it. At $3000 it's a huge layout of cash but don't you love the idea?

Beautiful Kaftans

Treat yourself to a Camilla Franks beautiful kaftan to throw over your costume (see www.camilla.com.au for stockists). Or pop into Bikini Island, 38 Campbell Parade, Bondi Beach, (tel: +612 9300 9446, www.bikiniisland.com.au) – on the beachfront at Bondi and choose from a fab range of swimmers.

Cupcakes

The Cupcake Bakery, Bakery, 438 Oxford St, Paddington, tel: +612 9332 370, www.thecupcakebakery.com.au) are baked fresh on site each day. Try the Chilli Choc cupcake for something a bit different or stick to an old favourite with Vanilla.

Amazing bikinis

The Zimmermann sisters – Simone and Nicki – are renowned for their hip little swimming costumes at Zimmermann, 387 Oxford Street, Paddington, (tel: +612 9357 4700, www.zimmermannwear.com). As local Sydney girls who live in the Eastern beaches and get much of their inspiration from Bondi their creations are eclectic and delectable.

Hip Bars

The Lincoln, 36 Bayswater Rd, Kings Cross (tel: +61 2 9331 2311, www.thelincoln. com.au). Pop downstairs to the 'disco' and check out the original poles still in place from when a pole dancing club stood there. Favela, 1 Kellett Way, Potts Point, (tel: +61 2 9357 1640, www.favela.com.au) - great bar, restaurant, club. Gazebo Wine Garden 2 Elizabeth Bay Rd, Elizabeth Bay tel: +61 2 9357 5333, www.gazebowinegarden.com. au) - won the best wine bar in Australia in 2006. Lotus 22 Challis Ave Potts Point (tel: +61 2 9326 9000, www.merivale.com.au) a really great cocktail bar. Shore Club 36 - 38 South Steyne, Manly (tel: +61 2 9977 6322, www.shoreclub.com.au) - on the beachfront, great views and the roof on the top level opens up for a super vantage point. Great for a Sunday bevvie.

Real Italian Cooking

Learn to cook authentic italian from scratch with Luciana Sampogna in her beautiful italianate home, see Cucina Italiana, 84 Johnston St, Annandale (tel: +61 2 8021 2699; www.cucinaitaliana.com.au).

Perfect spray tan and gorgeous swimmers

Tigerlily the label created by former model Jodhi Meares is the hippest name for beautiful swimmers in Australia. As well as a full range of swimwear at Jodhi Meares, 37 William Street, Paddington (www. tigerlilyswimwear.com.au) - the branch also does the best spray tan in Sydney.

Eats with friends

Jimmy Liks Restaurant & Bar, 186 - 188 Victoria Street, Potts Point (tel: +61 2 8354 1400, www.jimmyliks.com) - great venue, super food, atmosphere. We love

Macaroons

Can't make it to Paris to pick up a box of macaroons? Pick up some at the Lindt Café 53 Martin Place. (tel: +612 8257 1600) or Lindt Shop, 104-105 Cockle Bay Wharf, (tel: +612 9267 8064). I love the champagne, pistachio and chocolate flavoured macaroons best. Also the choccy ice-cream and choccy cakes are yum!

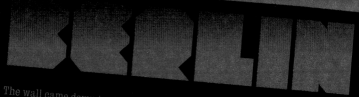

BERLIN

The wall came down in '89 and Berlin has become the club capital since. The Mitte neighbourhood, which was formerly East Berlin, is where it's all going down with boutiques, galleries and club nights. When in Berlin I don't want to come home. it's an Urban Goddess's nirvana.

SLEEP

Sleep Midrange
Propeller Island City Lodge, Albrecht Achiles Str 58, 10709 Berlin (tel: +49 30 891 9016, www.propeller-island.com). Sleep in a room with a flying bed on a wooden hill.

Sleep Budget
Circus Hostel, Weinbergsweg 1a,10119 Berlin (tel: +49 30 2839 1433, www.circus-hostel.de). Cheap as chips, well located accomodation, Circus hostel is a little jem. Here's a tip from our friends Bren and Lisa, book an apartment with a city view, that sleeps four people for only €140, and don't miss the all-you-can-eat €5 brekkie.

KaDeWe Tauentzienstr. 21-24, 10789 Berlin (tel:+49 302 1210, www.kadewe-berlin.de). A department store with a food hall to die for. Check the fourth floor for kitchen equipment, cutlery and china and the sixth for the magnificent food hall, Fauchon chocolates and Duncan Hines Devil's Food Cake Mix. Sushi anyone? Schneeweiss, Boenkestrasse 55, 13125 Berlin, (tel: +49 30 943 0575) does really nice food. Aroma, Warschauer strasse 69, 10243 Berlin, is a good café serving tons of different teas and teensey yummy brownies (although not as good as good as my friend Claire's on page 259). They use a little alarm clock here to brew your cuppa to perfection.

Titbit
Try the organic bratwurst ,pomme frites and currywurst some of Berlin's national snack food staples.

Best shop
Best Shop Berlin, Alte Schönhauserstrasse 6, 10119 Berlin (tel:
+49 30 24 63 24 85, www.bestshop-berlin.de) on a quiet street in Mitte,
like the name says, sells the 'best' including graphic art clothes and kicks.

Hidden Treasure
Andreas Murkudis, Münzstrasse 21, 1-2 hof 10178 Berlin. (www.
andreasmurkudis.net). Hidden in the shadows of Mitte, this boutique
stocks among other labels Germany's pulver dresses – a dress as a national
institution, who'd a thunk it?

European Stars
Apartment Galerie, Memhardstrasse 8, 10178 Mitte, Berlin (www.
apartmentberlin.de) sells the hippest labels from the avant-garde Berlin-based
labels Hui Hui and Klein Coprse to European stars like Cheap Monday.

A gallery of fashion
Konk, Kleine Hamburger Strasse 15 10117 (www.konk-berlin.de) houses Berlin's
superstar fashion designers and jewellers all in the one place. It's like a gallery
here with each room decked out like a conceptual-art project. Keep eyes peeled for
both C.neeon's and Cocotte Couture dresses. I love this place!

The new wrap dress
C'est Tout, Mulackstrasse 26, 10119 Mitte, Berlin (www.cesttout.de) If you like
Diane von Furstenberg's dresses then you'll luuuuurve C'est Tout's too. Their
wrap dresses suits all figure types. Beautiful and hard to find the the rest of
Europe which means rare.

Want something no one else has
Penkov, Invalidenstrasse 155, 10115 Mitte, Berlin, (tel:+49 (0)30 46 30 9047,
www.penkovberlin.com) Wow the most beautiful clothes ever!

Berlin's fashion stars
Pulver, Torstrasse 199, 10115 Mitte, Berlin, (tel+49 (0)30 27 90 7123, www.pulver-
studio.de) A four women design collective provide exciting, adorable designs.

Drool Jewels
Eva Niemand, Goldsmith Gallery at Kollwitzplatz, Knaakstr 45, 10435 Berlin
(tel:+49 30 44 315 892, www.eva-niemand.de). Have a gander at these on the
web, the work is really banging. I particularly like the dog wearing the tiara.
Nice touch that. Utter drool jewels!

BERLIN

MARKETS

Strasse des 17 Juni flea market (just outside the Tiergarten). Among the wares for sale here are chunks of the Berlin Wall.

Arkonaplatz, U8 Bernauer Str, 10435 Berlin - Mitte (tel: 49 30 786 9764). Opening times: Sun 10.00-18.00. In the heart of Mitte, this market is very cool. The stands towards the back hold the best secrets.

Boghagener Platz, 10245 Berlin, near Friedrichshain, U5 Frankfurter Tor or Tram 21. This flea market is a gem! Stuffed full of old folks, peddling relics of communist suburbia. Good for badges etc.

Turkischer markt, Maybachufer, (near Kottbusser Tor/Schonleinstr underground), takes place twice weekly (every Tuesday and Friday), where the Turkish community lays on this fantastic foodie market along the banks of the Landwehrkandal river on Maybachufer. What treats these are with Turkish bread stacked high, olives and pungent herbs. At unbeatable prices you'd be mad to miss this.

PARTEEEEE Til toast and tea

Fake Beach to Parteeeeeeee

The Badeschiff, (in English, "bathing ship") is an old ship's container which has been converted into a public safe swimming pool. Beached on the East Harbour section (Treptow) of the Spree River, it offers safe and sanitary swimming, (the Spree itself is waaaay too polluted for safe swims). In the winter it's all saunas and massages; in the summer a fake beach with a bar by the pool. Open til midnight, We're lovin' it !

Berlin and electronic music go together like butter and hot toast, for it was the washes of synthesizers, bass-lines, electric guitars and strings mixed in Berlin in the early 80s (known as the Berlin school) that spawned what Techno is today. Berlin still remains the capital of Techno. Check out www.myspace.com/iconclubberlin for the latest sounds.

Film and drinks

8mm bar, Schönhauser Allee 177, 10119 Berlin (tel: +49 30 4050 0624). There's one in every city, the dark little bar where everyone goes and doesn't leave until it's toast and tea time. Sit (or lie) back with friends and soak up the movies projected onto the walls while being drip-fed alcohol. Doesn't get much better then this.

Part and art

Party arty www.myspace.com/partyarty is an art party that moves. There's food, DJs, art by Berlin-based artists and (wait for it) backgammon play offs. Catch it around Friedrichshain and Kreuxberg (see myspace for details).

Live music

Schokoladen, Ackerstrasse 169, 10115 Berlin (tel: +49 30 282 6527, www. myspace.com/schokoladen – this is one of the cutest live band venues in town. Funny how this place used to be a squat and now hosts hip DJ sets, that's typical Berlin these days, check their myspace for details. Love their disco ball!

MYTUNES

1. Joris Voorn – Blank (www.myspace.com/jorisvoorn). Eight and a half minutes of pure joy!

2. Rekids – The Feeling John Daily Remix (www.myspace.com/rekids). Lovin' it!

3. Samuli Kemppi – Casual Care Samuli Kemppi (www.myspace.com/samulikemppi). A Techo God!

4. Robots in Disguise – La Nuit (www.myspace.com/robotsindisguise).

5. Marcel Fingler – Friction (www.myspace.com/marcelfengler).

6. Sven Vath (www.cocoon.net or www.myspace.com/cocoonrecordings).

7. Jacek Sienkiewicz – My Little Place. (In fact anything by this polish techno DJ will do, he's Fab!)

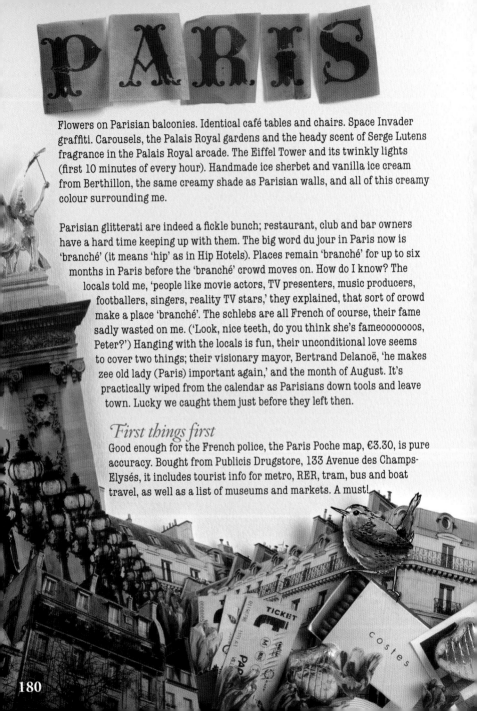

PARIS

Flowers on Parisian balconies. Identical café tables and chairs. Space Invader graffiti. Carousels, the Palais Royal gardens and the heady scent of Serge Lutens fragrance in the Palais Royal arcade. The Eiffel Tower and its twinkly lights (first 10 minutes of every hour). Handmade ice sherbet and vanilla ice cream from Berthillon, the same creamy shade as Parisian walls, and all of this creamy colour surrounding me.

Parisian glitterati are indeed a fickle bunch; restaurant, club and bar owners have a hard time keeping up with them. The big word du jour in Paris now is 'branché' (it means 'hip' as in Hip Hotels). Places remain 'branché' for up to six months in Paris before the 'branché' crowd moves on. How do I know? The locals told me, 'people like movie actors, TV presenters, music producers, footballers, singers, reality TV stars,' they explained, that sort of crowd make a place 'branché'. The schlebs are all French of course, their fame sadly wasted on me. ('Look, nice teeth, do you think she's fameooooooooos, Peter?') Hanging with the locals is fun, their unconditional love seems to cover two things; their visionary mayor, Bertrand Delanoë, 'he makes zee old lady (Paris) important again,' and the month of August. It's practically wiped from the calendar as Parisians down tools and leave town. Lucky we caught them just before they left then.

First things first

Good enough for the French police, the Paris Poche map, €3.30, is pure accuracy. Bought from Publicis Drugstore, 133 Avenue des Champs-Elysés, it includes tourist info for metro, RER, tram, bus and boat travel, as well as a list of museums and markets. A must!

Sleep Mid-Range

Hotel Bourg Tibourg, 19 rue du Bourg-Tibourg, 75004 Paris (tel: +33 1 42 78 47 39; www.hotelbourgtibourg.com). I always stay at this hotel; room 35 is my home when in Paris. €230 for a double room. Close your eyzes and breathe in the musk-scented air.

Sleep Mid-Range

A bit tired of the chintz and Parissy thang? Kube hotel, 1-5, passage Ruelle, 75018 Paris (tel: +33 1 42 05 20 00, www. kubehotel.com) offers something a bit more fresh and modern. €300 for a double room.

Sleep Luxury

Hotel Costes, 239, rue St. Honoré, 75001 Paris (tel: +33 1 42 44 50 00, www.hotelcostes.com) the bigger sister of Hotel Bourg Tibourg rooms are from €500.

Save a Few Euro

Prices go up in April so buy your museum and tour tickets before this at www. gotoParis.net and save a bit of dosh.

Titbit

April is the best month to visit Paris as it's the start of the al fresco outdoor concerts. I also love November and keep an eye peeled around the last week for the Rue de Bretagne brocante (roving flea market) to Christmas shop.

1. Emily Loizeau – L'Autre Bout Du Monde
2. Emilie Simon – Song of the storm
3. Yelle - "ACDG" Remix Electro VaVan Treaxy
4. Uffie – Pop the Glock www.myspace.com/uffie
5. Black Kids – I'm Not Going To Teach Your Boyfriend...
6. Justice (Et Justice Pour Tous) – DNVO Edit
7. DJ Mehdi – Pocket Piano
8. Frankie Valli /The Four Seasons – Beggin' (Pilooski re-edit)
9. Fuck Buttons – Sweet Love For Planet Earth
10. The Teenagers – Homecoming

Breafast

Breakfast at Rose Carrarini's bakery in the Dover Street Market Rose Bakery in London is always a nice little treat for me. Breakfast at her Rose Bakery at 46 rue des Martyrs 75009 Paris (tel: +33 1 42 82 12 80), is an even better experience.

Yummy lamb

Chez George, 273 Boulevard Pereire, 75017 Paris (tel: +33 1 45 74 31 00). The roast lamb with white beans, carved table side, is their speciality. If you can bring yourself to do it after dinner, havé the île flottante, a millefeuille filled with vanilla-flecked cream. Why not share it. (Or not.)

Fash packed lunch

Le Castiglione, 235 rue Saint Honoré, 75001 Paris (tel: +33 1 42 60 68 22). Good place to eat if you are around the Louvre or Tuileries. Good salads; it's rammed during fashion week.

Fresh langoustines

Le Duc, 243 Boulevard Raspail 75014 Paris (tel: +33 1 43 20 96 30) serves the best fresh langoustines with ginger and fennel gratin.

Marrow fat please

Au Boeuf Couronné, 188 avenue Jean-Jaurès, 75019 Paris (tel: +33 1 42 39 44 44, www.rest-gj.com). An old place (more than 100 years old) where I had the best marrow bones of my life. Three mahussive shins added to toast with a little salt followed by steak and yummy über-fries. Utter heaven. Easily the best bone marrow in Paris, I subsequently learned.

A quick Cuppa

Café de Flore, 172 boulevard Saint-Germain, 75006 Paris (tel: +33 1 45 48 55 26). My one tourist indulgence is a cup of tea here and an an hour or so to sort out my notebook.

Steak béarnaise

Chez George, 1 rue du Mail 75002 Paris (tel: +33 1 42 60 07 11). It never changes for me; this restaurant serves the best steak béarnaise and skinny frites in Paris.

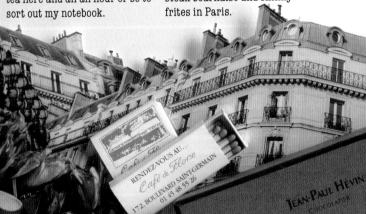

Late Night bites

Le Tambour, 41 rue Montmartre, 75002 Paris (tel:+33 1 42 33 06 90, www.restaurantletambour.com). French food eaten in a very casual set-up (bus-stop-sign bar stools anyone? Stays open until 3am. Le bienvenu, 42, rue Argout, 75002 Paris (tel: +33 1 42 33 31 08) serves food until 7am. (The cous cous is very good.)

Treats

Sadaharu Aoki, 35 rue de Vaugirard, 75006 Paris (tel: +33 1 45 44 48 90, www.sadaharuaoki.com) and 56 boulevard Port Royal 75005 Paris. The most beautiful éclairs, macaroons and pastries in a Japanese French style. This is where I had my 'It brag' moment. Pierre Hermé, 72 rue Bonaparte, 75006 Paris (tel:+33 1 43 54 47 77, www.pierreherme.com). Is this the most 'notable' macaroon in Paris? See page 40 and see if you agree. Pain de Sucre, 14 rue Rambuteau, 75003 Paris (tel: +33 1 45 74 68 92). Yummy cakes, pastries and breads. Galerie Lafayette Gourmet, 40 boulevard Haussmann 75009 Paris (tel: +33 1 42 85 12 00, www.galerieslafayette.com). Sadaharu Aoki has pastreis here as well as Pâtisseries from across Paris have counter space here, which saves you the cake schlep across the city.

Cake and Tea

Hit Le Grand Epicerie de Paris: 38, rue de Sèvres, 75007 Paris (tel: +33 1 44 39 81 00, www.lagrandeepicerie.fr) food market in Bon Marché for a cake or two (all the great patisseries have counters here). It's incredible. Top floor boasts one of the chicest rubber-necking spots in town, called Delicabar (tel: +33 1 42 22 10 12, www.delicabar.fr), this place is a real local secret.

Ice Cream

Handmade ice cream and sherbet from Berthillon, 31 rue Saint-Louis-en L'ile (tel: +33 1 43 54 31 61, www.berthillon-glacier.fr).

A Good All rounder

Colette, 213 rue Saint-Honoré, 75001 Paris (tel: +33 1 55 35 33 90, www.colette.fr). Full of energy and a magnet for the French bobo crowd. See my visit on page 58.

...and the rest

Madame André, 34, rue Mont-Thabor, 75001 Paris (tel: +33 1 42 96 27 24, www.madameandre.com) for accessories, lingerie and cutsey finds. Comme des Garcons, 54 rue du Faubourg Saint-Honoré, 75008 Paris (tel:+33 1 53 30 27 27). A mecca for everything Comme, the fragrances are particularly beautiful. E. Dehillerin, 18 rue Coquillière, 75001 Paris (tel: +33 1 42 36 53 13, www.e-dehillerin.fr). Oh my God, palpitations, they wrapped my madeleine tray in brown paper; it doesn't get any better than this. The place is stuffed with the very best bakeware in Europe (it's even on the ceiling). I buy one baking utensil here every single time I visit Paris. Hermès, 24 rue du Faubourg Saint-Honoré, 75008 Paris (tel: +33 1 40 17 46 00, www.hermes.com). Their horsey heritage gets me drooling with 'the want'. Repetto, 22 rue de la Paix 75002 Paris (tel: +33 1 44 71 83 12, www.repetto.com). I love, love, love Repetto. I had to queue to get in the door of this store and you know what a queue means in Paris, don't you? 'Notable' pumps made by the peeps who make professional ballet shoes for the Parisian ballet – these are top of my list for comfort. A.P.C., 112 rue Vieille-du-Temple, 75003 Paris (tel: +33 1 42 78 18 02, www.apc.fr) is the quintessential Parisian brand and I never leave Paris without buying a little something. EW, 21 rue Saint Paul 75004 Paris (tel:+33 1 42 77 55 11). Lace, linen and kitchenware – things that you would normally see at the markets. Isabel Marant, 47 rue de Saintonge 75003 Paris (tel: +33 1 42 78 19 24, www.isabelmarant.tm.fr). I have championed Isabel Marant's designs for a very long time. I'm obsessed with her beautiful work.

Sexy drawers

For the most beautiful sculptural drawer set, check out Tsé & Tsé Associées design at Astier De Villatte, 173 rue Saint-Honoré, 75001 Paris (tel: +33 1 42 60 74 13, www.astierdevillante.com).

Even Sexier drawers

Fifi Chachnil, 26 rue Cambon, 75001 Paris (tel: +33 1 42 60 38 86, www. fifichachnil.com). Very girlie lingerie for the Sex Goddess in you.

Designer labels

Last season's stock but who cares? At 40% to 70% off the regular price Annexe des Createurs, 19, rue Godot de Mauroy, 75009 (tel: +33 1 42 65 46 40, www. annexedescreateurs.com, metro Opéra, Auber, Madeleine) stocks big catwalk names. How many people do you know who can tell the difference between this year's Gucci trousers and last year's? I thought so. This place is a must.

The best vintage/second hand stores

Au Petit bonheur la chance, 13 Rue Saint-Paul 75004 Paris, (tel: +334 01 42 74 36 38). A mahussive collection of vintage café au lait bowls spans the entire wall. I drool at the vintage stationery here and the jam jars and vintage tins, oh I'm out of breath with 'the want'. 'Au Petit bonheur la chance' means 'the little happiness of random luck' and I'm so lucky to have found this little gem many, many years ago. Chez Mamie, 73 rue Rouchechouart 75009 Paris (tel: +33 42 82 09 98). Stocks the kind of vintage clothes and bags you can only dream of. Cuisinophile, 25 rue Bourg Tibourg 75004 Paris (tel: +33 40 29 07 32). Antique kitchenware found by the owner Anne Siquier at flea markets across France. Les Trios Marches de Catherine B, 1 rue Guisarde 75006 Paris. (www.catherine-b.com). If you've €4,000 lying spare you can pick up a second-hand Hermès Kelly bag here. The shop stocks a mahussive range of barely used designer bags. Réciproque, 88-101 rue de la Pompe 75016 Paris (tel: +33 1 47 04 30 28). From Galliano to Gucci, Westwood to Hermès this consignment shop is stuffed full of out of season stock. If you know what suits you this is a gold mine for staples. Rouge, 12 rue Mayran 75009 Paris. The owner hunts antique furniture and reconditions it; the pieces are gorgeous.

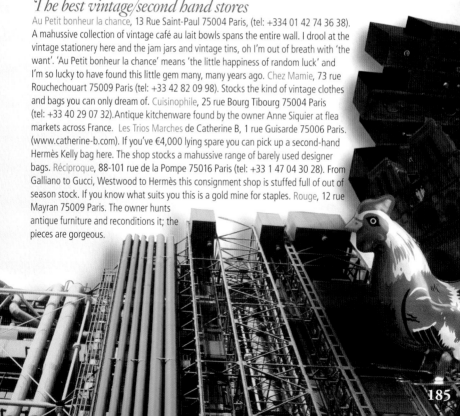

PARiZEEe

Favala Chic, 18, rue du Faubourg du Temple, 75011 Paris (tel: +33 1 40 21 38 14, www.favelachic.com/paris). This the original Favala (there's another in London's Shoreditch, 91-93 Great Eastern Street, EC2 (tel: +44 20 7613 5228, www.favelachic.com/london). Heels required (preferably Louboutins) to dance on the tables in this club/restaurant churning out Brazilian meets French beats. Le Baron, 6 avenue Marceau, 75008 Paris (tel: +33 1 47 20 04 01, www.clublebaron.com). DJ Olympia Le Tan spins great throwbacks; it's a rubber-neck paradise (stuffed with interesting characters). I love it because it's intimate and small. Le Fleche D'Or, 102 bis rue de Bagnolet, 75020 Paris (tel: +44 1 44 64 01 02, www. flechedor.fr). Parisian hipsters soak up pop electro and great indie (live). La Java, 105 rue du Faubourg du Temple, 75010 Paris (www. la-java.fr). A throwback to the Edith Piaf period with international artists and stand-up comedians. Le Paris Paris, 5 avenue de l'Opera, 75001 Paris (tel: +33 1 42 60 64 45, www.parisparis.com). Shake that bootie, child! De la bombe bébé... check out La French @Le Paris Paris on You Tube.

With the coolest location in Paris, Le Showcase, under le pont Alexandre III, 75008 Paris (www.showcase.fr) is nestled secretly under this historic bridge. (Shhhhhhhh!). Le Trabendo, Parc de la Villette, 211 avenue Jean Jaures, 75019 Paris (tel: +33 1 42 01 12 12, www.trabendo.fr). A great venue where I saw one of my NYC fave groups Au Revoir Simone (www.aurevoirsimone. com) play here. The night was fabby, fab, fab! Le Triptyque, 142, rue Montmarte, 75002 Paris (www.letriptyque.com). Boogie woogie til late, late, late. Yeeeeeehaw!

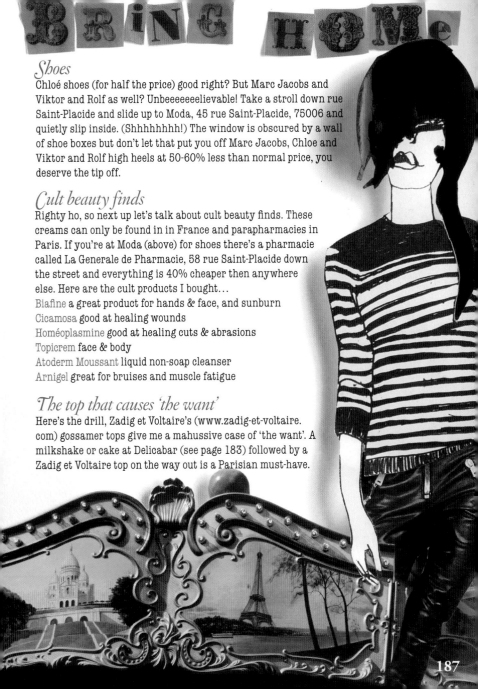

BRiNG HOMe

Shoes

Chloé shoes (for half the price) good right? But Marc Jacobs and
Viktor and Rolf as well? Unbeeeeeeelievable! Take a stroll down rue
Saint-Placide and slide up to Moda, 45 rue Saint-Placide, 75006 and
quietly slip inside. (Shhhhhhhh!) The window is obscured by a wall
of shoe boxes but don't let that put you off Marc Jacobs, Chloe and
Viktor and Rolf high heels at 50-60% less than normal price, you
deserve the tip off.

Cult beauty finds

Righty ho, so next up let's talk about cult beauty finds. These
creams can only be found in in France and parapharmacies in
Paris. If you're at Moda (above) for shoes there's a pharmacie
called La Generale de Pharmacie, 58 rue Saint-Placide down
the street and everything is 40% cheaper then anywhere
else. Here are the cult products I bought...
Biafine a great product for hands & face, and sunburn
Cicamosa good at healing wounds
Homéoplasmine good at healing cuts & abrasions
Topicrem face & body
Atoderm Moussant liquid non-soap cleanser
Arnigel great for bruises and muscle fatigue

The top that causes 'the want'

Here's the drill, Zadig et Voltaire's (www.zadig-et-voltaire.
com) gossamer tops give me a mahussive case of 'the want'. A
milkshake or cake at Delicabar (see page 183) followed by a
Zadig et Voltaire top on the way out is a Parisian must-have.

187

LONDON

I skip along with her, following one day into the next and then I look back in my notebook and look at all I've seen and heard. The A-Z, ice-cream and the Fortnum and Mason foodhall, the smell of real vintage, afternoon tea at Sketch, ES Magazine on a Friday with the Evening Standard, Smythson notebooks, pizza at Malletti's in Soho and then mind the Gap; these are a few of the things that I love about her and there are many, many, more, so where to start? How about here; I've organized London by area for you, this way it's easier to spend time in one place and enjoy a bunch of secret addresses close to each other all in one go. Let's kick off slap bang in the centre of Laaandon town shall we?

Bloomsbury & Fitzrovia

Nearest tubes: Bond Street; Baker Street; Oxford Circus; Tottenham Court Road

The Sanderson, 50 Berners Street London, England W1T (tel. +44 207 300 1400, www.sandersonlondon.com). Their Agua bathouse Spa, is one of the best spas in London. The Aromatherapy Associates Rose massage, pedis, manis, waxing, facials… the list goes on and on. Imagine treating yourself to the lot and then retiring to bed to fall into rose scented dreams. Utter bliss I tell ya! Utter bliss! Some great deals are to be had at this hotel so keep an eye on the website, rooms start at £250.

Persephone Books, 59 Lamb's Conduit Street, London, WC1 (tel: +44 207 242 9292, www.persephonebooks.co.uk). A fairytale of a place; Persephone is an independent publisher who specialize in re-issuing classics from the twentieth century. Their books look utterly stunning, all grey jackets with magnificent endpapers.

Planet Organic, 22 Torrington Place, London, WC1E (tel: +44 207 436 1929, www.planetorganic.com). A little supermarket that stocks organic beauty products and food, and there's a butchers, that's Daylesford organic.

Scandinavian Kitchen, 61 Great Titchfield Street, London, W1W (tel: +44 207 580 7161, www.scandikitchen.co.uk). When people hear 'Scandinavia' they say, 'What, like herring and stuff?' Ever wondered where to get some? Here! You can also buy good rye crisp bread etc, in this Scandinavian deli and grocery store.

Thorsten Van Elten, 22 Warren Street, London W1T (tel: +44 207 739 7237, www.thorstenvanelten.com). Thorston's philosophy has always worked with people he likes on products he loves. Clever lighting and home stuff and the odd quirky pieces.

MayFaiR & PicaDiLLy

Nearest tubes: Piccadilly Circus; Green Park; Oxford Circus; Bond Street.

A. Maitland & Co, 175 Piccadilly,W1J (tel: +44 207 493 1975). An old-fashioned chemist stocking beautiful products; I bought my Mason & Pearson hairbrush here.

The Chocolate Society, 32-34 Shepherd Market, W1J (tel: +44 207 495 0302, www. chocolate.co.uk). They stock a range of artisan hand-made chocolate brands. Oh how I love it, their tins of hot chocolate are the best.

Fortnum and Mason, 181 Piccadilly, London, W1A (tel:+44 207 734 8040, www. fortnumandmason.com). Stationery, their ice-cream parlour, tea and sugar mice, tea pots, jams, perfumes and tea cups. The stuff of dreams!

Maison Martin Margiela, 1-9 Bruton Place, London, W1J (tel: +44 207 629 2682, www.maisonmartinmargiela.com). Wonderfully inspiring fashion.

Matthew Williamson, 28 Bruton Street, London, W1J (tel: +44 207 629 6200, www.matthewwilliamson.com) can be relied upon to always add colour. His scarves are particularly divine (me being a scarf gal and everything).

Stella McCartney, 30 Bruton Street, London W1J (tel: +44 207 518 3100, www.stellamccartney.com) Stella can do no wrong, beauty, lingerie, fashion in the most gorgeous surroundings. Just look at the walls of this store as inspiration for your bedroom.

Penhaligon's, 16-17 Burlington Arcade, London, W1J (tel: +44 207 629 1416, www.penhaligons.co.uk). History in a bottle this.

COVENT GARDEN & SOHO

Nearest tubes: Oxford Circus; Tottenham Court Road; Leicester Square

Pizza

Malletti, 26 Noel Street, London, W1F (tel: +44 207 439 4096). By far the best pizza in London and Old Man Malletti is a hoot. There are always queues here at lunchtime and you know how excited I get about queues.

Romantic

Andrew Edmunds, 46 Lexington Street, London, W1 (tel: +44 207 437 5708) is cosy and reassuring; the handwritten menu, the well-sourced yet affordable wine, the comforting food (free-range chicken on artichoke or rib-eye steak anyone?). And they specialise in sherry which has left Granny's sideboard and become very hip to drink lately. Reserve a week in advance and ask for a ground floor table, the basement is waaaaay too cramped.

Organic

Leon, 35 Great Marlborough Street, London, W1 (tel: +44 207 437 5280, www.leonrestaurants. co.uk) for healthy lunch. The falafel, pitta bread and chicken with aioli are still my favourite things on the menu. There are seven more locations around the city including Spitalfields, Regent Street and Cannon Street.

Thai lunch and street watching

Busaba Eathai, 106-110 Wardour Street, Soho, London, W1 (tel: +44 207 255 8686) Grab a seat at the window and watch Soho drift by. Lovin the Thai green curry, rice served with crab meat, or the delicately textured tofu, lightly fried then served with a spicy yellow bean sauce. I'm hungry even thinking about it.

Fresh cream for scones

Neal's Yard Dairy, 17 Shorts Gardens, WC2H (tel: +44 207 240 5700, www.nealsyarddairy. co.uk) For cheese, cream and milk as it should taste. There's a larger branch at Borough Market.

Dim Sum/cake and tea

Yauatcha, 15-17 Broadwick Street, London, W1F (tel:+44 207 494 8888, www.yauatcha. com) I love the Dim sum here, har gao (prawn dumplings), char siu bun (baked venison puff), the congee (rice porridge) with preserved egg and pork and the salt and pepper quail are the highlights of the menu. The cake counter is magnificent too.

Buy

Cult status

Bape, 4 Upper James Street, London, W1F (tel: +44 20 7494 4924, www.bape.com) I'm sure you know about this Japanese cult brand, here's the address for those infamous little black monkey print hoodies.

Cakes/tea and fashion

Shop at Maison Bertaux, Basement, 27 Greek Street, London, W1D (tel: +44 20 7437 1259). Tucked away in the basement of a 135 year old French patisserie, are labels A.P.C, Sonia by Sonia Rykiel, Eley Kishimoto and Obey (street art on soft tees), plus there's Vivienne Westwood jewellery, Tocca products and odd teacups and plates for sale which will be gift wrapped for you in a cake box. Nothin for it but to buy some cakes on the way out I think.

Organic beauty

The Organic Pharmacy, 36 Neal Street, WC2H 9PS (tel: +44 207 836 3923, www.theorganicpharmacy.com) For every Earth Goddess, there's a product here. Their own organic beauty range is spectacular. There are also branches on the King's Road, Kensington High Street and Park Street in East London

I love this store

Liberty, Great Marlborough Street, London, W1B (tel: +44 207 734 1234, www.liberty.co.uk) Confession! I love this store, I love its creaky stairs, its stationery, its window displays and its range of antique perfume bottles and diaries. I could spend days poking around every last inch of this place. Nuff said.

Lomos and books

The Photographer's Gallery Bookshop, 5 & 8 Great Newport Street, WC2H tel: +44 207 831 1772 ext 201) This is where I bought my Holga (they also sell Lomos). They have a huge selection of photography books and rotating exhibitions.

Italian Deli

Lina Stores, 18 Brewer Street, London, W1F (tel: + 44 207 437 6482) Loving the green tiled walls of this delicatessen stuffed with all things Italian. Mmmmmmm!

BAPE

191

Markets

Great market

Borough Market, 8 Southwark Street, London SE1. Open Thursday 11am-5pm,
Friday 12-6pm, Saturdays 9am-4pm. See www.boroughmarket.org.uk for
details (Nearest tube London Bridge). Borough market, tucked under the roar
of the railway tracks by London Bridge, has a vast selection of street food; salt-
beef sandwiches, pies, for eating there and then and a market stuffed full of
darling little local produce stalls and yummy food treats to bring home.

The perfect Borough sambo

Pick up some (still warm) artisan bread, yummy French butter and Iberico
ham (from the Brindisa stall), then some cheese from Neal's Yard and put them
all together for a taste of Borough back home. Delish!

Pies

A pork pie from the Ginger Pig, Borough Market
Butchers, Borough Market, London, SE1 (tel: 020 7403
4721, www.thegingerpig.co.uk) is yumeeeee but their
filled pies which you take home and heat up offer an
even bigger dose of cheery-uppage on a chilly winter's
night. Mmmmmmmm!

Columbia Road Flower Market

The market opens 8am to 2pm every Sunday and apart
from the great selection of flowers there's a multitude
of great shops which only open on Sunday too
(www.columbia-flower-market.freewebspace.com).
I love hanging out here on Sundays with my pals.

BEYOND RETRO

EX. LARGE
HYDRANGEA

LONG. LASTING
CALLAS

REST ROSES

COLUMBIA
LOND

VINTAGE

For me, buying vintage is about the experience, the thrill of the chase. Trawling car-boots and charity shops for clothes and furniture has thrown up some great moments. Most places take cash only, so take along as much as you're prepared to spend as there may not be an ATM nearby. Always barter, (always) especially if you're buying more then one piece. Oh, and don't leave home without your measurements: even if it's a steal, there's no point lugging it home to find you have to winch that couch through your window or that dress is just too small.

Best vintage spots

Absolute Vintage, 15 Hanbury Street, Spitalfields, London E1 (tel: +44 207 247 3883, www.absolutevintage.co.uk).

Rokit, 107 Brick Lane, London E1 (tel: +44 207 247 3777, www.rokit.co.uk) plus four other London locations.

Beyond Retro, 110-112 Cheshire Street, London E2 (tel: +44 207 613 3636, www.beyondretro.com).

Rellik, 8 Golbourne Road, London W10 (tel: +44 208 962 0089, www.relliklondon.co.uk).

Vintage Heaven, 82 Columbia Road, E2 (tel: +44 (0)1277 215968, vintageheaven.co.uk)

London Vintage fashion, textiles and accessories fair, Hammersmith Town Hall, King Street, London W6. It takes place every five to six weeks from 10am to 5pm and you'll find details on www.pa-antiques.co.uk. The entrance fee is £10.00 from 8am-10am; £5 from 10am-5pm.

Second hand style

Check local press or subscribe to www.car-boot-sales-directory.co.uk for up-to-date listings of boot sales, markets and antique fairs. For charity shops in your area, look at www.charityshops.org.uk as most chains have dedicated furniture stores. Oxfam has 10 stores in the UK, plus a further 10 with separate departments. Check its website www.oxfam.org.uk.

Notting Hill

BUY

It's mint

Mint, 70 Wigmore Street, London W1U 2SF (tel: +44 207 224 4406; www.mintshop.co.uk). The droolage starts before I even get through the front door of this place. From the ceramics to unusual lamps and teapots, yes, everything here is Mint!

Antiques

Portobello Road (Antique Dealers Association), 223a Portobello Road, London W11 1LU (tel: +44 207 229 8354, www.portobelloroad.co.uk). Visit on a Friday or Saturday for a mahussive range of antique goods. Seeing as Portobello is in Notting Hill here are my other favourite spots nearby in West London.

Spices

The Spice Shop, 1 Blenheim Crescent, London W11 (tel: +44 207 221 4448, www.thespiceshop.co.uk). Loads of different spices and herbs sourced by spice trader Brigit Erath from across the globe. As well as running the shop Birgit also teaches at Books for Cooks (opposite the shop) and advises major TV chefs and cooks around the world.

Cookbooks

Books for Cooks, 4 Blenheim Crescent, London W11 (tel: +44 207 221 1992, www.booksforcooks.com). A shop that sells thousands of cookbooks and the best bit of all? Cookbooks are put to the test in their café at the back of the shop and there are cookery classes upstairs. Bliss for a Home Goddess!

Fabrics and linens

Ian Mankin, 109 Regents Park Road, London NW1 (tel: +44 207 722 0997, www.ianmankin.com). The most beautiful linens and interiors fabrics. He also has a shop at 271 Wandsworth Bridge Road, London SW6 (tel:+44 207 371 8825).

Wonderland

Vessel, 114 Kensington Park Road, London W1 (tel: +44 207 727 8001, www.vesselgallery.com). Hella Jongerius (www.jongeriuslab.com) is still by far my favourite ceramic designer. I love her snail plate for the historic German porcelain creators Nyphenburg.

Good lunch spot
Elecrtic Brasserie, 191 Portobello Road, London W11 (tel: +44 207 908 9696, www.electricbrasserie.com). Take a break from the hustle and bustle and treat yourself to some nice Lobster for lunch.

All things Sicilian
Arancina, 19 Pembridge Road, London W11 (tel: +44 207 221 7776, www.arancina.co.uk) Look for the bright orange car, you can't miss it and step inside for the best thin based pizza and deep-fried risorro balls this side of Sicily. Ever wondered what a Ciambella is? (Italian doughnuts), Or cannoli? Tube-shaped shells of fried pasty dough, filled with a sweet, creamy filling. You'll find the lot here.

Red Velvet Cake
Hummingbird Bakery, 133 Portobello Road, London W11 (tel: +44 207 229 6446, www.hummingbirdbakery.com). Cupcakes as big as your fist and the most decadent Red Velvet Cake in town. There's also a branch in South Kensington, 47 Old Brompton Road, London SW7 (tel: +44 207 584 0055) if you need a fix and you're in that area.

Lunch (and cakes)
Ottolenghi, 63 Ledbury Road, London, W11 (tel: +44 207 727 1121, www.ottolenghi.co.uk). The salads are to die for and the roast chicken and the desserts. Treat yourself to their cookbook and a cake for being so righteous. There are two bigger branches in Kensington and Angel.

Organic supplies
Planet Organic, 42 Westbourne Grove, London W2 (tel: +44 207 727 2227, www.planetorganic.com) A great spot to pick up organic dinner supplies and stock tons of natural beauty products (there are two other branches in Bloomsbury and Fulham.)

Ginger bread men
Tom's Deli, 226 Westbourne Grove, London, W11 (tel: +44 207 221 8818, www.tomsdelilondon.co.uk) A mahussive range of foodie type treats to bring home after a great day's shopping. I love this place.

EAST LONDON

(Nearest tubes Aldgate East; Old Street; Liverpool Street

Sleep Budget

The Hoxton, 81 Great Eastern Street, London, EC2 (tel: +44 207 550 1000, www.hoxtonhotels.com). What can I say that will in any way do justice to the Hoxton. It is totally fab! A five-minute walk from Old Street tube on the Northern Line (take exit three when leaving the station) this design hotel not only looks great but guess what? It's totally affordable too. There's a great lobby for chillin, a bar and a restaurant. And the rooms? When checking in, try to get a room on the third, fourth of fifth floor looking onto Willow Street (it's nice and quiet). Amenities in the room are good: tea and coffee-making facilities, a large bar of Pears soap, a five-foot bed, a flat screen TV, a good shower with a mahussive nozzle and free wi-fi. It's incredible. So how much does it cost G? From £1 on special offer days on the internet to £49. The most you'll ever pay is £149 when the hotel is busy. The trick here is to book early. I've had so much fun at this hotel, it's my favourite place in my favourite part of town.

Spanish food

Moro, 34 - 36 Exmouth Market, EC1R (tel: +44 207 833 8336, www. moro.co.uk)

Secret tea/oysters

Jones Dairy, 23 Ezra Street, London, E2 7RH (tel: +44 207 739 5372, www.jonesdairy.co.uk) This is a hidden little café in the archway which serves good tea and cake. Just outside there's usually a stand selling fresh oysters. Only open on Sundays.

Breakfast and grocery

The Grocery Cafe, 54 - 56 Kingsland Road, Shoreditch, E2 (tel:+44 207 729 6855, www.thegroceryshop.co.uk) has friendly staff, free wireless and great food. Does it get any better? Yes indeed it does, breakfast is served all day with eggs any style - £2 for yummy toast and soldiers (toast has barbecue marks on it and everything). There are also salads, soup, great desserts and organic juices. Snailey love it here. Their grocery also do good fruit, unprocessed, organic seasonal food and a range of beauty and home organic goodies make this one of my favourite places to buy supplies.

Deep Fried Calamari

Lee Seafood, Columbia Road, London E2 7RG. Order a little Styrofoam cup of the best deep-fried calamari from this little window overlooking the Columbia Road Flower Market. Only on Sundays too.

24 hour beigels

Brick Lane Beigel Bake, 159 Brick Lane, London E1 (tel: +44 207 729 0616). There are two bagel places next door to each other on Brick Lane, facing them you want the one with the white sign. It's open all night for bagels, cream cheese, salt beef and builder's tea. My friend MJar and I often drop in on early Sunday mornings.

Old world charm

A. Gold, 42 Brushfield Street, London, E1 6AG (tel: +44 207 247 2487), Pink sugar mice, assorted sweets, stacks of biscuit tins, Campbell's Tea, Dundee fruitcake and Dolly Smith's Brinjal Indian-style pickle are but a few of the British treats to be found in this little gem of a shop.

Treasure trove

Beedell Coram, 86 Commercial Street, London E1 (tel: +44 798155 9601), I was stopped in my tracks by the antique bell jars in the window, like the ones used in Dover Street Market for the taxidermy, I wanted the lot and everything else in this little place. I bought some antique medicine bottles, aren't they beautiful?

Treat yourself

Verde & Company, 40 Brushfield Street, London E1 (tel: +44 207 247 1924). Outside boxes of vegetables and inside sandwiches, coffee, soup, and high quality delicatessen goods are sold in an old curiosity shop setting. Copper kitchen implements fight for space alongside an old grandfather clock, homemade chutneys, jams and Pierre Marcolini chocolates. The author Jeanette Winterson owns the building and lives upstairs, it's magic!

Flowers

Columbia Road Flower Market, London, E2 7RG You want Cockney slang? There's plenty of it here as well as cut flowers and plants and streets lined with little homeware shops.

Perfume

Angela Flanders Aromatics, 96 Columbia Road, E2 (tel: +44 207 739 7555) Angela Flanders' pretty Victorian perfumery is in the thick of Columbia Road's flower market.

Artbooks

Artwords Bookshop, 65A Rivington Street, EC2A (tel: +44 207 729 2000, www.artwords.co.uk) A great little place to browse the most eclectic of titles featuring photography, illustration and art.

The biz!

Labour and Wait, 18 Cheshire Street, EC2 6EH (tel: +44 207 729 6253, www.labourandwait.co.uk) even the string and wooden pencil cases are cute here. This is the place to buy a pink little saucepan for boiling your egg in the morning or this Marseille soap, £4.

EaT

My favourite dining experiences in London

St John's Bread and Wine, 94-96 Commercial Street, London, E1 (tel: +44 207 251 0848, www.stjohnbreadandwine.com) near Spitalfields. It's where I love to have lunch. Try the cockscomb, hispi or the perfect bacon sandwich. For dinner I go with friends to its bigger sister in Clerkenwell St John's bar & Restaurant.

St John's bar & Restaurant, 26 St John Street, Smithfield, London, EC1 (tel:+44 20 7251 0848, www.stjohnbreadandwine.com) is a wonderful restaurant. Snailey loves the staff in both of these places, full of smiles they are and the food is superbly sourced and cooked, the Fergus Henderson soulful way ("nose to tail" is his philosophy – use every part of the animal), they serve everything from gulls eggs, chitterlings to roast bone marrow and parsley salad. Roast squirrel anyone? It blows my mind. If you eat nowhere else in London, try these two places first (and no, I haven't bought shares in the company!) Fergus Henderson's food is fan-bloody-tastic!

And guess what? One of the dessert choices at St John's Bread and Wine was an Eccles Cake & Lancashire Cheese. I love the taste of cheese and currents together. Why not try some Lancashire cheese with my current scone recipe on page 254?

Bistrotheque, 23-27 Wadeson Street, London E2 (tel: +44 208 983 7900, www. bistrotheque.com). Great food, super after-dinner drag cabaret in the basement, a top notch spot where you'll find me most weekends with friends if I'm not at....

Tayyabs, 83-89 Fieldgate Street, London E1 (020 7247 6400, www.tayyabs.co.uk). Forget Brick lane, this Pakistani restaurant hidden away in a secluded street in Whitechapel, is one of my very favourite secret places to eat. To me Tayyabs is special and here's why. First it's not fancey smancey. You queue with the locals and it's bustling, (top marks for atmosphere here), second you bring your own wine or beer and thirdly there's the food... the best spicy lamb chops ever. Also the chicken tikka (very tender), seekh kebabs (succulence meat with a green-chilli kick) and their freshly baked rotis, parathas and a keema naan (bread stuffed with minced lamb) go to make one of tastiest meals you're likely to ever encounter. It's a unique dining experience too and for no more than £20 it a great place to go with close pals. Please go, I guarantee you'll love it! I do because it's unique!

St. JOHN

BREAD and WINE

Malletti, 174-176 Clerkenwell Road, London, EC1 (tel: +44 207 713 8665). Extremely good thin-based pizza, a slice costs £3.35. The ingredients are quality and toppings change daily. It's like having a little slice of Naples in the East. There's also a branch in Soho 26 Noel St, London W1F (tel: +44 207 439 4096) both close on weekends but on weekdays you'll find Mr. Malletti senior in the Soho branch. He's great.

Rochelle Canteen, Rochelle School, Arnold Circus, London E2 (tel: +44 20 7729 5677, www.arnoldandhenderson.com) London's best-kept lunch secret, Rochelle Canteen has great food cooked simply. Margot Henderson runs this fantastic lunchtime restaurant set in the A-Foundation which is a resource for artists in a lovely Victorian school in London's East End. It's open Monday to Friday 9.30am to 4pm Lunch 12 to 3pm. It's as good as The River Café here.

Mangal Ocakbasi, 10 Arcola Street, E8, (tel: +44 207 275 8981, www.mangal1.com), go for the lamb, it's great, and if you're lucky you might spot the artists Gilbert and George they're here every day.

Worth leaving the East for, a trip to...

The Anchor and Hope, The Cut, Waterloo, London SE1 (tel:+44 207 928 9898). It's a gastropub with great, great food, if you can get a table that is (there's no booking, so you just have to wait patiently). If all else fails here's a tip Monday/Tuesday/Wednesday try afternoon time around 2.15pm or the same days around 9.45pm at night. And you can book Sunday lunch for a 2pm sit down to a set three course menu. Food is very good here, as is the wine.

Story Deli, 3 Dray Walk, The Old Truman Brewery, 91 Brick Lane, London E1 (tel: +44 207 247 3137). Story Deli is my most favourite communal table in London, and its organic pizzas are unbeatable! From coming here I now know all the staff and owners and Snailey loves them, smiles galore here. You can taste the truth in these pizzas and the atmosphere of sitting with friends at their communal tables while London hustles past onto Brick Lane. A really lovely spot any time of the year.

New York

Of all the cities, New York moves the fastest for me, too fast to be understood; in fact I always experience a sort of vertigo here, looking, up, up, up and then just when you think you've captured it, it dances away. The Manhattan skyline for first, second and even fifteenth timers (ahem), is still the most exciting thing for me, be all that as it may, I needed to stop looking up and start looking around me; I contacted a few of my friends who were locals there and the hunt was on.

"So how can you tell a real New Yorker?", I asked. "Not by their love of a favourite slice (pizza) but by a genuine attachment to Gray's Papaya, 402 Sixth Avenue, 539 Eighth Avenue 2090 Broadway.", I was told. This name is a New York institution, the skinny little hot dog sold at Gray's three eat-at-the-counter locations legendary among locals. The daaaaaaaawg, snaps "just-right" when you take a bite, and the buns are sinfully crusty. "This is what you look for in the perfect daaaaaaaaawg." The papaya namesake drink (guess what it's made from?) Papaya. Yes, well is nice too. A great little experience this one.

Where to start

Barneys, 660 Madison Avenue, New York, NY 10021 (tel: +1 212 826 8900). Bergdorf Goodman, 754 5th Avenue (58th Street), New York, NY10019 (tel: +1 212 753 7300). Henri Bendel, 712 5th Avenue, New York, NY 10019 (tel: +1 212 247 1100). Saks Fifth Avenue, 611 Fifth Avenue (between 49th and 50th Streets), New York, (US tel: +1 877 551 7257; international calls tel: +1 601 592 2860, www.saksfifthavenue.com). Takashimaya 693 5th Avenue, New York, NY 10022 (tel: +1 212 350 0100, www.takashimaya-ny.com). The origami packaging, is worth a purchase here alone.

The best blow dry

P.S. If you do decide to have a blow out (US tern for a blow dry), Shalom Sharon, 63 E 7th Street, 10003 (tel: +1 212 529 6712, www.shalomsharonhair.com) in the East Village is a god. It costs $65 including tip (a fat one) and he is FAB. He is a session stylist, one of Guido Paulo's protégés, and his salon has just two chairs. He cuts there on the days when he isn't shooting, to call ahead and ask if he's there, this a real insider tip, he's super talented.

Take skating lessons

$30 for a half hour's private tuition at the Rockefeller Centre Ice Rink, 5th Avenue between 49th and 50th streets, New York, NY 10020 (tel: +1 212 332 7654 for info and +1 212 332 7655 to book skating lessons, www.therinkatrockcenter. com). Re-opens for the season in October 2008.

Picture this

B&H photo, 420 9th Avenue, New York, NY 10001, (tel: +1 212 444 6700, www.bhphotovideo. com). I've been visitng New York For years and in the course of my to-ing and fro-ing, I've visited B&H many times. They sell equipment to just about everyone (even professional fashion photographers). This place is a mahussive 35,000sq store stuffed with all types of cameras (from state-of-the-art digital to vintage models). The store is owned and run by Orthodox Jews so plan your trip here anyday other then a Saturday.

Sleep

Sleep Luxury

The Gramercy Park Hotel, 2 Lexington Avenue, New York, NY 10010 (tel: +1 212 920 3300, www.gramercyparkhotel.com). Redesigned by Ian Schrager and the artist Julian Schnabel, The Gramercy even has its bars double as galleries for paintings by Andy Warhol, Jean-Michel Basquiat, and Cy Twombly. And an added bonus is that all guests are allowed entry to the exclusive, quiet, privately keyed Gramercy Park, just outside. Rooms start at $755. Tip: call and make reservations at the Rose Bar for cocktails as soon as you check in.

Sleep Luxury

The Mercer, at Prince & Mercer (tel: +1 212 966 6060, www.mercerhotel.com) in Soho is my favourite hotel in New York. Room 507 is my favourite room here, I just open up the windows and let the soud of bustling Soho float in from below. Everything I love is within walking distance. Room rate $640.

Sleep – Midrange

The Gaansvoort, 18 Ninth avenue, (tel: 212 206 6700, www. hotelgansevoort.com) not only has good rooms but a wonderful basement spa for pedis and manis which transforms into a club by night. Although the roof bar is still popular, the basement is the Manhattan velvet rope to slip past. A hotel key doesn't guarantee entry so arrange it upon check-in with the concierge. Room rate $450

EaT

Breakfast

On the Upper East Side there's Via Quadronno, 23rd E. 73rd Street (tel: +1 212 650 9880, www.vqnyc.com) (serves the best cappuccinos, espressos and flakey croissants in town) and Sant Ambroeus, 1000 Madison Avenue near 77th Street (tel: +1 212 570 22 11, www.santambroeus.com) for great breakfast coffee. In the meatpacking district there's Pastis, and Soho House, 29-35 9th Avenue, between 13th and 14th Street (tel:+1 212 627 9800, www.sohohouseny.com) a few doors up from it. In the West Village there Café Cluny, 284 West 12th Street (tel: +1 212 255 6900, www.cafecluny. com) and a downtown branch of Sant Ambroeus, 259 West 4th Street (tel: +1 212 604 9254, www.santambroeus.com), and in SoHo there's Balthazar, 80 Spring Street (tel: +1 212 965 1414, www.balthazarny.com).

Lunch

Grimaldi's pizza under the Brooklyn Bridge, 19 Old Fulton Street, Williamsburg, New York (tel: +1 718 858 4300). The best. The Burger Joint at Le Parker Meridien, 118 West 57th Street (tel: +1 212 245 5000, www.parkermeridien.com). Open 11 a.m.–11.30 p.m. (midnight Friday and Saturday). Shake Shack, Southeast corner of Madison Square Park, near Madison Avenue and East 23rd Street (tel: +1 212 889 6600, www.shakeshacknyc.com).

Lobstaaaa lunch

The lobster roll from this New York institution was the first thing on Tony Soprano lips when he came out of a coma in The Sopranos. Pearl Oyster Bar, 18 Cornelia Street, New York. NY 10014 tel: 212.691.8211.

Titbit

For New York-style lobster rolls, fill a warm, crusty baguette with chunks of cooked, beautiful lobster meat, mixed with chopped avocado, chopped scallions, some mayonnaise, a squeeze of lime juice and chopped tarragon

Meaty Subject

Shake Shack, Southeast corner of Madison Square Park, (tel: +1 212 889 6600, www.shakeshacknyc.com).

Picnic

The brownie ice-cream sandwiches, $5 each at Bierkraft, 191 Fifth Avenue Brooklyn, New York, NY 11217 (tel: +1 212 718 230 7600, www.bierkraft.com) for a truly decadent treat to take to the park on a picnic. The store also caries 250 artisan cheeses, over 100 gourmet chocolate bars and over 900 beers. 95 Orchard Street, (between Broome & Delancey Streets), New York, NY 10002 (tel +1 212 343 9922, www.labatoriodelgelato.com). Picnic in Prospect Park anyone?

Dinner

Matsuri, The Maritime Hotel, 363 West16 th Street, New York, NY 10011 (tel: +1 212 242 4300, www.themaritimehotel.com) and pop outside for cocktails to La Bottega. Morandi, 211 Waverly Place, New York, NY 10014 (tel: +1 212 627 7575, www. morandiny.com). An Italian joint owned by Keith McNally (of Pastis and Balthazar fame). The Spinach and ricotta ravioli with sage butter and my juicy roasted veal chop (at $45, yikes, it's the most expensive the menu) was very yum!
The River Café, 1 Water Street, Brooklyn (tel: +1 718 522 5200, www.rivercafe.com) has a spectacular view of Manhattan and good French food. The tablecloths are like white foldey cake icing they're so nice.

Cupcakes

Magnolia Bakery, Bleecker Street, New York 10014-2452 (tel: +1 212 462 2572, www.magnoliacupcakes.com). Magnolia Bakery, 200 Columbus Avenue, (tel: 001 212 724 8101) speaking of which…
Sugar Sweet Sunshine Bakery, 126 Rivington St, New York, NY 10003 (tel: +1 212 995 1960, www.sugarsweetsunshine.com). Owners Peggy and Debbie (former employees of the 'other' bakery) create the finest pistachio cupcakes on the planet; the icing alone is worth the trip. Other delights include comfy chairs and a Red Velvet cake that's indescribably good.
Billy's Bakery, 184 9th Avenue, New York, NY 10011 (tel: +1 212 647 9956, www.billysbakerynyc.com) for delicious $2 cupcakes. Yummm!

Communal Table

ABC Carpet and Home 888 Broadway at East 19th Street, New York, NY 10003, near Union Square, (tel: +1 212 473 3000, www.abchome.com) I like poking around here and their restaurant, Le Pain Quotidien, has a communal table that I have on my wish list as my new dining table.

Buy

Helena Christensen's fave

Castor & Pollux, 238 West 10th Street, New York, NY 10014 (tel:+1 212 645 6572, www.castorand-polluxstore.com). From the display cases taken from the fur department at Bergdorf Goodman retaining thier former glory, to the Castor & Pollux logo-wear inspired by a long time love of horses, this is one of Helena Christensen's favourite shops. Nuff said!

Urban Goddess Streetwear

Alife Rivington Club, 158 Rivington Street (tel:+ 1 212 375 8128 www.alifenyc.com). Seriously, if Nike made only a few hundred pairs of trainers, then they'd be nowhere else but here. Dave's Quality Meat, 7 East 3rd Street, New York, NY 10003 (tel: +1 212 505 7551, www.davesqualitymeat.com). Dope kicks, skateboards and graff tees. Ssur plus, 7 Spring Street, New York, NY 10012 (tel:+1 212 431 3152, http://www.ssurempirestate.com). Quality streetwear. Stussy, 140 Wooster Street, New York, NY 10012 (tel: +1 212 995 8787, www.stussy.com). Excellet for tees and hoodies. Vice, 252 Lafayette Street, between Prince and Houston Streets, SoHo (tel:+1 212 219 7788). Owned by the creators of Vice magazine, you know exactly the vibe, jeans, tees etc. And more dos than don'ts.

Books

Freebird Books & Goods, 123 Columbia St., near. Kane Street., Red Hook (tel: +1 718-643-8484), sit back on a comfy couch or visit the garden café and chose from their classics, nostalgic manuals, journals and thousands of zines.

192 Books, 192 10th Avenue on 21st Street, New York City (tel:+1 212 255 4022, www.192books.com). For unusual, hard to find titles, and unique things.

Global trinkets

Kiosk Kiosk, 95 Spring Street, 2nd Floor, New York, NY 10012 (tel: +1 212 226 5155, www.kioskkiosk.com). The most amazing kitchen finds from across the globe and a fantastic website too.

Great accessories

Pixie Market, 100 Stanton St; between Orchard & Ludlow, New York, NY 10002 (tel: +1 212 253 0953, www.pixiemarket.com). The house label is Maud but it's the Rheanna Lingham jewellery and AM Eyewear that I'm infatuated with. Drool!

New Shoes

Jeffrey, 449 West 14th Street, between 9th and 10th Avenue, New York, NY 10014 (tel: +1 212 206 1272, www.jeffreynewyork.com) for stunning shoes.

Petal pusher

Denise Porcaro's Flower shop at Ernest Sewn, 90 Orchard Street, New York, NY 10002 (tel: +1 212 979 5120; www.earnestsewn.com) is a superb place to pick up a bunch of blooms.

Limited Edition pieces

Albertine, 13 Christopher Street , New York City (tel: +1 212 924 8515, www. albertine-nyc.com) is one of three stores owned by the talented fashion eye Kyung Lee. The others are **Claudine**, 19 Christopher Street, New York City (tel:+1 212 414 4234) and **Leontine**, 226 Front Street, New York City (tel: +1 212 766 1066). These stores resemble doll's houses stuffed with ultra feminine styles from up and coming designers. **Anna**, 150 East 3rd Street, New York, NY 10009 (tel: +1 212 358 0195, www.annanyc.com). Kathy Kemp the designer/owner has been labelled as the new Diane von Furstenburg of New York and creates dresses truly fit for a Goddess.

Markets

Abingdon Square Greenmarket, Hudson Street, between West 12th & Bethune Streets, New York, NY 10014 (tel: +1 212 477 3220). Open Saturday 8am-1pm. **Essex Street Market**, 80 Essex Street, New York, NY 10002 (tel: +1 212 388 0449, www.essexstreetmarket. com). Open Monday to Saturday 8am-7pm. **Fort Greene Park Greenmarket**, Washington Park Avenue, between DeKalb & Willoughby Streets, Brooklyn, New York (tel: +1 212 477 3220). Open Saturday 8am-5pm. **Grand Army Plaza Greenmarket**, Northwest entrance to Prospect Park, Brooklyn, New York, NY 11238 (tel: +1 212 477 3220). Open Saturday 8am-4pm. **The Market NYC**, 286 Mulberry Street, New York, NY10012 (tel: +1 212 604 9766, www.themarketnyc.com). Open Saturday and Sunday 11am-7pm. **Tribeca Greenmarket**, Greenwich Street, between Chambers Street and Duane Street, New York +1 212 477 3220). Open Wednesday (April to December) and Saturday (all year) 8am-3pm. **Union Square Greenmarket**, Broadway and East 17th Street at Union Square Park, New York, NY 10012 (tel: +1 212 477 3220). Open Monday, Wednesday, Friday and Saturday 8am-6pm.

Vintage

Manhattan

Eleven, 15 Prince Street, New York, NY 10012 (tel: +1 212 334 5334, www.11nyc.com). Best selection of affordable boots in the city. **Dulcinee**, 127 Stanton Street, West Storefront, New York, NY 10002 (tel: +1 212 253 2534, www.dulcineenyc.com). Small, but a super selection of vintage Italian handbags and shoes, great coats, tops, dresses, and skirts too. **Edith and Daha**, 104 Rivington Street, New York, NY 10002 (tel: +1 212 979 9992). Best selection of vintage shoes and accessories in the city. Boots can cost anything from $80 and $95. .

Brooklyn

Blueberi 143 Front Street. Brooklyn, New York, NY 11201, (tel:+1 718 422 7724) just off the F train at york st. in dumbo, Blueberi features up and coming designers paired with the occasional vintage piece. **Beacon's Closet**, Williamsburg Store: 88 n, 11th Street, Brooklyn, New York, NY 11211; Park Slope Store: 220 5th Avenue, Brooklyn, New York, NY 11215 (www.beaconscloset.com). No list of vintage/second-hand clothing stores in NYC is complete without Beacon's. **Amarcord**, 223 Bedford Avenue, Brooklyn, New York, NY 11211 (tel: +1 718 963 4001). Amarcord stocks a host of well-selected pieces, the Italian pieces that turn up here are particularly great.

Hat trick

Eccentric millinery rules now, so avant-garde designer Gemma Kahng is one to buy a hat from: 232 West 37th Street, 2fl, New York, NY 10018 (tel: +1 212 868 6887, (www.gemmakahng.com).

New York does the greatest sample sales ever, great stores like...

Opening Ceremony, 35 Howard Street, New York, NY 10013 (tel: +1 212 219 2688, www.openingceremony.us). Steven Alan, 103 Franklin Street, New York, NY 10013 (tel: +1 212 343 0392, www.stevenalancollection.com).

One-off dresses

Ever since it quietly opened it doors four years ago No. 6, 6 Centre Market Place, between Broom and Grand Streets, New York, NY 10014 (tel: +1 212 226 5759, www.no6store.com), has been the best vintage boutique to hit New York. Some of the dresses are vintage and the No.6 designed dresses are all one-off pieces tweaked from vintage dresses ($130 to $245).

Listen to this... if Brooklyn was an independent city, it would be the fourth largest in the US. Isn't that mental? Just across the East River from Manhattan, much of the Williamsburg section of Brooklyn was industrial until the 1980s. As manufacturers moved out, artists moved in and now Brooklyn has become a byword for creativity.

Small boutiques that offer that Brooklyn individuality

Bird, 220 Smith Street, Cobble Hill, Brooklyn (tel: +1 718 797 3774) and 430 Seventh Avenue, Park Slope, Brooklyn (+1 718 768 4940, www. shopbird.com) Butter, 407 Atlantic Avenue, between Bond & Nevins Streets, Brooklyn (tel: +1 718 260 9033).Killer shoes and lots of Dries van Noten and the like. Ylli, 482 Driggs Avenue, Williamsburg, Brooklyn (tel: + 1 718 302 3555 www.yllibklyn.com). Dear Fieldbinder, 198 Smith Street, Cobble Hill, Brooklyn (tel: +1 718 852 3620, www.dearfieldbinder.com). Jumelle, 148 Bedford Avenue,Williamsburg, Brooklyn (tel: +1 718 388 9525, www. shopjumelle.com). Stuart & Wright, 85 Lafayette Avenue, Fort Greene, Brooklyn (tel: +1 718 797 0011, www. stuartandwright.com). Hip men's and women's clothing from two Steven Alan alumni. Suite Orchard, 145A Orchard Street at Rivington Street (tel:+1 212 533 4115).Girl-meets-rock style by Sonia and Cindy Huang.

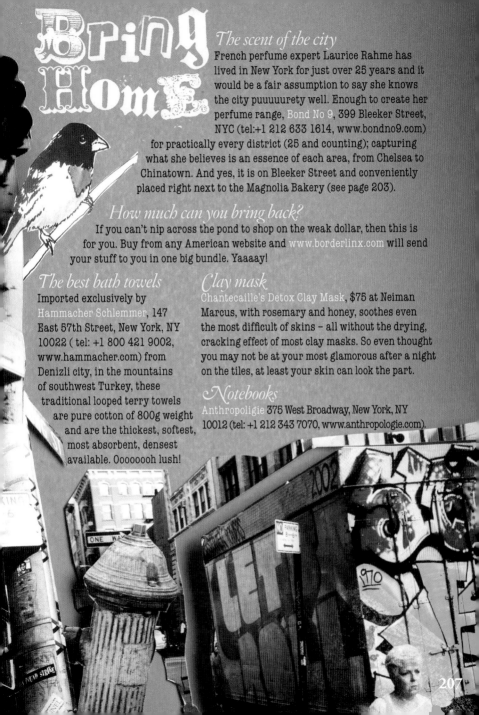

Bring Home

The scent of the city

French perfume expert Laurice Rahme has lived in New York for just over 25 years and it would be a fair assumption to say she knows the city puuuuurety well. Enough to create her perfume range, Bond No 9, 399 Bleeker Street, NYC (tel:+1 212 633 1614, www.bondno9.com) for practically every district (25 and counting); capturing what she believes is an essence of each area, from Chelsea to Chinatown. And yes, it is on Bleeker Street and conveniently placed right next to the Magnolia Bakery (see page 203).

How much can you bring back?

If you can't nip across the pond to shop on the weak dollar, then this is for you. Buy from any American website and www.borderlinx.com will send your stuff to you in one big bundle. Yaaaay!

The best bath towels

Imported exclusively by Hammacher Schlemmer, 147 East 57th Street, New York, NY 10022 (tel: +1 800 421 9002, www.hammacher.com) from Denizli city, in the mountains of southwest Turkey, these traditional looped terry towels are pure cotton of 800g weight and are the thickest, softest, most absorbent, densest available. Oooooooh lush!

Clay mask

Chantecaille's Detox Clay Mask, $75 at Neiman Marcus, with rosemary and honey, soothes even the most difficult of skins – all without the drying, cracking effect of most clay masks. So even thought you may not be at your most glamorous after a night on the tiles, at least your skin can look the part.

Notebooks

Anthropoligie 375 West Broadway, New York, NY 10012 (tel: +1 212 343 7070, www.anthropologie.com).

Hmmmmmmm. Home. To me the stuff of forts; the bed, the bath, the table, the couch, scraps of experience scavenged, brought home and put on display, dotted carefully about the place. Things, loaded with meaning, even the telly… by the way, is anyone still watching LOST? I'm guessing yes. Actually I've not been as keen on it lately; I couldn't get to grips with the fact that the passengers lost everything when Oceanic 815 crashed on that island and they still manage to look buff. It made me think. What if I lost everything in a plane crash? But never mind that, because I didn't need reminding as I boarded a plane from JFK (goodbye skyscrapers, hummers and Barack Obama, and hello my own bed).

Upon arriving home I jammed the key in the front door and it made that special clicky 'I'm Home' sound; closing it behind me it gave a unique little bang and a shudder. Have you ever noticed how putting the key in your front door and closing it behind you has sounded uniquely different in every house you've even lived and loved in? That tickled me to begin with… then I ran inside, and taking the stairs two at a time, piled my cases into my bedroom and flopped down on my bed and let out a relieved sigh. Lovely. Get sorted, get comfy, but back downstairs first.

I poked around the darkest recesses of the fridge and kitchen cupboards; there's always a respectable stash of chocolate biscuits tucked behind the rice cakes, so I found them before even reaching for a light switch – I have a blueprint in my head and know every inch of the walls and every floorboard. I flicked on a lamp and rifled through the post, the formula never varies in the coming home bit; I like it that way, I potter around in comfort and it's safe.

After the first few minutes of busy activity I paused and instantly felt like a trespasser, a cautious little trespasser, scanning every book, every picture, and every object to check that their stories were straight.

I eyed the lamps and, chewing a biscuit cautiously, I stopped 'Oh dear,' I mumbled, 'I don't like the look of this.' A pot plant looked crooked even though the space around it looked like a bombsite. Had there been a robbery? No, thank God. The message? Think, Gisèle, how lucky you were this time. All of this took place in about five minutes but it caused me to question the value of 'home'.

Around this point I said, 'this is weird, I've never come across this before.' as a thought in my head reasoned that home was more than just bricks and mortar, fancy wallpaper and a Smeg fridge. What if I took all of my stuff and moved it to another house? Where would home be then? The new house or the old house? Quick, Gisèle, think fast. I was standing in the place where I had accumulated two years of life's private experiences, so that was a start. It's where I cooked, ate, slept, woke, washed, played, made love, shared with friends, painted and wrote. It was a hiding place under the duvet, a ticking radiator when it was time to get up, a broken door latch in the garden, a creaky floorboard in the kitchen and a place I kept coming back to because that's where all my stuff was; the scratched chopping-board, my antique bed linen, my sketchbooks, my spoons.

Here in the half light my eyes focused on a tiny brown chair sitting in the corner. I'd had it since I was a baby and my dad gave it to me when I was 'home' last year. It reminded me instantly of my other home, the one I grew up in, a house in the south west of Ireland; the memories brought tears to my eyes. 'I'm going home for the weekend' always means I'm going to my parent's house. We all say it, don't we, and no one objects because they understand. But often I cannot get there and in its place I have this little chair. I have it and some other little things that make my life feel comfortable, warm and balanced – in the absence of my parents. In other words, they help me feel like I'm at home.

For the past two years I've travelled a lot, worked hard and learned to relax among my familiar childhood objects: a purple blanket, some antique pillowcases, a Cornish blue jug that belonged to my grandmother and books, huge piles of them that go back generations; every wall is lined with them and my home smells of an old library, full of leather and wood. The chair, though that's a piece of me from childhood, is very, very special. The house, I realized, was mere bricks and mortar, so apart from the little chair what else would I need to make it home? I wonder…?

Ex's

Recapture the hotel at home

'Home' is my own bed

So, back in my own bed, oooooooo, I love it. I feel that no matter how unsettled life becomes, there's one constant, one fixed place I adore. After returning from travelling, I long to sleep in my own bed, under my own duvet, on my own pillow. The first night back from travelling I dreamt of the beautiful places that had inspired me to personalize my bedroom.

Wish list

1. A beautiful fairy tale bed? 2. A treasured antique mirror? 3. A soft, silk pillow? 4. A beautiful fairy tale bed again? You've guessed it – hotel living, it felt very Goddessey, so I brought my wish list home…

My pillowcase felt stiff

My detergent was to blame. I added half a cup of baking soda to the wash – it's an excellent fabric softener – and I had super soft linen to dream on.

A Fairytale bed

I found a beautiful bed at La Maison, 107-108 Shoreditch High Street, London, E1 (tel: +44 207 729 9646, www.atlamaison. com). Their beds are unbelievably gorgeous and they hand make their mattresses.

Beautiful boudoir walls

One of my favourite pals, Mjar, introduced me to hip Shoreditch hair salon, Taylor Taylor, 137 Commercial Street, London, E1 (tel: +44 207 377 2737, www.taylortaylorlondon. com). I fancied my bedroom as a decadent French boudoir after seeing this wondrous place and being inspired. They have a 24 foot chandelier from BoDoMo (I know, wow, but for smaller ones see next page). They have a wall mural by Sacha Cohen (tel: +44 (0)7973 764943) that makes me gasp every time I pass the window. I know asking an artist to paint a mural might be a bit la-di-da but Sacha Cohen is a genius; her books on customizing your walls, from www.amazon.co.uk, help me dream.

Furniture

Taylor Taylor (same salon, different day) also has a chaise longue from Squint (see p00) and an aviary from the furniture shop Eccentricities, 46 Essex Road, Islington, London, N1 (tel: +44 207 359 5633), which contains two love birds that sing while you have your hair cut. Cool or what? I ached to buy a bird cage from a market (see p00) for my bedroom and fill it with books and antique bottles (Liberty does lovely old cologne bottles for about £23, tel: +44 207 734 1234, www.liberty.co.uk).

My feather pillow felt flat

I did what French viniculturists do? (No not French ventriloquists but viniculturists – wine makers to you and me). I took my pillows, popped them in a bath full of warm water and a mild detergent and treaded on them with my bare feet. This removed dirt and got the water and detergent through all the feathers. I spun them one by one in the washing machine and dried them naturally outside. They were cuddlier than ever.

Air con (no need)

Are you cold but your partner's roasting hot in bed? Check out the Chili Pad $999 (www.chilitechnology.com), for your own sleep experience, a matress pad which heats or cools seperate sides of the bed.

Titbit

Keep cold draughts at bay with a door curtain, which gives an extra layer of warmth to a room.

Silky sleep

What? You didn't know that sleeping on silk pillows and sheets prevents eye wrinkles and is good for your hair follicles? It's also hypoallergenic and won't mess up your hair like cotton does. You'll find silk pillows, £99.50 each (£179 for two), and pillowcases, £31 (55.80 for two), at Silkwood Silk (tel: +44 (0)7970 115557, www.silkwoodsilk.com). Also, try Gingerlily (tel:+44 (0)870 116 1368, www.gingerlily.co.uk) where a silk filled pillow costs £65 and a pillowcase £69. Gingerlily also does silk duvets, £190, as does Graham and Green (tel: +44 (0)845 130 6622, www.grahamandgreen.co.uk). You only need one to sleep on and the rest of your pillows can be feather. Smooooth!

An antique mirror

The hotels I stayed in always seemed bright (light makes me happy), so I got a large gilded antique mirror from Artefact, 273 Lillie Road, London, SW6 (tel: +44 207 381 2500). Popped about the house, mirrors reflect light into dark corners. Small ones look good on steps of stairs.

LET THERE BE LIGHT

A chandelier

Rainbow, 329 Lillie Road, Fulham, London SW6 (tel: +44 207 385 1323, www.rainbowlondon.com) are one of the best in London selling original Italian antique crystal chandeliers and reproductions which can be made to any size from £150 to £5000. Jones Antique Lighting, 194 Westbourne Grove, Notting Hill, London, W11, (tel: +44 207 229 6866, www.jonesantiquelighting.com) is also excellent. BoDoMo (tel: +44 (0) 845 643 2047, www. bodomo.biz) Want a chandelier like the one in Robbie Williams Rock DJ video? These guys supplied it along with chandeliers for Fifteen (Jamie Oliver's restaurant) and Alexander McQueen among others.

Cleaning a chandelier

Always turn off the power before cleaning a chandelier and make sure the circuit breaker is isolated. You will need some goggles, a lambswool duster, a spray bottle of water and vinegar mixed together in equal measures, little plastic bags and elastic bands, an umbrella and a stepladder. Dust the chandelier first. Then cover each light fitting with a small plastic bag secured with a rubber band so liquid doesn't get down into the electrical wiring. Hang the umbrella underneath it, hooking the handle over one of the arms of the chandelier. Spray the crystals thoroughly with the vinegar solution until they drip. The umbrella will catch all the dirty water. I feel a Del Boy moment coming on…

Lamp

Getting splodge-free mascara, flawless foundation and perfect brows seems easy in a hotel room because of the correct lighting installed around the mirrors. At home as the winter draws in it gets harder and harder to find the right light for the job. Position a lamp on your dressing table and simply remove the shade and use the light from the bare bulb to apply your make-up. It's as good as daylight as the winter mornings draw in and measn you won't end up with the dreaded two-tone jaw-line.

Scent you room like a beautiful hotel

Lovely hotels usually burn a scented signature scented candles like
Claridges in London, The Carlyle in New York and Hotel Costes or
Hotel Bourg Tibourg in Paris (the last is my favourite candle scent
by the way see p13). Anyway you don't even have to stay in these
hotels you can buy the candles in their gift departments, as well as
smelling beautiful the light from candles is beautiful too.

How come glass surfaces always look perfect in hotels?

It is possible to stop the build-up of lint and dust on glass-top
tables and other glass surfaces, using the following method:
add one tablespoon of liquid fabric-softener to about a litre
of warm water, then use a damp cloth to wash and coat the
surface with the solution. Not only will the fabric-softener
clean the glass, it will also help to prevent lint from gathering
again. This method can also used to keep computer screens
and TVs dust-free, although you should make sure that any
electrical appliance is switched off first.

LINEN

'Home' is... comfy blankets, snugly quilts and fresh, fresh linen sheets, tablecloths and napkins. Ohhhhhhhhh! Is it wrong to get this excited about sheets?

Ironing

The dreaded ironing! Firstly, I hear you say... Do I have to? Life's too short and it's perfectly fine to wash linen sheets, dry them and put them straight back on the bed, G. Yes I agree, but for hotel-style perfection, my little soldiers, iron we must (think beautifully pressed linen sheets, table cloths, napkins, drooool) so let's crack on and it won't hurt as much, I promise. I must confess I hate ironing too, not like vacuuming (I love that), so anything that will make it go quicker (radio, TV – watch the fingers don't get too caught up in Bones – and listening to a good book on tape) all good ideas.

Easy peasy ironing breezy

Iron linen while still damp (I find it's much easier to get rid of stubborn creases) – then fold and put in an airing cupboard or somewhere warm so it dries completely. Use a steam iron – the one below is the business - takes out creases fast as lightening. Linen water is a great invention – fragranced water that can be sprayed on as you iron. Who thought that up? Give them a Nobel prize I say. It not only helps take out creases but adds cherry uppage to the chore because it smells nice. Oooooooo! Don't get too caught up on the chess board creases which appear on sheets, duvet covers or table cloths that have been folded after ironing. I've seen this on sheets even in the snazziest of hotels. I don't really mind it, what do you feel?

If you want your table linen to say 'French bistro' use starch. It will also slightly protect the linen from staining. Ironing embroidered linen can be difficult, as the iron can get caught in the stitching and cause tears. If you place a piece of plain material over the top and iron the two together it prevents damage.

Titbit

If your linen starts to look slightly glazed, act quickly, it means your iron needs a wash. Turn off the iron, let it cool and use detergent, warm water and a cloth for non-stick irons. If your iron is not non-stick, try rubbing it with a fine-grade steel wool. The shine will disappear from the linen if you wash it again (Grooooan, I know).

214

Peacock Blue

Huge range of reasonably priced quilts, bedspreads and linen. Beautiful things. Made from silk and stitched by hand, their double quilt, £155, goes straight onto the happy list. Peacock Blue, (tel +44 (0)845 017 5566, www.mamut.net/peacockbluehome).

Nina Campbell

Gorgeous table napkins and fabrics. Nina Campbell, 9 Walton Street, London, SW3 (tel: +44 207 225 1011, www.ninacampbell.com).

Cologne & Cotton

Beautiful bed, bath and table linen in classic designs, made from natural cotton. (tel: + 44 (0)845 262 2212, www. cologneandcotton.com)

Ian Mankin

For anything for outdoors (oilcloth tablecloths) or indoors (linen table settings) and beautiful cushions and deckchairs. His linens are lush. Ian Mankin, 109 Regents Park Road, Primrose Hill, London, NW1 (tel:+44 (0) 207 722 0997; www.ianmankinonline.co.uk).

Cabbages & Roses

Cabbage & Roses, 3 Langton Street, London, SW10 (tel: +44 207 352 7333, www.cabbagesandroses.com). You can also shop online or order a catalogue. Among the unique items on offer are gorgeous French linens, which can be made into napkins and tablecloths, rose printed linens, and aprons fit for every Home Goddess. You can also find a selection of their items in some Jigsaw stores for example the Jigsaw at 49 South Molton Street, London. (nationwide).

The White Company

Their catalogue is a must, packed full of classic timeless white and neutral accessories for bed, bath and home, including clothing, bed linen, accessories and furniture. Their gift wrapping – a white box with a black ribbon is irresistible. The White Company, 12 Marylebone High Street, London, W1U and at Selfridges (tel +44 (0)870 900 9555, www. thewhitecompany.com).

Graham & Green

From printed duvet covers to designer furniture (stand-alone travel wardrobe trunk anyone?) Graham & Green has the most beautiful products sourced from around the world. Just ogling this site makes me went to own everything (tel: +44 (0)845 130 6622, www. grahamandgreen.co.uk).

The French House

Traditional, high-quality, embroidered bed and table linen, plus kitchenware and furniture. All items are made by artisans and small family firms based in France. Toile de Jouy single quilt £117 (tel: +44 (0)870 901 4547, www.thefrenchhouse.net).

Melin Tregwynt

Cosy blankets throws and cushions woven in Wales on traditional looms are brought up to date with gorgeous colour combinations. Prices range from £21 to £226. (tel: +44 (0)134 889 1644, www.melintregwynt.co.uk).

bathe

'Home' is a peaceful bathroom

Sign

Want to have the letters b-a-t-h-e or H2O or some personal word made for your bathroom wall? Check out (www.empirevintage.com.au) where Lyn Gardener creates these bespoke letters in white, black and red.

Statement piece

Any time I've been lucky enough to stay at either of Ian Shregar's hotels in London (The Sanderson and Saint Martin's Lane) I get particularly animated about the bathrooms. Then I happened across this chap called Jaime Hayon (a Madrid-born designer who has created the Hayon Collection (www. hayonstudio.com) for Spanish bathroom company ArtQuitect (tel: +34 93 844 4070, www.artquitect.net). His black ceramic washbasin (deep breath), £2,522 comes in gold, white, platinum and canary yellow and, let's be honest, it's mad expensive, but very beautiful – the table lamp seen here on it can be converted into a magnifying shaving (make-up) mirror. Anyway, this inspired me to get cracking on making my bathroom more beautiful, as for the sink? One can only dream.

Personalize

Invest in little box mirrored glass cabinets (Habitat do them), put a little row of them on the bathroom wall and dedicate one to each member of the family for their bits and bobs. When closed, these look really tidy and keep surfaces in the bathroom free of clutter.

Keep an orchid in the bathroom

Your Phalaenopsis orchid flowers and then what? Brown sticks in a pot that's what. Leave it in the bathroom and the combination of warmth and steam means that the orchid just comes back miraculously. Try it.

Titbit

Make sure your towel dries completely between uses by putting it on a hook rather than a towel rack. Graham and Green, 340 Kings Road, London, SW3 (tel: +44 207 352 1919 or mail order tel: +44 84 5130 6622, www. grahamandgreen.co.uk) do a great range of hooks.

Power shower

Most hotels pride themselves on massive manhole cover shower heads. Pimp your own shower at home with one of these monsters:

Classic rose (30.5cm diameter), £225, from Fired Earth, 34 Cross Street, Islington, London N1 (tel: +44 207 226 9700 www.firedearth.com). Customer service (tel: +44 (0)845 366 0400).

Oki arc swivel head and arm, £249 at The Bathstore, 33 Essex Road, Islington, London, N1 (tel: +44 207 354 4442, www.bathstore.com). Customer service (tel: +44 (0)800 023 2323).

Cloudburst luxury shower head at Colourwash, 223-225 Westbourne Park Road, Notting Hill, London W11 (tel: +44 207 243 3300, www.colourwash. co.uk). It's £650 (whoaaaaa expensive. That, apparently, is what you pay to feel like you're showering under a shower of rain).

Unsightly Deposits

If you live in a hard-water area then deposits will appear on your taps and shower doors… you can shift them with an old toothbrush dipped in vinegar.

Clogged shower-head?

Unscrew the head and pop it in a bowl of vinegar for 10-15 minutes. Remove the rubber washer (be careful not to lose it), clean any sediment out of the head with an old toothbrush, then put it all back together.

Titbit

If you want softer, fluffy bath towels, add a few drops of olive oil to the final rinse of your wash. A fabric softener sheet in the tumble dryer also helps to reduces static.

Kitchen Kit

Here is a selection of what I've put on my happy list. Expect to see these pots and pans getting regular use in the Food chapter and on www.thegoddessguide.com.

A mortar and pestle

What I love about this non-porous black granite mortar and pestle, £35, is that it's big enough to take on any grind I care to undertake. The design? It's made of hard stuff, with a good coarse grain in the interior. Pick one up at the Asian Market, Drury Street, Dublin or call CKS (tel: +44 (0)117 944 5226). It's a super housewarming gift, a heavyweight champion.

A dish for cooking potato dauphinoise/lasagne/roasting veg

Le Creuset rectangular dish in olive, with lifting handles, available from John Lewis (as before), House of Fraser (tel: +44 (0)870 160 7270, www.houseoffraser.co.uk), or call +44 (0)800 37 37 92, www.lecruset.com, for your nearest Le Creuset store, and check out Le Creuset oven, microwave, freezer and dishwasher safe rectangular dishes. Especially suitable for cooking potato-topped pies and lasagne and roasting vegetables. This colour is exclusive to John Lewis.

Titbit

Earth Natural Foods, 200 Kentish Town Road, London NW5 (tel: +44 207 482 2211, www.earthnaturalfoods.co.uk) do a wooden mortar and pestle, which is very light.

A roasting pan

For chicken and meat, John Lewis Stainless Steel Roasting Pans, John Lewis, Oxford St, London (tel: +44 (0)845 604 9049; www.johnlewis.com) are really the bizz.

Dishes for perfect gratins

Dishwasher-safe oval-eared Pillivuyt porcelain dishes, from £19.95, made in France. Available from the ceramic cookware range at Divertimenti, 227-229 Brompton Road, London, SW3 (tel: +44 207 581 8065, www.divertimenti.co.uk), or check out the West End branch of Divertimenti, 33/34 Marylebone High Street, London, W1U (tel: +44 207 935 0689).

Wear and tear

Silver restoration and replating service, £5 per piece, at Kensington Silver (tel: +44 207 602 5009 for an appointment).

Pasta pot

Stainless-steel saucepan by Hackman (26cm diameter), £185, Summerill & Bishop Limited, 100 Portland Road, London W11 (tel: +44 207 221 4566, www. summerillandbishop.com).

Chipped your Le Creuset?

Le Creuset doesn't do repairs (boo) but A.J Wells & Sons Vitreous Enamellers, Bishops Way, Newport, Isle of Wight, PO30 5WS (tel: +44 (0)198 353 7766, www. ajwells.com) does (yay). Although it costs around £50 and takes about three weeks, it's cheaper than buying a new Le Creuset pot. They also re-enamel cast iron baths and even old Agas. Can't see anyone putting one of those in the post though!

Tea towels

Wide Stripes tea towels, £2.95, from The Conran Shop, 55 Marylebone High Street, London W1U (tel:+44 207 723 2223, www.conranshop.co.uk).

A stock pot

My KitchenAid Meyer stockpot, £44, from Meyer (tel: +44 (0)151 482 8282; www.meyeruk.com) is great for boiling potatoes. Once the lid is clicked into place, I can drain water from the pot through the holes at the side without having to try and precariously balance the cover.

My favourite homewares website

A hand whisk by the Amish people of Pennsylvania, from Manufactum (tel: +44 (0)800 096 0938, www.manufactum.co.uk) and a Jenaer Measuring Jug. This is one of my favourite home wares sites.

Magic Oven Liner

Hate cleaning the oven? Then don't! Line it with a PTFE coated heavy-duty non-stick fabric, £9.99, from Lakeland (tel: +44 (0)153 948 8100, www.lakeland.co.uk). It's heat resistant up to an amazing 260°C, easy to remove for cleaning and will withstand 5 years or more of constant use, and can be cut to size. Even the most stubborn, burnt-on spills will glide off. (Suitable for use in all ovens, except where the heating element is in the base.)

Tableware

This tableware is made in the style of old French crockery, from £8.50 for a side plate; ivory slender-handled cutlery, £75 for a 24-piece set. All from Dibor at department stores nationwide. These are dishwasher safe, which is a bonus.

DITCH the DIRt

While travelling it was all; dum dee dum luxuraaaay and then it was home, back to my own place, and I started to notice things weren't exactly perfect. Lacking a troop of cleaners, I set about doing it myself with a few chambermaids' tips I'd picked up along the way. Try them!

Tidy up with cupboards

Hotel rooms always have built in cupboards and presses. To squirrel away clothing at home I installed a huge French wardrobe in the bedroom, which holds loads. In the dining room, discreet built-in cupboards help de clutter. You can have your nicest things out on display but everything you don't want people to see (gas bills and the stereo) can be hidden away.

Why don't windows in cute restaurants steam up?

Washing-up liquid, I was told in Berlin. A tiny amount on a good quality smooth, dry cloth, rubbed in a very thin film over the windows, and they won't steam up when you're cooking. Also works on any other glass surfaces in the house.

Dirty wall

Remove smokey radiator scorch marks on a light coloured wall by lightly scrubbing them with a soft brush dipped in a solution of water and washing-up liquid. Always start at the bottom and work your way up to the top and rinse each section in the same way to prevent streaking.

Perfect glasses

To restore wineglasses that have become cloudy in the dishwasher, stop using the dishwasher. Glasses should be washed by hand in hot water with a little detergent, then rinsed in warm water and dried with a clean cloth.

Perfect silver cutlery

Place a sheet of aluminium foil (tin foil) and a tablespoon of washing soda (sodium carbonate) into a plastic basin. Add the cutlery, ensuring that every piece is in contact with the foil. Then cover with boiling water. Leave for approximately 15 minutes, then wash as normal and re-polish if required.

Tarnished cutlery

Soak a wine cork in water and dip it in scouring powder. Rub the cutlery with the cork, rinse well, then buff with a soft cloth.

Dirty wallpaper

Remove light stains from wallpaper by rubbing with a piece of stale bread.

Greasy microwave

Boil half a lemon in a bowl of water in the microwave for a few minutes. The lemon steam will vaporize the greasy stains and also get rid of nasty smells. Prevent grease from forming in your microwave by wrapping greasy foods in paper towels when microwaving it.

Garden furniture

How come white resin plastic garden furniture always looks spotless outside gastropubs? Toothpaste my friends; rub hard for a few minutes with a scrubbing brush covered in a few squirts of whitening toothpaste and add water, just like teeth, then buff with a cloth. And relax!

Smelly presses

An open bottle of vanilla essence can help or put a bowl of bicarbonate of soda in the cupboards as it absorbs nasty smells.

Titbit

Of course there nothing more satisfying than keeping the nest clean and tidy.

Silk lampshades

Wash using a small amount of washing powder. Add two lumps of sugar to the final rinse to give the silk a lovely sheen.

Grubby stainless steel

Wash the appliance with a hot-water and washing-up liquid mix. Rinse with clean water and wipe dry with a soft cloth. Wiping dry is the secret to maintaining the gleam of stainless steel, so don't leave your pans dripping on the draining board or water droplets on your appliances and accessories. Wiping dry is especially important in hard-water areas as it prevents the build-up of grey coloured film caused by limescale deposits. Avoid using abrasive cleaners and wire-wool pads, as they leave scratches.

Dirty wallpaper

Remove light stains from wallpaper by rubbing with a piece of stale bread.

Stained cups and mugs

Scour them with a damp cloth and either salt or bicarbonate of soda, or bleach them, but be sure to rinse thoroughly afterwards.

Smelly fridge

No probs. Turn the fridge off, mix 1 capful of Milton with 3 pints of water and give the fridge a once-over with a sponge, avoiding all metal parts. Wipe the fridge dry and turn it back on.

Blood stain on a carpet

1. Sponge the stains with cold water (never hot; it sets the stain). 2. Soak up with a towel until it's faded. 3. Wash the spot with carpet shampoo. 4. Walk down to the police station and hand yourself in.

THE DINING TABLE

'Home' is a kitchen table (scratches and all)

At my parent's house, growing up we ate breakfast together at the dinner table every morning and ate dinner together there every weekend. My special area of responsibility was to remove the cutlery, plates and condiments and to clean the table completely. Rectangular, long, oak, I'd clean and polish every inch of it until it gleamed. During the summer the glare was so high we'd sometimes have to wear sunglasses to eat lunch at it, its glossy, grainy top reflecting in the sunshine.

I remember it made a creaking noise at my dad's end when he leaned his elbows on it and at I remember one corner had a chip and a scorch mark the shape of an arc where I accidentally scorched it with a hot pot. It was a beautiful flaw, which I'd rub my palm over and smile silently; I didn't get punished for that scorch because a minute later I burnt my hand also (I diiiiiiiid). I loved that flaw and I loved that table; it meant fun, laughter and lots of shared stories. Looking at my parents seated at either end last Christmas, I wondered if I'd ever have a great table with my own family sitting around it. Have you tried to shop for a dining table in the last year? Brutal, that's all I can say, two words bru tal.

I shuffled off with my friend Mark to Ikea in London and we laughed at the size of the £23 'dining' table that was on sale there. The shop assistant told us that it was the most popular model, 'no one wants a big dining table these days, they're old news'. Was she mental? The Ikea job that she was suggesting was so small it would only fit Snow White and, say, about, three dwarves, (five at a push) but no way the whole seven. 'Utter crrrrramp!' I said, and I don't often get out of my box.

222

At the Conran Shop (still in London), a table by Gregor Jenkins with a zinc top on it showed promise; get this, as the metal ages, different patterns will appear on it. Hmmmm speckled with little marks – an archive of my experience – sounded promising but too small and too expensive at £2,995 for 210cm x 90cm. See, I value individuality in a piece of furniture more then anything, but I value common sense more and I'm not so keen on spending nearly three grand on something just because it's flashy. No way.

So where does that leave me? Sitting at a great big dining room table? Better than sitting at one, eating at one with friends, but sadly not in my home. In London, I laid my knife and fork on a dining room table to die for. What sort? Oak I think. The point is that it had several marks on it and with a fair bit of ooooing and aaahing on my part, the owner told me that it was a salvage job. That table is in a great little organic pizza place just off Brick Lane called Stori Deli. It sits just inside the window and I've left a little G mark on underneath it, already thick with loads of other marks and dents, I didn't think they'd mind. Each mark is an echo of an experience there, its surface a map of the great times I and others have spent there eating pizza and having chirps. It's big, old(ish) and heavy, and is large enough to seat all my closest pals at one sitting. When I find a table like that (I've got the titbits below lined up already) I'm going to cook a massive feast and load it up like Christmas. Surely I'll have my own table sorted by then. Fingers crossed.

Clever casters
Casters under table legs prevent it leaving marks on a wooden floor or carpet. Most peeps use squares of carpet but then I saw these heavy antique ashtrays used as casters in Germany. Just slip them under the table legs, they look very glam.

Stori Deli
Check out travel (page 199) and www.thegoddessguide.com to see the Stori Deli table and a host of other communal tables that I'm ker-razy for.

Scratches?
Crack open a walnut, rub the nut on the scratch and watch the nut's resin make the scratch disappear. Where'd it go?

MAKING IT YOUR OWN

Certain things capture our hearts from the moment we see them. So what things have become and will become pieces of you? Here's how to enhance the things that you love.

Line

A huge French antique wardrobe is an ingenious way to hide knick knacks while making a room feminine. You can buy huge French wardrobes from Judy Greenwood antiques. Judy Greenwood Antiques, 657 Fulham Road, London SW6 (tel: +44 207 736 6037). Customize it and brighten up your room by lining the inside (including shelves) with your favourite paper, it'll cheer you up every morning when you open your wardrobe to get clothes.

With knobs on

Pick up a few jewel-like knobs from Graham & Green, (tel: +44 207 352 1919 or mail order tel: +44 (0)845 130 6622, www.grahamandgreen.co.uk) and dress up a wardrobe, kitchen cupboard or drawer. Available in 2 sizes (£2.95-£3.75) they come in blue, crystal, green, pink, smoke, turquoise and amethyst.

Beautiful colour

Squint, 178 Shoreditch High Street, London E1 (tel: +44 207 739 9275, www.squintlimited.com) features chairs and sofas dressed in a patchwork of vintage fabrics; a very beautiful way to add colour to a couch or a chair.

Beautiful cushions

Cacharel Home (for a full list of stockists call tel: +44 (0)1672 521594). Designers Guild 277 Kings Road, London, SW3 (tel: +44 207 893 7400, www.designersguild.com). Devoré velvet feels beautiful and the Montplaisir cut velvet cushion, £65 is sooo gorge. Marimekko 16/17 St Christopher's Place, London, W1U (tel: +44 207 486 6454, www.marimekko.co.uk). Lelievre 1/19 Chelsea Harbour Design Centre, London, SW10 (tel: +44 207 352 4798, www.lelievre-tissus.com) Beautiful fabrics to create cushions from.

Wallpaper your room – these are still my favourite peeps

Cole & Son, Ground Floor 10, Chelsea Harbour Design Centre, Lots Road, London, SW10 (tel: +44 207 376 4628, www.cole-and-son.com). Founded in 1873, C&S has a huge heritage portfolio and continues to make a selection of the 20th century's greatest hits. Their wallpaper is beautiful. Claire Coles (tel: +44 207 371 7303, www.clairecolesdesign.co.uk) her stitched bird wallpaper is sublime! De Gournay 112 Old Church Street, Chelsea, London SW3 (tel: +44 207 823 7316, www.degournay.com). Look on their website and bring a tissue for the droolage. A wall of Earlham print Chinoiserie wallpaper graces British fashion designer Matthew Williamson's shop wall at 28 Bruton Street, Mayfair, London W1J (tel: +44 207 629 6200, www.matthewwilliamson.com) and you can see the results on their website. Williamson embellished the birds' tails on the print with a thin brush and fluorescent paint to make them stand out more. He then added brooches to the birds' beaks and pinned them onto different branches of the trees in the print for sparkle. Luscious! Deborah Bowness (tel: +44 (0)781 780 7504, www.deborahbowness.com) makes beautiful bird-themed wallpaper. Kuboaa 24 Barton Street, Baynes, Bath, BA1 1HG (tel: +44 (0)122 548 4997 www.kuboaa.co.uk) strong graphic prints. Louise Body (tel: +44 (0)773 490 7357, www.louisebodywallprint.com) also offers bird themed paper. Timorous Beasties, 384 Great Western Road, Glasgow G4 9HT and 46 Amwell Street, London EC1R (tel: +44 (0)141 959 3331, www.timorousbeasties.com). Innovative, contemporary and clever wall covering. Tracy Kendell (tel: +44 207 640 9071, www.tracykendall.com) I love her wallpaper that shows stacks of books and plates. How great are they?

225

CHAIRS | 'Home' is a beautiful chair

Architectural Salvage
Secret Addresses (Shhhhhhhh!)

Salvage merchants can provide seriously good furniture if you want a period look for your home. Stock can include anything from beautiful birdcages at Lassco to cast-iron baths, old school radiators, chairs and panelling. Antique perfume bottles or laboratory cabinets anyone? Check out www.salvo.co.uk to find salvage pieces online.

Architectural Antiques, 351 and 324 King Street, Hammersmith, London W6 (tel: +44 208 741 7883, www.aa-fireplaces.co.uk). Specialists in English and French fireplaces, mirrors and other decorative artefacts. Love it! Architectural Classics, Princess Court, Gloucester Street South, Dublin 2, Ireland (tel: +44 208 144 1377, Ireland tel: +353 1850 246001, Worldwide +44 208 144 1377, www.architecturalclassics.com). Fireplaces, grates and door fixtures. Church Antiques, Rivernook Farm, Sunnyside, Walton-on-Thames, Surrey KT12 2ET (tel +44 (0)1932 252736; www.churchantiques.com). Ecclesiastical furnishings can look surprisingly modern in the right environment; no I don't mean a converted church. Drummonds Architectural Antiques, The Kirkpatrick Buildings, 25 London Road, Hindhead, Surrey GU26 6AB (tel: +44 (0)142 860 9444; www.drummonds-arch.co.uk). Lassco, St Michael's, Mark Street, London EC2 (tel: +44 207 749 9944, www.lassco.co.uk). An inspirational sort of place for me, where I've often struggled to walk away without a dentist's chair, a rocking horse or a mahussive bird cage. I have to be dragged screaming from this place. Love it all. Retrouvius, 2A Ravensworth Road, Kensal Green, London NW10 (tel: +44 208 960 6060; www.retrouvius.com). If you can't find what you're looking for here they'll source it for you. South West Reclamation, Wireworks Estate, Bristol Road, Bridgwater, Somerset TA6 4AP (tel: +44 (0)127 844 4141; www.southwest-rec.co.uk). Baths, sinks, doors, staircases — good for bathroom stuff.

Going, going, Gone!

If you're into vintage, then to really squeeze the best experience possible from it you have to get to an auction. They're great places to pick up special pieces and get your pulse racing. Oooooo yeah! visit www.invaluable.com to find reputable auction houses.

Modern Classics

If you have neither the time nor the inclination to hunt down your second-hand finds, try a reputable modern interiors store instead. 'Classic' pieces are still made under license with the original specifications in terms of materials, techniques and dimensions, and meet the standards that make them enduring classics, and therefore solid, sound investments for your home. Doesn't hurt either that they're insanely gorgeous.

Aram, 110 Drury Lane, Covent Garden, London WC2B (tel: +44 207 557 7557, www.aram.co.uk) for loads of interiors gems, and also holds the license for Eileen Gray's deco designs. Atomic Interiors, Plumtre Square, Nottingham NG1 1JF (tel: +44 (0)115 941 5577, www.atomicinteriors.co.uk). Designshop, 116-120 Causewayside, Edinburgh EH9 1PU (tel: +44 (0)131 667 7078; www.designshopuk. com). Europe By Net, (tel: +44 207 734 3100, www.europebynet.com) a really great website packed full of classic favourites including Mies Van Der Rohe daybeds, and Henry Bertoia wire chairs, Arco floor lamps and the Tufty Time sofa. Droooool! Fusion Lifestyle, 30 Church Street, Birmingham, B3 2NP (tel: +44 (0)121 236 1020, www.fusionlifestyle.co.uk) Italian and Scandinavian design dominate this packed mahussive store. Margaret Howell, 34 Wigmore Street, London W1U (tel: +44 207 009 9006, www. margarethowell.co.uk) Howell, a fashion designer, has collaborated with Ercol to reissue five original designs. I love the butterfly chair, it's gorgeous. Places and Spaces, 30 Old Town, Clapham, London SW4 (tel: +44 207 498 0998, www.placesandspaces.com). An impressive roll call of designers here from Norman Cherner (palpitate – see the chair) to Eero Saarinen. Pop UK, 278 Upper Richmond Road, Putney, London SW15 (tel: +44 208 788 8811, www.popuk.com). An extensive collection of gems from Charles and Ray Eames and Le Corbusier. Vitra, 30 Clerkenwell Road, London EC1M (tel: +44 207 608 6200, www.vitra.com) I press my face, Oliver Twist style, up against their window on my way through Clerkenwell to Shoreditch on the bike. I love, love, love their chairs even though the atmosphere is a bit business-like here, often broken by me bouncing up and down with excitement in front of a Charles and Ray Eames Ottoman and Chair.

My first vivid experience of umami (didn't know it was called that back then) took place one Thursday lunchtime when I was taken out of school at the age of five for an afternoon trip by my father. The day turned out to be a diamond. All hell broke loose as kids screamed and waved and chewed the ends off pencils with the excitement of having a grown-up enter the classroom. I remember this moment precisely because I was holding aloft my first real piece of school art – a blue snail that I had carefully made from magic marla (plasticine). I named him Snailey and smuggled him out in my coat pocket instead of returning him to the school art supplies cupboard. (Oh the guilt!) Still, Mrs Reidy, if you're reading, I've got Snailey, he's been around the world but just in case you've been worrying about him, I thought I'd put your mind at rest now.

Thursday was by far the busiest day of the week for my dad as he brought other people's cows (sometimes his own) to the local mart in Listowel for selling. We padded around in our wellies, Dad moving within the mart's belly in the dimly lit pens stuffed full of animals, me sliding about in the wash of brown-green sludge outside the cattle pens trying to keep my red wellies dry. The heat from the pens was extraordinary. Nothing much more inviting than echoey air sweet with cows' bellows and hot cows' breath. And there was the smell of tractor and lorry diesel too and the sweet meaty aroma of some kind of 'newness'.

'What do you think that is?' asked Dad, sniffing the air in the direction of the canteen. 'Don't know,' I answered. 'It's soup,' he explained, beef oxtail, a big pot of it bubbling away for lunch in the canteen. A peculiar hush settled over the pens for a few moments. 'That'll be the cows smelling oxtail, it always goes quiet here at lunchtime.' Our deal was if I behaved, I'd get to taste a bowl. My mouth salivating at the promise of that deep dark sweetness which wafted across the cow pens, I kept Snailey close to hand, whispering to him that soon we'd have lovely tasty treats.

On the ground the brown water slipped along the sloping ground into gullies and, if kicked quickly enough, the brown fermenting puddles parted completely to uncover clean grey concrete. 'Who are those men?' I asked. 'What men?' Dad said. 'Those men wearing different kinds of green wellies?' 'Oh, they're all farmers.' After a while I turned my attention to counting the different shades of green that the farmers' wellies came in, as they hovered like giants above me. And then there it was, the small decision that altered the course of the rest of my life as we headed in the direction of the soup, a thick plume of steam coming from a vent in the canteen wall.

Stepping inside, my clothes soaked up Woodbines and caffeine, toast, soup and ham sandwiches. I loved the cold smoothness of the table tops, I counted up the salts and peppers, the sugar shakers and the chairs, like counting with Mrs. Reidy. A ham sandwich arrived with plasticky-tasting margarine and waaaaaaay too much yellow Colman's mustard. Settling down with a Styrofoam cup I took my first mouthful of packet oxtail soup. 'Well? Is it nice?' 'It tastes a bit funny because of the melting Styrofoam,' my voice rang across the canteen. A waitress happened to be passing and swapped the soup into a small china cup. 'All right then,' she said sweetly, pushing a Wagon Wheel towards my dad, smiling. For anyone interested, i.e. me, and maybe my mum, this was a turning point for me.

That cup of soup was a very special brown colour – not as dark as HP Sauce yet darker than milk chocolate – and it had a very special taste, a delicious lingering after-effect. I remember drinking it and something in my brain changing. But as soon as I'd finished it the hot sticky brownness began fading. 'Amazing, wasn't it?' I whispered to Snailey. 'Nice soup then?' Dad asked. 'Dad,' I said, gathering my thoughts, 'it tasted kinda special, like the word soup, all warm and smack-your-lips-together cosy.' It was the first and last time I'd experience that sensation, the first and last time until this...

So back in the present, there I was looking out over the noise and mess of loveliness that is Vietnam and a flash of that day struck me – it felt pretty good. It had something to do with what I was eating, the taste. What sort? Don't know. It was a sort of saltiness. I was eating a bowl of steamed sticky rice with spicy and salty toppings. I didn't realize then, but I realize now that what I was experiencing was umami. I'd experienced it for the very first time drinking that cup of oxtail soup. It was only when I started discussing this taste with others that I found out this ...

The Hunt for Umami

Even before I was halfway through my lunch in Vietnam, I sensed somewhere inside me a reawakening. So what happened? What happened was something that I'd eaten had sparked that cup of oxtail soup with my dad memory to return vividly. A taste. I took a few moments to relive it and then nibbled round my meal to backtrack. Salted shrimp and rice in the first bowl, pleasant but nothing special; going along nicely, I tried the fish sauce, mmmmm a bit fishy and a tiny bit meaty but no oxtail yet, and the powdered fish? Nothing. And then the fourth mouthful made me wake up and sit up straight and be serious. The stuff in the last bowl was called ikan billis (crispy anchovies) and it was bang on, an exact oxtail match, in a strange inexplicable sort of way. I thought: hold on, someone is bound to know what they're doing here, so I looked around and (as so often is the way when you taste something notable or extraordinary in a small restaurant) the chef loved his job and told me that that something I was experiencing was umami – the fifth taste.

Now if I find a thing I like, I get obsessed (by now we know that, don't we?). I ignore everything else in the world around me and jump into that experience again and again and again for days on end until I've bounced the fun right out of it like a good mattress. I decided to do just that with the fifth taste, or umami (pronounced like someone who's really excited at seeing their mammy: Oooo Ma Meee!).

So the G went on an umami bender, a no-holds-barred taste loop. And it was that repetition, I think, of the umami taste reminding me of my first cup of oxtail, plus the after-effects of weeks of jet lag that accounted for the flood of genuine feeling that all but engulfed me for the rest of the day in that restaurant.

I put my head on my hand and listened to the chef explain how he used umami every day as he went about his business. 'Umami is the fifth basic taste,' he explained. 'It is an inexplicable meaty, savoury, intense sensation in the mouth and comes in fermented fish sauces, soy sauces, and meat and vegetable extracts, even in little things like stock cubes. Asian cooking is full of it.' 'And Italian!' A frail old Italian American couple sitting next to me added their opinion to the pot. They were enacting a timeless mime, her trying to serve him extra rice for dinner, him refusing, her insisting, him gesturing no with a wave of his hand. She continued to explain … 'Umami is the Japanese for "deliciousness", did you know that?' she asked with a slight Italian inflection. Her English was perfect so I wrote all this down.

As locals clutched umbrellas against a shower outside, weaving their way home balancing immense burdens, I strained to hear what else the Italian lady was saying over the raindrops rebounding off the plastic roof. 'The processes of ripening, drying, curing, ageing and fermenting in any food culture create a chemical reaction which releases umami (or glutamic acid or glutamate, as it's also called). Cured pork products have it … chorizo in Spain, pepperoni in Italy, bacon in Ireland, and frankfurters in Germany. Fresh ripe foods have it too – a ripe tomato has ten times more glutamate than an unripe tomato. And dried shiitake mushrooms contain waaaaay more than fresh ones.'

So what about my ikan billis? 'Salt-cured,' the Italian lady explained. 'Salt helps the anchovies ferment and while they cure, umami is formed within them. And although salt does not impart umami, a little salted preserved food, such as artichoke hearts, capers, olives, or gherkins help enhance the umami of a dish containing anchovies or tomatoes, which are both umami-rich foods.' 'Yee-ha,' her partner added Tony Soprano style. 'Anchovies (fresh, dried, whatever), they're full of that umami stuff. And bacon, bresaola (cured Italian beef), capers, caper berries, caviar, chorizo, clams or clam juice, olives, prosciutto, ham, lox, sardines, baccalà (salt cod), Italian food, you can't get any better,' he crowed.

'Yes, but Asian food is packed with umami ingredients too,' explained the chef. 'Fermented black beans, fish sauce, glasswort, samphire, niboshi (Japanese dried sardines), nori, oysters or oyster sauce, shrimp paste, soy sauce, tamari, and look at all of the dark sauces in England like Worcestershire sauce, Bovril ...' 'And Australian Marmite,' I added.

'Yee-ha, but who'd wanna eat any of that rubbish?' said the old Italian, as he finished off a second bowl of rice and wiped the sweat from his brow. 'Hot weather, it's overrated, isn't it?' (There's me going on the Irish weather thing again.) 'Can't get any work done and what would life be without work, eh?' With such fine informants on hand, umami hunting, I reckoned, was good for a few more pages in my notebook. After all, this elderly couple seemed to know tons as they bickered about it, so I listened on.

'Puttanesca, now there's an Italian dish full of the good stuff,' the Italian man added. 'It's the dish I'm most proud of. Being an old Italian.' 'How did I know you were going to say that, Dante?' his wife poked. 'Puttanesca was eaten by the – how can I say this? – "ladies of the night" between clients because it was quick to make but tasty and filling,' she whispered in embarrassment. 'Yee-ha, but it's gooooood. It's got the anchovies, the tomatoes, the Parmesan, the lot.' 'Yeah, yeah, OK, I suppose you're right! The anchovies in the olive oil bring out the sweetness of the pasta and boost the umami in the tomatoes.' 'Hey, have you ever had anchovies on scrambled egg on buttered toast for breakfast? Or anchovies in a Caesar salad or on lamb or steak?' I had. 'Whadda leeeeeettle super fish, eh?'

So what does umami taste of? I know sweet means sugary, bitter a good lemon tart, or a crackin' gin and tonic. But what food has the most amount of umami? 'Puttanesca,' Dante smiled. 'I mean, what single food has the most umami, Dante?' 'Parmesan,' the Italian couple chimed. 'Yee-ha,' said Dante, 'one up for the Italians.' 'Yes, but soy sauce is high up there too,' said the Vietnamese chef. I opened my iPhone. 'Listen, lads, I can roam the planet here without even leaving the restaurant, money on the table which has more umami, Parmesan or the soy sauce?'

As they all watched on, I got quite interested in the BBC website for some reason. 'Heeeeeya, whad you doin'?' the Italian said impatiently. 'Calling your papa?' The thing I love most about the Italians and even Italian Americans is that somehow, although they have some of the best fashion designers and cars in the world, they've managed to retain a unique sense of tradition – I like to call it 'village'. Nothing at all wrong with it. That's why I was lucky to have met these guys, much better then watching guff on the telly or spending hours with scientists making it complicated. Jaysus, I'd be bored stiff.

Google turned up this lot: 'Umami was first named in 1908 when a professor at the University of Tokyo called Kikunae Ikeda isolated the source of the taste and christened it. He became interested in the delicious flavour that a seaweed broth lent to anything flavoured with it. The seaweed was kombu, known in English as giant sea kelp. Ikeda discovered that the active taste ingredient in kombu was glutamic acid. Ikeda named this umami [which, although it sounds all la-di-da to us normal folk, in Japanese actually means something close to "yummy"]. In the years that followed, scientists in Japan proved to their satisfaction that umami was an independent extra basic taste alongside sweet, sour, salty and bitter, hence it's called the fifth taste.' Facts over … bets on … Parmesan or soy sauce?

Here are the figures ... mature Parmesan cheese came in at 1,200mg per 100g, top of the list according to t'internet. 'See, I told ya.' The Italian stretched out his hand for his winnings. 'Wait a minute!' said the chef. 'Where's my soy sauce?' 'Second, sorry,' I commiserated; soy sauce came in at 1,090mg per 100g. The list went on – walnuts were third (658) then fresh tomato juice (260). Good old Bloody Mary, eh? Then grape juice (258) and then peas (200). 'That's young peas,' Dante nodded. 'Old tomatoes and young peas, Italian rules. What's next?'

Mushrooms – cooked and dried, especially porcini and shiitake (180). 'Hey, hey, we're winning this hands down, Connie,' Dante chirped, getting younger as he sat upright in the chair. Then broccoli (176), tomatoes – roasted and sundried (140), oysters, lobster, prawns (cooked from raw) (137), corn (130), potatoes (102), chicken (44). 'It's the natural juices that run off a roasted bird and coagulate as brown bits in the corners,' explained the chef. 'The same is true for quail and turkey.' And finally there was mackerel (36), beef (33), eggs (23) and human milk (22). For obvious reasons I didn't read out the last one.

'Eh, beef, aged beef has more umami than fresh stuff,' explained Dante. 'And that ham in Spain where the pigs eat acorns, what's that called, Connie?' 'Iberico ham.' 'How do you think umami got into my oxtail soup at the mart with my dad when I was five then?' 'Easy,' explained the chef whose name was brutally hard to pronounce. 'MSG (monosodium glutamate) gives a concentrated umami hit.' MSG – isn't that the stuff that gets the bad stick in Chinese food? I learned that it first went into commercial production soon after Ikeda's discovery, first as an extract of kombu seaweed itself, and then as a fermented substance derived from molasses or sugar beet, composed of 78 per cent glutamic acid and 12 per cent sodium. It has been speculated that the sodium in MSG creates the umami effect. It's used in great quantities by the food industry in soups and stews and nearly all dried food on supermarket shelves. 'It's safe,' the chef explained, 'hype, that's all. In Asia it's a popular flavour enhancer.'

We went our separate ways, they back to their hotel, me towards the restaurant kitchen. I thought about what they'd said, not the umami bits, but the bit about 'Heeeeeya, whad you doin'? Calling your papa?' Well, I'm as bound to my family as the next person. So I rang my dad. 'Where you off to next?' New York, Dad – maybe I'd see Dante and Connie. 'Is umami the reason why Americans love pizza and pasta with Parmesan cheese so much, why they smother their steaks in blue cheese and their French fries and hamburgers in tomatoey ketchup, do you think?' 'I'll find out, Dad.'

Before that, though, it was home to try to cook an umami-laced puttanesca with Peter. We got chopping immediately. 'Don't fo get da vodka,' Peter said, Tony Soprano style like Dante. 'What vodka?' 'The vodka shots that you must add after slow-roasting ripe vine tomatoes in the oven. I saw old Italian ladies cook this in Rome when I lived there.' Old ladies, you say, eh? I rummaged among my reams of umami research like a mad professor and guess what? Vodka acts as a solvent and releases the umami in tomatoes. Brilliant! It was all happening now! The puttanesca was gorgeous (see the recipe on page 236). And then there was the pea soup that we ate at our friend BrenB's house, packed full of good Parmesan and pea-ness. What did Dante say? Oh yeah, I remember: 'old tomatoes, young peas'. And the burgers that Richard and Lucy cooked for us with their own special recipe, they were umami-laden and even better than the ones we hunted down in New York (see pages 243-245).

But there was something else nagging away at me, some obstacle between me and happiness. What was it? Oh yeah, that was it ... I wanted to share the recipes that I've collected while on my umami hunt. An urgent stabbing desire to give you the lot stole up on me. So I have. Enjoy! x

Perfect rice

My secret way to cook rice like basmati, jasmine and Asian

1. For Asian rice soak the rice in water for 3 hours or overnight. Drain.
2. If using basmati or jasmine there's no need to soak.
3. Measure your rice using a cup (I find that 1 cup of rice is enough for 2 people).
4. Throw your rice into a bowl and swish it around in cold water with your fingers for 1 minute to rinse out the starch. Drain in a colander and repeat.
5. Now pop the rice into a heavy-bottomed saucepan and add 1¼ cups of water for each cup of rice you are cooking. Add a little salt and let the rice boil for 2 minutes on high.
6. Then turn to a low heat, cover the saucepan and let the rice simmer gently for 6 minutes.
7. Take the rice off the heat and leave it to steam in the covered saucepan for 12 minutes. The easy way to remember all the times is 2-6-12.
8. When the rice is finished steaming run a fork through it and behold its fluffiness. Ta-dah! The G's perfect rice.

Titbit

Although I love my Le Creuset pans, risotto and rice always scorch and stick in them.
I use this stainless-steel stockpot (32cm diameter), £42.95, from Kitchen Ideas, 70 Westbourne Grove, London W2 (tel: +44 207 221 2777), for my soups, risottos and perfect rice instead.

Puttanesca

Serves 6 as a starter/
4 as a main course
Cooking time: 35 minutes

400g plum tomatoes
salt and ground black pepper
4 garlic cloves, chopped
1 red chilli, finely chopped and seeded
4 tbsp olive oil
1 cup chopped oregano
6 mashed anchovy fillets
60g capers
150g chopped and pitted Kalamata olives
2 shots of vodka
500g penne
100g grated Parmesan
½ cup chopped flat-leaf parsley

1. Season the tomatoes with pepper and roast in a preheated oven for 20 minutes. When they're cooked, mash them up with the back of a fork.
2. Now for the sauce ... gently cook the garlic and chilli in olive oil in a pan for about 1 minute without allowing them to brown (charred garlic tastes bitter).
3. Add the chopped oregano, anchovies, capers and olives to the pan then pour in the vodka and stir for another minute. (Vodka optimizes the release of umami from tomatoes).
4. Add the roasted tomatoes to the pan and season with black pepper. Once all this is stirred together let the whole lot simmer for 15 minutes.
5. Meanwhile, boil a large pot of water with a dash of salt and cook the pasta.
6. Drain the pasta and add it to the sauce. Serve with grated Parmesan and chopped parsley. Parmesan, tomatoes and anchovies make this dish one big umami treat. Enjoy!

BRENB'S P SOUP

Serves 6
Cooking time: 80 mins

4 heads of garlic
4 shallots
olive oil
500g frozen garden peas
80g salted butter
550ml of chicken stock
1/2 cup of parmesan
400g of low fat crème fraîche
salt, black and red pepper

Not only does our pal BrenB
rock a great pea soup, but he's
a cracking illustrator too.
He cooked it, he drew it, we ate
it and it was yummy. You can
see more of his work at
www.brenb.net.

1. Take the heads of garlic and slice the tops off, then remove the loose papery skin (the garlic cloves should still bejoined together as a whole head of garlic). Make tin foil squares and place each head garlic in the centre and cup the foil around it like a bag. Make a larger tin foil bag for the peeled shallots. Drizzle with the oil and loosely close the foil. Place them all in a preheated oven at 200 C for about 45 minutes. Check occasionally to make sure they are not burnt or too brown, they should be soft when done.
2. Boil the peas like normal, in salted water. Drain and throw into the blender. Now the messy part. Take the roasted garlic and squeeze the soft pulp into the blender. Surprisingly the garlic does not stink due to it being roasted so get your fingers covered in the stuff. Add the butter shallots, Parmesan and half the stock and blitz.
3. Pour it all into a pot and add the remaining stock, adding the crème fraîche to taste.
4. Heat the soup on a medium heat, season with salt and pepper and get stuck in. YUMMY!

Gx's ROASTED CHICKEN

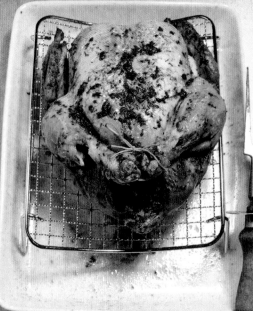

Don't feel like you have to apologize by saying, 'It's nothing special, just chicken for dinner.' Chicken is yum! As it roasts you'll notice crispy brown little bits forming on the skin and in the roasting tin; these are packed with umami flavour. This recipe may be simple but the results are truly wicked!

Serves 6
Roasting time: 1 hour 10 minutes

1.8kg chicken, preferably free-range
1 unwaxed lemon
115g butter
2 good handfuls of chopped thyme
sea salt
cracked black pepper
2 garlic cloves, finely chopped
1 onion, finely diced
150g fresh breadcrumbs
5 sprigs of thyme
4 tbsp chopped parsley and sage

1. Put an appropriately sized roasting tray in the oven and preheat to 220°C/425°F.
2. Wash your chicken inside and out and pat dry with kitchen paper.
3. Working carefully from the opening in the chicken, ease your fingers up under the breast skin and separate it from the meat, giving you a pocket in which to stuff some flavoured butter (so let's make that now).
4. Into a bowl grate the lemon for the citrusy fresh yellow rind and put the fruit aside to be used later (optional).
5. Add 60g of the butter, 1 tsp chopped fresh thyme, sea salt, cracked black pepper and the two finely chopped garlic cloves to the bowl and squish everything together to make a beautiful thyme butter for seasoning the chicken's skin.
6. Rub this thyme butter between the breast skin and meat and rub it around the chicken to coat the skin before roasting (this is all good, well worth the hassle).

7. Righty ho, so do you want to put your stuffing inside your chicken or not? Your call. If not, cut the lemon in half and pop inside the chicken and make the stuffing to bake in a shallow dish in the oven separately.

8. To make the stuffing, melt the remaining butter in a heavy-bottomed frying pan (Le Creuset is good) and gently fry the diced onions while moving them around the pan with your wooden spoon to stop them from burning.

9. When the onions are translucent, add the breadcrumbs gradually and let them soak up the butter from the onions in the pan. Add more butter if the breadcrumbs are still white and dry.

10. When the breadcrumbs are a yellowish colour in the pan add the thyme by pulling your fingers along the stems and letting it fall into the stuffing mixture.

11. Add some finely chopped sage, parsley or rosemary and season with sea salt and cracked black pepper

12. If stuffing your chicken, spoon your stuffing loosely into the cavity of the chicken. If the stuffing is packed too tightly, it won't heat all the way through.

13. Using cotton string, tie the legs of the chicken together so that they are almost touching. This helps the chicken hold the stuffing in while roasting.

14. Don't bother tying the chicken's legs together if you haven't stuffed it and there's just a lemon inside.

15. Slash and gash the thighs to allow the heat to reach into the flesh. Put your chicken in the hot roasting tray and let it cook in the oven for 1 hour and 10 minutes.

20. When cooked, remove from the oven and leave to rest for 10 minutes. Once the meat has been removed, a little light

gravy can be made in the tray on the hob, if the tray is metal, otherwise scrape the juices from the tray into a pan and make the gravy on the hob with a splash of wine and stock.

Don't want your stuffing in the chicken?

Same stuffing, different cooking method I've been making this stuffing with my mum since I was eight and my younger brother Michael loves it. He prefers it crisp and crunchy so instead of stuffing it in the chicken, I bake it in the oven in a shallow dish with a piece of buttered baking parchment over it to prevent the tips of the breadcrumbs from charring. It only takes 15 minutes and it goes beautifully brown.

Titbit

To test whether the chicken is cooked, skewer the flesh at the thickest point – under the leg, about 8cm in, on the fleshy part of the thigh. The chicken is ready when the juices run clear, not pink.

CX'S UMAMI LAMB

This recipe I learnt from an old Italian woman as she studded a leg of lamb with rosemary, garlic and anchovies. You might think it a bit strange, but let me tell you, anchovies bring lamb alive. I've been using this recipe since returning from Italy and everyone asks about the richness of the meat and its gorgeous gravy. The anchovy doesn't come across as fishy-tasting at all – it simply lends a savoury note that blends beautifully with the meat. It's what umami's all about.

Serves 6
Marinating time: 1 hour
Cooking time: 1 hour 20 minutes

1 x 2–2.5kg leg of lamb
6 garlic cloves, peeled and cut into slivers
4 sprigs of rosemary
50g anchovies (1 tin or a bottle in oil), patted dry
75g butter, softened
freshly ground black pepper
juice of ½ lemon
juice of ½ lime
4 tbs olive oil

1. Using a sharp little paring knife, make several small 2.5cm-deep slits into the fleshy side of the lamb. Push in a tiny sliver of garlic, followed by a sprig of rosemary and half an anchovy fillet, making sure you get them right down into the holes. Most of it will fall out during cooking, but it will still give the meat and resulting gravy the most fantastic flavour.
2. Cream the butter with any remaining anchovies and rub this marinade all over the surface of the lamb with your hands.
3. Season the lamb well with freshly ground black pepper and marinate it, loosely

covered, at room temperature for 1 hour.
4. Preheat the oven to 170°C/325°F/Gas
3 while the lamb is marinating.
5. Place the lamb fat side up in a roasting
tin. Pour over the lemon and lime juice
(the acidity of the citrus juices acts
almost like a mint sauce).
6. Cover with tin foil and pop it in the
preheated oven for about an hour or
slightly more, depending on how you like
your meat. Baste from time to time.
7. Take the meat out of the oven and
leave to rest in a warm place covered in
foil for 15 minutes before carving.

8. During roasting, the cooking juices
from the lamb should have reduced and
mingled with the anchovy butter to make
a delicious gravy. If it's too thin, a quick
bubble on the hob should thicken it.
9. Carve the lamb into chunky slices.
Serve the sliced lamb with Parmesan
mash. An absolute umami showstopper.

Titbit

Lamb can be studded, marinated,
covered and chilled for up to 5 hours.
Bring to room temperature for about 1
hour before roasting.

Perfect Roast Potatoes

You can cook your roast potatoes in the same roasting tin as your lamb or if you'd
prefer to be more prepared, boil the potatoes ahead of time, score them and have
them ready to pop in the oven at the same time as your lamb in a separate tin. From
experience I've learned that you get optimum results by doing them separately.

Serves 6
Boiling time: 8–10 minutes
Roasting time: 45 minutes (plus
a 10-minute blast at the end if
they need crisping up)

2kg floury potatoes such as Cara,
Maris Piper or King Edward
fine sea salt
freshly ground black pepper
goose fat

1. Peel the spuds and cut them into
smallish chunks the size of a plum.
2. Put in a pan, cover with water, salt well
and bring to the boil. Simmer for 8–10
minutes, then drain and leave to cool.

3. Once cold, score the potatoes with a
fork and toss with a little salt.
4. Put enough goose fat in a large roasting
dish to cover the base by about 4mm
and put it in the oven to preheat to
220°C/425°F/Gas 7.
5. When the fat is spitting hot, add the
potatoes, toss them in the fat to coat
them completely and push the roasting
tin back in the oven. Turn the potatoes a
couple of times while they're cooking.
6. You may feel that your potatoes could
be a bit crisper, in which case leave
your potatoes to roast for a further 10
minutes.
7. Season with salt and pepper
before serving.

BURGERS

So, there I was, in New York, touched down the first week in May for a spate of Goddess research. What a great month May is, the fifth month in the Gregorian calendar. I wonder is it because it's Taurus, the bull, that it's National Hamburger Month in the US? Hmmm!

So you're probably thinking I didn't eat any burgers, right? That I'm one of those gals who just mentions food and lets everyone else do the chomping. Wrong! New York is the birthplace of the burger, I immediately got myself involved with that … but only about three times. Or possibly six. Seven burgers. OK, twelve. And maybe tentatively nibbled (at first) and then totally devoured.

My first day in New York and I was reminded again how everything really is much bigger in the US; Big Hummers, Big pretzels, Big bottoms and Big burgers; the burgers are mahussive, some too big to even squish into your mouth without getting stuff all around your nose.

UK-based Michelin-star chef Heston Blumenthal, proprietor of the Fat Duck in Bray, devoted one full episode of his BBC TV programme *In Search of Perfection* to creating the perfect hamburger. On his search, he too had visited New York. Anyway Heston (the only person I know called Heston) is my food hero, and in his research he spoke to a man called Jon Prinz, a chewing expert (among other subjects) at Wageningen University in the Netherlands. (Ooh yeah! Very Oceans Twelve.) Prinz had previously advised Heston that beef, toppings and bun together should be no bigger than two inches. This is what two inches looks like … it's not much, is it?

DB Bistro Moderne
Burgers
(like a hooker)
High $50

And guess what Prinz also told him? That most people find the experience of opening their mouths further than two inches uncomfortable. To test this discomfort, press your three middle fingers together, turn them sideways and then jam in your mouth, go on, try it, can't you feel that little stretch? To avoid this feeling while eating, we instinctively press a burger together tightly with our hands to make it flatter, and inadvertently squeeze out all of its lovely juices, and that's counterproductive to experiencing the full flavour. The bun's function (apart from keeping the sandwich together that is) is to keep most of this juice from escaping. In G-speak I think that means no burger bits or juice should escape up your sleeve or up into your nose.

So what happened next? I think we know, don't we? Off I went, all Dorothy (Lion, Scarecrow, Tin Man), to forage in New York's burger joints for the best burger that matched up to my two-inch rule (of course, as well as being the right size, it had to taste great). It also had to have great meat, great accessories and a good bun, with enough surface area and soakage to keep together its entire contents. Spent weeks at it between shop visits. Got quite serious at one point. So here are snack club's results…

The first day, I started with one of the most infamous burgers in New York City. This burger set the trend for celebrity chefs to start creating signature burgers in 2001. Daniel Boulud's $27 hamburger at DB Bistro Moderne, 55 West 44th Street (tel: +1 212 391 2400, www.danielnyc.com/dbbistro) is vulgar, no two ways about it. Way over the two-inch mark, with a small bun trying to contain ground sirloin stuffed with braised short ribs, foie gras and truffles, it looked like a Wag in her fifties in a miniskirt trying to squeeze everything in. Oooooooh, nearly there! Bits were pouring out everywhere. Just way OTT as food goes. In his defence let me just say this: Boulud's burger accounts for 30 per cent of the bistro's food sales. So some people somewhere love it. Sadly, not me!

I'd gone through ten burgers and was doing OK. Not Heston Blumenthal, not Anthony Bourdain either, but getting there. At the end of the second week though I hit pay dirt at numbers eight, nine and ten. I should have stopped there, but I didn't and burgers eleven and twelve were disappointing. Especially twelve … it was hideous: stodgy, fatty and the meat had the grey pallor of a Russian Blue (that's a cat … ummmmmmm, maybe it was, a cat, I mean). After eating it, I felt immobilised for hours, exhausted, disorientated and was found wandering aimlessly around Williamsburg mumbling incoherently, something about Barneys and finding bigger jeans, I think. Later that evening, I huffed away over my notes in my notebook and in pole position there was this lovely specimen: the Burger Joint burger (the ninth burger I'd tried in the city). Here's why it made me the happiest.

The Burger Joint at the Le Parker Meridien hotel

The Burger Joint at Le Parker Meridien, 118 West 57th Street, sent my happiness Richter scale into overdrive. It wasn't the trample through the Le Parker Meridien hotel lobby with it's fancy-smancy high ceiling, I decided, or the experience of stumbling down a normal dark corridor, or the pushing aside of a black curtain, a heavy rippling sound as a gap opened beneath the neon sign (Dorothy meets David Lynch, how are you?), or the vinyl-covered chairs and benches, or the menu written in marker on the side of a ripped-up cardboard box outlining all the burgers on the wall. Or rather, it's all of those things, but not any one thing in particular. Maybe clubbed together they account for 20 per cent of my happiness.

And another 10 per cent would go to the mix of shoes queuing to place burger orders, leather brogues, trainers, steel toe caps, our shoes (Peter's, Charlie's, mine). No, I'll up that mark to a 15 here because that's democracy and Snailey loves it. No, I take it back, I give it 10, yes 10, 10's my final answer because I need the 5 to give to the little fact that the $6.50 burger is a whopping $20 if you're staying in the hotel and order it room service upstairs. (Suckers!)

And then another 5 must go to the ordering system. As ever I ask for my burger done 'rare to medium with lettuce, tomato, onion, pickle, ketchup, mayo and mustard ... the works and some fries. Thank you very much. And a whole gherkin. And what's to drink? I'll take a milk shake. It cost $4.50.' (I'd heard that the thick strawberry milk shake was the business.) It was.

Thanking you.' Order quickly or go to the end of the line. That's their motto. And the line at lunchtime is long. This little lot costs? $11.25, which they insist on, in cash, immediately. They also insist on knowing your name and then shout it back at you when your burger comes off the grill. How New Yawk is that?

But the main chunk of my marks, the – what's left over? – the 50 per cent that I have kept, the 50 per cent that turned this eating experience into something close to nirvana was that I was there with my friends who could also appreciate this joint's use of well-sourced ingredients to make a brilliant meal. My burger, handed over wrapped in waxy paper with my chips in a paper bag, was ace.

So the burger, why was the burger so perfect? Where do I start? The bun was like a good pillow: fluffy, plain and free of lumps and bumps, i.e. sesame seeds. The breadth and thickness of the Burger Joint's buns are scaled to match the burgers and don't eclipse them (note that that's important for when we make our own at home later). The gherkin was crunchy, the tomato firm, and the meat, juicy and tender, striped on the grill but still pink inside. The beef patty is made of ground top sirloin and shoulder, the quality of which seemed to be flawless. It possessed in abundance what I was hunting for: umami. Even the tomato ketchup helped with this. I'd be hard pressed to do as good a burger myself at home.

Back in Dublin, (Rathmines to be exact), a tall (ish) blonde (ish) guy (let's call him blondie) walked into Jo'Burger and sat not far from where they keep the Beano menus with his partner (wife maybe?) and two small children. "Well" said Peter, "which burger do you fancy?" My eyes narrowed to read the menu. We were seated at a communal table –and I scanned the burger list nestled inside a vintage copy of the Beano (everything in Jo'Burger is organic – even the sauces, juices and the cola). I opted for the Beef Pimville, which came with fresh salsa and avocado, (there's a choice of over 20 fillings) and there was also a large slice of tomato and a mahussive lettuce leaf nestled in between the giant Breton buns. Along with Bush fries with piri piri seasoning, (€3.95), old-school fried potato slices and a portion of Ruby coleslaw (€3.95) - red because they add beetroot, this was the most lip-smackingly good, burger I've ever had in Dublin. Sprinkle some smiley staff on top and Snailey was ready with the 8 out of 10 mark! And thus did I find myself faced with the best burger in Dublin and an ex-love interest staring past his (wife, girlfriend?) every five seconds as I negotiated every single bite of it. Has that ever happened to you? I swapped seats and turned my back to him immediately, on a mission as important as this, it's always has to be about the food.

New York - The Burger Joint at Le Parker Meridien, 118 West 57th Street (tel: +1 212 245 5000, www.parkermeridien.com). Open 11 a.m.–11.30 p.m. (midnight Friday and Saturday). Shake Shack, Southeast corner of Madison Square Park, near Madison Avenue and East 23rd Street (tel: +1 212 889 6600, www.shakeshacknyc.com) and also 77th and Columbus Avenue. Open 11 a.m.–9 p.m. Corner Bistro 331 West Fourth Street (Jane Street) Manhattan, NY tel: +1 212 242 9502. Nuf Said!

Dublin - Jo'Burger, 137 Rathmines Road, Dublin 6 (tel: +353 1 4913731, www.joburger.ie).

London - Hanburger Union, 22–25 Dean Street, W1 (tel: +44 207 437 6004, www.hamburgerunion.com). Peter and I had a burger here with Pat McCabe and his wife Margo. Good burger, what I remember of it, as we'd been in the pub before-hand and were in no position to judge.

Ricky's Burgers

Next, Snack club had a meet at our friends Richard and Lucy's house in Dublin. My conclusion? Threefold. First, condiments are key – the more the merrier – they offer a real bespoke experience to everyone dressing their own burger. Second, if you start with great meat then you have to add very little to it. Ask your butcher to mince the steak for you if you plan to make your own. Third, seeing as each of us ate not one but two burgers, I can safely say that (Adopt Gordon Ramsay accent ...) Ricky's Gourmet Burgers will make you stuff your mouth. DONE.

Bottom half
Smear of Dijon mustard
Seared red onion
Cashel Blue cheese (put on the bottom to make sure it melts)
Oven-roasted sliced peppers (soaked in olive oil and balsamic vinegar)

Middle
Beef or lamb burger (Fallon & Byrne, Dublin, see page 248). Two slices of smoked back rashersFor a lower-fat option marinate a free-range chicken breast in dark rum, smoked paprika and some pepper and serve in place of the burger

Top Half
Fresh rocket
Mango and almond chutney
Ketchup
Pickles
Mayo

Titbit
Ideally served with oven-roasted potato wedges which are parboiled and then smothered in smoked paprika, salt, pepper and olive oil. Make sure to put the olive oil into the oven first and then, when parboiled, roll the potatoes in the hot oil to get maximum effect. Cook until crispy.

Goddess Umami Burger

Serves 6
Cooking time:
10 minutes

1kg lean minced beef steak
12 garlic cloves, chopped or crushed
2 tbsp sundried tomato paste
1–2 tbsp dark soy sauce
1 medium egg, beaten
2 tsp Worcester sauce
1 tsp dried oregano
60g stale bread, wetted, squeezed dry
and crumbled
6 rolls
8 tbsp caramelized onion sauce or confit
1 packet mixed leaf or herb salad
1 red onion, sliced into rings
tomato ketchup and mustard
salt and freshly ground black pepper

1. Heat the grill to high. Put half of the
minced beef steak into a food processor
with the garlic, tomato paste, soy sauce, egg,
Worcester sauce, oregano and bread. Whiz
in 5-second bursts, to form a sticky paste (do
not over-mix to a sausage-like texture).
2. Transfer mixture to a large bowl. Add the
remaining mince and knead until smooth.
Shape into 4 burgers, each approx. 150g.
3. Grill the burgers for 3–4 minutes on each
side until cooked through.
4. Halve each roll, spread the base with
caramelized onion sauce, then add salad
leaves and a burger. Top with red onion and
serve with your favourite condiments.
I like mustard and ketchup.

Buy ready-made

Pipers Farm steak burgers (£11.29 per
kg), as well as lamb, chicken and venison
burgers (tel: +44 1392 881380, www.
pipersfarm.com). In Dublin, Fallon &
Byrne, 11–17 Exchequer Street, Dublin 2
(tel: +353 1 472 1010) do good beef and
lamb burgers.

Titbit

I like my burgers a little lighter so I
add egg and breadcrumbs. If you have
enough fat content in the meat, it'll
stop your burger becoming one
big solid lump. I like to make
my own because I'm in control
of the umami content and the
ingredients.

Ketchup

I admit I only picked up a bottle of Tiptree's tomato sauce from the Sainsbury's shelf because of the sticker. Each one has the name of the person who 'finished' it. I had the choice of Susan or Marilyn. I chose Marilyn because of Monroe. After tasting it, I don't think I'll be going back to Heinz. They do an organic one too, the best for my perfect burger.

Where to buy: Devotees of Heinz may dispute the authenticity of flavour, but if you are looking for alternatives, Tiptree's Tomato Sauce (at Sainsbury's) is sweet and tomatoey, while Daylesford Organic's version comes in a cool swing-top bottle (£7.95 for 500ml). Goodness Direct (+44 871 8716611, www.goodnessdirect.co.uk) has a range of organic ketchups, including Meridian, which is made with 68 per cent organic Italian tomatoes and unrefined sugar (£1.09 for 285g).

Mayonnaise

The list of ingredients in mayo should be short and to the point: oil, eggs, lemon juice and vinegar. A rambling list on the jar means a ton of additives and preservatives. Some peeps say that it's fattening, but a spoon or two won't do any harm to spruce up a sambo or burger. Anyway I'd prefer two spoonfuls of something full-fat and natural instead of a whole load of something low-fat and riddled with E numbers.

Pollen Organics, £1.80 (tel: +44 1428 608870, www.pollenorganics.com) is made from locally grown organic ingredients and is a beautiful yellow colour with a really rich flavour – the nearest we could find to the real thing. Garner's Extra Special, £1.59, at Waitrose (tel: +44 800 188884 for other stockists), is smooth and really lovely with chips. Failing that there's always the old favourite, Hellmann's Light, £1.39.

Wholegrain mustard

Grey Poupon Harvest Coarse Ground, £1.09, or Maille Wholegrain Mustard, 99p. Both are good and not vinegary. Great with all meats and looooovly on Emmental cheese sambos.

BAKING KIT

Everything you'll need to crack on with some serious cakey-bakeyness.

Titbit

Use a copper bowl and a balloon whisk to create the stiffest egg whites for meringues and soufflés. The best egg bowls, are £58, from Divertimenti, 227–229 Brompton Road, London SW3 (tel: +44 207 581 8065, www.divertimenti.co.uk) – or check out the West End branch of Divertimenti, 33/34 Marylebone High Street, London, W1U 4PT (tel: +44 207 935 0689). They're made of heavy-gauge beaten copper. To ensure the bowl is perfectly clean before use, scrub the inside with salt and half a lemon then rinse and dry thoroughly. Hand wash only.

Serve on one-off bespoke plates

Lou Rota is fast becoming known for her witty transformations. Whether it's a vintage French desk or a salvaged polypropylene stacking chair, a 1950s mirror or 1960s glass coffee table, each piece is unique ... Suitable for decorative use or as occasional serving plates, she has one-off pieces at affordable prices. Small, medium and large plates £20/£25/£30. Lou Rota furniture and home accessories (tel: +44 (0)7941 357981 www.lourota.com) also retail at Liberty, Regent Street, London W1, Selfridges and Caravan, Spitalfields, London E1.

Baking sheet

A metallic cookie sheet, £14.95 (plus p&p), at The Conran Shop, 55 Marylebone High Street, London W1 (tel: +44 207 723 2223, www.conranshop.co.uk) is a baking must.

Madeleines

Williams-Sonoma madeleine pan (www. williams-sonoma.com). Madeleines are easy to bake – and even easier in this flexible, non-stick pan.

Copper retinning

Copper retinning is essential if you use your tinned copper frequently. If you cook directly on copper, without a tin layer, you can risk inclusion of copper oxide in your food which in some cases can be poisonous. Divertimenti offer a professional retinning service which takes about two weeks.

Kitchen scales

Retro scales in pink by Typhoon, £25, at John Lewis; also available at Debenhams and Typhoon Housewares Ltd, Oakcroft Road, Chessington, Surrey, KT9 1RH (www.typhoonhousewares.com). The scales also come in peppermint and limousine black, and check out the beautiful limousine black colander for £10. Who can resist those prices?

A proper cake stand

Ceramic cake stand, £82.50, at Summerill & Bishop Limited, 100 Portland Road, London W11 (tel: +44 207 221 4566, www.summerillandbishop.com) or white scalloped cake stand, $54, at www.williams-sonoma.com – they will make even the simplest cookies or cake look special.

An E-cloth

My E-cloth is brilliant at cleaning stainless-steel surfaces. It gets rid of prints and marks, and no soap is required – you just rinse it in water to clean it. Buy at www.e-cloth.com or John Lewis.

An electric mixer

It makes shipping up a batch of cupcakes so much easier. Braun Multiquick Fresh System £99 (tel: +44 (0)800 783 7010, www.braun.com). This four-in-one, multi-purpose kitchen tool can crush ice, blend, chop, purée, whisk and even preserve food with a unique vacuum tool. It comes with freezer- and oven-safe Pyrex boxes. KitchenAid retro mixer I know I bang on about this but I'd be lost without mine. Treat yourself to this classic mixer by KitchenAid (tel: +44 (0)800 381 04026, http://international.kitchenaid.com/main.asp).

Bring your cupcakes to the office

Cup-A-Cakes, blue, set of 3, $10.50 at www.williams-sonoma.com. The predicament of transporting iced cupcakes has been resolved once and for all by a team of mothers. They designed these clever containers to each hold a single cupcake or muffin, so it arrives at its destination in pristine condition. Good job they only come in sets of three, limits the daily calorie intake.

Cupcake cases

Choose from a really great selection at Jane Asher (www.janeasher.co.uk).

Mechanical pastry bag

Much easier to control than a conventional pastry bag, this pastry decorating tool comes with ten attachments for you to personalize cakes. The stainless-steel barrel is dishwasher safe. Pure cake porn. (www.williams-sonoma.com)

Baby passion fruit/blackberry meringues

Makes 24 meringues
Preparation time: 15 minutes
Cooking time: 45–50 minutes
Cooling time: 1–2 hours

6 **medium** egg whites
300g golden **caster** sugar
100g palm sugar, chilled
and grated

For the passion fruit cream
250ml whipping cream
Pulp from 6 ripe passion fruit
to serve add a few sprigs of
mint and some blackberries

1. Preheat the oven to 120ºC/284ºF/Gas 1.
2. Line 2 large baking sheets with non-stick parchment.
3. In a large copper bowl, whisk the egg whites with an
electric hand whisk or a balloon whisk (see Baking Kit)
until they form stiff but not dry peaks.
4. Gradually whisk in the caster sugar until the
meringue is thick and glossy.
5. Gently fold in the palm sugar with a large metal
spoon.
6. Scoop 6cm dollops of the meringue mixture onto
the prepared baking trays, spaced well apart. Make an
indent in the centre of each meringue with the back of
a spoon.
7. Bake in the oven for 45–50 minutes or until firm.
8. Cool in the turned-off oven for 1–2 hours.

To make the passion fruit cream

1. Whip the cream until it just begins to stiffen.
2. Top each meringue with the cream, then the passion fruit pulp.
3. Push blackberries in around the cream in a random fashion.
4. Finally, add some finely chopped mint and serve. (That bit's optional.)

Titbit

Unrefined sugars are great for baking as they're strong in natural molasses's buttery flavour. You don't need all of these but it's nice to know a little about them if you want to try making something new.

Golden caster – A classic baking sugar, it has a mild buttery taste. I find it great in meringues, cakes and biscuits. **Light muscovado** – A soft light brown sugar with a fudgy flavour, it's excellent in cakes and toffee sauce. **Dark muscovado** – I use it in meat marinades, fruit cakes and chutneys. **Demerara** – A crunchy golden sugar – nothing else will do for the top of an apple crumble. **Molasses** – The darkest sugar available, it's packed with natural cane molasses. It has the deepest and richest flavour of all sugars.

Titbit

Thai palm sugar is often sold in plastic tubs and looks like solid creamed honey. If you can't get hold of it, substitute it with another brand or with equal quantities of soft brown muscovado sugar and maple syrup although the taste will not be the same.

Titbit

It is important to let your egg whites come to room temperature, as this will help you get the most volume. Also, make sure all your bowls, whisks, etc., are spotlessly clean and free of any grease.

Titbit

Add a tiny pinch of salt to the large bowl before you beat the egg whites in it. This ensures that there's no grease in the bowl and the egg whites whisk **to** form better peaks in **any** meringue recipe.

Titbit

These meringues are wheat-free, gluten-free, yeast-free, but still fun!

S
U
G
A
R

Icing Sugar

Unrefined Demerara

Unrefined Golden Caster Sugar

Unrefined Light Muscovado

Unrefined Dark Muscovado

ROMANCING THE SCONE

How happy am I? Woke up to this on a Saturday morning, jumped out of bed at 10 a.m. and set about baking Mum's secret recipe and had that cakey-bakey stare in my eye. Scones warm from the oven with proper Irish butter? Un-bee-lievable! Proper farmhouse cream and jam made with chunky fruit. Happy? Over-the-moon ecstatic more like!

Makes 12–15 scones
Prep. time: 20 minutes
Resting time: 15 minutes
Baking time: 20 minutes

150g salted butter, cubed
600g plain flour
150g caster sugar
40g baking powder
280g sultanas
190g double cream
190ml milk
2 eggs, beaten
1 egg, beaten with
a pinch of sugar
and salt for
an egg wash

Titbit

To keep scones or cake from going stale, just put half an apple in the cake tin with them. They stay fresher for much longer and it keeps them company.

1. Preheat the oven to 220°C.
2. Rub the butter into the flour in a mixing bowl. Add the sugar and baking powder.
3. Add the sultanas and mix until they are evenly distributed.
4. Whisk the cream, milk and eggs then make a well in the dry mixture. Pour the liquid into the well and mix with your hands until all the ingredients are bound together.
5. Lightly dust your work surface with flour and turn the dough out onto it.
6. Press down, then fold it in half; then press down again and fold the opposite way. Repeat until you have a rough square.
7. Flour the top and bottom of the dough, cover with a tea towel and rest in a cool place for 15 minutes.
8. To shape the scones, lightly flour the work surface and then roll the dough out to a thickness of 2.5–3cm. Brush off any excess flour. Flour the edges of a tea cup and turn it upside down to cut out the scone shapes.
9. Lay them on a baking tray, making sure they are not too close together. Roll out any scraps of dough and cut some more scones until you have used all the dough.
10. Glaze the scones with the egg wash. Wait for 2 minutes, then glaze again. Turn down the heat in the preheated oven to 200°C and bake for around 20 minutes until well risen and golden. Enjoy!

Titbits

Clarence Court eggs (tel: +44 (0)1579 345718, www.clarencecourt.co.uk) from major supermarkets. Unbleached stone-ground white flour from **Stoate's** (tel: +44 (0)1747 852475, www.stoatesflour.co.uk). **Ouse Valley Jam** (tel: +44 (0)1273 891893, www.ousevalleyfoods.com) at Fresh & Wild, 196 Old Street, London EC1 (tel: +44 207 250 1708). **Wild Rose Jam** £4.95, from the Bekaa valley in Lebanon at Mortimer & Bennett, 33 Turnham Green Terrace, London W4 (tel: +44 208 995 4145, www.mortimerandbennett.co.uk) or buy online. Aromatic, perfumed, gorgeous! **Ivy House butter**, milk and clotted cream at La Fromagerie, 2–6 Moxon Street, London W1 (+44 207 935 0341, www.lafromagerie.co.uk) or Neal's Yard Dairy (tel: +44 207 645 3554, www.nealsyarddairy.co.uk). **Kerrygold Butter** (www.kerrygold.com) yummy!

CHOCOLATE

We'd been collecting all sorts of chocolate as we travelled. Then disaster, Lent struck and we had to put them away under lock and key. If happiness is built on anything in Catholic Ireland it's built on pure denial. The temptation was brutal. Have you seen chocolate ads lately? Hinting that the brown stuff is as good as a good seeing-to. Trust me I've had both, and while chocolate tastes a bit nicer, it's no substitute for sex.

Anyway after Lent we built our own chocolate city and I took half an hour out of my busy schedule to eat half of it. It was Peter's birthday the day we built it. Well he built it actually and I promised I'd help er, ummmmmm… help eat it, that is….. I took the Valhrona skyscraper supporting the King Kong type character down first just in case of further attack and tucked it away to make his birthday cake (see p260 nice recipe). Then I immediately nibbled the third building from the right, it had a racy name "François Pralus" one of the most respected chocolate makers in France at least that's what the man who sold it to us in Paris said (only two other chocolate makers exist), Francois even has his own cacao plantation in Madagascar.

Of course for years I stuck loyally to Green & Black since its birth in 1991 and its enticing range of world ingredients (the stem ginger one is especially nice). I rummaged around the city and plucked a bit of Mayan Gold for old time's sake and then I tried a bit off the building fourth from the right "What's that?" asked Peter "Funny you should ask?" I said "it's this thing called Dolfin Milk chocolate with Konacha green tea from Japan and there's a Dolphin Milk chocolate with green tea & jasmine from Morocco over there on the right of King Kong too.

I'd never had it before (Dolfin, I had discovered five minutes earlier, was invented in 1989 by the Poncelet brothers in Belgium. To protect the fine aromas, the bars come, like finest tobaccos, in a specially wrapped wallet. At least that's what I gleaned from the packet anyway.) "What?" said Peter mishearing me, "they're making chocolate with tobacco in it now are they?" What next? Heroin? Whiskey? Nice bar of Gin?" So that was fun while it lasted.

Then Peter held up a pink wrapper which actually said Gin & Tonic chocolate. Who's that by then? "Cocoa Bean Chocolates, they're Irish artisan chocolate makers and each bar is hand wrapped." "Show me so I can see the volume of booze in it". They'd used lime zest and crushed juniper berries in the bar to create the gin and tonic flavour. Mmmm, it was luscious. After that the Toblerones met with a swift end (lovin' them) and then what to do about the last eight? There was nothing for it but to use them to bake chocolate goodies in the kitchen. So that's what I did. See the recipes next.

Chocolate Addresses

Francois Pralus (www.chocolats-pralus.com) available from www.chocolatetradingco. com, Monmouth, 27 Monmouth Street, Covent Garden, London, WC2 (tel: +44 207 379 3516; www.monmouthcoffee.co.uk and Fresh and Wild, 69-75 Brewer St. London W1F (tel: +44 207 434.3179; www.wholefoodsmarket.com. Green and Blacks www.greenandblacks.com (nationwide). Dolphin, www.dolfin.be www.chocolatesdirect.co.uk sell 8 small bars for £8.00 Cocoa Bean Chocolates, www.cocoabeanchocolates.com are available at Fallon & Byrne and Harvey Nichols Nationwide. Valrhona, £3.99 each (tel: +44 (0) 845 2308899, www.chocolate.co.uk) See further chocolate cities and Snack Club meets at www.thegoddessguide.com

The G's Chocolate Bomb

A chocolate pudding with a gooey centre – many a Masterchef finalist fell at this hurdle, I can tell you. Well, with practice I've mastered it – the secret is the cooking time; it's crucial and you'll need to set a timer for this.

Serves 6
Preparation time:
1 hour 20 minutes
(includes 1 hour chilling)
Cooking time: 12 minutes

300g good-quality dark chocolate, chopped (I like Valrhona)
150g butter, chopped
4 eggs
3 egg yolks
150g unrefined golden caster sugar
6 tbs plain flour

1. Rub a thick layer of butter onto 6 metal pudding moulds and then dust with flour. Chill the buttered and floured moulds in the freezer while you make the mixture.
2. Melt the chocolate and butter in a heatproof dish on top of a small saucepan of simmering water on the hob, stirring occasionally to prevent lumps – it needs to be completely smooth.
3. Beat the eggs, egg yolks and sugar for 4–5 minutes until thick. It will take on a palish colour. Gradually mix in the melted chocolate mixture until everything is completely combined.
4. Sift in the flour and fold it through until everything appears smooth.
5. Remove moulds from the freezer and spoon the mixture into them, filling them almost to the top.
6. Transfer them to the fridge and chill them for at least an hour (they can be refrigerated for up to 24 hours).
7. Heat the oven to 200°C/Gas 6. Bake for 12 minutes (this bit is by far the most important) and have a look at them.
8. If they're done they should have risen slightly and the tops should be just firm to the touch but not sticky or damp. Put them back in the oven for an extra minute or two, if needed. Remove from the oven and let them sit in their tins for 2 minutes (it's important to do this bit too).
9. Loosen the puddings by running a knife around the inside edge of the mould. Turn each tin upside down on a serving plate until the chocolate pudding pops out.
10. Serve with a dollop of crème fraîche (buy extra if you're making BrenB's pea soup as a starter) or with a few scoops of vanilla ice cream.

Titbit

These puds can be made ahead of time and stored in the fridge for up to 24 hours. Alternatively they can be frozen (uncooked) for up to a month – they can then be cooked for 25 minutes from frozen. How cool is that?

Claire's Brownies

These brownies stopped me in my tracks the first time I tasted them. My editor Claire Bord at HarperCollins brought them in to share one day when I was in with her for a girlie chat and a cup of tea. They are by far the best brownies that I have ever tasted. Here's Claire's secret recipe – like the chocolate it's all in the timing, baby ... Thanks for sharing, Claire. x

Makes 10-12
(but I always like to double up!)
Preparation time: 20 minutes
Cooking time: 30-40 minutes

250g unsalted butter
100g plain flour (sieved)
400g dark chocolate
(use a couple of bars of Bourneville)
3 eggs
250g dark muscovado sugar
1tsp baking powder
Pinch of salt

1. Firstly, pre-heat the over to 170/325 F or Gas Mark 3
2. Grease and flour a rectangular cake tin and line the base with greaseproof paper.
3. Put the butter in a saucepan, break-up the chocolate and throw that in, melt over a low heat to be sure the chocolate doesn't burn.
4. Whisk the eggs and add the sugar a spoonful at a time.
5. Mix in the melted chocolate mixture and carefully fold in the flour, baking powder and pinch of salt.
6. Pour the mixture into the tin and bake in the oven for 30 -40 minutes. The key to perfect brownies is to undercook them ever so slightly – poke a skewer in the mixture and if there is a little bit clinging to the end then they're perfect.
7. Take them out the oven and let them cool slightly before transferring onto a cooling tray.
8. You can keep them for a while in an airtight container either in the fridge or in a tin.

Titbit
for a quick dessert, warm the brownies in the oven and serve with good vanilla ice cream.

Goddess Wicked Chocolate Cake

This is the cake that I bake for Peter's birthday or for friends I love who stay with us for weekends. It's utterly lush and is well impressive. For cake sake get baking!

220g unsalted butter, chopped
110g unrefined golden caster sugar
110g light muscovado sugar
4 eggs
142ml/small tub of sour cream
120ml corn oil
300ml chilled water
4 tbsp ground almonds
220g self-raising flour
pinch of sea salt
60g good cocoa powder

Serves 10
Preparation time: 20 minutes plus chilling
Cooking time: 50–55 minutes

For the fudge icing
220g golden caster sugar
220ml milk
280g good-quality (minimum 70% cocoa solids) dark chocolate, chopped (I like Valrhona)
110g unsalted butter
4 tbsp double cream

1. Preheat the oven to 180°C/350°F/Gas 4.
2. Butter and line two 18cm cake tins with greaseproof paper.
3. Using a freestanding or handheld electric mixer (I love my KitchenAid), cream the butter and both sugars and whip until light and fluffy. Add the eggs and sour cream and beat again, then add the corn oil and water and beat further.
4. Add the ground almonds and give a quick whirl on the KitchenAid.
5. Sift the flour, salt and cocoa together and fold into the butter mixture gently.
6. Spoon this into the prepared cake tins, and bake in the oven for 50–55 minutes or until a skewer comes out dry and clean.
7. Leave in the tins for a while on a wire rack, then turn out onto the wire rack and leave both cakes to cool completely.

To make the icing
1. Place the sugar and milk in a pan and heat to dissolve the sugar. Bring to the boil and simmer for 8 minutes. Take the pan off the heat, add the chocolate and allow to melt.
2. Then add the butter and cream and stir together until everything has melted. Place the icing in the fridge to chill until thick enough to spread.

Assembly
Cut both cakes in half horizontally, then sandwich the four layers together, using a third of the icing. Spread the rest over the cake using a large palette knife or a rubber spatula. Utterly gorge!

Goddess Wicked Swirl Cupcakes

These treats look great and taste gorgeous. Who'd a thunk Nutella was so useful? Sandwiched between biscuits it's yummy, but swirled in these cupcakes it's gorge.

Makes 12
Preparation time: 20 minutes plus chilling
Cooking time: 20 minutes

140g butter, softened
85g unrefined golden caster sugar
3 eggs
½ tsp vanilla
200g sifted plain flour
¼ tsp salt
2 tsp baking powder
120g of Nutella

1. Preheat oven to 160°C/325°F/Gas ?.
2. Butter and line a 12-cup muffin tin with paper liners.
3. Using a freestanding or handheld electric mixer (I use my KitchenAid), cream together butter and sugar until light, which takes about 2 minutes.
4. Add the eggs one at a time and keep mixing until fully incorporated. Don't worry if the batter doesn't look smooth.
5. Add vanilla then stir in the flour, salt and baking powder until batter is uniform and no flour remains.
6. Using an ice-cream scoop or a spoon, fill each muffin liner with batter. They should be three-quarters full.
7. Top each cake with 1 tsp Nutella. Swirl it in with a toothpick, making sure to fold a bit of batter up over the Nutella to give it a swirled-in effect.
8. Bake for 20 minutes and then remove to a wire rack to cool completely.

FREDDIE'S CHIC FRITES

So we've drowned ourselves in chocolate now it's time to pay

Back on pages 84- 95 you may have glanced quickly at the bits about our time spent in Paris with Vivienne Westwood. Thing is, I forgot to put in a bit where she (Vivienne) told me that she prefers her models to be interesting and curvy rather then boring and thin. I don't mind admitting that I was pretty pleased with her for just saying that, but hold on, what's this? Am I seriously trying to use her words so that I can scoff loads more chocolate?

I rang my friend Freddie and got to chirping. By the way, Freddie is Parisian and what she doesn't know about fashion.....at the half way point of the phone call I decided, cue trumpet blast, I'd go off the chocolate, you know, slim down a little bit. It's a dull old business, dieting; involves loads of negative chirps: doesn't it? You can't do this, you can't do that, say no to everything. Yawn! After the call I made myself a cuppa and had a Cadbury's cream egg anyway. Unwrap it, bite the top off and then nibble it down a bit while trying not to get the yellow and white stuff on your clothes, bit like trying to control a real egg at breakfast time isn't it?

Actually, for two days after that, I coaxed myself into self-denial, ate only salads and fruit, drank gallons of water and lost the will to live. Then I had a bright idea. Why don't we forget about this stupid diet lark? Then Freddie started to tell me this great insider tip from her super skinny friends back in Paris "they are losing pounds without suffering too much... having largoose low fat frites a few times a week as part of their regime" she said. A chip that tastes deep-fried but has the calories of a carrot. Don't get much better than that. The following Sunday I was up to Freddie's for a demonstration.

Blue tit

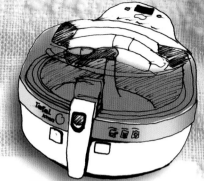

Freddie's Chic frites
Preparation time: 15 minutes
Cooking Time: 20 minutes
Makes enough for 6 people

Freddie took 8 floury potatoes, (Maris Piper or King Edward are perfect), peeled them (keep unpeeled if you prefer the texture), chopped them into 2cm thick shapes with one of these plastic chopping thingeys and placed them in a bowl of cold water. She then rinsed and drained them well and patted them dry with kitchen paper.

Measuring out 1 tablespoon of olive oil she piled the freshly cut chips into her new secret weapon and popped the 1 tablespoon (yes you read correctly) of olive oil in on top of them, Ta dah! Drum roll please… let me introduce to you ladies and gentlefolk the Tefal Actifry at £149.99 (www.tefal.co.uk). It's the latest hot new thing on the continent. The whole of Paris is raving about it. So how does it work? By circulating hot air around, whilst the mixing paddle evenly disperses the oil, the chips come out crispy on the outside, soft on the inside, with only 3% fat content. And where can you bag one of these fashionable babies? "Why largoose of course", chirped Freddie it took me a while to realise what largoose is erm Parisian for. Translated carefully it's Argos.

Tit Bit
Lakeland Limited chip cutter £9.95 (tel: +44 (0)153 948 8100, www.lakelandlimited.co.uk A top cutter that turns out perfectly formed home-made chips for the Tefal Actifry.

BEAUTY

So, beauty. It's a big ask, worth a new page in the notebook to begin with. Flicking back to the food bits with my friends, I smiled – they made me happy. You'll recall the astoundingly calorific saga of the hunt for the perfect burger? (I enjoyed that one immensely. May in New York it was.) Obviously, the G had the body of Kylie and Julia Roberts's body double in *Pretty Woman* just in time for summer after that one. And were you with me for snack club's foray into dessertage? Anything better than having cake and tea with pals? Hmmmmm, I struggled to think.

Actually, no, there was. Sunshine. Shoving the plates to one side (laters), I decided to work off some calories. Outdoors, after breakfast, pounding the ground, sun shining, it's not just great, it's wicked. Lunging down really low until my right knee touched the floor, then hold … one, two, three … Leaning on the wardrobe, I was looking for a vest and some baggy bottoms, yes, quite the athlete me. Whoa! I caught sight of myself in the mirror just there. For a split second I didn't recognise myself. That ever happened to you? And I think we know, don't we, what happened next? Yes, I paced around the bathroom like a madwoman, taking it all in, 360 style. There was some work to be done on the G for her reflection to go on her Happy List – just as well I'd written the word 'beauty' into my notebook then.

Before I'd even left the house for the first jog of the summer, I got a call from a girlfriend. 'Heyyyy, Mandy.' Picking our way down a list of subjects, we got talking about lipstick. 'What's your favourite luxury, Mandy?' 'Red lipstick, Gisèle. I need a new one.' Could the hunt for a beauty product ever be as rewarding as the hunt for other things for me? Umami, for instance. Would I ever really find a lipstick useful? I couldn't see it. Unless I was kidnapped while jogging maybe. I could use lipstick to scrawl PLEAS… (shit, lip gloss just doesn't do van windows, does it? I'm a lip gloss ladeeee). OK so it's nice to have a lipstick in the make-up bag. Anyway Mandy swore that if they stopped making her favourite shade, she'd go into meltdown. Riiiiiiiiiiight! So off I went for my jog to have a think about that.

Listen, I was thinking, what would you do if your all-time favourite beauty products were discontinued. Would you go mad? Why do you love them? Why do they make you happy? Practicality? Luxury? Whichever, it's a feeling of comfort, isn't it? See Mandy got me thinking ... what would you do if your favourite product was no more? What if you couldn't get another one? That's the desire talking now, watch him, he's brutal. For me the worst would be fragrance. Of all beauty products my relationship with fragrance is the strongest, it even extends to body products that are fragranced, like Decléor's Aromessence Body Concentrate. I should like to recommend it. I apply it to every inch of my body each night before I go to bed without fail, even when I've been out partying. If I didn't apply it I'd feel naked. I literally slide out of bed because I put so much on. If that were discontinued I'd go mental. Of course I'd find it on Google and eBay for a bit, but then what?

Would you email or write to complain if your favourite products were discontinued? I would. And do you know something? In reality, I don't need them at all, they're a fleeting luxury. But I have fallen in love with Decléor's Aromessence Body Concentrate and at the moment it's easy peasy to find. Imagine if (God forbid) it was a limited edition? Imagine after three months if it was discontinued? Did you know that sometimes there's such a hoo haa when a limited edition is discontinued that a company often has to fold and make the product part of the main line (for good).

Ah yes, beauty's a tricky business, but this one little bottle of Decléor oil is a lot more than a business to me. It's a staple. Am I vain or have I been duped by Decléor? Actually neither ... I've used this product for years; like the Pierre Hermé macaroon, it's outside fashion and trends and hype and marketing; it's 'notable' because it gives me real results. The thought of it disappearing gave me 'the fear'. After a few weeks of thinking about and poking around the subject of classics appearing and disappearing guess what I learned? We count. Yes, you and little old me, our opinion is the most important thing to the beauty companies; they will reinstate a product if we request it often enough, because without us buying what we like, they're profitless.

CLEANSe

I've started to relax now while
doing my cleansing routine and
these products help me wipe
away the rottenness of moods.

Eve Lom Cleanser

Eve Lom Cleanser and muslin cloth, £48
(mail order tel: +44 208 665 0112), available
from Space NK (tel: +44 208 740 2085, www.
spacenk.com), is a real treat. The hot cloth opens
your pores and then the waxy balm latches onto dead
skin cells and decongests them. Smells beautiful but
don't use it on your eye make-up. Too scratchy!

Organic wash-off cleanser

Liz Earle's Cleanse & Polish Hot Cloth Cleanser, £10.75, (mail order
tel: +44 (0)1983 813 913, www.lizearle.com) removes make-up including
mascara and is truly a wonder if you have sensitive skin. It's 100 per cent
natural as is The Organic Pharmacy Carrot Butter Cleanser, £24, at the
Organic Pharmacy, 23 Great Marlborough Street, London W1 (tel: +44 207
287 1607, www.theorganicpharmacy.com), which has won the CEW 2008
award for best organic skincare product (it's the beauty industry's highest
honour). Both these cleansers use a wash-off system using a muslin
cloth like Eve Lom (above). These all cheer me up in different ways.

Tone

Alcohol-laced toners dry out skin and upset oily skin's balance
so ensure that if you tone you use one that's completely
alcohol-free like Amanda Lacey's Persian Rosewater (tel:
+44 207 351 4443, www.amandalacey.com), or Rose Water
by Neal's Yard (tel: +44 (0)1747 834634 for your nearest
stockist, www.nealsyardremedies.com). Liz Earle's
Instant Boost Skin Tonic (mail order tel: +44 (0)1983
813 913, www.lizearle.com) with its aloe vera juice,
cucumber and calendula is also gentle.

Cleansing oil

Shu Uemura High Performance Balancing Cleansing Oil, £20, at Shu Uemura, 24 Neal Street, London WC2 (tel: +44 207 240 7635, www.shuuemura.co.uk) removes water-resistant make-up and regulates your skin's oil production.

Cleansing milks

Sisley's Cleansing Milk with White Lily (tel: +44 207 491 2722, www.sisleya.com) is my favourite wipe-off milk cleanser. Its beautiful scent and creamy texture are an incentive for me to cleanse thoroughly before crashing into bed after a night's clubbing. It leaves skin dewy, glowing and lush. For another organic milk that smells gorgeous try Dr Hauschka Cleansing Milk, £21 (tel: +44 (0)1386 791 022, www.drhauschka.co.uk).

Smoker?

If you're looking for fewer fine lines and wrinkles on very dry skin opt for NV Perricone Olive Oil Polyphenols Gentle Cleanser with DMAE, £36 (tel: +44 207 329 2000; www.nvperriconemd.co.uk), available at Harvey Nichols. It's also a great cleanser for skin suffering from the drying effects of air conditioning or central heating in an office, so cheer up Office Goddess.

Organic eye make-up remover

I'm currently using Dr Andrew Weil for Origins Mega-Mushroom Eye Makeup Remover Pads, £18 (tel: +44 (0)870 034 2888, www.origins.co.uk); they're full of natural goodness and the beautiful scent makes me smile.

Waterproof mascara

Bliss Lid+Lash Wash, £18 (www.strawberry.net) gently removes even the strongest waterproof mascara and eye make-up while still leaving lashes on eyes. It's fanfeckintastic!

Titbit

Keep your toner in the fridge and let it soothe. Ahhh!

The Tools

Sponge - Ramer's Classic Make-up Sponge, £1.20 (tel: +44 (0)1252 845292, www.spongerama.com), deepens a cleanser's pore-clearing effectiveness. Wash it with Carex antibacterial soap, 99p, after each use to combat germs. **Wipe** - These cotton balls are superb for cleaning up milks like Sisley's Cleansing Milk with White Lily and Dr Hauschka Cleansing Milk and perfect for applying toners. **Wash** - Liz Earle Muslin Cloths, £2.50 for 2 (mail order tel: +44 (0)1983 813 913, www.lizearle.com). An exfoliating cloth that lifts grime from congested faces.

HYDRATE DAY

Skin savers that work

'Moisturizing. It's a complete conversation killer, fact!' my younger sister Barbara pointed out to me one day as I browsed the skincare counter of a department store. Back in my bedroom, I had a choice between two purchases: a moisturizing cream or a youth-giving serum. I'd bought both earlier to soothe my frazzled 'shop face' you see. I chose the cream because it was ... well, creamy, and hours later? I've got to say, frankly, I was disappointed, it was crrrrrrrap. Why hadn't it given me that eighteen-year-old's complexion that it had promised on the telly ad? It had let me down. Ah well.

But hold on a minute, why was it that every time something went wrong with a beauty product there was no one to grill about it? 'Give me that phone there.' I made an appointment to see Dr Andrew Markey, the fancy-smancy dermatologist at London's Lister Hospital ... questions needed to be answered, goddamnit! I kicked off with 'Why can't I have the skin of those girls off the tv, Doc?' Twenty minutes with him and I wished I'd never spent time in the sun as a child without sun cream (who knew?), I wished I'd never started smoking (been off them seven years) and I wished I'd chosen bed over bars more often while travelling. 'No cream can make you look eighteen again, Gisèle.' 'Yeah, thanks, Doc, but is there anything that'll make me look ... say nineteen?'

Among the most enjoyable of those twenty minutes with Dr Markey were the handful spent talking about solutions. I explained that the closest I'd ever come to superhero glowiness was a detox I did in Switzerland two years ago. Thereby hangs a huge tale in itself, no time to tell it here though, time is ticking, Doc, and none of us are getting any younger-looking. 'Look,' I said, 'break it down for me, I can take it.' Turns out it wasn't all doom and gloom, in fact with the proper creams, I could achieve superhero glowiness in no time. Anyway I'd jumped the gun a bit judging the product so quickly earlier; seemingly it takes a few months to see a difference with a new cream.

A few days later, still obsessed, still searching for superhero glowiness (oh the want), I recalled what I'd scribbled in my notebook at Dr Markey's. Oh yeah, there it was, there was a bit about starting a preventative anti-ageing routine with a big NB written next to it. A skincare routine should be broken up into morning and evening. Morning is about protection (sun protection and antioxidants) after a thorough cleansing. Night-time, after cleansing, it's about repair (peptides, vitamin A, vitamin C). 'Right,' I said, 'now we're getting somewhere.' My superhero glowiness mission was to track down the creams next. Surely one of them would give me the glow of that girl on TV?

Daytime protection

I started by learning all about daytime protection. Backstage models told me about applying SPF 30 sunscreen every morning to their faces, necks, chests and hands to protect skin from UVA and UVB damage. Incidentally a moisturizer containing sunscreen will do also. Wear either, under your make-up. Try Clarins UV Plus Protective Day Screen SPF 40, £25, or Clinique City Block Sheer SPF 15, £12.50. Both are oil-free. Also Estée Lauder DayWear Plus SPF 15, £28 (tel: +44 (0)870 034 2566), and Olay Total Effects 7x Day Cream SPF 15, £14.99.

Apply an antioxidant cream every morning

Yes, sunscreen is essential, but strong UV rays can get through it and bash away at your skin. A good antioxidant cream will prevent that. You wear it on top of one of the creams mentioned in the previous paragraph – oh and if you're a smoker one of these will help your face. Try SkinCeuticals C E Ferulic, £60 (tel: +44 208 997 8541), Caudalie Vinoperfect Day Perfecting Cream SPF 15, £33 (tel: +44 (0)800 4429 2424), Ole Henriksen Express the Truth moisturizer, £55, at www.hqhair.com or Nivea Visage Anti-Wrinkle Q10 Day Cream, £6.79.

Titbit

Want SPF (UVA and UVB protection) and antioxidants in the one cream? Try Super Charged SPF 15 Day Cream, £16.95, by dermatologist Dr Nick Lowe at Boots.

Night creams containing retinoids

Two words. Vitamin A (is 'A' a word, do you think?) Most good night creams use a derivative of vitamin A known as retinoid to zap wrinkles. Boots No 7 Protect & Perfect Beauty Serum, £16.75, has it (remember the queues for this one after the Horizon programme scientists proved that it gave the best anti-wrinkle results?) The following creams also have it: Elizabeth Arden Ceramide Gold Ultra Restorative Capsules, £52 for 60; MD Formulations Vit-A-Plus Anti-Aging Lotion, £45, at www.hqhair.com; L'Oréal Dermo Expertise Revitalift Anti-Wrinkle Night, £12.99. These are all excellent wrinkle zappers while you sleep.

Night creams containing peptides

Sometimes a retinoid can irritate so instead try a cream containing peptides. Olay did a big fancy-smancy test comparing peptides and retinol (retinoid) products and found both performed the same (wrinkle depth shrank by the same amount). Peptides plump the skin, keeping it youthful (I like the sound of that don't you?). Two of the best are Olay Regenerist Night Cream, £19.50, and Estée Lauder Perfectionist (CP+) Correcting Serum, £42. Magic results!

Night creams containing vitamin C

And if neither retinol nor peptides take your fancy you can always try a night cream containing vitamin C (it's usually written on a cream's label as ascorbic acid). Vitamin C stimulates collagen growth and plumps skin so smooths out wrinkles. Try Philosophy Hope and a Prayer Topical Vitamin C Powder, £28 (tel: +44 (0)870 990 8452); Skin Wisdom Age Delay Vitamin C Youth Boost Serum, £7.97, from Tesco; Vitage Vitamin C Serum, £45, and Mask, £24 (tel: +44 (0)845 555 2121).

Titbit

Estée Lauder Advanced Night Repair, £47. It delivers high levels of hyaluronic acid, nature's moisture magnet', and repairs skin while you sleep. Magic results!

ESTÉE LAUDER

Advanced
Night Repair

Protective
Recovery Complex

Protecteur et accélérateur
de réparation cellulaire

TRUTH SERUMS

When serums first hit the shelves, to be honest I was a bit put out. As if the exfoliating and the cleansing and the toning and the moisturizing and the tanning weren't enough (phew, I'm worn out from it), now I had to deal with the added complication of adding more potions to my skincare kit. Seeing the benefits though, that's another matter: a serum's tiny molecules mean it offers immediate results and reaches parts that moisturizer can't. So do they really work? I was on a mission to find out ...

One evening after a night on the tiles with pals my skin was grey as a geriatric badger. I thought, 'I know, I'll chance a bit of serum, see if it'll help me hide the truth about my night-time shenanigans.' The word 'serum', you see, made me think of Jack Bower and him administering a dose of 'truth' serum to me (very 24). Within minutes of applying it all evidence of the previous night's naughtiness was camouflaged (not a bit of evidence that I'd been drinking or casual smoking (tut tut!) or that I hadn't managed the recommended eight hours' sleep). If you've a problem with fine lines, sensitivity, dehydration, blotchiness or you're sporting a grey hangover face there's a serum here for you to hide behind. I've tried loads and these are the best.

Illuminating

One of the best 100 per cent natural serums to give miracle results is iRejuvenate Step 2, Regenerating Skin Serum, £36, by Dr Barbara Olioso at Forest Secrets Skincare (tel: +44 208 242 4746, www.forestsecret-sskincare.com). Made from a powerful blend of hydrating and softening ingredients, after ten minutes it's like you've taken a nap in the rain. Beautiful!

Calming

If you've sensitive skin, L'Occitane's Ultra Comforting Serum, £26, by L'Occitane, 9 the Market, Covent Garden, London, WC2E 8RB (tel: +44 207 379 6040, www.uk.loccitane.com), gives soothing relief to irritation and redness from the moment it goes on (I said they were fast, didn't I?). It's free from parabens, fragrance, colorant, preservatives and alcohol.

Titbit

Always apply serum to bare skin so it can be absorbed, applying your moisturizer on top if needed. The cream acts as a protective layer, so the serum works twice as hard underneath.

Wrinkle-fighting serum

Crème de la Mer Lifting Face Serum and Lifting Intensifier, £220, are two bottles containing blue algae and azurite crystal that work together to visibly plump lines and make skin glow. This system is so fancy-smancy it's like rubbing gold buillion all over your face.

Spot-busting

Apply Prescriptives Custom Concentrates Anti-Blemish Serum, £21 (tel: +44 (0)177 302 3566, +44 (0)870 034 2566, www.prescriptives.com), daily all over the face to purify and calm blocked pores and blemishes. Gives a glass-like smoothness to the skin.

Hydrating

Is your face like cardboard? Chanel's Hydramax + Active Serum, £63 (www.chanel.com), is based around an ingredient derived from the fruit of the Moroccan carob tree which gives instant moisture which makes your skin plump up and full of moisture as if you've just spent the day running and doing the odd twirly, twirl in the rain.

BATHE

Of course you know how to take a shower – get wet, lather up and rinse off, right? But there's a bit more to it than that if you're looking for a glowing complexion. Here are a few things you might like to know about shower time.

Protect

Did you know that the chlorine in your water can fade and change your hair colour? Swap your shower head for the Methven Satinjet Maia, £280, available on www.amazon.com. Created by Santa Monica dermatologist Karyn Grossman for Methven, it contains a vitamin C cartridge which removes the chlorine. It does loads of other cool stuff too.

Loofah junkie

OK, if you're hooked like a crack junkie to your radioactive scrubber, at least clean it after each use, either with an antibacterial soap like Lever 2000 (bring home from the US) or buy Carex, 99p, available from your supermarket. Pop it in the washing machine once a week and let it dry in an open area. Always replace it once a month.

Back to basics

Your scrubby thingy could be depositing more germs than it's scrubbing off you! Gross, I know. I'm not a fan of loofahs and puffy scrubbers any more because they're the perfect place for bacteria which can cause skin infections. Think about it, all that sloughed-off skin and moisture? Recipe for disaster. Natural loofahs are the worst, but synthetic nylon scrubbers are only slightly better. I've binned mine! The alternative? A plain white facecloth – after use I just throw it in the washing machine every couple of days and it lasts ages.

Before you shower

If you like to stay in the shower for more than ten minutes, coat your entire body in a body oil before showering (everywhere except your feet, that is); use L'Occitane Almond Shower Oil, £14.50, by L'Occitane, 9 the Market, Covent Garden, London, WC2E 8RB (tel: +44 207 379 6040, www.uk.loccitane.com) or in Dublin at L'Occitane, 15 Wicklow Street, Dublin 2 (tel: +331 6797223). Lisa Hoffman Spa Shower Body Oil, $34 (www.lisahoffmanskincare.com), available at Harvey Nichols, is another great oil to slather on before you step into the water. These oils help prevent water from drying out your skin. A good buy if you're visiting the US is Nivea Body Smooth Sensation Body Oil, $4; it's cheap and great lashed on all over before you shower.

The water in your shower should be around 75 to 80 degrees rather than roasting.

Titbit

Switch to a multiblade refillable razor instead of a one-blade disposable for underarm and leg shaving (this prevents red lumps and nasty nicks).

Titbit

If you notice a chalky build-up on the shower door, you have hard water, which is drying to hair and skin. You can counteract it with moisturizing shampoo and body wash.

Body wash

Skin becomes dull and flaky over time and needs a good exfoliation. Use your washcloth every day with a no-chemical body wash like Ren Moroccan Rose Otto Body Oil, £22.50 (tel: +44 (0)845 225 5600, www.renskincare.com), available at Space NK, if you like the scent of roses or The Organic Pharmacy Sicilian Lemon, Seaweed & Eucalyptus body scrub, £20 (tel: +44 207 351 2232, www.theorganicpharmacy.com), if you like eucalyptus. It removes dead skin, detoxifies and moisturizes with no use of chemicals.

Defuzz

Coat your legs in moisturizing shaving cream and use at least a triple-blade razor. Gillette Venus Breeze Razor, £7.99, is a bar with in-built shave gel; just wet and go. For the closest shave, draw it in strokes from the ankles upwards (if skin is sensitive use downward strokes). Repeat the process on your underarms.

Bluebell

The Bluebell Bath-oil by Penhaligons, 16 Burlington Arcade, W1J (tel:020 7629 1416, www.penhaligons.com) not only smells great but is a sumptuous addition to your bathroom shelf.

Exfoliate

Once a week massage Lancôme Resurface Microdermabrasion Body, £30.50, onto wet skin and shower off. It contains finely ground pumice stone, helps to fade pigmentation, and also tackles dry heels and elbows if applied on dry skin before showering. (If skin is oily, use a scrub twice a week.) Or try Brown Sugar Body Polish by Fresh, 94 Marylebone High Street, London W1 (tel: +44 207 486 4100, www.fresh.com), $65. Go lightly on the chest, and skip scrubbing your legs on a day you plan to shave them.

GLOW

Apart from cycling (doesn't suit everyone) and after-dark bouncy boyfriend bedtime fun (doesn't suit everyone either), there are several less sweaty ways to get that just-exercised radiance – take these neat little tubes and jars for example. To whoever came up with these formulas, excellent work, well done, feel free to pull your shirt over your head and run around the office. One thing, people asking you if you've been on holiday ... is that a side-effect of these good creams?

Right, dull skin and how I cured it. The rubbing, the flaking, the rinsing! Me bent over the bath, tongue stuck out to the side in concentration. Oh the effort! But say what you like about beauty routines, I still love finding new, hard-working road-testable stuff. So I feel a challenge coming on. Anyone out there know the secret to perfect radiance? Any takers? I hadn't a clue myself until I found these.

Exfoliate

Heavy duty microdermabrasors (sounds painful) were originally only available as salon treatments, but now there are tons of microdermabrasion kits on offer that you can use yourself at home. Take the controlled peel, Philosophy Microdelivery Mini Peel Pads, £28 (tel: +44 (0)870 990 08452, www.philosophy. com), a great little glow giver. As is Lancôme's Resurface-C Microdermabrasion, £61, which comes with a serum rich in vitamin C that makes a great base for flawless party make-up. Speaking of which, no good having a great face and a dull chest and arms, is it? MD Skincare by Dr Gross Alpha Beta Daily Body Peel, £69 (www.hqhair.com), should leave your body glowing to match your face. My conclusions? All of these products deep-clean and polish the skin's surface so you look sparkly and healthy before you even touch your make-up bag.

Illuminate

Next up, it's time to add some radiance. I kicked off with Chanel's Précision line. The first product, Chanel Éclat Maximum Radiance Cream, £46, I tried after cleansing (even popped it in the fridge beforehand as an extra treat, very cool, very refreshing). Then I added the Chanel Éclat Original Serum, £51, on top. The results? They created a soft film that acted like a second glowing skin for me to apply my foundation over. Respect to Chanel, these products are grrrrrrrrreat and best of all ...they give a kick-ass glow. Looked as if I'd just had a cycle race against a guy on a BMX Top Gear style ... über radiant! But my obsession didn't stop there; no, in a rare display of energy, after seeing the über glowiness, I decided to experiment to see if there were a few more things that I could use to achieve that superhero glow. A waste of time? Come on, you know me by now.

...

Make-up base

Trying out a batch of illuminating make-up bases, I settled on Clarins Instant Smooth Perfecting Touch, £20, and, applied before my foundation, it worked the hardest. Guess what? It caught the light, bounced it around the room and made me look all superhero-esque. All that going on under my foundation. It can't get much better than this now, can it? All done? As if ...

Feast your peepers on these guys ...

Clinique's Up-Lighting Liquid Illuminator, £17.50 (tel: +44 870 034 2566, www.clinique.co.uk); Shu Uemura's Base Control in Pearl, £12, at Shu Uemura, 24 Neal Street, London WC2 (tel: +44 20 7240 7635, www.shuuemura.co.uk); and my own personal faves, MAC's Strobe Cream, £18.50 (www.maccosmetics. co.uk) and Shiseido The Make-up Sheer Enhancer Base $32 (also comes in brown which can be worn alone for a sunkissed glow). Any of these illuminators (take your pick) when tapped sparingly with fingers onto the cheekbones and across the forehead (after applying your foundation, concealer, blushers, etc. – see X), give added radiance. Real superhero stuff, this little lot!

FOUNDATION

Have you found that wearing the same make-up shades and using the same techniques in the winter as you do in mid-July just doesn't cut it? It's like wearing a bikini in a blizzard. Fact is foundation needs to be a little darker after September and concealer and bronzer are also a must to avoid that winter pastiness (it just creeps up, doesn't it?), but more about bronzing and contouring later; for now let's get a few new foundation basics added to your make-up bag. A good foundation (and concealer) alone can make a huge difference to your complexion. Here are the ones that I've found fantastic!

Winter foundation

In winter it's a good idea to change over to a foundation with an inbuilt moisturizer. Chanel's Vitalumière Satin Smoothing Fluid Makeup, £23 (tel: +44 207 493 3836, www.chanel.com), is a beautiful liquid foundation which really lifts winter skin (comes in seven colours). Another great one is Clinique's Dewy Smooth Anti-Ageing Make-up SPF 15, £18 (tel: +44 (0)870 034 2566, www.clinique.co.uk), which comes in 8 different shades and, speaking of shades, Clinique makes 12 different foundations with 100 shades to choose from, so hopefully there's something there for you.

Rethink your foundation for summer

It may sound obvious but it's amazing how many people don't think to invest in a new foundation for summer. What you need is a liquid foundation that'll give a natural glow. The trick is to try several different shades along the jaw line before choosing. The one that disappears into your skin is your summer colour and the one we're looking for.

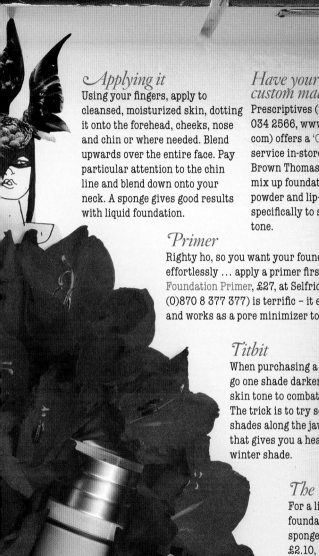

Applying it

Using your fingers, apply to cleansed, moisturized skin, dotting it onto the forehead, cheeks, nose and chin or where needed. Blend upwards over the entire face. Pay particular attention to the chin line and blend down onto your neck. A sponge gives good results with liquid foundation.

Have your foundation custom made

Prescriptives (tel: +44 (0)870 034 2566, www.prescriptives. com) offers a 'Custom Blend' service in-store at Harrods and Brown Thomas, Dublin, that will mix up foundation, concealer, powder and lip-gloss shades specifically to suit your skin tone.

Primer

Righty ho, so you want your foundation to glide on effortlessly ... apply a primer first. Laura Mercier Foundation Primer, £27, at Selfridges (tel: +44 (0)870 8 377 377) is terrific – it evens out cracks and works as a pore minimizer too.

Titbit

When purchasing a winter foundation go one shade darker than your natural skin tone to combat winter paleness. The trick is to try several different shades along the jaw line and the one that gives you a healthy glow is your winter shade.

The Tools – Sponges

For a light finish to a foundation, use a damp sponge. Buy latex wedges, £2.10, at Sally Hair and Beauty Supplies (www. sallybeauty.com). MAC Cosmetics stock great sponges too.

CONCEAL

Dark circles, broken capillaries around the nose and blemishes due to central heating can all be camouflaged with a good concealer. Like a good bra or superhero, a good concealer works best when it's totally undetectable.

Applying concealer over or under foundation?

Applied over your foundation, a concealer such as Secret Camouflage by Laura Mercier, £25, at Selfridges (tel: +44 (0)870 837 7377) is the bizz. There's a light and dark shade in each compact which allows you to blend them to your exact colour. Sometimes you may not even need foundation – just apply your concealer where you need it and finish with a touch of powder to keep in place. For a silky fine pressed powder opt for Shiseido Pressed Powder, £24 (tel: +44 207 313 4774, www.shiseido.co.uk), and apply with a brush.

Picking a concealer

Since skin undertones vary, visit a make-up counter and let a professional help you pick your colour. As a general rule, you want a yellow-tone concealer if your dark under-eye circles have a blue cast, a peachy one if your circles have a brown or yellowish tint and a tone that matches your skin exactly to camouflage redness.

Applying it

Use your ring finger, which has the lightest touch, to pat eye cream all around your eyes. Light-reflecting particles minimize the appearance of dark circles so choose an eye cream that contains them like Liz Earle's Instant Boost Skin Tonic, £12.25 (mail order tel: +44 (0)1983 813 913, www.lizearle.com) or pat a product designed to brighten the area such as Bobbi Brown Eye Brightener, £26, or Prescriptives Vibrant Instant Eye Brightener for Dark Circles and Puffiness, £24, over your regular eye cream.

Give your eye product a minute to sink in, and during this time, apply your foundation or tinted moisturizer (previous page). You can also apply your eye make-up now too; this way, you avoid bits of fallen eye shadow or smudged mascara landing on freshly applied concealer.

If concealer cakes or settles in lines under your eyes, dip a cotton swab in a drop of eye cream or moisturizer and lightly sweep over any colour that has gathered.

Titbit

Make-up artists use concealer brushes made with synthetic hair because the bristles pick up more colour than natural hair. Try Synthetic 12 by Shu Uemura, £25, or L'Oreal Paris Makeup Artiste Concealer Brush. For touch-ups, keep a retractable lip brush in your bag.

Hiding spots

Use a heavier concealer for red spots. Press it on and pat with your fingers to blend. To cover a blemish, dot concealer on top, then brush tiny strokes around the area. Erase obvious edges around the spot by rubbing with a wedge sponge like the Starcluster non-latex wedges, 4 for £1.35 (tel: +44 (0)1252 845292, www.spongerama.com), or MAC's latex wedge sponge, £2.50 (www.maccosmetics.co.uk). Loose powder sets concealer, so dust Lancôme Photôgenic Skin-Illuminating Sheer Loose Powder in Translucent or Bobbi Brown (tel: +44 (0)800 525 501) or my own personal favourite Chanel Natural Finish Loose Powder £25 over your concealer (everywhere except around the eyes).

Covering dark eye circles

In natural light, dot creamy concealer on the inner corner of your eye with a brush. Start around your tear duct and work outwards, covering only the dark areas. Use your fingertips to gently press – not rub – the dots of colour into the skin. Apply a second layer where skin still seems dark, and repeat the process on the other eye.

Titbit

Never put concealer on eyelids as it can make them look too heavy. To cover redness in eyelids, dip your fingertip in a drop of foundation and tap onto your lids.

The Tools

Experts use a large eye-shadow brush to dust powder over concealer because it's precise and won't deposit too much. Try **Natural 10 by Shu Uemura**, £45 (tel: +44 207 240 7635). **YSL Touche Eclat**, £21: a pen-brush for adding a touch of light to dark areas (under your eyes or at the sides of your nose), disguising dark shadows or even perfecting your lip line, Touche Eclat has yet to be bettered. It has many imitators but none of them has the texture – or delicacy of light-reflective particles – that puts Touche Eclat in a league of its own and makes this kind of no-see make-up correction foolproof.

CONtoUR

Whether it's chiselled cheekbones or a razor-sharp jaw line, these contouring tricks will help you look great.

The big ask for make-up is how to make it look naturally contoured, yet totally individual like the make-up gurus do backstage for super modules (my madey-uppey word for super models – God, how I envy their chiselled cheekbones!). I've tried various methods of giving myself a chiselled catwalk profile: a fringe, V necks, sucking my cheeks in really hard; however, after years of scribbling notes diligently backstage I have finally cracked the code. A tiny word of warning before we kick off here: be careful applying this little lot the first few times, the mere touch of heavy-handedness and it's Dallas all over again.

Prep

Start by applying a tiny bit of your lightweight liquid summer foundation and then dot on a concealer to hide any blemishes. Like I said on the previous page, Laura Mercier Secret Camouflage, £25, is the bizz applied with a Synthetic 12 Shu Uemura brush £25 (tel:+44 207 240 7635, www.shuuemura.com).

Applying bronzer

Standing under a light and looking at yourself in a mirror, study how the light falls on your face shape, what are your contours? Using a two-tone bronzing palette (the Duo, remember?), apply the paler shade under your cheekbones with a good blusher brush and sweep the colour out towards the temple. 14H Pony Brush by Shu Uemura, £16, is a good one (blends nose and eyes too). If you want a stronger look, use the darker bronze over the top and build until you have a well-contoured cheekbone. To make everything symmetrical, mix your brush in both the light shade and dark shade of the Duo palette and brush it down the centre of your nose.

Slim jaw line

To slim a heavy jaw line, use the dark shade from your bronzing palette below the jaw line to enhance a deep shadow effect and use the lighter shade just above the jaw line to give a more chiselled jaw.

Liquid blush

To achieve contours and warmth in summer, use the Duo if you want a powdery textured finish to your blusher, but for a more dewy finish, swap to a liquid blush. The best are Daniel Sandler's Watercolours, £11 each (tel: +44 (0)1923 845 370, www.beautique.com). One drop of these sheer liquids blends seamlessly into the skin to give a natural glow with staying power. The coral colour especially looks fantastic on tanned or black skin.

Bronzer

Deep breath, here comes the magic ... Glam Bronze Blonde/ Brunette Duo Sun Powders by L'Oréal Paris, £9.99 (it's a mouthful so let's just call it 'The Duo'). It's a two-tone bronzing powder with dark powder on one side of the palette and light on the other. There's Glam Bronze in Blonde Harmony 101 for blondes and Glam Bronze in Brunette Harmony 102 (yes, not rocket science) for brunettes. It's a staple for any make-up bag and wait until you see what it can do.

Plump lips

For a lip-plumping effect, apply the pale bronze of your bronzing palette (or any pale powder) along your Cupid's bow, dusting it on with your finger. Finish with a nearly-nude pink gloss like Stila Melon Mint Plumping Lip Glaze, £15, or Stila's regular Watermelon, £15, in a pen applicator with built-in brush making it easy to apply. Perfect!

A great all-rounder

Stila Convertible Colour Dual Lip and Cheek Cream, £18 (www.hqhair.com). A delicate peachy glow, with a light, dewy texture that enhances cheekbones.

Titbit

Remember: stick with matt products and avoid the sparkles if you don't want to be transported back to the eighties.

BROWs

Want to look waaaaaaay younger? Nothing beats a pair of perfectly groomed brows, for getting an instant face-lifting effect.

Light brows

Want to darken brows without making them look fake? Apply a clear brow gel – Max Factor No Colour Mascara (available nationwide) or Anastasia brow gels (in either clear or blonde), available at Harrods Urban Retreat, should be enough to shape and darken them subtly. Also if you have light-brown brows and want more depth, try a coloured gel. Benefit Speed Brow (tel: +44 (0)808 238 0230, www.benefitcosmetics.com) is a good choice.

Thin brows

Another option is to take your brown mascara, wipe the wand until a tiny amount remains, then brush it through your brows lightly. To make your brows look thicker (but not darker) use two shades of brow pencil, both close to your natural colour and apply them in feathery strokes softly through your brows. Take a little time to practise this and eventually you'll achieve natural texture and depth.

Disastrous eyebrow wax or plucked too thin?

Leave over-plucked brows to rest for a couple of months to allow time for them to recuperate. In the meantime, brush hairs in the direction they naturally grow with a Brow Comb and Lash Brush by Giorgio Armani, £12 (tel: +44 207 493 3836, www.giorgioarmanibeauty.co.uk), and fill in bald patches with a powder such as Chanel Perfect Brows in Brun, £26.50 (tel: +44 207 493 3836, www.chanel.com), or MAC Eye Brows in Foolproof, £10, feathered along the brow will help make them look thicker. Once the hairs have grown back have them reshaped by a pro: Vaishaly Patel (page 295) is the best in the business.

Permanent make-up

Or why not try having some semi-permanent make-up applied to your eyebrows? Brows Perfection, £495, at Debra Robson Lawrence, 144 Harley Street, London W1G 7LE (tel: +44 (0)845 230 2021, www.permanent-makeup.com), gives amazing results. It's worth having your eyeliner done here too while you're at it. It's also an option if you've lost your brows due to an illness or have been affected by alopecia.

A classic

Maybelline Great Lash Mascara, £4.99. Why do 200 million women love this? Simplicity. Nuf said.

Feline flick

My scarves and my feline flick are my trademarks. I like my flick to be razor sharp and wear very little other eye make-up. I've tried many liquid eyeliners over the years, currently these are my favourites: Liquid Eye Liner by MAC, £12 (www.maccosmetics.co.uk), Guerlain Divinora Eyeliner in Noir Ebène (tel: +44 (0)193 223 3909, www.guerlain.com), Chanel Ligne Extreme, £16 (tel: +44 207 493 3836), Prescriptives Lucky Stroke, £15 (tel: +44 (0)870 034 2566, www.prescriptives.com). Meeeeeeeow!

The Tools – Tweezers

Tweezerman (tel: +44 (0)1730 811811) for precision plucking. Lightweight, accurate and not too sharp. The storage tube, lifetime guarantee and free sharpening are all bonuses. **MAC concrete eye powder** and **MAC 266 brush**, £ , has a slanted tip which makes it perfect for filling in sparse areas between brow hairs. Here's a tip, wet the brush and use with Mac's eye powder in concrete to draw a light line over your brow. Perfect!

LASHES

Time to have a flutter

Flutter bunny

Now, if you're anything like me, you're a last-minute Goddess. Occasion is looming and as usual I've left it too late to book an appointment to have an eyelash tint. Well, here comes Boots to the rescue with their lovely ad song Here Come the Girls and their Eylure Dylash, £7.50. It's real easy to dye lashes at home with this – the applicator is shaped like a mascara wand.

Good mascaras

Clinique Lash Doubling Mascara in brown, £12.50 (www.clinique.co.uk), is perfect for daywear. Estée Lauder MagnaScopic Maximum Volume Mascara, £17 (www.esteelauder.co.uk), is brilliant for ramping up lashes at night. Dior Diorshow Mascara, £18 (tel: +44 207 7216 0216), gets phenomenal results. Vroom, vroom!

Application

Well-defined, clump-free lashes are as much to do with method as mascara. A common mistake is to put mascara on too fast – this way it goes clumpy. Wait for a few seconds between each stroke for the layers to dry. If it comes off underneath your eyes you are either putting too much on or applying too soon after moisturizing – oiliness makes it run. When you apply it to your lower lashes, rest the brush on them and wiggle it a bit so the mascara gets between them.

Don't want falsies?

Lancôme's Cils Design Pro Mascara, £24.50 (available nationwide), has a brush each end containing a different formula. One lengthens lashes and the other, wax-based, thickens them. It comes in black, grey, brown or blue.

How to create luscious lashes with the tools (below)

Smudge a soft brown or black kohl pencil into the roots of your top lashes and then, to look wide awake, use an eyelash curler (Shu Uemura do the best). Apply your mascara from the roots to the tips of the top side of the lashes before coating the underside of the lashes upwards. Apply a single sweep of mascara to the lower lashes. Finally, comb out any clumps. For more defined result, use a lash primer (see below) before applying mascara, or try some individual false eyelashes.

Titbit

If you're after a fresh-faced look, apply mascara to your top lashes only.

Try a colour

Everyone sticks to black mascara for its drama, however Chanel's Cils à Cils in Marine mascara (tel: +44 207 493 3836, www.chanel.com) or in Violet really makes me smile. An added benefit is that it makes the whites of my eyes sparkle.

Titbits

Soft plum-coloured mascara suits older skin or Too Faced Chocolate Brown Mascara, £12.50, at HQ Hair, 2 New Burlington Street, London W1 (tel: +44 (0)871 220 4141, www.hqhair.com), is a good shade if you're fair. And Jan Marini Lash Mascara, £90 (tel: +44 208 868 4411, www.jmsreurope.com) stimulates growth.

The Tools

Cotton buds - Have a pack of Shu Uemura's Cotton Buds, £4.50, from Shu Uemura, 24 Neal Street, London WC2 (tel: +44 207 240 7635, www.shuuemura.co.uk) nearby in case of smudges. The Shu Uemura Eyelash Curlers, £9.95, are also the best in the business; they're hypoallergenic, suit everyone and give a great curl. The bunnies here are wearing Shu Uemura Eyelashes in Black, £10 for 6, and blue £12, thay're the very, very best eyelash brand. Lash primer - Blinc Lash Primer, £12.50, at HQ Hair & Beautystore, 2 New Burlington Street, London (tel: +44 (0)871 220 4141, www.hqhair.com) offers tiny lashes condition and a larger base to work with. Applied before mascara, it delivers incredible volume. Eyelash comb - Ruby & Millie Folding Lash & Brow Comb, £7.50 (available at selected Boots nationwide), combs clogged mascara from lashes quickly. Eye pencil - Valerie Smudgey Pharaoh, £15 (and Pencil Sharpener, £8), from Valerie in LA (www.victoriahealth.com) has very good staying power and looks really black.

Sweep Dreams

Like all great artists, good tools mean excellent application and keeping your tool kit up-to-date. Here are the basic tools favoured by the pros and product care tips that I picked up backstage at fashion weeks.

The brush

Divas are obsessed with the make-up range called Shu Uemura, but did you know that Shu Uemura is a real person? He lives and works in Tokyo and his hand-crafted brushes and custom made lashes are the only brand peeps like Jennifer Lopez and Madonna will use. (Jennifer Lopez wore a pair of his red fox-fur lashes to the 2001 Oscars and Madonna's make-up artist ordered 30 mink pairs for Madge's 2004 Re:Invention tour. But back to the brushes and the most famous of the lot is this. Ta-da! Feast your eyeses on this... the Shu Uemura Pure Kolinsky 5 £36, from Shu Uemura, 24 Neal Street, London WC2 (tel: +44 207 240 7635, www.shuuemura.co.uk). This brush is made of sable hair with a rounded tip suitable for almost everything (it can blend highlighter onto cheeks, smoke up an eye, oh and Geishas use it to apply lip colour.) For brushes, Shu Uemura is the biz and this one brush is a super investment.

The perfect brush kit

The Shu Uemura brush kit is what your ultimate make-up brush kit should be (budget permitting); this is the brush kit to ask Santa for... it also makes for a super-duper gift for any Goddess; the blusher brush Natural 20, £33, a shading brush Natural 10, £45, a lip brush Natural Portable Compact Lip, £16, foundation brush, Syhthetic 12, £25 and a brow brush, Natural 60B, £17, all by Shu Uemura are the make-up application secrets of many backstage pros.

How to keep them clean

After each use rub your brushes with tissue to remove excess product. Wash regularly in baby shampoo and water and leave to dry naturally in the air lying flat. Clinique and Bobbi Brown do brush cleaners but I prefer just plain washing.

5R   pure kolinsky

Expiry Date

Once a product is opened, it's going to start to deteriorate because of a few things, the first is exposure to air. The second is if you put your fingers in it, you can introduce bacteria into the product so try not to touch the product with your hands and use the little scoopy thing they supply instead. Never leave a product on a window sill in the sun as this will drastically shorten its shelf life and potency. Check for this symbol, (known as the pot symbol) which is found on packaging and tells you how long the item will stay fresh for from the moment of opening. I always forget the day, month or sometimes even year I opened a product so now I jot it into the back of my diary – anal? Just a little bit, but better then having weeping eyes me thinks.

How long do products last? In descending order...

Mascara: 3-6 months maximum (never share it with anyone).

Moisturisers and cleansers natural and/or organic: 6-9 months.

Eye cream: 6 months-1 year.

Self-tanning products: 6 months – this counts also for moisturisers that allow you to gain a glow gradually.

Sun screen: 6 months only. In fact, two weeks in the sun should finish a bottle easily so you shouldn't have any left.

Lipstick: 12-18 months (tops).

Foundations: 12-18 months

Blush, eye shadow, bronzing powder: 12-18 months

Nail polish: 1-2 years (Keep it in the fridge when opened. It will chip and peel if too old.)

Pencils: (brow, eye, lip) 2-3 years.

Powder: (loose) 2-3 years.

Moisturisers non-natural (plus those with UV protection): 18-24 months.

Fragrance: 24-30 months – keep it in the box away from heat and light and it should last well.

shu uemura

shu uemura

Doctor Who?

As ever in doctors' offices I feel like a trespasser, a confused disorientated mess, who lolls about pointlessly eating biscuits and drinking cuppas waiting to poke out the next bit of beauty crack. I've had office visits with this little lot for a few years now (well, er, not visits as such, more like an hour or two here and there when they can fit me into their diaries between regular guest spots on TV shows (Oprah etc.) Yes, they're all well famous in schleb-land for stopping the march of time across schlebrities' faces and bodies. So, what are the hottest new treatments docs?

Dr who? Frederic Brandt, Sixth Floor, 317 E. 34th Street, New York (tel: +1 212 889 7096, www.drbrandtskincare.com)
Treatment: Easily one of the most famous dermatologists (he keeps Madonna looking supa. Nuf said, right?) His new thaaaang is a kick-ass procedure called the Botox boob job. Available exclusively in the States, it involves decreasing the use of the muscle under the breast so that the top muscle has to overcompensate. Result: perkier boobs that need topping up every twelve weeks.
Ching ching: Boob Botox £700.
Bring home: Dr Brandt Infinite Moisture, £49, at Space NK (www.spacenk.com) – he's the Botox king so naturally this is a great anti-ageing product.

Dr who? Jean-Louis Sebagh, 25 Wimpole Street, London W1 (tel: +44 207 637 0548, www.drsebagh.com)
Treatment: Working from both Paris and London, he does Botox for many, many schlebs. His skincare products are magic.
Ching ching: Botox and fillers start at £300.
Bring home: Dr Sebagh Pure Vitamin C Powder Cream, £72 – a rich formula for the face which aids collagen production at Space NK (www.spacenk.com).

Dr who? Norman Leaf, 36 North Bedford Drive, Suite 103 Beverly Hills, California 90210 (tel: +1 310 274 8001, www.drnormanleaf.com) and his nurse Rand Rusher (a Botox specialist) set up the Leaf & Rusher® Medical Skincare Clinic (tel: +1 310 276 5558, www.leafandrusher.com).
Treatment: Leaf is the man who shapes Hollywood (he's famous for his 'no scar' platysma face lifts) but I'm more into his super-duper product range.
Ching ching: Botox starts at $500.
Bring home: Leaf & Rusher Tx Eyes, £74, at Space NK (www.spacenk.com). After thirty days lines reduce – Hollywood has gone nuts for this stuff.

Dr who? Andrew Weil (www.drweil.com)

Treatment: Dr Andrew Weil is a Harvard-educated doctor and botanist. There's big love for him in America for his command of integrative medicine. Besides being an all-round genial guy (he looks like Santa) and an advocate of alternative remedies, he was one of Time Magazine's Most Influential People last year.

Ching ching: He doesn't take personal appointments so ching ching can go on his products, his range for Origins is worth every penny.

Bring home: Dr Andrew Weil for Origins Mega-Mushroom Face Cream, £45 at Origins, 24 Neal Street, Covent Garden, London W1 (tel: +44 207 836 9603, www.origins.co.uk), contains mushrooms and natural ingredients. The range is wicked!

Dr who? Nick Lowe, Cranley Clinic, 19a Cavendish Square, London W1 (tel: +44 207 499 3223, ww.drnicklowe.com)

Treatment: A dermatological surgeon, he specializes in Botox and Thermage (a non-surgical radio-wave treatment which improves chicken neck, tightens jowls, cheeks, and helps older hands look young again). He also offers non-surgical skin resurfacing with a Fraxel laser (treats acne, age spots, brown spots and wrinkles, especially around the eyes).

Ching ching: Botox from £300; Thermage from £1,500.

Bring home: Look out for Dr Lowe's new range in Boots. Super Charged SPF 15 Day Cream, £16.95, has high UVA and UVB protection, and antioxidants.

Dr who? Andrew Markey, The Lister Hospital, Chelsea Bridge Road, London SW3 (tel: +44 207 730 3417).

Treatment: A dermatological surgeon, he specialises in very natural Botox.

Ching ching: £800 for Botox – it's a flat rate (you're paying for sublety).

Dr who? Rita Rakus, 34 Hans Road, London SW3 (tel: +44 207 460 7324, www.drriterakus.com).

Treatment: OK, where to start? She offers IPL, Fraxel, Thermage and drum roll... Velasmooth (a light- and radio-wave treatment) which zaps cellulite. Yes, I said zap! Oh and it also tightens jiggly arms for an instantly toned result. She's also 'London's lip queen' – she does all the big names smackers.

Ching ching: Botox starts at £210, Velasmooth is £150 a session (six is norm).

Leave It to The Experts

Oily skin/open pores

Treatment: La Prairie Cellular Purifying Treatment, £90 for 90 minutes by La Prairie at Urban Retreat, 5th Floor, Harrods (tel: +44 207 730 1234, www.urbanretreat. co.uk)

The experience: Two La Prairie cleansing masks were used to tackle dead skin and then pores were minimized and mattified. A really lovely experience here was enhanced by the La Prairie girls who were terrific. (Excellent facial by the way.)

Bring home: La Cellular Cellular Normalizing Serum, £90 absorbs excess oil and brevents oil breakthrough.

Wrinkles/smoker?

Treatment: Dr Sebagh Advanced Anti-ageing Facial, £115 for 90 minutes at The Spa at Browns (tel: +44 207 727 8002, www.drsebagh.com)

The experience: No unblocking of pores here, it's strictly down to the business of combating wrinkles and dull skin. This would be a great facial for a smoker.

Bring home: Dr Sebagh's Deep Exfoliating Mask, £52. It melts away dead skin and made my face glow.

Blocked pores

Treatment: The Ultimate Cleanse Eve Lom Facial, £80 for one hour at Space NK (tel: +44 207 727 8002, www.spacenk.co.uk)

The experience: I use Eve Lom cleanser and if I've had weeks of running about, this is the best facial for a really deep cleanse. After a thorough cleansing, paraffin wax was used to draw out everything lurking in my pores. Then a half-hour relaxing acupressure massage decongested my lymph system. Squeaky-clean skin and very relaxing.

Bring home: Eve Lom Cleanser and muslin cloth, £48 (mail order tel: +44 208 665 0112)

Late nights/work stress

Treatment: Triple Oxygen Facial, £145 for 85 minutes at Bliss (tel: +44 207 584 3888)

The experience: After a very thorough cleansing and exfoliation I was treated with an oxygen wrap and fruit washes to brighten and hydrate. I've since had this facial in New York as well and both times it was amazing.

Bring home: Bliss Triple Oxygen Facial in a Bottle, £38. (tel: +44 (0)808 1004 151).

Dull complexion/ dehydrated skin

Treatment: Decléor Aroma Expert Facial, £105 for 70 minutes at Spa Illuminata, 63 Audley Street, London W1 (tel: +44 207 499 7777), or salons nationwide (tel: +44 207 313 8780)
The experience: This facial was unbelievable: not only did it leave my thirsty skin plump and hydrated, but there was a diagnostic back massage, a hand massage and a foot massage too.
Bring home: I buy Decléor Aromessence Spa Relax body oil, £37, for rehydrating after showering and Decléor Neroli facial oil, £38 (100 per cent natural and smells divine).

Sagging jowls, puffiness

Treatment: Hydradermie Lift Deluxe by Guinot, £80 for 1 hour 15 minutes at Guinot salons (tel: +44 800 590 094, www.guinotuk.com)
The experience: Right, first off, this one involved magic wands – well, not actual magic wands but you know what I mean. My facialist used little rods to administer electrotherapy micro currents which moved through the rods and through the different products. The current drained the lymphatic system of my face and tightened my facial contours. I had a razor-sharp jaw and chiselled cheekbones for a few weeks afterwards.
Bring home: Guinot's Masque Energie Lift, £35, nourishes and firms skin and restores radiance. A brilliant tightening product.

Grey complexion/tired

Treatment: Aromatherapy Associates Renew Rose Radiance Facial, £50 for one hour at Agua at The Sanderson Hotel (tel: +44 207 300 1414) or salons nationwide (tel: +44 208 569 7030. www.aromatherapyassociates.com)
The experience: I knew that this facial was going to be ultra luxurious when it started with the inhalation of frankincense and a scalp massage. After an exfoliation the facialist applied a hydrator and then set to work on massaging my arms and hands with rose oil while it worked. I was floating after this one and smelling of roses.
Bring home: Aromatherapy Associates Deep Relax Bath and Shower Oil, £30. In fact any of the bath oils. Aromatherapy Associates Support Breathe Essence, £12.50: dabbed on a tissue and inhaled, this anti-bacterial essential oil will protect you from colds, flus and nasty germs on flights.

FaciaLists

On the hunt for the perfect complexion? Treat yourself to a tiny piece of luxury from these renowned experts; they're at the top of their game and will help you rewind the years.

Facialist: Anastasia Achilleos
Treatment: Anastasia Achilleos Signature Facial, £130 for 90 minutes (tel: +44 (0)79 3933 1889)
The experience: Anastasia is very, very special. She soothes both body and soul, and her cranio-sacral massage, reiki and gentle healing powers help with the release of bottled-up stress and tension. This is not just a facial, it's a bespoke experience where Anastasia caters to what your body needs.
Bring home: I could wax lyrical all day about Anastasia and her products, which are available at Harrods Urban Retreat not least her Urban Retreat Inhalessence, £10. Mix a few drops of this blend of specially selected essential oils in a sink full of warm water, and then inhale the vapours deeply to revive and relax you before your cleansing ritual at home.

Facialist: Amanda Lacey
Treatment: Amanda Lacey Signature Facial, £130 for one hour at Amanda Lacey, 46 Walton Street, London SW3 1RB (tel: +44 207 351 4443, www.amandalacey.com)
The experience: She's so good that dermatologists refer patients with skin problems to her for treatments. A few minutes into the treatment and I could see why the schlebs love her touch – reportedly she's Gwyneth Paltrow's favourite. It consisted of a no-nonsense mix of lymphatic-drainage massage and unplugging of blackheads.
Bring home: Amanda Lacey Persian Rosewater, £48 (www.amandalacey.com). Made from 100 per cent organic Persian rose oil, this is a luxurious toner which nourishes the skin and is totally natural. Brand-new Amanda Lacey Pink Serum, £85, is an incredible anti-ageing serum: the opalescent lotion contains light-diffusing particles which give skin an instant youthful, healthy glow whilst potent ingredients work for longer-lasting benefits. To use, apply a small amount of serum in the morning under moisturizer, or in the evening as a make-up base to give skin luminosity.

Facialist: Vaishaly Patel

Treatment: Vaishaly Patel Facial, £110 for 1 hour at the Vaishaly Clinic, 51 Paddington Street, London W1 (tel: +44 207 224 6088, www.vaishaly.com)

The experience: An expert facialist, Vaishaly is also known as London's eyebrow queen and has a gargantuan waiting list. Her clients include Elle Macpherson, Nigella Lawson, Sophie Dahl, and, ummm, me. All her treatments are spectacular. In her hands my one hour felt like three. Her approach was very holistic. Although Vaishaly only touched my face, I felt like I'd had a full body massage.

Bring home: Vaishaly Patel Night Nourisher, £65 (tel: +44 (0)808 144 6700). A syrupy blend of aromatherapy oils free of parabens (the chemicals used as preservatives in cosmetics), it's both miraculous and exquisite. Vaishaly products are available at Vaishaly Clinic, Harvey Nichols and via mail order (tel: +44 207 224 6088).

Facialist: Kirsty McLeod

Treatment: Kirsty McLeod Muscle Sculpture Massage Facial, £95 for one hour at Kirsty McLeod, 34 Moreton Street, London SW1 (tel: +44 208 34 0101, www.kirstymcleod.com)

The experience: Skin was double cleansed followed by two exfoliations and then a hot stones neck and shoulder massage. Bliss! After deep pore extractions and a muscle-resculpting massage using her Revitalising Vitamin Booster Oil my skin was plump, oxygenated and glowing. A very luxurious experience.

Bring home: Kirsty McLeod Smooth & Lift Serum, £58. Use it under make-up and whenever your skin looks fatigued to give instant radiance. Kirsty McLeod Revitalising Vitamin Booster Oil, £48. Both are available at Selfridges (mail order tel: +44 207 123 4567) and at www.kirstymcleod.com.

Facialist: Una Brennan

Treatment: Una Brennan Muscle Sculpture Massage Facial, £95 for 90 minutes at 41 Moorhouse Road, Notting Hill, London W2 (tel: +44 207 313 9835 or +44 (0)79 5216 8678)

The experience: Skin was double cleansed using her favoured dermatological brand, SkinCeuticals. Then to soften pores, she painted on warm wax. She removed imperfections carefully (very hands on) and massaged my face (incredible). Then ice-cold compresses were applied to stimulate blood flow – the facial equivalent of a dip in a plunge pool. She is also a genius at treating pregnancy hyperpigmentation. Una Brennan is one in a million.

Bring home: SkinCeuticals C E Ferulic, £60 (tel: +44 20 8997 8541). A potent antioxidant serum that protects against daily environmental agressors.

Happy?

For as long as I can remember I've wanted to be an artist. Had the basic kit from Dad at six – a biro tied to a piece of string worn around my neck and a copybook. I'd fly up trees like a pussycat, haul myself along to settle myself on my favourite branch and stay up there looking down at the plants and the animals for hours. I seldom thought of the consequences of falling, if the branch gave way and the string snagged and choked me. I crossed my spindly little legs and fishing around below, asked myself "As an Indian squaw is there anything more exciting than disappearing off over the horizon on a white pony, a biro and copybook flapping on a piece of sting round my neck in the wind?" I chewed the biro and thought...

Actually no, there was. Better than waiting for that chance encounter I'd make it happen. Six feet up, melting into the foliage, silent and patient I waited and then wham! I made an aerial dismount, launching a belly full of cake and lemonade onto one of our grazing donkeys, Ted. Plaits flying, I landed squarely on Ted's back right in the middle of the crossy bit, ('it's his gift for carrying Mary full of Jesus to Bethlehem', my Mum said).

Ted went mental and I managed to stay on for oh, all of five seconds. Immediately, he bucked me to the ground and I broke my right wrist. I blamed Ted the donkey for me losing months of vital practice on my drawing skills and life was never really the same again after that – the pain of broken bones makes you older somehow. The plaster of paris (great three words these, plaster of paris and until now, probably never been used in the same sentence as donkey in retelling of great wild-west adventure stories. Usually these other stories involve the words, "big", "white" and "horse"). But hey, it's time to come clean. It's time to move on.

Back home at my parents house last summer I laid my notebook and pen on the kitchen table and smiled when I looked out the window at that tree which I had dived out of. It was up that tree that I decided to launch myself out into the world as a writer, you know take a chance. I toyed with is for years as a teenager, picked it up, put it down, twirled it around a bit in my noggin, will I won't I, oh hell, yeah, why not? The town I grew up near (Listowel) is a fairytale kind of place, a land of dreamers and famous storytellers, John B Keane, Brian McMahon, and it was here that my identity was formed. So let's start at the bottom… looking up the length of that tree trunk, I felt an urge to risk the climb again for old times sake, (what is it that I read in one of Mum's big thick Shakey Spear books years ago?) Oh yeah, that Julius Caesar chap in the path of death said to his wife, 'cowards die many times before their deaths, the valiant never taste of death but once', that made me want to do it even more. So up I went. Hauling myself up the trunk, I wanted to climb higher, as high as I possibly could…So what happened then?

As I shuffled along the branches, I felt a few raindrops on my forehead and as I settled on one with a good view, suddenly I understood what real happiness was… knowing my sense of place, knowing where I belonged. I thought: G, this is it, alone, up a tree, in the rain, in Kerry, with a notebook and a biro. This is freedom. My notebook and a pen stuffed securely in my pocket, I was ready to climb down when a horse sauntered very close to the tree trunk. So what did I do? Well I kind of made an attempt jump didn't I? Kind of slipped and hit the ground and then looked around to see if I was alone and clambered my way up onto the poor unsuspecting animal. "Take me to the rainbow and beyond Tonto."

Back in Dublin, Sunday morning, hours before light, rain lashing against the bedroom window, I sat upright in bed. It's at times like this that I need to steady myself, so I did, I made tea, cup held captive in my hands in the kitchen, my suitcase peeping in from the hall. "Are you coming or are you going?" I asked myself. Silence… lamps, suitcase, furniture, everything sleeping. The heavy rain had wrenched me from the most magnificent dreamland…I had found myself in a pen shop in Paris and then there was a taxi driver named Victor… Peter and Charlie were there and we were striking out into the world. And there were other people and macaroons, queues everywhere… and perfume and a blue plasterine snail, ker-razy stuff. If I went into all the details of it you'd think I'd scoffed a truck load of LSD. Next in rolled Vivienne Westwood on a roaring tide of ink splashes. Sitting there in an empty kitchen drinking tea as the last fading echoes of my picture-perfect dream, died away to silence. Surely nothing as exciting as this could ever happen to me in real life. I sighed and opened my notebook, carried on a tide of roaring ink splashes I made out these.

The Happy List Continues...

It all started simply in Paris with some ink splashes, a Rorschach and a burning question "what if I filled this notebook with the things that make me happy", I wrote. Or words to that effect. As I flicked through the pages I could see different little things poking out from among the splashes, things like shoes with heels the colour of conkers, the word conker and then that made me think of how clothes moths don't like conkers so does that mean that moths hate Horse Chestnut trees too? See that's the way Happy Listing gets you thinking and I now had a notebook full of this kind of stuff. Do you mind if I tell you about the things that made me the happiest? Now, let me see what's on this page here, ah yes, toast and warm butter...deep breath, here goes.

I like Poilane bread toasted and spread with Kerrygold butter the two melting into each other like lovers on a first date.

And I like Poilane because they ship bread from Paris to Robert de Niro (loved him in Raging Bull, nuff said.) And I like a perfect club sandwich fashioned from Poilane bread and no other with, Clarence Court eggs (happy chickens), chicken for my sandwich (unhappy chickens), mayo, grilled bacon and green salad.

Poilâne, 8 rue du Cherche-Midi, 70006 Paris tel: (tel: +33 1 45 48 42 59) in the Saint Germain des Prés district of Paris. In London: Poilâne, 46 Elizabeth Street, London, SW1 (tel: +44 207 808 4910, www.poilane.fr). Also available in Selfridges Food Hall.

I like newspapers and the crinkly sound they make

And I like lemon aid

Pop some sliced lemons in a freezer bag and into the freezer with them. Super idea from Dodo. Fancy a quick G&T? Just pluck one from the freezer. Good tip that.

And I like pod hotels

Have you tried the Pod Hotel at Heathrow airport? It's a great idea if you're knackered at the airport and just want to chill and watch TV (www.yotel.com).

And I like pop-up stores

Dover Street Market (www.guerrilla-store.com) have done them in Asia and Europe and everyone from Nike to Target have in the US.

And I like the smell of Christmas

Take 1 orange, 1 lemon and 1 satsuma peel, 1 sliced apple, some pine cones, a few pine twigs with needles nipped from the crimble tree, some rosemary, half a handful of cloves, two cinnamon sticks, and eucalyptus. Bake it in the oven on a very low heat for a couple of hours until it dries out and then place around the room in little bowls. Total Crimble! (as told to me by a shop owner in Paris who cooked this up at home and then placed inside the air con system in his shop.)

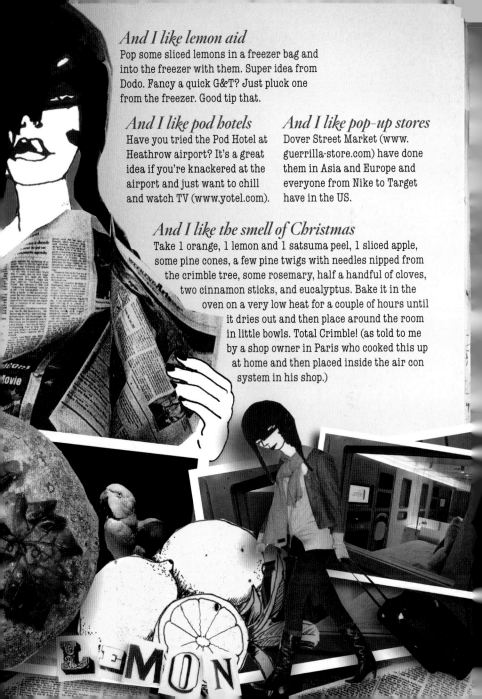

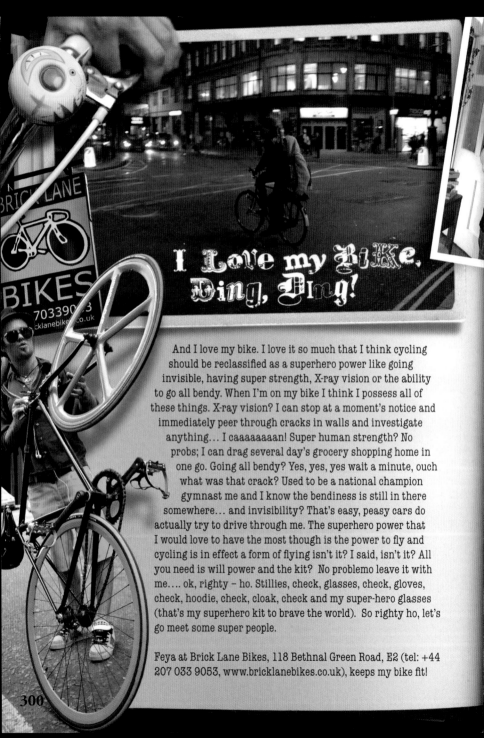

I Love my Bike, Ding, Ding!

And I love my bike. I love it so much that I think cycling should be reclassified as a superhero power like going invisible, having super strength, X-ray vision or the ability to go all bendy. When I'm on my bike I think I possess all of these things. X-ray vision? I can stop at a moment's notice and immediately peer through cracks in walls and investigate anything… I caaaaaaan! Super human strength? No probs; I can drag several day's grocery shopping home in one go. Going all bendy? Yes, yes, yes wait a minute, ouch what was that crack? Used to be a national champion gymnast me and I know the bendiness is still in there somewhere… and invisibility? That's easy, peasy cars do actually try to drive through me. The superhero power that I would love to have the most though is the power to fly and cycling is in effect a form of flying isn't it? I said, isn't it? All you need is will power and the kit? No problemo leave it with me…. ok, righty – ho. Stillies, check, glasses, check, gloves, check, hoodie, check, cloak, check and my super-hero glasses (that's my superhero kit to brave the world). So righty ho, let's go meet some super people.

Feya at Brick Lane Bikes, 118 Bethnal Green Road, E2 (tel: +44 207 033 9053, www.bricklanebikes.co.uk), keeps my bike fit!

King ADz

And I like King Adz and his forthcoming Urban Cookbook, the man sure has been busy traversing the globe and cooking for graffiti artists, photographers and designers along the way. With such a great appreciation of street culture, I wondered what his take on luxury was.

What makes you Happy?

Spending time with my family (Wilma, Kaiya & Casius) and watching them all flourish; having an seemingly unlimited supply of ideas and possibilities and then making them become real; reading books by people like Eric Hansen, Tama Janowitz, RK Narayan, watching films by Nick Broomfield, Werner Herzog and Lars von Trier and on a superficial level: Masala Dosa!

What is my Luxury?

A voyage of discovery without a brief (or deadline!) but with a decent budget; not being part of the 9 to 5 rat race and working at home (when I'm not on the road); Not reading newspapers or watching TV, but reading wicked books and watching great films...and last but not least being able to live with peace & love and not having to worry about anything really bad (unlike a lot of the world who live in fear of war, oppression or American troops).

I like secret Rooms in New York (Shhhhhh!)

Crif Dogs, 113 St. Marks Pl., New York, NY 10009 near. Ave A (tel:+1 212 614 2728) this looks like any other hot-dog place, but behind the vintage phone booth lies a hidden cocktail bar called Please Don't Tell. Beatrice Inn, 285 W. 12th St., New York, NY 10014 nr. 4th St. (tel: +1 212 243 4626) a cosy little bar in the West Village that's not dissimilar from a gentelman's club. There's a juke-box (Yay) and a back room (Woooo) where you can dance til you fall down.

And I like these choons

Dizzee Rascal – Dance wiv me
Scroobius Pip – Thou Shalt Always Kill
Peggy Sue and the Pirates – Spare Parts
The Knife – Heartbeat
Bat for Lashes – What's A Girl to Do
Skinnyman – Council Estate of Mind
Micachu – Golden Phone
The Flaming Lips – The Yeah Yeah Yeah
Lykke Li – I'm Good I'm Gone
Fleet Foxes - White Winter Hymnal

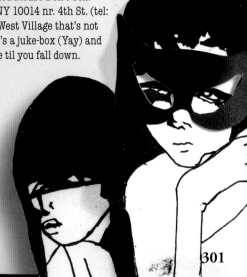

SCROOBIUS PIP

And I like Scroobius, he's one of my favourite sounds at the moment, his urban poetry is phenomenal, this man writes some killer lines, so what makes him tick

What makes you happy?

Being onstage makes me happy. This is something I have only found in the last two years. It really is amazing that, at this moment, I am lucky enough to be going all over the world, from Japan to America to Europe and getting to experience the feeling of standing in front of such varied crowds and cultures and doing what you love. Can't complain one bit!

What is your luxury?

My luxury at the moment would have to be DVD boxsets! I, like many addicts, am not sure if it is a luxury or an addiction. It is certainly something that gives me many a great escape though!

LAURA DOCKRILL

And I like Laura Dockrill, watch out for her in 2008 (also known as Dockers MC) she's a poet and artist from South London. Her debut book Mistakes in the Background is out this autumn.

What makes you happy?

At the moment its a good nights sleep, I like it when I'm hot in bed and when I flip the pillow over and it's really cold, I like the idea of drinking coffee and red wine really late at night telling some profound stories... this never happens – both make me drowsy, I like it when I write a poem I'm proud of, I like giving people unexpected presents, when the train or bus comes straight away, the odd occasion when my mum washes my clothes, playing hide and seek with my boyfriend, fruit salads, finishing a book, starting a book, when I see my art work used on stuff – cd covers, mugs, yoyo's – I like it when I get a fresh cup of tea and I could do this forever so better make this a good one...when I get something done that I've been meaning to do for ages – I have a tendancy of ignoring stuff – I love the relief of getting stuff off my shoulders...phewwwwww.

DAMIEN HIRST

And I like Damien Hirst and his diamond skull called "For The Love of God." Visiting it was a seminal moment for me in my research for this book. There was a ton of hoopla about it at the time and as I queued to see it with Peter and our friends Chloe Early and Conor Harrington (artists themselves) we got to chirpin about the little matter that it was valued at 50 million quid. Now if that ain't luxury, I don't know what is. 50 million big ones. For the half hour that we queued to see the diamond studded skull in a glass box in a darkened room, the four of us ate some consolatory chocolate and discussed as artists what else we could cover in diamonds.

Of course the whole queuing thing got me all excited, the skull was being displayed in a dark room and even had its own body guard who gave us a little speech about standing well back from the display case. In TV land they call this 'the big reveal'. Aaaaaanyway, in we all went along with seven others, me lagging behind still trying to think up cool things that I could plaster with diamonds. I managed to get so close to the skull that my breath fogged the glass up and although it was waaaaay smaller than I expected, it was utterly magnificent, a true metaphor for exuberance and luxury. I wanted to ask Damien Hirst what his luxury was, so here goes...

What's your luxury?
My luxury is buying art, it's unfuckinbelievable that I'm in this position to be able to afford to buy paintings and sculpture by artists that I could only look at in books and art galleries and museums when I was a boy and put them on my walls.

What makes you happy?
My kids make me happiest, not drinking makes me happy 'cos when I was drinking, I thought I'd lost something and when I stopped I realised I'd still got it, life and friendships make me happy, sunlight on flowers, I fuckin love this planet.

And I like literary festivals

A Weekend of entertainment, the Flat Lake Literary & Arts Festival (www.theflatlakefestival.com) held on the grounds of Hilton Park, a country estate near Clones, is curated by film director Kevin Allen and novelist Pat McCabe. It was among the cultural highlights of 2008 with highlights from Pat McCabe with his Radio Butty and a Talent Contest titled the X-Tractor.

Listowel Writers Week

And I like Listowel Writer's Week (www.writersweek.ie) - Ireland's longest established literary festival. I met all sorts there in 2007 including, Roddy Doyle, Pat McCabe, Alain de Botton and Irvine Welsh. There are workshops on subjects as diverse as poetry, freelance journalism, writing for theatre and thriller writing, all booked out pretty much instantly. And there are readings daily by some of the world's most famous writers. This festival and the people who run it are really terrific, but then I would say that as Listowel is where I grew up and I'll always see it as home.

And I like second-hand books

Abe Books (www.abebooks.com) is a super website for second-hand books.

And I like these bookstores

Koenig Books, 80 Charing Cross Road, London WC2H (tel:+44 207 240 8190, www.koenigbooks.co.uk) From fashion to art to photography I've been known to spend a full day reading here. There's also a branch at The Serpentine Gallery. Claire de Rouen Books, Specialist Photography, First Level, 125 Charing Cross Road London WC2H OEA (tel: +44 207 287 1813, www.clairederouenbooks.com) RD Franks, 5 Winsley Street, London, W1W (tel: +44 207 636 1244, www.rdfranks.co.uk). Magma, 117 Clerkenwell Road, London EC1R 5BY (tel: +44 20 7242 9503, www.magmabooks.com). Ocean Books, 127 Stoke Newington Church Street, Stoke Newington, London, N16 (tel: +44 207 502 6319).

I like an unputdownable book

I recommend..

Perfume – Patrick Süskind
Brave New World – Aldous Huxley
Birdsong – Sebastian Faulks
The Catcher in The Rye – JD Salinger
Rebecca – Daphne du Maurier
Anything by Roald Dahl

PAT McCABE

And I like having time to read my favourite titles, can't wait to read The Holy City (Bloomsbury) by Irish author Pat McCabe, what this man does with words is pure magic.

What makes you happy?

What makes me happy is this: Thinking about sitting at home watching an episode of Fair City and thinking: 'This isn't as good as last night's show' when suddenly and quite unexpectedly there is a knock on the door and when I go out who do I find there? Only a futuristic-looking fellow, an alien if you will, with a shiny suit and a visor on him but best of all, in his hands for me a great big parcel wrapped up in brown paper which when opened is found to contain that much-prized item the jet-pack cum time-travel machine which when activated takes me back to when I was 21, full of beer and wondering what I was going to be, then on to marriage and the Tool Box Murders, which was the film my wife and I went to see on our honeymoon before zipping away on there through the time-space continuum to that place where, glory be to God, your mother and father are alive again, and not only that but all the people that they knew and when they see me, cry: 'There he goes now,' and 'Oh my, didn't he do good.' Daft though it is, thinking about that – it just makes me happy.

What is your favourite luxury?

Buying the maddest shit ever on ebay, including stamps and coloured jumpers and sweepstake tickets from 1962. I could do that for hours and, believe me, I do. Oh and lots of Meccano sets as well. And bagetelles. It's great.

PATRICK McCABE

LAUREN LAVERNE

And I like Lauren Laverne. She's everything you need to brighten up a Tuesday night's telly; an abundance of beauty, wisdom and wit: Lauren Laverne of the BBC's The Culture Show gives us her take on books art and music and chirps enough good sense to make your ears bleed. Good heavens! Could it be that she's all for equality when it comes to cultural appreciation? She is a true Urban Goddess.

Photograph by Nicky Johnston, Camera Press London

What makes you happy? Well, let me think, my son makes me happy, his dad makes me happy usually! And a fantastic pair of shoes always makes me happy.

What's your luxury? I think my luxury is pottering. Free time just bumbling around, doing ordinary things, riffling through a second hand shop to find some excellent junk that someone else has discarded that I'm going to love. Playing with building blocks with my little boy, building towers for him to knock down. Going for walks, looking at trees. That's my luxury. Free time.

The definition of luxury seems to be about money, what do you make of that? No I don't think luxury is materialistic. It's easy to make that distinction but luxury for me is about abundance. For me its having freedom and time and room to pursue pleasure.

Why do your friends love you? I'm so busy that sometime I feel that I'm a rubbish friend as I'm always working. I'm quite funny when I have a cocktail or two inside me and I can make them laugh. I'm a good listener because I really enjoy listening and that's the secret to being a good conversationalist I think, to be able to listen well. I love my friends so I try and be the friend I would want to have. My friends know that I would always drop everything and be there for them if it came down to it, I'm very loyal.

And when working on the culture show you're exposed to paintings, poetry and music? What genre do you particularly love? Music is the big passion in my life and it's funny really because it's the thing that has been the north star for the course of my life. The friends I made came through music and I ended up doing the job that I do because I was in a band and because I love music. I know a reasonable amount about records, its just my big passion that somehow ended up forging the shape of the life I'm living now which is really weird but I can't think of anything nicer than doing a job that comes out of your biggest love.

What do you yourself love music-wise? I've got very broad music tastes, everything from 1940's bar songs by Louie Jordan and really old blues right through to very current dance music. I can't think of a genre of music that I don't like some of.

You're very accessible for people to watch, you make the very high-brow stuff very palatable. I've kind of got a no-brow approach to it all really. I don't think there is such a thing as high-brow or low-brow.

Better than a mono-brow! Yeah exactly, as long as you haven't got a mono-brow you're doing alright! I think culture is something that belongs to everybody and whatever your opinion is, whether it's on a poem, painting, book or piece of music it's very subjective and so your opinion is right. I think the problem comes when people try and take ownership and say well we understand this and you don't, this is for us and not for you. We'll decide who gets this and really you know, that's all bollocks. The key to it is to have confidence in your own taste and know what you like and don't be ashamed of it. Follow your bliss, you've got the right too.

Who are your British Icons? Paul McCartney, Mark E. Smith, Vivienne Westwood would definitely be British icons and Kate Moss for definite. There's tons of music ones but Macca and Mark are definitely my big two.

You specialise in books? There is a book called Apples by Richard Milward who is a friend from Middlesbrough that I did a VT on and I'm going to interview Chuck Palahniuk next week which I'm really excited about. He's the author who wrote Fight Club. I also did a piece on Dickens at the Edinburgh festival because I'm a bit of a Dickens fan.

Would Fightclub be one of your favourite books then? Choke is one of my favourite Chuck books. I love The Amazing Adventures of Kavalier and Clay by Michael Chabon – which is pretty Dickensian, has loads of characters in it and is utterly absorbing and will make you cry on public transport. I really like Clockwork Orange as well. And you've got to read Fear and Loathing before you die.

ANNA PiaGGi

And I like Anna Piaggi the fashion icon whose collages for Italian Vogue are legendary. Near the end of a chat with her, I asked: 'because you work in fashion it doesn't obviously cost you a lot for luxurious things does it? Her answer stunned me - I've replayed the tape a few times. She said: 'But I don't really spend, I don't have the money to buy expensive clothes.' The rest of her answers were as honest: on what makes her happy? 'Myself. I'm happy. I try to find a good reason to be happy.'

And what was her luxury. 'My luxury is taking care of myself because I am alone now because I don't have anymore my husband and my boyfriend? I try to live as I learn with them, I love my work, I love fashion. So this makes me at ease.'

I asked her if she had a millions pounds what would she do with it? 'I really don't know, I never thought, I am so used to living with limited means'

But you look so beautiful are you not molto moto rich non? (Oh yeah, quite the linguist, there's about three languages in that last sentence). 'Non really not at all, it is really a challenge every time for me. Not at all, maybe poverty is good challenge.' Poverty a good challenge? I repeated. What a refreshing concept. 'Yes it is' she continued 'if you have some aim to reach, if you are studying, if you are researching, it doesn't matter the money. I think that it is very good to give out an expression of intelligence, of curiosity and so the money is not really the main thing.'

Talking to her felt like talking to (or, more accurately, listening to) a very real person - like listening to a very clever aunt displaying the freedom of just having returned from a trip around the world. Much of what she said was brilliant. She is sensible. She is rooted and loves her work (remember Victor? 'My attitude since I've been working in magazines for many years is that fashion is just styling, it's putting things together, there are old ones and new ones and poor ones, it doesn't matter, it's just the pleasure of making something compact which gives out a graphic expression.'

Anna Piaggi

And I like week long birthdays and the Hulger

My friend Nik Roope (www.vi-r-us.com), (look he designed the Hulger (www.hulger.com) telephone isn't it gorgeous?) came up with a super plan last year. To avoid getting cloned he pretended to the social networks that he belonged to, that his actual birth date was on different dates. Just a day or two out here and there but enough to be incorrect. And to his delight this meant that birthday congratulations rolled in all week. He recommends creating a good spread of fakey dates so on one day your plaxo friends are all congratulating you and on the next your facebook buddies are sending their best wishes. Keep adding to them and you've extended your birthday into a week long mini festival. Great idea, I love it!

And I like healthy nails

An Irish Chapple manicure, at The Nail Studio, 3 Spanish Place, W1U (tel:+44 (0)7956 307 392) takes care of that bit. She spends a full hour just concentrating on nail health and a slow-air dry (machines make polish brittle) means a French manicure lasts for weeks. I keep a Ruby and Millie glass nail file £13 from Boot (tel: 845 070 8090, www.boots.com) in my bag as glass is the kindest type of file for your nails to prevent splintering and a Dr Hauschka Neem Nail Oil Pen, £12 (tel: +44 (0)1386 7926420) for nourishing my nails on the go.

And I like patent boots

They're on my winter wish list. To keep them good as new, I'll fix them with Opi (tel: +44 (0)1923 240 010) nail polish or Morello Futura 2000 £5.50 plus p&p (tel: +44 (0)845 241 6293. www.millsleathergoods.co.uk).

And I like dressing table powder

Pink Orchidée loose powder, £26, by T Le.Clerc (brightens) and lilac Parme, lightens the complexion. Banane (it's yellow) illuminates most skintones. Available in 22 shades at Fenwick (for mail order, call +44 207 629 9161).

And I like all these labels

Charles Anastase at www.brownsfashion.com or www.start-london.com. Tibi at Harvey Nichols, www.fenwick.co.uk and www.net-a-porter.com All Saints www.allsaintsshop.co.uk. David Szeto (also at Browns and Start). Philip Lim at Harvey Nichols www.matchesfashion.com and www.net-a-porter.com

CHLOE EARLY

With her vibrant palette and abstracted urban landscapes, Chloe Early is one of the art world's darkest horses.

Her recent work is putting her right where she belongs: in the spotlight. Tucked away in a corner of her East London studio, the kettle is boiling, "I always thought I'd be a painter when I grew up," she says while making us tea. Every once in a while she sips, but for the most part she's completely absorbed in mixing and applying her delicate colours. As a medium, oil painting takes long hours of concentration and weeks, (if not years) to dry. Overload a canvas too much, and you'll end up with an unyielding, sprawl of messiness: let things get too loose, and the work is shapeless to the eye. A less patient painter would have moved onto the next painting, but Irish-born, and now London-based Early has persevered – her attention to colour, astonishing, her sell out show at D*Face's Stolen Space gallery off Brick Lane; a result of years of honing her skill. She admits that painting and working with colour is all consuming. It was actually quite daunting to watch her work with oils, who better then to ask about real beauty.

What makes you happy?
Bright evenings, long days, swimming in the sea, starting paintings, finishing paintings and everything in between.

What is your luxury? Tea and lemon tart.

What is beauty?
Beauty is an enigma I strive for but the reality of imperfection is more appealing to me. Mistakes or accidents stumbled upon in the process of trying to create something beautiful are the real treasures of painting. I spend a lot of time thinking about what works, does the composition work, do the colours work? Everything can be working but nothing is happening, painting needs a spark, a pulse of its own. That is why I don't plan too much, I want to be open to the unexpected.

Beauty in art is often frowned upon. But the nature of the painting process is very beautiful, you can take an extreme shocking image of death and destruction and paint it in a certain way. It will be beautiful, it will change from a depiction of, to a meditation on death and destruction. Painting removes us from reality and everyday painting provides a place for me to go to, a beautiful messy uncontrollable place where anything can happen.

See Chloe's work on www.chloeearly.com. Or contact her representation at Stolenspace Gallery, Dray Walk, The Old Truman Brewery, 91 Brick Lane, E1 (tel: +44 207 247 2684; www.stolenspace.com)

HUNT *for the* PERFECT CUPPA

The three questions I get asked the most often are 1) How did you become a writer? 2) Do you love travelling? 3) What's with the obsession with the milky tea? To these the answers are: 1) Dunno, just kinda happened. 2) Yes I love travelling and the last one's the one I'd like to clarify, I have been drinking tea this colour since I was five.

Aaaaanyway. What I thought I would do is go on the hunt around the place to see if I could poke out the best cake and cuppa. The nature of the detective business is that you never know what cake joint your investigations are going to take you to, so after casing about twenty joints here are some gems...

The Wolsley is packed to the rafters with posh peeps, titled folk. What no Big Brother winners G? No not a sausage. The whole point of The Wolsely is that it's posh, but a place is no fun without ordinary peeps so off I went with Snailey to get the ball rolling.

Upon entering the room, I find it simply breathtaking, my but the ceiling alone is lush. The menu is abbreviated brasserie – eggs Benedict, salade nicoise, Coq au Vin, crème brûlée, bosh, bosh, bosh, bosh, and the room, with its gilt edged bird cagey feel is goldey art-deco and I love it. I felt all ladey-di-da, puncturing my two boiled egg with my soldiers (£6.50) – breakfast being the new lunch and all of that crack. Then it was time to get down to tea talk, the breakfast tea was perfect. A few days later I doubled back for the cream tea (3.30-5.30) £9.75. Great selection of cakes here along with good scones, clotted cream and tasty jam and by the way you can order cups of tea all the way up until midnight if the mood strikes you. Is there nothing this place can't do well? Now from the sublime to the meticulous.

Next up, I have another really great spot for you, sorry, you must think I'm going soft in the head. I haven't crucified anywhere yet and for the sake of balance there needs to be a lambasting of a bit of tea and cake somewhere, it's the reason AA Gill has a job right? But really why would I do that? It's a waste of good space. Or is it? Take **Yauatcha** in Soho for example, which serves all-day cocktails, tea and dim sum, it's a beautiful place where tea and cake has become extra chi chi. Richard Rogers designed the building and much has been written about the dim sum since it opened in 2004 but the real pull is the cake bar, which stays open until 11.45pm (10.45pm Sundays). Their most expensive tea costs £75 here, yeah no dot between the seven and the five in there either. Steeeep! So I swaggered past the 'Sino-European' fusion pastries (their words not mine) displayed like museum pieces into light and lovely surroundings. It feels all calming and Japaneesey, in the way that Japan (well, Tokyo) actually isn't, but good Japanese restaurants in London always are.

Check out this amazing cake that Fiona Cairns (tel: +44 (0)116 240 2888, www. fionacairns.com) baked for us here at Goddess Guide HQ. Her cakes and cupcakes are available at Harrods, Fortnum & Mason, Selfridges, Waitrose and Sainsbury's. Even the la-di-da Parisians have fallen for her sweet sweet creations as Le Bon Marché can't keep her is stock

If there's a stinker here (and boy did I poke about to find one), it's the staff, they're a bit how can I put this? Slooooooooow is how Snailey described it and that's coming from a snail. But forget my mumbling and grumbling here between bites of Shanghai Lily - an almond rose biscuit topped with rose confit, a ballerina's tutu of a snack - because the tea and cakes are absolutely wonderful; pretty little cakes that mix traditional chocolate and creams with sake butter, cold rice and green tea. And there was a Jade Ganache topped by a frilly pale green mound of absinth cream, which was truly a beautiful little thing to see. The tea was good too. This place, the colours, the textures, the wrapping of fluorescent boxes and ribbon, the whole experience, sumptuous and feminine. So one day it's Japaneesey, the next it's Frenchy...

Equally chi-chi but with smilier staff is **The Parlour** at **Sketch**. They serve avant-garde cakes; petit gateaux, each just a couple of inches square but intricately constructed, glazed and presented. It's like a band of fairies made them. Fairies with cakey bakey faces, yeah. You are supposed to nibble and appreciate the brief moment when the different ingredients harmonise. In addition to serving all-day cake and tea, the parlour offers a varied swellection of individual cakes (from £5, you order in advance) and they're packed into beautiful boxes and tied with ribbon for you to take home. My cake here was gorgeous and the tea was excellent too served in beautiful old china. The décor is luscious; Japanese wall paintings and Italian chandeliers. Tasting the pastries I could taste their "obsessiveness". At Sketch they've been trying to perfect the croissant for years. I like it here and tea and cake comes to £7.50. Fan-bloody-tastic. I was so high on sugar it's all a bit of a haze.

At **Sun Luen** (Little Newport Street, Soho) my pineapple bun was warmed in the microwave (I heard the ping). The result? Sponge so soft and light it floated. A pot of jasmine tea and this Chinatown cake was £2.30. There aren't many non-Chinese cake places in Chinatown, I like it, you can be completely anonymous here, to think in peace. At C&R café they serve Malay cakes: a sticky pyramid of white rice topped with coconut and wrapped in a banana leaf costs just one pound. It is delicious and gentle. I ate it with a plastic spoon and ordered a cuppa. Nice tea here but I'm much more a breakfast tea gal.

Fact, I love **Fortnum & Mason** and the smart move here is to avoid the mezzanine Patio Restaurant – in the middle of their noisy food-floor-and take the lift to the fourth floor St James Restaurant. A huge, room cast in alabaster and pale green. It's mausoleum style. The staff were friendly so Snailey was flying, even the pianist while tinkling a lame 'Moon River', cracked a smile. Ah yes, dum, deee, dum, dum, di, dum, di, deeeeeeee, aaah sorry, getting carried away there. I didn't order the £20 afternoon tea; I went 'a La Carte'. One pot of Darjeeling (excellent) and two small cakes please £9.50 (a minute raspberry tart with fruit and perfect custard and a strawberry mousse, wrapped in white chocolate) were wonderful. But I'm not into nobbing around with tiny bits of pastry, so I should have gone for the bigger option. The staff are very nice here and you can just chill for ages so it's a nice and friendly place. I sat there for an hour, or was it longer? With all the papers around me it was heaven; the only thing to break me from a good bit of JK Rowling type scribbling was the tapping of spoons on fine bone china and the pianist occasionally hitting a wrong note. Overall a very relaxed tea experience.

315

E. PELLICCI

So what's this about saving the best till last and all of that? Off we schlepped next morning to **E. Pellicci's** on Bethnal Green Road, to test the tea and have a mahussive breakfast café style (sorry scratch that) caff is a far more appropriate word, yeah a mahussive caff relax. It's very honest, very anti-fashion, a refreshing middle finger raised to the

fancy smancy cakey bakey places I'd seen all week. We rocked up and queued for a table, inside it was bustling, a small room with a counter and scrum of tables. The menu is laminated and includes "Full English, Lasagne, Spaghetti Bolognese, etc.", Shepherd's Pie, I think, and Steak and Kidney Pudding. A proper caff.

I asked for the Full English and was seduced by Mr Pellicci senior behind the counter in charge of tea brewing. The man taking our order was Mr. Pellicci junior, his son (their both called Nevio). It was a very jolly place, everyone local, proper East Enders havin it their own way, no one just there to be seen, my kind of place. And then Mr Pellicci senior asked, "are you having the Full English and the jam Roley Poley?" When I said that I was, he said: "The thing is you'll never fit both. Have the fry and see how you feel." A meal for £5.80? Astounding value. Smiley, smiley people. Snailey went into spasmic melt-down when Mr. Pellicci senior offered to show us how to make the prefect cup, scald the cup, in with the tea, add the milk. "Keep everything nice and hot." I'd never met nicer. The fry was the business with beans (proper order). Mr. Pellicini junior pointed to the hatch at the back of the caff "my Mama do a good fry up eh?" and the tea? It's the best cup easily. I swear to you, it's worth the trip to Bethnal Green alone. At odd times this place comes to mind and I fly down there and hammer on the door till they feed me up good and proper. Who'd be anything but normal when you can find an honest cup like this?

Looking back through my notes I thought of all of the cups of tea and all the bits of cake that I'd sampled. The cakes were rich and were eaten slowly, they worked hard to help me forget about regular city-time. Then I got into

it and learned to enjoy the decadence of it all. And the truth? To get the most from any of these places the experience must last at least an hour. Starbucks etc. must be ignored bad cake, disgusting tea in cardboard cups. Yuck! A good tea place for me is a retreat against modernity, a place that makes me want to talk to strangers, write a novel or fly to the moon (with enough good cake inside you wouldn't even need a rocket). Good tea makes anything possible. It's the number one thing on my happy list, a good cup of tea.

PELLICCI'S
Cafe-Restaurant
332 Bethnal Green Rd
London E2 0AG
Tel: 020 7739 4873

£ 11·60

Cakey Bakey Shops

Baker & Spice, 54-56 Elizabeth Street, Belgravia, SW1 (tel:+44 207 730 3033, www.bakerandspice.com). Beard Papa, 143 Oxford Street Store, London W1D 2JB (tel: +44 207 494 9020, www.beardpapa.co.uk) the world's best Japanese choux puffs filled with whipped cream custard – I defy you to resist them. C&R Café Rupert Court, London W1D (tel: +44 207 7434 1128). Fortnum and Mason, 181 Piccadilly, London W1A 1ER, (tel: +44 207 734 8040, www.fortnumandmason. com). Hummingbird Bakery, 133 Portobello Road, W11 2DY (tel: +44 207 229 6446, www.hummingbirdbakery.com). The best cupcakes and Red Velvet cake in London. There is a branch at 47 Old Brompton Road, SW7 (tel: +44 207 584 0055). Maison Berteaux, 27 Greek Street, Soho, London W1D (tel: +44 207 437 6007) see the lovely array of cakes, pictured below, and buy mismatched china in the shop downstairs. Ottolenghi, 287 Upper Street, N1 (tel:+44 207 288 1454, www.ottolenghi.co.uk). Bigger than the Notting Hill branch this Ottolenghi's is a perfect place for a Sunday brunch or afternoon tea. Patisserie Valerie, 44 Old Compton Street, Soho W1D, (tel: +44 207 437 3466, www.patisserie-valerie.co.uk). Peyton and Byrne at Heals, 196 Tottenham Court Road, London W1T (tel: +44 207 580 3451, www.peytonandbyrne. com) cupcakes, cupcakes and more cupcakes. Sketch, 9 Conduit Street, W1 (tel:+44 870 777 4488, www.sketch.uk.com). Sue Luen, 14 Little Newport Street, London WC2 (tel:+44 207 437 7468). Treacle, 110-112 Columbia Road, E2 (tel: +44 207 729 5657, www.treacleworld.com). Stuffed with tableware for sale and a vintage wooden cabinet filled with the best cupcakes. I love it here, but it is only open on Sundays though! The Wolseley, 160 Picadilly, London W1J (tel: +44 207 499 6996, www.thewolseley.com). Yauatcha, Broadwick House, 15 Broadwick St W1 (tel: +44 207 494 8088). Louis Patisserie, 32 Heath Street, Hampstead London NW3 (tel: (tel: +44 207 437 1694).

Hello friends! So it's onto la-di-da delf now; cups and dinky little caekê plates. Excuse my appalling typing skills; I'm afraid my usual finger fluency has been disrupted by my big fat fringers. I mean fingers from eating bins (sorry buns) and cake. And apart from snack club's cake tasting excursions, I'd noticed something else about cakey bakey places their la-di-da delf was just grrrrreat.

Check out our pictures…proof that in the best tea emporiums in town they're serving tea and cakes in, around and on mis-matched plates, cups and saucers and guess what? You don't have to go to the markets either to find mismatched stuff. Big, big pottery companies are creating interesting, individual pieces that you can mix and match to suit your own mood. Lovin it! Now here are the peeps making cups and plates unique.

Hella Jongerius (www.jongeriuslab.com), my favourite ceramic designer continues to design a range of wares for the renowned German porcelain creators, Nymphenburg. Her hand-painted plates (1), tea-pots (2) and snail plate (3) are available at hip art-cum-craft galleries like Vessel, 114 Kensington Park Road, London W1 (tel: +44 207 727 8001, www. vesselgallery.com). At the antique end of the market is The Dining Room Shop, 62-64 White Heart Lane, Barnes, London SW13 OPZ (tel: +44 208 878 1020, www.thediningroomshop.co.uk) it's stuffed full of antiquey treats. While Becky MacKenzie at Mint, 70 Wigmore Street, London W1U (tel: +44 207 224 4406, www.mintshop. co.uk) has produced some stunning ceramics. A very affordable treat is the robin breakfast cup and saucer (4), £12, Oka, 103 Lancaster Road, Notting Hill, London W11 1QN (tel: +44 207 792 1425, www.okadirect.com or tel: +44 (0)844 815 7380 mail order), they're cute as buttons as is the Robinia cup (5) and saucer £101 at Meissen, 81 Walton Street, SW (tel: +44 207 589 0128, www.meissen-porcelain.co.uk).

And I like the weather; sunshine, snow, wind and torrential downpours.

Why do BBC weather forecasters always do the droopy mouth thing when forecasting rain? And I like the BBC news lots and lots and the special tune which echoes a welcome as the only English language thing in a foreign hotel room. And I like dim sum in the world's greatest China towns, Marks & Spencer's lemonade and breakfasts at home. And I like the smell of bonfires on drizzly Halloween evenings and Halloween in general, and Guillermo Del Toro movies, and spiderwebs because of the way they collect raindrops and I like the smell of horses and the sound of their hooves and the way they sound different on dry roads and wet puddles and I love the world puddle. Simple things like that.

And I like C&C t-shirts at Selfridges and Jonathan Kelsey stilettos and Reese Peanut Butter cups and swallow dives. And pub quizzes and the first cup of tea in the morning and friendly cab drivers and leather based perfume. And I like Americanisms like 'Good Jaaaaawb!' and East Enderisms like Tom foolery (jewellery)

And I like being a girl and shopping for lingerie, and derelict buildings. And I like saving my favourite flavours in a little pile on my plate when eating my dinner so that my last bite can taste of that flavour. And I like fresh scones, fluffy clouds, squirrels and lamps. And I like street art and flower markets, and giraffes and macaroons.

And I like sheltering from torrential downpours in New York on Broadway, watching two types of peeps running for cover from the rain. The grumblers hidden away and the splashers, they giggle and don't mind the puddles. And I like running out of doorways and doing twirly twirls with the gigglers. So did I? Do twirly twirls on Broadway in Monsoon weather? Indeed I did and got soaked to the bone. But did I care? Did I what...

Happiness is the freedom you feel doing twirly twirls in the rain.

EBAY

And I like surprises, like Ebay and Amazon and crimble card time. And I like the anticipation of EBay and Amazon - it's the secret to thier success. The anticipation of receiving the gift/book whatever in the post. I like that, I like that millions. And I like the ker-razy stories about the things that have sold on EBay, like Diane Duyser, from Florida, claimed that a 10-year old image of the Virgin Mary on a toasted sandwich had brought her luck-including (wait for it) $70,000 dollars in casino wins. 1.7 million peeps viewed the auction on Ebay before Golden Palace an online casino, bought the sandwich for $28,000 to take on a world tour. It was not long before another Ebay seller offered a sandwich toaster able to produce Virgin Mary toast.

And I like sweet beginnings
My friend Lisa is the Curly Wurly queen. She told me that a Curly will lasts ages if popped in the freezer and chilled for a few hours. She's right, they're pretty low in calories and after freezing, the chew lasts much longer so you can prolong the experience. Frozen and all, I ate this one in three minutes.

...and I like nicely wrapped pressies, with foreign stamps on them

TO: GISÈLE SCANLON

Cadbury
CURLYWURLY
26 g (Net)

322

And I like big frames whatever the season

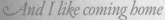

Just because the summer's over (sob) I don't have
to ditch the shades. It's winter 11am and I've
arrived on a flight from the US, but thanks to the
fabulous Linda Farrow glasses I'm totally getting
away with it. Girls, when you go out on a large
one don't forget a pair of serious fashion frames!!
Linda Farrow, 51 Calthorpe Street, WC1 (tel:
+44 207 713 1105, www.lindafarrowvintage.
com). SImon Jablon discovered hundreds of
pairs of vintage sunglassses while poking
around his mothers warehouse. These now
form the basis of the Linda Farrow Vintage
sungalsssess collection. They're fab!

And I like coming home

The previous evening - my last night in New York,
happy I'd found the perfect burger, I had a revelation.
I thought: I love this freedom, but I don't have to be
here. I thought: sod it. I'm off home. And I was. The
main component of my wanting to go home, the what's
left?- 70 per cent that turns dislike into something close to horror, was a deep
aversion to strange beds. This aversion is so strong that although I wanted to see
more of New York, I wanted to leave more. So I did. And I'd forgotten how great that
felt, a fully functioning individual once again, home in time for a cup of tea and A
Touch Of Frost, wonderful. And that was pretty much that. Sound of the key in the
door, sound of key turning, parking suitcase in the hall, until I venture out again,
this was all the happiness I needed.

And most of all I like my own bed

I lay back down on my pillow to return to dreamland, a new notebook and pen by
my bedside. I'd take tomorrow off and do nothing. Take the time that everybody
was telling me was their luxury. And then what? Learn Japanese, travel the
world first class? No, I'm gonna take the time to read lots more books and
hopefully write some. Nice thought isn't it? What would I fill my next notebook
with? Hmmmmmm, now let me see, let's tippy toe through a dream here. I love the
word tippy and I love the word toe and I love that I'm a writer and nothing much
more and I love that that takes me on many new adventures. Night, night. Click!

THE END